The Impact of eConveyancing on Title Registration

Gabriel Brennan

The Impact of eConveyancing on Title Registration

A Risk Assessment

Springer

Gabriel Brennan
Dublin
Ireland

ISBN 978-3-319-10340-2 ISBN 978-3-319-10341-9 (eBook)
DOI 10.1007/978-3-319-10341-9
Springer Cham Heidelberg New York Dordrecht London

Library of Congress Control Number: 2014955461

Printed on acid-free paper

Springer is part of Springer Science+Business Media (www.springer.com)

Table of Cases

Cases

Acknowledgements

Most especially I would like to thank Graham Ferris and Gary Wilson for their excellent guidance and advice. Their insight and encouragement has proved invaluable. Special thanks is also due to Professor Michael Cardwell.

I am hugely indebted to Mary Keane and T P Kennedy who supported me in this endeavour and Professor Adrian Walters for his input. I am also grateful to Dennis Barnhart, John O'Sullivan, Greg McDermott, James O'Boyle, Kate Murray, Ken Crawford, Alexandra Radley, Dr. Paddy Prendergast, Agostino Russo, Vicki McArthur and Nuala Casey who found the time to discuss ideas, provide information and make suggestions for improvement. Thank you all for your assistance.

Finally, I would like to thank my friends, family and in particular my husband for his continuing support and my children for their love and laughter.

All opinions expressed are my own.

Contents

List of Figures

List of Tables

Chapter 1
Introduction

> *In this book is told a tale of two innocents, one who owned land (he thought) and wished to sell it (he thought) and another who had money to spend (he thought) and wished to buy that land (he thought). Nothing could be simpler (they thought). Little foresaw they the dark and dangerous depths of the 'wide and sometimes largely uncharted sea' to which they entrusted their ship of fortune (Farrand (1983), p. 3 referring to* Lee-*Parker v. Izzet* [1971] 3 All ER 1099).

1.1 Context

Since the 1980s the passing of title to land by way of sale and purchase or gift, commonly known as conveyancing, has been undergoing transformation on an international and unprecedented scale. This transformation is due to the application of technological advances to what was previously a paper based process. The application of technology to this process, known as electronic conveyancing, e-conveyancing or herein referred to as eConveyancing, has thrown up many important issues for land owners and others who have an interest in the conveyancing process such as consumers, professionals, academics and policy makers.[1] These issues include the roles of stakeholders in the process, the need for process improvements, security, costs, removal of paper, incidences of liability and the quality of title.

One of the foremost issues concerns the management of risk. Does the application of technology to such a traditional process have any effect on the management of risk? What, if any, are the actual and potential effects of this technological transformation on the management of risk in conveyancing? Is the shift in technology risk neutral? While the management of risk has always been a compelling concern in the conveyancing process, with legal practitioners fighting a continual duel in the sale and purchase of property to protect their clients' interests, how to

[1] Harpum (2000), p. 1 notes that the business of conveyancing is a significant political issue because of the time and expense involved.

G. Brennan, *The Impact of eConveyancing on Title Registration*,
DOI 10.1007/978-3-319-10341-9_1

deal with existing and new risks becomes a vital and dominant feature once you try adapt the process to a modern electronic environment. The development of eConveyancing provides the impetus for change to the process that can have unforeseen consequences on the incidence of risk.

eConveyancing moves the conveyancing process from being a paper based system of effecting and recording transactions to a modern electronic system via the creation and empowerment of electronic communication networks. The potential impact of this change on the distribution of legal risk in conveyancing transactions with particular reference to Ontario and Ireland is investigated.

There are a broad range of different models and systems of eConveyancing.[2] The development of eConveyancing has primarily taken place in common law jurisdictions and Ontario and Ireland are two common law jurisdictions that represent opposite ends of the spectrum in terms of integration of technology into the conveyancing process. Ireland's Law Reform Commission has acknowledged that the Ontario model offers the approach that best fits the Irish environment.[3]

> Ontario is recognised as the most progressive eConveyancing solution currently in operation and is widely acknowledged as a reference source for new eConveyancing solutions in other jurisdictions....The Ontario solution is the closest "end-to-end" eConveyancing solution that is currently in existence with functional models such as: property registration, solicitor communication facilities, online searches, online mapping functions and dealings with financial institutions.[4]

Thus many commentators have recognised Ontario as the oldest most developed operating system of eConveyancing in the world and it was the first jurisdiction to introduce full electronic document registration.[5]

This analysis explores the perception that it is by far the most developed eConveyancing system by articulating the key components of eConveyancing, examining the extent of the Ontario system and comparing experiences in other jurisdictions which have undergone reform in this area. These jurisdictions include Australia, Scotland, New Zealand, British Columbia, England and Wales and Northern Ireland.

By contrast Ireland is only beginning to develop the initial stages of its eConveyancing project and thus has much to learn in order to take advantage of advances already made in this arena. Ireland is entering a period of reform and it is timely that research is done to inform the debate. The fact that Ireland is distinctively behind many other states[6] is seen as an advantage as it can try to emulate the successes of other jurisdictions while avoiding the pitfalls that they have already encountered.

There has been widespread acceptance that eConveyancing is a change for the better[7] and certainly many benefits of electronic advances in conveyancing have

---

[2] Harpum (2004), p. 5.

[3] The Law Reform Commission (2006), p. 8.

[4] The Law Reform Commission (2006), p. 89.

[5] Murray (2004), p. 21. See also Low (2005), pp. 155–178 and Christensen (2004).

[6] Killilea (2010), p. 11.

[7] Perry (2003), p. 26 and Coffin and Pierre (2005), p. 7.

been articulated.[8] However, many of these efficiencies and benefits primarily assist the professionals or state agencies involved in the conveyancing process. Writers and researchers have to a lesser degree explored the impact on land owners and third parties or property claimants. This analysis fills this gap by describing and articulating current conveyancing systems in order to project the likely impact of technological change on those with, or seeking to assert, rights and interests in land.

Risks are inherent in the conveyancing process and any change to that process will impact on the risk landscape. This effect, where risks are created, re-assigned or otherwise effected by the introduction of eConveyancing, is the impact that is explored. Thus the word 'impact' in this context should not be understood as referring to an empirical study. Instead legal, descriptive, analytical and comparative techniques have been deployed in order to anticipate how, and to what extent, a change in transactional process may unintentionally affect the distribution of substantive legal risk within property law systems.

In effect this comprises a risk assessment constituting risk identification, risk analysis and then risk evaluation. The term 'risk' in this context is the consequence of change and the likelihood of that consequence having a negative effect. This risk assessment allows for risk management[9] which can minimise or eliminate the consequences and thereby the negative impact.

This is premised on the understanding that risks are inherent in the conveyancing process[10] and any change in that process, here the move towards eConveyancing, will affect or impact that risk landscape.[11]

1.2 Focus

The management of risk in the conveyancing process in Ontario and Ireland is investigated in light of moves from a paper-based conveyancing system towards eConveyancing in these and other common law jurisdictions. While the primary focus is on Ontario and Ireland the experience in other common law jurisdictions, which have undergone reform in this area, has also been drawn upon. These include

[8] Gahan (2008), p. 15; Wylie (2004), p. 11; Treacy and O'Sullivan (2004), p. 6; and Murray (2004), p. 20.

[9] It is interesting to note that Susskind identified the legal risk manager as one of the five main future roles for lawyers. See Susskind (2008), p. 272.

[10] No activity is without risk and action involves a judgement of the balance between risk and reward. A higher degree of risk may be accepted if there is a greater probability of reward depending on the parties appetite for or aversion to risk.

[11] In consultations with stakeholders in Australia a preference was expressed for 'no change' in risk and liability exposure. The risk assessment carried out by Sneddon and his team showed that this would be unlikely given the introduction of new processes and requirements in NECS (now PEXA) which do not exist in paper conveyancing. Instead a preference was expressed for the objective 'no material net increase' which they considered to be the closest achievable objective to 'no change'. See Sneddon (2007), p. 10.

Australia, Scotland, New Zealand, British Columbia and Northern Ireland. In particular the move towards eConveyancing in England and Wales is referred to as both the Ontario and Irish land title systems developed from that source.

Developments in land administration, title registration and title insurance are also explored. Thus elements of property transactions in America, Europe and Eastern Europe, Asia and Scandinavia are also examined.

Given the broad nature of the conveyancing process it is not possible to deal with all the potential risks that might lead to loss in the course of the operation of a conveyancing system (whether electronic or not). Thus, the focus is solely on risks which impact on title registration and the security, protection or lack thereof that this registration offers to land owners, third parties and property claimants.

Other aspects of the conveyancing process are not examined. These include:

(a) the pre contract enquiries generally carried out by transferees relating to matters such as the size, physical condition or location of the property, outgoings and services;
(b) the legal and procedural requirements for completing the conveyancing transaction;
(c) the requirements to be fulfilled in order to comply with planning and environmental laws;
(d) the mapping requirements laid down by the registering authority; and
(e) compliance with the law on taxation.

Other aspects of the conveyancing process are dealt with but only in so far as they impose on the main focus; risks impacting on title registration. These include:

(a) the legal and procedural requirements for drafting contracts or deeds;
(b) the legal right or capacity of the land owner to sell or gift title to land;
(c) searches of the title register, deeds register, judgments[12] and other registers to establish encumbrances on the title;
(d) post contract enquiries.[13] These relate to matters such as boundaries, rights of way, identity, bankruptcy, possession, notices and proceedings relating to the property.
(e) other enquiries to be carried out by the transferee so that he or she is on notice of all the matters that are pertinent to the transaction[14];
(f) the entitlement of a lender holding under a charge; and
(g) the legal and procedural requirements for registration of title to land in the title register.

[12] The term execution is used in Ontario.

[13] In Ireland these are known as Requisitions on Title and are published in a standard format by the Law Society of Ireland.

[14] The law will generally protect the transaction from being undermined by anything that could not be discovered by a transferee for value who carried out all reasonable enquiries.

There are numerous stakeholders with an interest in the conveyancing process. However, this analysis focuses exclusively on the risks posed to land owners, third parties and property claimants. It excludes those with an interest in the process alone, such as legal or other professionals.

This analysis also focuses on single residential conveyancing transactions. This is where a typical consumer[15] is purchasing a single house for occupation. Sale of part of land from a scheme is excluded, as is the perspective of a developer or someone purchasing a buy to let property. Instead the focus is on a consumer who is a one off purchaser of a home. As Viitanen points out "it is easiest to find the basic elements of transaction processes in the normal house transaction of families."[16] Among rural families in Ireland this family home is often built on land that is gifted from the farm and thus this scenario is also addressed.

The analysis is not concerned with problems common to the development of information technology systems. Thus it excludes the specific types of problem that are common to all electronic processes e.g. authorisation, identity verification, electronic signatures and passwords.[17] These electronic processes and their associated difficulties are referred to but only in the context of shedding light on the main focus.

Some risks may be affected by eConveyancing but are not produced by it whereas other new risks may be produced by the development of eConveyancing. Thus the risks examined are both novel and traditional.

1.3 Approach

The risk assessment is both descriptive and capable of identifying normative possibilities for reform based on determining:

1. What is conveyancing?
2. What is eConveyancing?
3. What is title registration?
4. Who are the parties to a conveyancing transaction?
5. Who bears the risk in that transaction?
6. What risks impact on title registration?
7. What party is subject to that risk?
8. How is the risk impacted by the move to eConveyancing?
9. How might that party be protected in an eConveyancing system?

---

[15] The law tends to distinguish between a consumer who is purchasing property for their own use as a family home and a business person who is only interested in the property as a financial investment. The law provides more protection to consumers as they are seen as not having the same business acumen as an investor.

[16] Viitanen (2003), p. 55.

[17] For an examination of these issues in the context of eConveyancing see Keating (2012).

10. Is such protection desirable and feasible?
11. If not, what other party should bear the risk?

The answers to these questions are arranged in terms of a clear unifying purpose; risk and its incidence in paper and electronic conveyancing.

A broad international and multidisciplinary approach has been taken in that the analysis draws from law, economics and social science literature as well as doctrinal property law. It examines not just black letter property law but also the policy and procedure of conveyancing practice. Thus the approach is not restricted to an examination of formal legal rules and includes relevant contributions from practitioners and theorists from legal and non legal spheres.

Some difficulties were encountered as follows:

(a) the lack of an accepted definition of what constitutes eConveyancing[18];
(b) inconsistent use of terminology by researchers and commentators;
(c) continual development of the law, systems, processes and procedures in each jurisdiction.

There is a difference in terminology between jurisdictions not just in conveyancing but also eConveyancing and thus a new vocabulary needed to be generated. This new neutral vocabulary has been articulated in Chap. 2 so as to provide commonality across jurisdictions and systems. This neutral vocabulary provides a set of clear definitions and minimises the difficulties caused by inconsistent use of terminology by other writers.

This area of research relates to current live and developing eConveyancing projects and thus elements are constantly being withdrawn and new initiatives launched. This requires a continual review of the literature.

1.4 Method

In order to identify any relevant risks a transaction analysis is done through the use of a model or abstracted process. This involves the creation of abstract or model conveyancing transactions and the allocation of risk to the parties to those transactions. The use of abstract transactions with abstracted participants generalises the problematic and allows the risks to be identified and allocated. "The goal of any model is to simplify and provide an abstraction of a complex and diverse world."[19] In this way "[m]odels are useful precisely because they abstract from irrelevant

[18] Sneddon (2007), p. 2 says that eConveyancing does not have a precise meaning but encompasses a range of activities in the process of recording, searching and transferring interests in land which may be effected using electronic (or digital) communications and/or electronic (or digital) processing.

[19] Astke et al. (2004).

details and thereby allow us to focus on the aspects of the domain we are interested in."[20]

Thus modeling is not used to give a detailed description of all possible real or theoretical conveyancing transactions. Instead the concept of modeling is used to illustrate the most general transactions and the most general relations between different parties that arise during those transactions.

Šumrada explains that:

> [m]odels help us to understand, learn and shape both a problem domain and its solution domain. A model is a simplification of the selected part of reality that helps us to master a large and complex system, which cannot be comprehended easily it its entirety. The model is intended to be easier to use for certain purposes than the complete system observed. Models therefore unable (sic) us to organize, retrieve, examine and analyse data about large systems.[21]

Visser and Schlieder point out that modelling real property transactions "is not a trivial task. We have to model static knowledge (e.g. parcels, buildings etc.). We also have to deal with processes, and we have to deal with abstract entities such as rights."[22]

The development of a process model allows for a theoretical, descriptive and analytical examination of risk. This model is presented using visuals. This use of visualisation[23] in law is increasingly used as a means to present complex ideas simply.[24]

The two most common conveyancing transactions are modeled; an arms length transaction and a gift. The risks are identified, analysed and allocated to the participants. This requires an examination of which of the participants suffers if the risk leads to a loss. This impact on land owners, third parties and property claimants is explored through the creation of abstract participants in the abstracted model of the conveyancing process. The conveyancing process is examined from the standpoint of each abstract participant thus examining how risk is distributed between those participants.

This use of standpoint, as articulated by Holmes,[25] Hart[26] and Twining[27] provides a framework for identifying the tension between different claimants, all arguing for the upholding of their property rights. Thus the laws of each jurisdiction

---

[20] Visser and Bench-Capon (1998), p. 28.

[21] Šumrada (2003), p. 140.

[22] Visser and Schlieder (2003), p. 111.

[23] For example, charts and diagrams. Lawyers tend to be expert at using language and words to persuade and debate; they are less familiar with using visual techniques but these can be a powerful tool of communication.

[24] For examples see Mahler (2010). See also Haapio (2010), pp. 391–394 and Berger-Walliser et al. (2011).

[25] Holmes (1896–1897), pp. 457–478.

[26] Hart (1959), pp. 233–240.

[27] Twining (1972–1973), pp. 275–303.

are considered from the standpoint of a transferor, transferee, donor, donee, lender, third party and property claimant in order to identify the risks peculiar to each party. This incidence of risk between the security of the transferor and donor or transferee and donee and the security of those interested in the land (lender, third party or property claimant) is examined in the context of the continual tension in a conveyancing transaction between dynamic security and static security.

This transactional based account of property law is expressed in the under-articulated but well established practice of using an abstracted conveyancing transaction to organise the law. Function is determined by transactional context so this approach meets the needs of a comparative analysis.

Examples of the practice of this transactional type of analysis in the law of real property is provided by commentators such as Hewitt and Overton,[28] Williams and Lightwood[29] and more recently Farrand.[30] These classic accounts of the law of unregistered title conveyancing adopted this schematic focus for the law of real property. As Williams and Lightwood explain the text is designed to discuss the incidents of a contract for the sale of land as they are usually presented to the notice of conveyancers i.e. in order of time.[31] Thus the incidents are set out as a transaction would unfold. Cooke and O'Connor[32] provide a contemporary example in the use of this organising technique.

Once actual and potential new risks are identified and allocated, there is an evaluation to determine if the person to whom the risk was allocated (either by design or not) should be protected from the effects of the risk being realised. If such protection is not feasible or desirable then consideration is given to the allocation of the risk. A number of choices are examined in determining the allocation. The risk could be;

(a) left with the party subject to it; or
(b) re-allocated to another party or entity; or
(c) it could be socialised through the use of insurance either as a feature of the system or through the establishment of a market.

This examination requires a comparison and evaluation of competing risks and a determination as who or what entity should bear the risk. Thus mechanisms for removing, minimising or distributing the risk are examined or the view taken that the risk is worth bearing given other accrued benefits.

---

[28] Hewitt and Overton (1929).

[29] Williams and Lightwood (1936).

[30] Farrand (1983).

[31] Williams and Lightwood (1936), p. (v).

[32] Cooke and O'Connor (2004), pp. 640–666.

1.5 Scholarship

eConveyancing systems have not been extensively discussed in legal literature. Thus this research is a ground breaking piece of legal scholarship in the Irish context and more generally. This research is the first research done in Ireland on the incidence of risk in the conveyancing process in light of moves towards eConveyancing. Thus it offers an insight into the possible effects of eConveyancing on risk management in the Irish conveyancing system.

As Ireland is entering a period of reform in this area this research has the ability to influence policy at a critical point. It will inform policy development and also further academic debate as to the degree to which Ireland should make fundamental changes to its conveyancing system in the move towards eConveyancing. It identifies normative possibilities for reform of conveyancing in Ireland.

The design of this research involves the novel use of organising concepts through the creation and articulation of a model or abstracted process to determine risks in the conveyancing process. This abstraction provides a mechanism for ignoring those aspects that were not relevant to the research in order to focus more fully on those that were. While the use of models in property law is not new they are rarely articulated.[33]

The abstracted model of the conveyancing process in this research is based on modelling the participants. It involves the creation of abstract participants in dealings with title to land. This is original within the context of the doctrinal law of Ireland and in terms of methodology within the legal discipline. This modelling allowed the separation of the descriptive aspects and the identification of normative possibilities for reform by exploring how things might happen thus revealing emergent properties.

1.6 Legislation

All legislation will initially be referred to by its full title but thereafter Irish legislation will be referenced according to the year of its enactment (e.g. the 1964 Act) whereas the Ontario legislation will be referenced according to its title (e.g. the Land Titles Act).

[33] See Miceli et al. (2002), pp. 565–582 for an example.

1.7 Summary

This book is divided into nine chapters, the first being this chapter by way of introduction.

Chapter 2 explains in detail the methodology of the research and sets the research in context. It also provides a neutral vocabulary for the research.

In Chap. 3 eConveyancing is defined and the relationship between its constituent parts is explored. The move towards eConveyancing in Ontario and Ireland is also examined.

Chapter 4 looks at land administration, land registration, the nature of title registration and the systems operating currently in Ontario and Ireland.

Chapter 5 sets out the model of the conveyancing transactions, identifies the abstract participants and their standpoint. It identifies the risks borne by each participant and categorises the key risks to be examined.

Chapters 6–8 then examine each of the risk categories and determine the impact of eConveyancing. Does an eConveyancing environment lead to no change in the risk profile of each participant or is there increased or decreased risk? Who, if anyone, suffers if the risk leads to a loss in an eConveyancing environment?

In Chap. 6 the risks posed by the registration gap and the formalities for registration are explored. Chapter 7 looks at errors in the register. Chapter 8 explores interests off the register which affect title, the destructive effects of a registered transaction and interests which are not recognised and not capable of registration.

Chapter 9 is the concluding chapter. It provides an overarching view on the impact of eConveyancing on risk and examines potential mechanisms for removing, minimising or distributing the risk or takes the view that the risk is worth bearing given the other benefits accrued. Finally it seeks to draw conclusions to inform the reform process in Ireland.

All of this analysis is set within the context of moves towards eConveyancing and developments in title registration in other jurisdictions across the globe.

References

Astke, H., Mulholland, G., & Hyarady, R. (2004). *Profile definition for a standardized cadastral model*. In FIG Conference on Standardization in the Cadastral Domain. http://www.fig.net/commission7/bamberg_2004/papers/ts_02_04_asthe_mulholland.pdf. Accessed 14 May 2014.

Berger-Walliser, G., Haapio, H., & Rekola, K. (2011). *Contracts as roadmap for performance: Enhancing cross-disciplinary understanding through contract visualization*. In Institute for Supply Management, Working Paper for the 21st Annual North American Research Symposium on Purchasing and Supply Chain Management 17 March 2011.

Christensen, S. (2004). Electronic land dealings in Canada, New Zealand and the United Kingdom: Lessons for Australia. *Murdoch University Electronic Journal of Law, 11*(4). http://www.murdoch.edu.au/elaw/issues/v11n4/christensen114_text.html. Accessed 14 May 2014.

Coffin, M., & Pierre, K. (2005). *Land registration: The Nova Scotia experience*. Caris 2005 Mapping a Seamless Society. http://www.caris.com/conferences/caris2005/proceedings/papers/11.pdf. Accessed 29 Jan 2009.

Cooke, E., & O'Connor, P. (2004). Purchaser liability to third parties in the English land registration system: A comparative perspective. *Law Quarterly Review, 120*.

Farrand, J. T. (1983). *Contract and conveyance* (4th ed.). London: Oyez Longman.

Gahan, E. (2008). Taking full advantage of the possibilities of eGovernment. *Public Affairs Ireland, 51*.

Haapio, H. (2010). Visualising contracts and legal rules for greater clarity. *The Law Teacher, 44* (3).

Harpum, C. (2000). *Property in an electronic age. Modern studies in property law* (Vol. 1). Oxford: Hart.

Harpum, C. (2004). *English experience: Title by registration – Preparation for e-conveyancing*. In Law Reform Commission Annual Conference. http://www.lawreform.ie/Annual%20Conference%202004.PDF. Accessed 18 Feb 2009.

Hart, H. L. A. (1959). Scandinavian realism. *Cambridge Law Journal, 1959*.

Hewitt, E. P., & Overton, M. R. C. (1929). *Dart's treatise on the law and practice relating to vendors and purchasers of real estate* (8th ed.). London: Stevens and Sons Ltd.

Holmes, O. W. (1896–1897). The path of the law. *Harvard Law Review, 10*.

Keating, S. (2012). *Digital signatures and electronic conveyancing* (LL.M. thesis). National University of Ireland, Galway.

Killilea, M. (2010, April). *eRegistration in Ireland – An assessment of the transferability of the Queensland model* (Dissertation). Dublin Institute of Public Administration.

Law Reform Commission. (2006). *eConveyancing: Modelling of the Irish conveyancing system*. The Law Reform Commission (LRC 79 – 2006). http://www.lawreform.ie/Reports_Published/Default.135.html.

Low, R. (2005). Maintaining the integrity of the Torrens system in a digital environment: A comparative overview of the safeguards used within the electronic land systems in Canada, New Zealand, United Kingdom and Singapore. *Australian Property Law Journal, 11*(2).

Mahler, T. (2010). *Legal risk management* (Ph.D. thesis). University of Oslo.

Miceli, T. J., Munneke, H. J., Sirmans, C. F., & Turnbull, G. K. (2002). Title systems and land values. *Journal of Law and Economics, 45*.

Murray, K. (2004). *Electronic registration and other modernization initiatives in Ontario's land registration system*. In Law Reform Commission Annual Conference. http://www.lawreform.ie/Annual%20Conference%202004.PDF. Accessed 18 Feb 2009.

Perry, R. (2003). E-conveyancing – A critical view. *Conveyancing & Property Law Journal, 8*(2).

Sneddon, M. (2007). *Risk assessment and management in electronic conveyancing*. In Registering the World Conference, Dublin, 26–28 September 2007. http://www.prai.ie/uploadedfiles/conference20071/papers/s4p1.pdf. Accessed 14 May 2014.

Šumrada, R. (2003). Conceptual modelling of cadastral information system structures. In H. Stuckenschmidt, E. Stubkjær, & C. Schlieder (Eds.), *The ontology and modelling of real estate transactions*. England: Ashgate.

Susskind, R. (2008). *The end of lawyers? Rethinking the nature of legal services*. Oxford: Oxford University Press.

Treacy, C., & O'Sullivan, J. (2004). *Land registration in Ireland – Current position and future developments*. In Law Reform Commission Annual Conference. http://www.lawreform.ie/Annual%20Conference%202004.PDF. Accessed 10 Mar 2009.

Twining, W. (1972–1973). The bad man revisited. *Cornell Law Review, 58*.

Viitanen, K. (2003). Purchase of real property in Finland. In H. Stuckenschmidt et al. (Eds.), *The ontology and modelling of real estate transactions*. England: Ashgate.

Visser, P., & Bench-Capon, T. (1998). A comparison of four ontologies for the design of legal knowledge systems. *Artificial Intelligence and Law, 6*.

Visser, U., & Schlieder, C. (2003). Modelling real estate transactions: The potential role of ontologies. In H. Stuckenschmidt, E. Stubkjær, & C. Schlieder (Eds.), *The ontology and modelling of real estate transactions*. England: Ashgate.

Williams, T. C., & Lightwood, J. M. (1936). *A treatise on the law of vendor and purchaser of real estate and chattels real, intended for the use of conveyancers of either branch of the profession* (4th ed.). London: Sweet and Maxwell.

Wylie, J. (2004). *Keynote address: Need for a modern legislative framework*. In Law Reform Commission Annual Conference. http://www.lawreform.ie/Annual%20Conference%202004.PDF. Accessed 29 Jan 2009.

Chapter 2
Methodology

2.1 Introduction

This chapter explains in detail the methodology and provides a neutral vocabulary thus setting the framework for the creation of the abstracted model of the conveyancing process.

2.2 Methodology

The methodology is primarily based upon doctrinal legal scholarship in the comparative law tradition. This approach advocated by Zweigert and Kötz[1] attempts to use a functional analysis of legal processes to describe the substantive and systemic aspects of different legal systems. There may be little or no convergence between the systems and their terminology but many legal systems attempt to protect similar interests. Only rules which perform the same function or address the same problem can profitably be compared. Similar concepts won't have the same label and thus researchers must move past the formal label into function. Thus an examination of the function of the rules within each system must be carried out. Rules or laws with similar functions, in this instance to protect different property rights, will yield common ground for research.

Through this comparative study of the systems in Ontario and Ireland weaknesses and strengths are highlighted and any strengths of the Ontario system can be followed and weaknesses avoided. As Ireland is in the early stages of eConveyancing a comparative study is appropriate to assist in the development of its system. Zweigert and Kötz refer to this as modern comparative law developed in

[1] Zweigert and Kötz (1998).

G. Brennan, *The Impact of eConveyancing on Title Registration*,
DOI 10.1007/978-3-319-10341-9_2

the early nineteenth century which has a practical purpose, namely reform and improvement of the law at home.[2]

Different systems are generally striving to achieve the same ends though often by diverse means. Restricting comparison to similar systems may exclude other better ideas but for such a comparison to be feasible there must be some common ground between the items being compared. Ontario and Ireland have many key similarities which provided the rationale for a comparison of their systems.

Ontario and Ireland are western developed societies and have long established market economies. Ireland and Canada are members of the OECD[3] and WTO,[4] UN[5] and IMF.[6] Both have a tradition of democratic governance and achieved statehood through independence from the United Kingdom. They have common rather than civil law legal systems and are English speaking. The two jurisdictions have a practice of secured lending for the purchase of property with a tradition of relatively unrestricted freedom of lifetime disposition of property. Both jurisdictions have a similar division between deeds and title registration and the model of land registration for both Ireland and Ontario developed from the English system. Thus a comparison of the systems in Ontario and Ireland is feasible.

Table 2.1 shows some key comparators between the two jurisdictions.

There is however criticism of comparative law and the view of Zweigert and Kötz that functionality is the basic methodological principle of all comparative law.[7]

Teubner calls this functional equivalence but he takes issue with it and argues that attempts at unifying law[8] or convergence will result in new cleavages.[9] Legal institutions cannot really be transplanted from a foreign to a domestic culture but instead they become a legal irritant which,

> cannot be domesticated; they are not transformed from something alien into something familiar, not adapted to a new cultural context, rather they will unleash an evolutionary dynamic in which the external rule's meaning will be reconstructed and internal context will undergo fundamental change.[10]

He is of the view that globalising tendencies produce new divergences as their unintended consequences.[11]

Another critical view is offered by Legrand who is strident in his opinion that legal transplants are impossible as legal rules cannot travel.[12] He argues that law

---

[2] Zweigert and Kötz (1998), p. 54.

[3] Organisation for Economic Co-operation and Development.

[4] World Trade Organisation.

[5] United Nations.

[6] International Monetary Fund.

[7] Zweigert and Kötz (1998), p. 34.

[8] In his commentary European contract law.

[9] Teubner (1998), pp. 12–13.

[10] Teubner (1998), p. 12.

[11] Teubner (1998), p. 13. See also Kahn-Freund (1974), p. 1.

[12] Legrand (1997), p. 114. At p. 111 he equates transplant to displacement. Another negative view is offered by Paasch who states that internationalisation of law, including visions of legal integration and even unification of legal systems is an old dream. See Paasch (2007), p. 167.

Table 2.1 Comparison of Ireland and Ontario

	Ireland	Ontario
Population	4.58 million[a]	13.2 million[b]
GDP[c]	203[d]	1,522 (Canada)[e]
Total housing stock (dwellings only)	2 million[f]	4.88 million[g]
Average house prices (including apartments)	€231,011 (new) €257,462 (second hand)[h]	$650,721[i] (almost €447,006)[j]
Total land area	70,295 (km^2)[k]	917,741 (km^2)[l]
Estimated percentage of total land mass registered in the registering authority with registered title	Circa 96 %[m] (estimated to be 200,000–250,000 unregistered titles)[n]	13 % (87 % of the land mass is crown land[o] and there are only 36,000 unregistered titles)[p]
Estimated percentage of legal titles registered in the registering authority	Circa 92 %[q]	Almost 100 %[r]
Number of registered title land parcels	2.14 million folios[s]	5.8 million parcels[t]
Percentage of home ownership	79 % total[u]	67 % total 35 % with mortgage 32 % without mortgage[v]
Tax on property as a % of GDP[w]	1.8	3.3 (Canada)
House prices (% change over previous period)[x]	−12.8	4.8 (Canada)
Tax revenue on property as a % of total taxation[y]	6.5	10.7 (Canada)
Value of new mortgage lending for residential property	€568 million[z]	$10 billion (new construction) (€6.86 billion)[aa] $89 billion (existing residential property)[ab] (€61 billion)[ac]

[a]Census as of 10 April 2011. See preliminary results accessed 14 May 2014 at http://www.cso.ie/en/media/csoie/census/documents/Prelim,complete.pdf

[b]Preliminary figure as of 1 July 2010. Statistics Canada (2011)

[c]Gross Domestic Product. 2013 statistics as billions of US dollars accessed 14 May 2014 at http://www.oecd-ilibrary.org/economics/gross-domestic-product-in-us-dollars_2074384x-table3

[d]Estimated value

[e]Ontario represents almost 40 % of Canada's GDP. See http://www.investinontario.com/en/Pages/WO_SGE_default.aspx, accessed 14 May 2014

[f]Census as of 10 April 2011. See preliminary results accessed 14 May 2014 at http://www.cso.ie/en/media/csoie/census/documents/Prelim,complete.pdf

[g]2011 Census at http://www.statcan.gc.ca/tables-tableaux/sum-som/l01/cst01/famil55b-eng.htm, accessed 14 May 2014

[h]As of quarter 4 2013; accessed 14 May 2014 at http://www.environ.ie/en/Publications/StatisticsandRegularPublications/HousingStatistics/FileDownLoad,15295,en.XLS

[i]As of quarter 1 2014. Canada Mortgage and Housing Corporation (2014)

[j]As at 27 June 2014

[k]Dol and Haffner (2010)

[l]http://www.statcan.gc.ca/tables-tableaux/sum-som/l01/cst01/phys01-eng.htm, accessed 14 May 2014

[m]Deeney (2014), p. 3

(continued)

Table 2.1 (continued)

[n]James O'Boyle Financial Controller Property Registration Authority by email 13 June 2014
[o]The land registration system administered by the Ministry of Government Services only administers land that has been patented by the Crown. Jurisdiction for land that has not been patented is given to the Ministry of Natural Resources and this land falls outside the land registration system. Vicki McArthur Teranet by email 15 June 2012
[p]Alex Radley Legal and Technical Officer Service Ontario by email 7 June 2012
[q]Deeney (2014), p. 3
[r]Alex Radley Legal and Technical Officer Service Ontario by email 7 June 2012
[s]James O'Boyle Financial Controller Property Registration Authority by email 13 June 2014. See Property Registration Authority (2013), p. 10 for the growth in numbers of registered land parcels since 2008
[t]Alex Radley Legal and Technical Officer Service Ontario by email 7 June 2012
[u]As at 2004. Dol and Haffner (2010)
[v]As of 2009. Statistics Canada (2011)
[w]2012 statistics accessed 14 May 2014 at http://www.oecd-ilibrary.org/taxation/taxes-on-property_20758510-table7. Since then Ireland has introduced a residential property tax
[x]2012 statistics accessed 14 May 2014 at http://www.oecd-ilibrary.org/economics/house-prices_2074384x-table17
[y]2012 statistics accessed 14 May 2014 at http://www.oecd-ilibrary.org/taxation/tax-revenue-by-sector-2008_20758510-table8. Since then Ireland has introduced a residential property tax
[z]Irish Banking Federation/PriceWaterhouseCoopers Mortgage Market Profile Quarter 1 (2014)
[aa]As at 27 June 2014
[ab]http://www.statcan.gc.ca/tables-tableaux/sum-som/l01/cst01/manuf03b-eng.htm, accessed 14 May 2014
[ac]As at 27 June 2014

would need to be segregated from society to travel across jurisdictions and this could only occur if law was a "somewhat autonomous entity unencumbered by historical, epistemological, or cultural baggage."[13]

A contrary perspective is offered by Watson who says we do legal transplant or 'borrowing' all the time and that "[i]n most places at most times borrowing is the most fruitful source of legal change."[14] The reality is likely somewhere in the middle of these two divergent perspectives though the failures of 'borrowing' probably generate more attention than the successes.

For example Meadows and Griffin are of the view that previous title registration initiatives were "perceived to have failed to address the specific requirements of Bermuda and instead sought to impose an existing system from another jurisdiction."[15] These attempted transplantation initiatives are blamed by them for the failure to introduce title registration into Bermuda.

These arguments have merit however the aim is not to unify or converge the law in Ontario and Ireland. If the aim was to 'transplant' the Ontario system in its entirety into Ireland there is no doubt it would become a major 'irritant'. While the

[13] Legrand (1997), p. 114.
[14] Watson (1996), p. 335. See also Ewald (1995), pp. 489–510.
[15] Meadows and Griffin (2007), p. 5.

jurisdictions share a common history their legal systems are by no means the same. Instead the aim is to learn lessons from the Ontario system so as to determine how risk is to be managed in a system of eConveyancing in Ireland.

As Lepaulle has said "[t]o see things in their true light, we must see them from a certain distance, as strangers, which is impossible when we study any phenomena of our own country."[16] Sen also refers to the need to transcend the limitations of our positional perspectives.[17] He explores the search for some kind of position-independent understanding but acknowledges that we cannot hope to succeed fully in this endeavour as this is the view from nowhere.[18]

While acknowledging Sen's argument this 'view from nowhere' proves unhelpful in this context as it is only by looking at the conveyancing process from the perspective of Ireland's land law system that the benefit or negative effect of any change can be evaluated. As Chodosh points out decision-makers and scholars cannot be expected to understand the foreign without comparison to the familiar.[19]

Similarly Legrand states that:

> unless the comparatist can learn to think of law as a culturally-situated phenomenon and accept that the law lives in a profound way within a culture-specific – and therefore contingent – discourse, comparison rapidly becomes a pointless venture.[20]

The act of interpretation of legal rules is embedded unconsciously in the language and tradition of the interpreter.[21] Thus law has to be looked at in context.

The context here is the conveyancing systems in Ireland and Ontario. The functional analysis is based upon the management of risk in the conveyancing process across the two jurisdictions and in particular the identification, analysis, allocation, comparison and evaluation of risks.

Despite the similarities between the two jurisdictions there are fundamental differences in concepts and terminology. In order to overcome these differences a neutral vocabulary has been generated. This clarification of terminology and meaning sets the stage for the creation of the abstracted model to be applied across the two legal systems.

The necessity for this neutral vocabulary to overcome diversity between the two jurisdictions is explored initially before the neutral vocabulary is articulated.

---

[16] Lepaulle (1921–1922), p. 858.

[17] Sen (2009), p. 155.

[18] Sen (2009), pp. 161 and 169.

[19] Chodosh (1998–1999), p. 1056.

[20] Legrand (1997), p. 124.

[21] Legrand (1997), pp. 114–115.

2.3 Neutral Vocabulary

2.3.1 Context

> It has often been said that law and language are intimately linked, as language structures the way we think and, consequently, the way we think as lawyers. . .It is accepted wisdom that unification or even harmonisation of the law is neither possible without the creation of uniform legal terminology, preferably laid down in a limited number of 'authentic' language versions, nor without a superior authority (frequently a court) that is responsible for reaching uniform interpretation.[22]

The lack of a uniform legal terminology and uniform interpretation also arises in comparative law research.

Jurisdictions have differing systems with fundamental differences in key concepts and terminology within that system. This presents difficulties for comparative law researchers who wish to compare these concepts or terms across jurisdictions. The question of the *tertium comparationis* or the comparability of the items of comparison arises i.e. is comparison possible?

Ferlan and his colleagues recommend deciding at an early stage what the comparison will entail and:

> using reasonably simplified methods, to identify manageable and comparable conditions in different countries so that the person making the comparison will not need to master the whole body of each country's property law. Comparisons have to be standardised, despite the risks that this entails.[23]

Hence the importance of being self-aware in modelling conveyancing transactions and the importance of identifying key concepts that perform the same role across legal systems.

Fundamental differences may arise not just in relation to the systems being compared but also the labels or terminology used. In addition even when similar or the same terminology is used across jurisdictions the meaning assigned to that term may be different. Transplantation of terminology and concepts may not prove too problematic between jurisdictions in the common law family particularly where many of the key concepts have continued to develop along similar lines. However, such transplantation would likely prove more difficult between jurisdictions without these similarities though some commentators are of the view that "even in the area of property law civil and common law share more principles and underlying policies than meets the eye at first glance."[24]

Akhtar sees eConveyancing as the way of delivering harmonisation of European property law[25] but other commentators note that the "diversity of individual

---

[22] Van Erp (2003b).

[23] Ferlan et al. (2007), p. 28.

[24] Van Erp (2002).

[25] Akhtar (2014), pp. 106–122.

economies and associated legal practices alone makes the concept of a common land market model unrealistic."[26]

Clancy acknowledges the impetus towards convergence but he is of the view that comparison of procedures between the common law and civil law systems is like comparing apples with oranges.[27] He refers to the adversarial system in common law jurisdictions where conveyancing is based on the principle of *caveat emptor* versus the civil law system where there is an independent statutory official and the vendor has a duty of disclosure. This independent statutory official known as the notary or *notaire* acts on behalf of both vendor and purchaser and is an agent of the State.

Many of these countries have complete eRegistration systems but will never progress to full eConveyancing as there is little, if any, part of the conveyancing process taking place outside the role of the notary. A clear example of this is Estonia where the notary performs all the necessary inquiries and prepares all the documentation which is digitally signed and sent electronically to the land registry where it is automatically registered.[28] Commentators often refer to these systems as eConveyancing systems but a fundamental tenet of eConveyancing is the creation of a central hub between multiple stakeholders both private and public, not just between different arms or branches of the state.[29]

Clancy also notes that business processes can be benchmarked due to a common understanding of the terminology but "[t]his is not the case with land administration, which operates at jurisdictional level and inherits terminology that is often peculiar to the particular jurisdiction being evaluated."[30] Akhtar notes that real property law is now one of the few legal branches which has remained essentially national and in which differences among national laws remain greatest.[31] Lemmen *et al.* also point out the lack of a shared set of concepts and terminology between cadastral[32] and land registry systems.[33]

This lack of a shared set of concepts and terminology is being partly addressed in Europe by the UN[34] and the publication of a glossary of terms by the European

---

[26] Dale et al. (2006), p. 3.

[27] Clancy (2007), p. 11.

[28] Rätsep (2008), p. 3 provides a simple explanation of the conveyancing procedure in Estonia.

[29] See Chap. 3 for a detailed examination of the elements required for eConveyancing.

[30] Clancy (2007), p. 5.

[31] Akhtar (2014), p. 120.

[32] Stubkjær distinguishes between the cadastre with its spatial focus and the land register with its legal focus. See Stubkjær (2003), pp. 227–238. The cadastre which exists in Norway and many other west-European countries, once under the command of Napoleon, generally deals with mapping, land use and land values for taxation. Land registration often sits alongside this cadastre. Together they can be defined as the land administration system (LAS). The distinction between cadastral and land registry systems is explored further in Chap. 4.

[33] Lemmen et al (2005).

[34] The Food and Agriculture Organization of the United Nations (2003) sets out a comprehensive thesaurus of terminology.

Land Information Service (EULIS).[35] Paasch sees this as an important contribution in spreading knowledge of national real property domains to interested parties but points out that it does not provide a fully standardised description of the information.[36] The UN has also published guidelines on real property units and identifiers aimed at supporting efficient and effective national land administration and management. The guidelines include a survey of the real property rights in 18 countries in Europe which prove to illustrate a great degree of diversity.[37]

Another publication across the world wide stage is the Inventory of Land Administration Systems in Europe and North America produced by the Land Registry of England and Wales on behalf of the UN Economic Commission for Europe Working Party on Land Administration (UNECE WPLA).[38] Though this is an inventory of systems and organisations rather than a thesaurus or glossary this also demonstrates the diversity of real property rights[39] and the disparity in systems and processes.

The difficulties as they apply to property law are already acknowledged. Zevenbergen and his colleagues note that the actors and procedures involved in transactions in real property appear to differ even between countries with comparable economies.[40] Stubkjær and his colleagues, who were working on the same research project, note that different legal traditions in different European countries created terminological and semantic difficulties in achieving comparable descriptions.[41] Comparison across countries is difficult because the same term may be used differently and there may be no exact correspondence between concepts.[42] Thus clarification of terminology and meaning is crucial.

In order to address these problems Zweigert and Kötz state that comparative lawyers must cut themselves loose from their own doctrinal and juridical preconceptions and liberate themselves from their own cultural context in order to discover 'neutral' concepts.[43] Thus rather than transplant and adopt the meaning or term assigned by one system or the other, a new system neutral vocabulary can be generated to incorporate the terms for each jurisdiction. Neutral vocabulary can provide a degree of commonality across the jurisdictions and systems being

---

35 http://www.eulis.eu/.

36 Paasch (2007), p. 168. Paasch also refers at pp. 168–169 to the standardised core cadastral model developed by Van Oosterom and his colleagues which does not focus enough on the problems with establishing a common terminology in the domain. See Van Oosterom et al. (2006), pp. 627–660.

37 United Nations Economic Commission for Europe (2004).

38 HM Land Registry on behalf of the United Nations Economic Commission for Europe Working Party on Land Administration (2005). For more up to date information in draft see the United Nations Economic Commission for Europe Working Party on Land Administration (2014).

39 Paasch (2007), p. 168.

40 Zevenbergen et al. (2007), preface.

41 Stubkjær et al. (2007), p. 3.

42 Stubkjær et al. (2007), p. 5.

43 Zweigert and Kötz (1998), p. 10.

examined. The development of this neutral vocabulary increases the prospect of finding parallel provisions or an echo of similar type provisions in each system.

Paasch is of the view that:

> [t]he establishing of a standardised terminology for the classification of the different rights and restrictions would make it possible to 'match' the different real property rights and restrictions existing in one national legal system with their counterparts existing in another legal system, even if they are not created by the same legal process and have a different terminology.[44]

This view demonstrates the importance of developing a common terminology without distorting the systems being compared.

The lack of an accepted definition of what constitutes eConveyancing, inconsistent use of terminology by researchers and commentators and the difference in terminology between jurisdictions, not just in conveyancing but also in eConveyancing, thus required that a new vocabulary be generated.

This difficulty with terminology and scope is demonstrated by the use of the term electronic conveyancing in a new cross border European initiative. This project called Cross Border Electronic Conveyancing (CROBECO)[45] was initiated by the European Land Registry Association (ELRA)[46] as a cross border transaction scheme which allows purchasers to buy foreign immovable property in other member states. The scheme provides a bilingual contract and allows the purchaser to apply the laws of their own country thus protecting them against "the unknown consequences of contracting a sale in a foreign legal system that is not familiar to them".[47] The current focus is on English and Dutch buyers of property rights in Spain and Portugal.

O'Sullivan refers to the fact that in some jurisdictions the terms eRegistration and eConveyancing and related concepts are ill-defined and used somewhat interchangeably.[48] He attributes this to differences in legal systems and sometimes to the use of language. Thus in outlining the developments in Ireland he proposed the following working definitions:

> eApplications: this covers ordering documents and services online. . . .eLodgement: relates to the lodgement of applications resulting in *changes to the register* ('registration'). . . . eRegistration: lodgement of documents occurs in electronic format only (paper documents are not lodged) and all registrations are made on an electronic register. . . .eConveyancing: the term envisages paperless transactions through most or all of the stages of the conveyancing process from pre-sale to post completion of the transaction.[49]

These definitions were presented at the Registering the World Conference[50] in Dublin in 2007 where most, if not all, of the jurisdictions involved in eRegistration

---

[44] Paasch (2007), p. 177.

[45] http://www.elra.eu/elra-european-land-registry-association/crobeco/crobeco-ii/.

[46] http://www.elra.eu/about-elra/what-is-elra/.

[47] Akhtar (2014), p. 114.

[48] O'Sullivan (2007), p. 5. See also Killilea (2010), p. 2.

[49] O'Sullivan (2007), p. 5.

[50] Registering the World Conference Dublin (2007).

and eConveyancing advances were represented.[51] They have remained unchallenged since that time and have become internationally accepted.[52] These definitions are drawn upon, amended and expanded substantially in order to generate a neutral vocabulary for this research.

This neutral vocabulary as set out below provides commonality and a consistent set of terms that can be applied across jurisdictions and systems. It provides an explication of knowledge and meaning in order to overcome diversity between jurisdictions. It attempts to provide unambiguously defined concepts for the modeling process by setting out the meaning for terms in the model. This vocabulary also limits the boundaries and sets out the parties to the conveyancing transactions to be examined.

While the phrase neutral vocabulary is used here, other commentators and researches have chosen to use different terms. For example Paasch refers to standardised terminology[53] while O'Sullivan refers to working definitions.[54] Visser and Schlieder use the term ontology to mean a language of shared concepts.[55] They point out that while there are already ontologies available in the law domain these have been confined to legal reasoning and spatio-temporal ontologies and, in their view, the inability of these ontologies to describe processes might be one reason why they have not been used frequently in the development of models of real property transactions.[56] Thus Visser and Schlieder and their colleagues turned to software engineering to build their model of real estate transactions.

Visser and Bench-Capon point out that few authors have explicitly specified their conceptualisation of the legal domains in a (semi-) formal language.[57] Having compared four legal ontologies they also come to the conclusion that none of the ontologies seem to have adequate provisions to specify legal procedures. They point out many of the difficulties with comparing legal ontologies and suggest the creation of libraries of legal ontologies, indexed on task, legal subdomain, applicability, and abstraction level.[58]

Hage and Verheij present an abstract model of the law as 'a top ontology'.[59] Their aim is to find heuristic guidelines for legal knowledge representation by a model based on two crucial characteristics of the law. Firstly, that the law is a

---

[51] Fifteen jurisdictions were represented including Canada, Ireland, England and Wales, Australia and New Zealand.

[52] United Nations Economic and Social Council (2007), p. 4.

[53] Paasch (2007), p. 177.

[54] O'Sullivan (2007), p. 5.

[55] Visser and Schlieder (2003). This book is the opening book for research conducted between 2001 and 2005. The concluding book is Zevenbergen et al. (2007) available at http://repository.tudelft.nl/view/ir/uuid%3Ace45bcf6-2cc8-46a3-9305-8526df914887/. See also http://costg9.plan.aau.dk/ for further details of this study and ongoing commentary and research.

[56] Visser and Schlieder (2003), p. 111. For an examination of these ontologies see pp. 109–111.

[57] Visser and Bench-Capon (1998), p. 32.

[58] Visser and Bench-Capon (1998), pp. 53–55.

[59] Hage and Verheij (1999), pp. 1043–1077.

dynamic system of states of affairs and secondly that these states of affairs are interconnected.[60] In this way they take account of events thus reflecting the sequential nature of the legal process.

These commentators are using the term ontology to express language as a method of organising and structuring information about law and legal systems. They are of the view that the ontologies already available in the law domain are flawed in that they do not take account of law as a process or sequence of events and this is why they have not been used frequently in models of real property transactions.

There is no doubt that many aspects of law are governed by the sequential nature of legal transactions and this is particularly evident in conveyancing where one step is often predicated on a prior step in the process.[61]

In articulating the terms forming the framework for this examination the term neutral vocabulary was chosen as providing a simple yet accurate reflection of the purpose for its inclusion. A specific attempt has been made to keep the language clear and unambiguous so as to open this analysis to those without any detailed knowledge of the conveyancing or registration process. Though much of the vocabulary stems from a common law legal perspective and this may confuse a reader from a civil law background.

This neutral vocabulary is as follows:

2.3.2 Neutral vocabulary

eRecords

This is the first phase of eConveyancing. It requires the registering authority to convert all its paper records to an electronic format. This phase is a subset of eApplication and eRegistration.

eApplication

This is also a subset of eRegistration and is the second stage of a wider eRegistration and eConveyancing project. It involves electronic messaging or data transfer from the lawyer to the registering authority but this must subsequently be followed by the lodgement of paper. This may also be referred to as eLodgement.[62] It is a precursor to eRegistration and may become obsolete when full eRegistration is introduced. Until then eApplication and eRegistration may operate in parallel.

---

[60] Hage and Verheij (1999), p. 1043. Signing a sales contract is one of the legal topics modeled. See pp. 1049–1050 and also p. 1054.

[61] This aspect is explored further at Sect. 5.7 and in Chap. 6.

[62] Note that O'Sullivan divided the initial stages into eApplication and eLodgement. See O'Sullivan (2007), p. 5.

eRegistration

eRegistration is the application of technology solely to the registration element of a conveyancing transaction. This will involve electronic messaging or data transfer from the lawyer to the registering authority. No paper documents are lodged.[63] This is an essential element of eConveyancing and is usually a precursor to it. It is the third phase before the final development of eConveyancing.

eConveyancing

The application of information technology to the conveyancing process (often referred to as electronic conveyancing or e-conveyancing). O'Connor says that electronic conveyancing or EC is not a term of art, but can refer to any part of the conveyancing process being done through the transmission of digital data.[64] It moves conveyancing from being a paper based system of recording transactions and documents to an electronic system via the creation of a secure electronic network and a set of processes underpinned by technology.

The network can take various forms. These include a desktop application between each stakeholder group, a desktop application for all stakeholder groups, a stakeholder portal or a central hub. The differences between these options and an assessment of their respective advantages and disadvantages are set out in the Irish Law Reform Commission Report on eConveyancing.[65] The Commission recommends the central hub model as the most appropriate model for Ireland[66] however not everyone agrees.

Connolly is of the view that this model is unnecessary and too cumbersome for Ireland.[67] Instead she is in favour of a stakeholder portal.[68] In another study Killilea found that generally the Queensland model of eRegistration met the requirements of a successful service for Ireland.[69] He dismissed the Ontario hub model as being expensive to develop and maintain due to the use of electronic signature technology[70] however any eConveyancing system will require some form of authentication usually involving an advanced electronic signature.

eConveyancing is defined in more detail in Chap. 3 which also explores the relationship between eRecords, eApplication, eRegistration and eConveyancing.

---

[63] O'Sullivan (2007), p. 5.

[64] O'Connor (2006).

[65] The Law Reform Commission (2006), pp. 121–134.

[66] The Law Reform Commission (2006), p. 136.

[67] Connolly (2007), p. 61.

[68] Connolly (2007), p. 56.

[69] Killilea (2010), p. 80.

[70] Killilea (2010), p. ii and p. 3.

Lawyer

Refers to a solicitor in Ireland, a solicitor or barrister in Ontario and a similar professional in other jurisdictions. These professionals have authority to practice conveyancing in Ireland and real estate practice in Ontario.

Conveyancing

The passing of an estate or title to land by way of sale to a purchaser or by gift from one land owner to another land owner. Also the practice of property law by lawyers who facilitate the purchase and sale or gift of title to land. In Ontario this is more commonly referred to as real estate practice but the term conveyancing will be used. This passing of title to land occurs by means of a process or set of procedures that must be complied with in order for one land owner to dispose legally of their title to another who thereby becomes the owner of the land. Sale and purchase are used to describe a single transaction, such usage depending upon context and standpoint.

Conveyancing Transaction

This includes a purchase and sale or gift, of the whole or part of the title to land, whether freehold or leasehold, and also includes the granting of a lease or the creation of a charge in favour of a lender. In general usage it may also refer to the creation of other rights or interests such as easements, restrictive covenants or trusts in land.

Land Registration

The system under which titles to land are recorded. There are two basic divisions; deeds registration and title registration. Many commentators use alternative terminology to mark this division. For example Miceli refers to the title registration system as the Torrens system and the deeds registration system as the recording title system.[71] He, along with many other commentators, marks the division on the basis of the role of government in guaranteeing land title. The Torrens system is so called after Sir Robert Torrens, an Irishman, who introduced it first in South Australia in 1858.

O'Connor notes that the term 'Torrens system' is an ambiguous one[72] as it has been used in the general sense and also in a genealogical sense. In the general sense it is used to mean a system that registers land titles and not deeds or instruments. In

[71] Miceli et al. (2002), p. 565.
[72] O'Connor (2003), p. 82.

the genealogical sense it refers to the family of land title systems that derive, either directly or indirectly, from the statutes enacted in Australia at the instigation of Sir Robert Torrens.[73] The two key characteristics that members of this family share are that indefeasible title[74] guaranteed by the state is obtained by registration and the system includes a system of compensation to ameliorate the risk of an error in the register erroneously depriving a person of their interest in land.[75] However the type of indefeasible title and also the operation of the compensation system may differ.[76]

Indefeasible title may only arise in relation to the first registration of the title thus 'cleansing' it of all prior defects. It may be conferred on each purchaser (immediate indefeasibility) or, alternatively, if there is a defect in a transaction then that purchaser's title may not be indefeasible but a subsequent purchaser's title may be (deferred indefeasibility). There are also exceptions which may make the title defeasible. For example if the title was obtained through fraud[77] or there was some moral wrong-doing resulting in an *in personam* action.[78]

Similarly recourse to compensation may be limited in various ways. There may be criteria that have to be met. For example the party wronged may have to claim against the wrongdoer first so that the compensation fund is only a last recourse. In other jurisdictions the party may make a claim *ab initio*. Claimants may need to show that they did not cause the loss, fraud, neglect or default or the amount of compensation may be limited.

Indefeasibility and the compensation scheme are examined in Chaps. 4 and 7 with particular reference to Ontario and Ireland.

Deeds Registration (or Unregistered Title)

In Ireland deeds are registered in the Registry of Deeds. The deed (document) is registered but the title is not, so the title is commonly referred to as unregistered title.

---

[73] O'Connor (2003), p. 81.

[74] Conclusive and unimpeachable. See Ruoff (1952), p. 118.

[75] Flaws notes that state compensation may only have been introduced to entice lawyers to accept the Torrens system and he references law reform proposals in New South Wales as identifying Malaysia, Sudan, Fiji, West Germany and Austria as jurisdictions where registration systems operate without compensation. See Flaws (2003), p. 400.

[76] These aspects are explored in detail in Chaps. 4 and 7.

[77] There is no statutory definition in Ireland. In Ontario fraudulent instrument and fraudulent person are defined in section 1 of the Land Titles Act R.S.O. 1990, CHAPTER L. 5.

[78] A registered owner should not be allowed to refuse to perform contracts he had made and anyone who entered into such a contract should be entitled to claim such relief in law or in equity as a Court may grant. This includes specific performance or enforcement of a trust and may result in the Court ordering the registered owner to part with his title.

"Systems of deeds registration do not abrogate the principle that a chain of title is only as strong as its weakest link."[79] Thus under the deeds registration system the title must be investigated *de novo* every time the property is transferred.

In Ontario this system is referred to as the Registry system. In both jurisdictions this is the older system. As part of the move towards eConveyancing both jurisdictions have changed their deeds registration system to make it more similar to the title registration system so that in time the deeds system can be closed or merged into the title registration system.[80] In this analysis the term deeds registration or unregistered title denotes unregistered title in Ireland and deeds registered in the Registry system in Ontario.

Title Registration (or Registered Title)

In Ireland title is registered in the Land Registry. This is commonly referred to as registered land or title. In Ontario this system is referred to as the land titles system. In both jurisdictions the title is registered and not the deed as in a deeds register.

In this analysis the term title registration or registered title denotes registered title in both Ireland and Ontario. Many commentators have maintained that eConveyancing can only be successful in a title registration system and this has provided the impetus for both jurisdictions to move away from deeds registration towards title registration.

Neave sets out the triad of principles that underpin title registration; the 'mirror principle' (the register as a mirror of the state of the title),[81] the 'curtain principle' (behind which the purchaser need not investigate)[82] and the 'insurance principle' (the state guarantees the accuracy of the register and compensates any person suffering loss if there is an inaccuracy).[83] Together these concepts form 'the principle of indefeasibility'.[84]

Registering Authority (Registration Authority or Registry)

The authority which manages and controls land registration in each jurisdiction. In Ireland the Registry of Deeds and Land Registry are managed and controlled by the Property Registration Authority (PRA). The PRA (or PRAI) operates under the

[79] Neave (1976), p. 173.

[80] See Donahue et al. (2003), p. 1 in relation to Ontario.

[81] The question arises as to whether this means the state of the legal title or should it reflect the truth on the ground.

[82] The danger is that the 'real' ownership could be hidden behind this curtain.

[83] Neave (1976), p. 174. These three fundamental principles are attributed to Ruoff. See Ruoff (1952), p. 118.

[84] Neave (1976), p. 174.

auspices of the Department of Justice and Equality. In Ontario the Registry system and the Land Titles system are governed by the Ministry of Government Services (Ontario Ministry or Ministry). Both are under the control of central government.

Title Register (Register or Land Register)

The record of registered titles i.e. the title register held and maintained by the registering authority. The term title register is used as the term land register is close to land registration which encompasses both the title register and the deeds register.

The term land register may arise in quotations and unless otherwise indicated this should be read to mean the title register. The term register may also be used and again this should be read to mean the title register (and not the deeds register).

Deeds Register

The record of documents dealing with unregistered titles i.e. the register of deeds held and maintained by the registering authority.

Registrar

Generally this is an official in the registering authority who can alter the title register and who has statutory powers relating to the management and operation of land registration.

In Ireland this role is known as the Registrar of Titles however since 2006 the powers are vested in the PRA. Thus the terms Land Registry, registrar and PRA (or PRAI) in relation to Ireland may be used interchangeably.

In Ontario there are a number of roles; the Director of Titles, the Director of Land Registration and individual land registrars who cover the 54 land registry offices.[85] In simple terms the Director of Land Registration authorises access to the eRegistration system; the Director of Titles determines policy and regulates any matter relating to title and, while the individual land registrars can change the register if there is an error, only the Director of Titles can determine matters relating to fraud. References to the registrar in Ontario will refer to the Director of Titles unless otherwise stated.

---

[85] There are three individual land registrars. Interview with Ken Crawford Sr. Legal and Technical Analyst Service Ontario 12 July 2012.

Registration

The process of registration of

(a) title (an estate, right or interest in land);
(b) the deed, transfer or electronic transfer;
(c) encumbrance; and
(d) the deed of encumbrance, court order or other document which gives validity to the encumbrance.

Registrant

Person who alters the title register by means of an electronically sent message or data e.g. electronic transfer to the registering authority. This person is not employed by the registering authority and is usually a lawyer. This role does not arise outside of eRegistration or eConveyancing. As the person is not employed by the registering authority they are not under the direct management of central government. Their actions and authority are controlled by the business rules and policies laid down as part of the system design which is demonstrated via format and form.

Automatic

A change in the title register is automatic if it is triggered immediately by the registrant without any intervention by staff in the registering authority. It is automatic as no 'human' input is required from the registering authority. Arruñada refers to this as agency registration.[86]

Automated

A change in the title register may be automated without being automatic.[87] The process occurs via electronic channels but the registrar or staff in the registering authority need to act upon the message or data before a change in the title register can take place. Thus it is automated but not automatic. This 'human' input by the registering authority can involve processing of the data or a substantive check. eRegistration involves the automating of applications to the registering authority.

---

[86] Arruñada (2010), pp. 115–120. The implications of agency registration is explored further in Chap. 3.

[87] The United Nations Economic and Social Council (2007), p. 4 notes that the choice between automatic or automated access will often be determined by the nature of the registry guarantee or indemnity.

Applicant

Person, usually a lawyer, who makes an electronic application to the registrar but who cannot alter the title register. The word applicant is generally used when referring to the eApplication phase of eConveyancing where there remains lodgement of paper.

Transferor

Is the seller (or vendor) of registered title for value. For value means that the title is sold for its value in money or an equivalent. This is referred to as the consideration. In this analysis the term purchase monies is used. 'A' is the transferor[88] in the schematic in Chap. 5.

Transferee (or *Bona fide* Purchaser for Value)

Is the buyer (or purchaser) of registered title for value. This person is also called a *bona fide* purchaser for value.[89] 'B' is the transferee[90] in the schematic.

Donor

Is the person giving a gift of registered title not for value. 'X' is the donor in the schematic in Chap. 5.

Donee (or Volunteer)

Is the person receiving the gift of registered title not for value. This person is also called a volunteer.[91] 'Y' is the donee in the schematic.

[88] Used as a term of art for vendor in Ireland and hence this is used rather than following the more general England usage of 'vendor'.

[89] See Sect. 5.5 for a more detailed explanation.

[90] Used as a term of art for purchaser in Ireland and hence this is used rather than following the more general England usage of 'purchaser'.

[91] See Sect. 5.5 for a more detailed explanation.

Lender

This is the provider of secured finance for a conveyancing transaction. The finance is secured on the basis of a legal charge on the title to land. Also known as secured lender, chargee or mortgagee. In Ireland the lender is often treated the same as the transferee. Section 3 of the Land and Conveyancing Law Reform Act 2009[92] (hereafter the 2009 Act) provides that the definition of purchaser includes a mortgagee. This contrasts with the position in Ontario where the lender and transferee may be treated differently.[93]

The lender's role in a conveyancing transaction can be split into two specific functions. These functions can be carried out by the same provider or by two different providers. The **prior lender** will be seeking to have its charge paid in full from the purchase monies and the **acquisition lender** will be seeking to have a first legal charge registered against the title on foot of the monies advanced to the transferee for the conveyancing transaction. The prior lender is 'T' in the schematic and the acquisition lender is 'C'.

In Ireland standard practice is to have a first legal charge for 'all sums due' and any further monies advanced later by the same lender would be secured by that charge. Where additional monies are advanced by another lender there is the possibility of a second, or other subsequent charges, on the title and these would be common in commercial lending. The creation of second charges to release equity in family homes did occur to some extent during Ireland's property boom but many homes are now in negative equity and lending rules have tightened to the extent that such lending is now rare. Thus the role of such subsequent lenders does not form part of the schematic.

Where the land owner re-mortgages after the transaction is completed the new finance provider will step into the shoes of the acquisition lender and thus is dealt with as part of 'C's role in the schematic.

Chargor (or Mortgagor)

Holder of title to land who grants a legal charge (or mortgage) to a lender. When a mortgage is created the title is transferred to the lender who covenants to transfer the title back when the loan is repaid (redeemed). When a charge is created the title is not transferred to the lender but the charge becomes an encumbrance on the title. The terms mortgage and charge will be used interchangeably to denote a legal charge on title to land.

---

[92] No. 27 of 2009.

[93] In Ontario lenders are not members of the prescribed class given more favourable treatment for the recovery of compensation from the registrar. These aspects are explored more fully in Chap. 7.

Subsequent Purchaser

Person who subsequently purchases the property from the transferee, B, or the donee, Y. This is a *bona fide* purchaser for value[94] and does not include a subsequent lender. The subsequent purchaser is 'D' in the schematic.

Contract

The legally binding agreement between the transferor and transferee setting out the terms and conditions of the conveyancing transaction. This will be for value; generally no contract is completed in the case of a gift.

Deed

The formal document which passes title from a transferor to a transferee or from a donor to a donee. This is handed over at completion of the transaction and it gives effect to the contract. A deed of conveyance is the document which passes unregistered freehold title and a deed of assignment is the document which passes unregistered leasehold title. For registered title the deed is called a transfer.

Transfer (or Deed of Transfer)

The document which passes registered title (freehold and leasehold) from a transferor to a transferee or from a donor to a donee. This is handed over at completion of the transaction. It gives effect to the contract.

Electronic Transfer

The electronic form, message or series thereof which passes registered title from a transferor to a transferee or from a donor to a donee. This will be transmitted to the registering authority at or immediately after completion of the transaction. It gives effect to the contract.

Assurance

Generic term to include deed, transfer and electronic transfer.[95]

[94] See Sect. 5.5 for a more detailed explanation.

[95] For deeds registration this term would include a conveyance and assignment.

Completion (or Closing)

The legal and procedural requirements for finalising the conveyancing transaction. Moore and Globe refer to this as closing the deal[96] and in some jurisdictions it is referred to as settlement. The deed or transfer and vacant possession is exchanged for the purchase monies. In eConveyancing the electronic transfer is transmitted to the registering authority and there is electronic funds transfer (EFT) of the purchase monies. Thus completion may involve payment, transfer and registration of title. Generally physical possession or the right to physical possession of the property passes at the point of completion.

It is difficult to tie down a specific point of completion. This is due to the sequential nature of the conveyancing transaction and the fact that completion may involve a number of specific steps. In a paper environment the paper documents and keys may be exchanged physically for a cheque or bank draft. This exchange will then be referred to as the closing or completion of the deal. In an electronic environment there may be no exact point of exchange. Instead completion may occur at the push of a computer key.

From a transferor's perspective, completion is likely to be when the balance of the purchase monies is released to him or her. A transferee will likely say that completion occurs when they get the keys and thus possession. From a legal perspective completion occurs at an earlier point.

In Ireland the paper deed or transfer and any other closing documents, together with the keys, are exchanged for the purchase monies. This may occur in person or by post. After completion the transferee's lawyer will pay the stamp duty and then lodge the deed or transfer for registration. Thus completion occurs prior to registration.

In Ontario documents are signed electronically by the lawyers pursuant to a signed Acknowledgement and Direction[97] from the client.[98] The transaction is then closed and documents are registered in accordance with a Document Registration Agreement (DRA)[99] between the lawyers. A separate Acknowledgement and Direction and DRA will be required for each registration in the e-reg system[100]

---

[96] Moore and Globe (2003), p. 339.

[97] This must be retained in the lawyer's file as written verification of the clients' instructions and authority for electronic document registration. See The Law Society of Upper Canada (2002).

[98] The Acknowledgement and Direction confirms the client's approval of the electronic document and authorises the lawyer to sign and register electronically. It also authorises the lawyer to enter into a DRA and close in escrow on behalf of the client. See Moore and Globe (2003), pp. 418–419 for an example of an Acknowledgement and Direction. See also https://www.teranetexpress.ca/content/support/pdf/ADR.pdf.

[99] This is in a recommended form published by the Joint Law Society of Upper Canada–Canadian Bar Association Committee on Electronic Registration of Title Documents. See Moore and Globe (2003), pp. 421–422. See also http://rc.lsuc.on.ca/pdf/eReg/dramarch04.pdf.

[100] eRegistration system in Ontario.

i.e. a transfer, discharge of a charge or creation of a new charge. Electronic transactions are closed online in escrow.

As in traditional escrow closings the funds, keys and documents are held in trust until each lawyer has confirmed receipt and approval of their respective requirements. The transferree's lawyer will usually register the transfer and other documents according to the list set out in Schedule A of the DRA. This lists the documents being registered and also the order or priority in which they are to be registered. The sequence is usually as follows[101]:

1. the transferor's lawyer delivers the closing documents that are not to be registered to the transferee's lawyer
2. the transferee's lawyer delivers the closing documents that are not to be registered to the transferor's lawyer together with a certified cheque for the closing proceeds
3. all these non registration documents and the purchase monies are held in escrow
4. once each lawyer is satisfied with the closing deliveries due to them, the transferor's lawyer logs on to the Teraview system[102] and authorises the release of the registration documents
5. the transferee's lawyer then logs onto the system and completes a final search to confirm that there has been no change to the title
6. once this is confirmed the transferee's lawyer instructs the system to proceed with registration
7. the system automatically searches for executions[103] before registration is completed
8. once registration is completed the transferee's solicitor contacts the transferor's solicitor to confirm the registration and then all documents and monies are released from the escrow.

This is the sequence where the DRA provides for the release from escrow to occur following notice that registration has been completed. The DRA also allows for this release to occur at a closing time referred to in the agreement of purchase and sale.

A registration confirmation report which lists the documents and their registration numbers will be printed immediately following closing. In addition the parcel register[104] may be printed in order to confirm registration. Fees are transferred in the Teraview account for payment of registry fees and taxes. The final closing searches are also done online.

[101] Donahue et al. (2003), pp. 267–273.

[102] Teraview is the eRegistration software. This software delivers the land registration system under contract from the Ontario Ministry. See Sect. 3.4.2 for more detail.

[103] Judgments.

[104] The title register in Ontario is called a parcel whereas in Ireland it is referred to as a folio.

The standard form provides for two alternative completion options, completion to occur after registration or at an earlier closing time, but Donahue and his colleagues note that despite the risks:

> current practice is to complete purchases and mortgage advances just as one would do under the [unregistered] Registry system and not await the certification of the instrument.[105]

Thus in both Ireland and generally in Ontario closing occurs in advance of registration. Funds and non-registration documents are exchanged in advance of electronic registration in Ontario. In Ireland funds and all documents are exchanged in advance of paper registration.

The issue of completion is explored further in Chap. 6 as the time gap between completion and registration is one of the key risks examined.

Land Owner

Generic term to include transferor, transferee, donor and donee i.e. 'A', 'B', 'X' and 'Y' in the schematic in Chap. 5.

Encumbrance

Encumbrance is a burden or restriction on the title to land and includes charges held by a lender, rights or interests held by third parties and judgments against the title.

Property Claimant

Someone claiming or asserting a new right or interest in the land. The potential time available for claiming or asserting such a right or interest is usually limited. 'V' is the property claimant in the schematic.

Examples might include a non owning spouse who has the right to challenge a transaction that took place without their consent, someone claiming a right of pre-emption on foot of a contract or option to purchase, a claim of proprietary estoppel or part performance or someone who contributed to the purchase price and is thus claiming the existence of a trust.

The claim may be unsuccessful or may succeed but be deemed not to create a new right or interest in the land. In these instances the property claim fails. The successful property claimant will become a third party or encumbrancer.

---

105 Donahue et al. (2003), p. 35.

Third Party (or Encumbrancer)

Someone other than the land owner or lender who wishes to protect their existing right or interest in land. A successful property claimant becomes a third party or encumbrancer. This third party has a proprietary interest in the land. For example someone holding an easement or an equitable interest. Such third party rights do not fall within the registrable estates but instead may appear as burdens upon registered titles. The third party is ‘U’ in the schematic.

Pre Contract

The initial negotiation and enquiries carried out in a conveyancing transaction prior to execution of the contract.[106] For example there may be some negotiation about the exact purchase monies and completion date. The enquiries may relate to the size and physical condition or location of the property, planning, occupation, outgoings and services.[107]

Post Contract

The stage of the conveyancing transaction after execution of the contract and before completion. During this stage the transferor and transferee are legally bound to complete the transaction and cannot back out save as provided for by the terms of the contract.

The exact point at which the contract becomes binding will differ according to the jurisdiction and the terms of the contract. It may be when the contract is signed by both parties (executed) or when it is signed and delivered (or exchanged) or it may not be binding until a deposit is paid.

Alternatively the contract may be executed subject to some conditions and will only become binding when these conditions are met. In both Ontario and Ireland the contract will usually be subject to such conditions. This contract is in a standard form. In Ireland it is a precedent document issued by the Law Society.[108] In Ontario it is usually in a printed form prepared by a legal stationer or by the local real estate board.[109]

---

[106] In Ireland the contract is referred to as the contract or conditions of sale. In Ontario it is called an agreement of purchase and sale.

[107] See Brennan and Casey (2014), pp. 18–29 for examples relevant to Ireland.

[108] Brennan and Casey (2014), Appendix 6.1 and see pp. 111–117 for examples of conditions that may be included.

[109] Donahue et al. (2003), p. 206 and see Appendix 6 and 7 for examples of Agreements of Purchase and Sale. See also pp. 221–227 for examples of conditions that may be included.

Post Completion

The legal and procedural formalities to be done after completion. These will often include payment and discharge of the prior charge and registration of the transferee's title and the new charge. It will also include practical matters such as the transferee taking occupation of the property and notifying service providers of the new ownership.

Title to Land

"Both 'who can be an owner' and 'what can be owned' are defined by law.... Ownership can only exist if it is acknowledged and properly enforced within a society."[110] In legal terms what is owned is not the land or property, the physical entity, but an estate or interest in that entity which denotes the nature and extent of land ownership.[111] The student of property law expects to study physical objects but instead encounters abstractions.[112] Often this is referred to as having title to land.

Title to land can be divided into two fundamental groups; estates and interests. Interests are more minor and fall short of estates which confer major rights in respect of the land. In simple terms an estate gives the right to possession or occupation to the exclusion of others while an interests confers a limited right to land owned by another.

> The notion of dividing ownership according to different periods of time is what makes land ownership under a common law system flexible. It enshrines the fundamental principle that what is owned is not the physical entity, the land, but rather some estate (giving substantial rights in respect of the land such as the right to occupy it) or interest (giving less substantial rights such as the limited use given by an easement comprising, for example, a right of way over a road on the land, or a *profit à prendre* comprising a right to cut and take away turf) in the land. . ..How many of the various estates and interests will exist in respect of a particular parcel of land will vary from case to case.[113]

Different people may own different estates and interests at the same time or in succession in respect of the same land. Engle notes that the "concept of absolute exclusivity and precisely defined right is completely alien to contemporary legal thought, which sees [property] rights as relative, divisible, and somewhat amorphous."[114]

---

[110] Ottens and Stubkjær (2007), p. 151.

[111] Gray and Gray (1998), at p. 15 note that property is not a thing but rather a relationship which one has with a thing.

[112] Lawson and Rudden (1982), p. 15.

[113] Explanatory memorandum Land and Conveyancing Law Reform Act 2009, p. 3.

[114] Engle (2010), pp. 84–107.

For Calabresi and Melamed the law decides entitlement, so as to determine who will prevail among two conflicting parties, and having made that initial choice must then enforce it through state intervention.[115] In relation to conflicting property rights this will be reflected in how a property registration system operates.

Not every estate or interest can avail of the protection offered by registration in the registering authority. Those capable of registration in the title register are seen as being more advantageous than those capable of registration in the deeds register as the title register is backed by a state guarantee. Chapter 4 examines in detail the estates and interests that can be registered in Ontario and Ireland.

In general property law seeks to classify property rather than to define it. The classifications govern the way property interests are protected in law by registration and the way they are transmitted which is procedural. Lawson and Rudden note that property law defines types of user as 'property' which will be protected against third parties and is alienable and is divided into those which bind regardless of notice (overriding interests)[116] and those that depend on notice (registration).[117]

The four dimensions that determine how property is classified are length, height, breadth and time. In seeking ways to make sense of this classification commentators have used varying methods of explaining the nature of ownership. Lawson and Rudden provide some examples based on the principle of the fragmentation of ownership.[118] Birks uses five keys: time, space, reality, duality and formality.[119]

These principles and the concept of estates and interests flowing from them recognise the flexible division of ownership including the division between legal and equitable ownership. In addition the inchoate nature of the common law equitable system often allows for the growth of categories of estates and interests which are not limited and may be expanded to meet the needs and demands of the market place.

This is in stark contrast to the *numerus clausus* doctrine which applies in civil law countries.

> The numerus clausus – principle states that nature and content of the German real rights are regulated by law. . ..in legal dealings rights have to be selected from a self-contained pool of real rights. This might appear to you. . .as being restrictive. . ..However, it is a fact that German 19th century lawmakers were ruled by a desire for legal certainty, clarity, and uniformity.[120]

As Lawson and Rudden point out:

> [i]f property law had been codified after the Continental fashion, the codifiers would have introduced more order into it, and in particular would have asked whether certain generalizations accepted for one kind of property were acceptable for others.[121]

[115] Calabresi and Melamed (1972), p. 1090.

[116] These interests are examined later in this chapter.

[117] Lawson and Rudden (1982), p. 218.

[118] Lawson and Rudden (1982), p. 218.

[119] Birks (1998), p. 460.

[120] Wilsch (2008), p. 6 in referring to the application of the principle.

[121] Lawson and Rudden (1982), p. 224.

Instead they note a lack of co-ordination in English property law and the different ways of dealing with property in that it may be enjoyed as a physical object or as an investment "of which the money value alone is relevant....[This distinction] may be expressed summarily as one between objects and wealth, or between use-value and exchange-value."[122] The differing values which can be imposed on property ownership is a recurring theme throughout this analysis.

The push towards eConveyancing has given impetus to the drive for similar legal certainty, clarity and uniformity in common law jurisdictions and there is a possibility that a move towards *numerus clausus* will become the norm. It is more difficult to build an electronic system that is flexible enough to accommodate estates and interests that may not be determined for some years to come. This aspect of eConveyancing is explored in Chap. 8.[123]

Estates

In both Ontario and Ireland ownership of land is defined according to common law principles which are less absolute and more flexible than the civil law system in continental Europe referred to earlier.

> Land is 'held' (not 'owned' in the civil law sense) and the tenant is entitled to an 'estate'. Various types of estates can be distinguished, but an essential characteristic of each estate is time. The two major types are the freehold (unlimited duration) and the leasehold (limited duration).[124]

Many jurisdictions, including Ontario and Ireland, limit the number of legal estates to these two. The first being a freehold (also know as the fee simple) and the second being a leasehold which is a limited estate in that it only exists for a term of years. It may be said that each estate is conferred with powers, rights, privileges and liberties.[125] Each estate confers rights together with obligations on the land owner and property law often attempts to balance these in the one estate and also between different land owners.

In Ontario the Crown has the ultimate or underlying title however this has been described as a legal fiction.[126] Rights are held from the crown in the form of tenures, estates and interests. When Ontario was settled all land in the province was claimed by the Crown and the only way settlers could get title was to obtain a Crown Patent.[127] Donahue notes that only by examining the Crown Patent can you

---

[122] Lawson and Rudden (1982), p. 226.

[123] See Sect. 8.5.

[124] Van Erp (2003a).

[125] On the nature of rights see Hohfeld (1913), pp. 16–59 and for a commentary see Engle (2010), pp. 84–107.

[126] Pienaar (2008), p. 2.

[127] Donahue et al. (2003), p. 2.

ascertain what interests are retained by the Crown and this information does not appear in the registry except for patents issued since 1 October 1965.[128]

In Ireland the 2009 Act[129] abolished feudal tenure[130] and the old feudal notion that all land was held ultimately from the Crown. The explanatory memorandum states that this concept is not compatible with the relationship between the State and its citizens as prescribed by the Constitution.[131] However the position of the State as ultimate intestate successor to a deceased person's property under section 73 of the Succession Act 1965 was preserved.[132] The word tenure continues to be used to denote the terms and conditions under which someone holds land while the doctrine of estates is used to denote the duration or time for which the land is held.[133]

The 2009 Act preserved the notion of estates and interests in land,[134] both freehold and leasehold. The only legal estates that may be created or disposed of are the freehold and leasehold estates specified by section 11. Section 11(4) set out the legal interests in land that could be created or disposed of. Whether they are legal or equitable will depend on how the interest was created. Failure to comply with the necessary formalities may lead to an equitable interest only being created.[135]

Section 11(2) provides that a freehold estate means a fee simple in possession and includes

(a) a determinable fee,[136]
(b) a fee simple subject to a right of entry or of re-entry,[137]
(c) a fee simple subject only to
    (i) a power of revocation,
    (ii) an annuity or other payment of capital or income for the advancement, maintenance or other benefit of any person, or
    (iii) a right of residence which is not an exclusive right over the whole land.

---

[128] See Donahue et al. (2003), p. 2. If the patent issued prior to 1 October 1965 a search must be made in the Ministry of Natural Resources and if the lands were reserved as Indian lands then searches must be made elsewhere.

[129] Note that one of the guiding principles of this Act as listed in the explanatory memorandum was to facilitate the introduction of an eConveyancing system as soon as possible.

[130] Section 9(2).

[131] P. 3.

[132] Section 9(3)(a)(ii). Other statutory limits on ownership also continue to apply e.g. planning legislation.

[133] Lyall (2010), p. 63.

[134] Section 10(1).

[135] See Battersby (1998).

[136] This is a qualified fee simple. It is subject to the possibility that it may end prematurely.

[137] The fee simple may be subject to the right of some other person to entry or re-entry. The right of entry will be to take possession temporarily whereas the right of re-entry will be to take permanently. In the case of re-entry the previous owner's estate or interest will be forfeit.

Section 11(3) provides that a leasehold estate means the estate which arises when a tenancy is created for any period of time or any recurring period and irrespective of whether or not the estate

(a) takes effect in immediate possession or in future, or
(b) is subject to another legal estate or interest, or
(c) is for a term which is uncertain or liable to termination by notice, re-entry or operation of law or by virtue of a provision for cessor on redemption or for any other reason.

Such a tenancy creates the relationship of landlord and tenant which is based on the parties' contract or agreement and not on tenure.[138] A tenancy may be for a fixed period of time or for any recurring period. These recurring tenancies are known as periodic tenancies and may be weekly, monthly or yearly. They will run for such successive periods until either party serves notice terminating the tenancy.

Interests (or Rights in Land)

Section 11(4) sets out the legal interests in land which may be created or disposed of. These are more minor and fall short of estates which confer major rights in respect of the land. An estate gives the right to possession or occupation to the exclusion of others while an interests confers a limited right to land owned by another. Legal interests are limited to the following;

(a) an easement,[139]
(b) a freehold covenant,[140]
(c) an incumbrance,[141]
(d) a rent payable under a tenancy,[142]
(e) a possibility of reverter,[143]
(f) a *profit à prendre*, including a mining right,[144]
(g) a public or customary right,[145]
(h) a rentcharge,[146]

[138] See section 3 of the Landlord and Tenant Law Amendment Act, Ireland 1860 (known as Deasy's Act).

[139] These include a right to light, right of way or a right of support.

[140] Such a covenant may require a fence to be erected or may restrict usage.

[141] Under section 3 this includes annuities, liens and other charges over land which may be created in favour of others. Examples include the payment of a capital sum or funds to provide an income or the creation of a mortgage or judgment mortgage.

[142] This is an interest that can be assigned.

[143] Again this is an interest that can be assigned.

[144] The holder has the right to go onto someone else's land and take something natural from it. Examples are the right to cut turf (turbary) and graze animals (pasture).

[145] Examples include a public right of way or the right to use parkland.

[146] The rent is a charge on the land and arises separate to the relationship of landlord and tenant.

(i) a right of entry or of re-entry attached to a legal estate,[147]
(j) a wayleave or other right to lay cables, pipes, wires or other conduits,[148]
(k) any other legal interest created by any statutory provision.[149]

Thus further legal interests can be created by statute. Other estates and interests take effect as equitable interests only but this does not prevent the creation of the above estates and interests as equitable interests.[150] Also nothing in the 2009 Act affects judicial recognition of equitable interests.[151] Thus the courts remain free to exercise their equitable jurisdiction to develop the law in order to accommodate the changing needs of Irish society. Recent examples include the

> equitable doctrines of proprietary estoppel and constructive and resulting trusts, whereby a person who is the strict legal owner of land may be regarded as holding it subject to some equitable interest of another person.[152]

As previously noted Canada has retained the feudal principle that all land is held or owned by the Crown. "Where no original Crown patent was issued for a piece of land, no private ownership can exist in law, even today."[153] Subject, however, to that underlying Crown ownership, individual owners hold estates. Again the two basic categories are freehold and leasehold. The freehold can be a fee simple and though less common a conditional fee simple, a determinable fee simple or a life estate. The leasehold estate can be fixed or periodic. These are the only legal estates that can exist.

The distinction between legal and equitable interests is important. The general rule is that legal interests will bind successors in title whereas a mere equitable interest may lose priority to subsequent purchasers of a legal estate. Thus legal interests confer a greater degree of protection on the holder. While additional legal interests can be created by legislation and equitable interests can be created by the courts, only two legal estates exist; the freehold and leasehold.

These interests or rights with reference to Ireland and Ontario include:

- easements
- rights of non owning spouses, civil partners or cohabitees during the life of the land owner
- judgment mortgagor
- the proprietary interests of anyone in actual occupation
- someone holding under adverse possession

[147] The right to entry or re-entry may arise in relation to a freehold or leasehold estate. The right of entry will be temporary whereas the right to re-entry will lead to forfeiture of the previous owner's estate or interest.

[148] Utility companies supplying water, gas and electricity commonly hold these interests.

[149] Section 11(4).

[150] Section 11(6).

[151] Section 11(7).

[152] Explanatory memorandum Land and Conveyancing Law Reform Act 2009, p. 5.

[153] Moore and Globe (2003), p. 2.

- trespassers
- lender holding under a charge
- spouses, civil partners, cohabitees or children on the death of the land owner
- those holding under a trust or settlement
- those holding the benefit of a restrictive covenant
- rights of enlargement
- remedial rights
- right of state or Crown in relation to non payment of taxes[154]
- someone holding a construction lien[155]
- any title or lien acquired by an adjoining owner due to improvements[156]
- any right of expropriation, access or user, or any other right, conferred upon or reserved or vested in the state or Crown[157]
- right to payment of any periodic sum of money (except rent under a lease or tenancy)
- public rights
- any other rights or equitable interests not already listed above

Such rights may be legal or equitable and some are capable of being registered as an encumbrance on the title register. Some may also have status as overriding interests. This list excludes personal rights that cannot be enforced against title to land. Those holding under a lease or tenancy[158] hold an estate and thus are not listed here.

The distinction between different rights in land can be confusing as many commentators use the words rights and interests interchangeably and may even use these terms when they actually mean estates.[159] Also estates that are capable of being registered in the title register are commonly called registered or registrable interests. Chapter 5 explores the categorisation of rights in more detail.[160]

Chapter 4 explores the estates and interests that can be registered in the title register in both Ontario and Ireland.

[154] Including any rights accruing to the local authorities in Ireland or the municipal authorities in Ontario.

[155] There is no comparable right in Irish law.

[156] There is no comparable right in Irish law.

[157] Including any rights accruing to the local authorities in Ireland or the municipal authorities in Ontario or any other public or statutory bodies in both jurisdictions. This includes the right of escheat or forfeiture to the Crown which is still a feature of the Ontario system. In Ireland the notion of escheat was abolished by section 11(3) of the Succession Act 1965.

[158] Tenancy usually refers to a short term lease of a residential property. It may be oral or in writing. Lease generally refers to a longer term interest that is set out in writing and it may be of residential or commercial property.

[159] Birks notes that the word 'interests' is slightly evasive. See Birks (1998), p. 460.

[160] See Sect. 5.6.

Overriding Interests

Overriding interests are those that affect title without registration in the title register.

The Ontario government guarantees the registered title vested in a land owner subject to the liabilities, rights and interests in section 44(1) of the Land Titles Act R.S.O. 1990[161] (hereafter the Land Titles Act) and these are deemed not to be encumbrances within the meaning of the Act. Section 44(1) contains a list of 13 liabilities, rights and interests to which registered land remains subject. Donahue *et al.* note that it is a formidable list.[162]

Similarly the Irish Land Registry guarantees registered title subject to some exceptions. Section 72(1) as amended[163] of the Registration of Title Act, 1964[164] (hereafter the 1964 Act) sets out the class that affects without registration though notice of any section 72 burden may be entered on the register under section 72 (3).[165]

The 19 overriding interests in Ireland are listed below and where there is commonality with the 13 in Ontario this is indicated in brackets and italics.

1. duties and taxes (*provincial taxes and succession duties*)
2. charges re land improvement and drainage
3. annuities or rentcharges under the Land Purchase Acts
4. rights of the Land Commission or of any person under an order made or published under the Land Purchase Acts
5. rights of the Land Commission under an order for possession
6. public rights (*any public highway*)
7. customary rights arising from tenure
8. easement and profits a prendre unless created by express grant or reservation after the first registration of the land (*any right of way, watercourse, and right of water, and other easements*)
9. wayleaves
10. tenancies created for any term not exceeding 21 years or for any less estate or interest, in cases where there is an occupation under such tenancies (*short term leases with an unexpired term for less than three years where there is actual occupation*)[166]
11. the rights of every person in actual occupation of the land or in receipt of the rents and profits thereof, save where, upon enquiry made of such person the

[161] Land Titles Act R.S.O. 1990, CHAPTER L. 5.

[162] Donahue et al. (2003), p. 27.

[163] The 1964 Act has been amended on numerous occasions.

[164] No 16 of 1964.

[165] This is subject to the consent of the registered owner or an order of the Court.

[166] Leases for longer terms must be registered.

rights are not disclosed (*possessory rights in the matrimonial home of the spouse of the registered owner under Part II of the Family Law Act*[167])[168]

12. in the case of land registered with a possessory, qualified or good leasehold title, all rights excepted from the effect of registration
13. a perpetual yearly superior rent
14. covenants and conditions created in an instrument creating the superior rent
15. purchase annuity for a cottage under the Labourers Act 1936
16. restrictions on the mortgaging or charging of such cottages
17. rights acquired or in the course of being acquired under the Statute of Limitations 1957 i.e. adverse possession (*any title or lien that, by possession or improvements, the owner or person interested in any adjoining land has acquired to or in respect of the land*)[169]
18. burdens to which section 59 (prohibition or restriction on alienation, assignment, subdivision or sub-letting) or 73 (mines, minerals and mining rights) applies
19. covenants which continue in force after enlargement

Those arising in Ontario with no comparable interest in Ireland are:

a. a construction lien (in Ireland a creditor would obtain a judgment mortgage)
b. any right of expropriation, access or user, or any other right, conferred upon or reserved or vested in the Crown (though this does have a degree of commonality with 2–5, 15 and 16 above)
c. any liabilities, rights and interests created under section 38 of the Public Transportation and Highway Improvement Act
d. Any by-law passed under section 34 of the Planning Act
e. planning act violations under sections 50 and 50.1 of the Planning Act[170]
f. where the registered owner is or was previously a railway company
g. any right of the wife of the person registered as owner to dower in case of surviving the owner

The impact of these overriding interests on risk is dealt with in Chap. 8.

---

[167] Family Law Act R.S.O. 1990 c. F. 3.

[168] In Ontario this is confined to spouses. In Ireland it is extended to all persons which will also include spouses. The case of *Guckian v. Brennan* [1981] I.R. 478 held that the power of a spouse to refuse consent to a transfer of the family home is not a section 72 burden though such a spouse may have an overriding interest if in occupation. In the absence of evidence that the assignment had been invalidated Gannon J. held that the plaintiffs could rely on their registration as full owners with an absolute title and on the conclusiveness of the register. See also *Murray v. Diamond* [1982] I.L.R.M. 113 which affirmed that the right of a spouse to veto a transaction in relation to the family home is not an overriding interest as section 72 relates to property rights only. The spouse must hold an estate or interest in the land. In England and Wales the matrimonial home rights of a spouse cannot be an overriding interest. See section 31(10)(b) of the Family Law Act 1996.

[169] Note that in Ontario this is limited to adjoining land.

[170] Donahue et al. (2003), p. 28 note that this exception creates a serious flaw in the registered title system.

Registrable Interests (or Registered Title)

Not every estate or interest is capable of being registered in the title register. Generally estates are capable of substantive registration but in the case of a lease this may depend on the length. Other rights may also be capable of registration but only as burdens on the registered title e.g. a charge. These rights need to be registered to gain priority.

There are a number of different quality or classes of title. In Ontario section 32 (2) of the Land Titles Act provides that land may be registered with an absolute, possessory, qualified or leasehold title. In Ireland the classes are absolute, possessory, qualified and good leasehold title.[171]

In Ontario two new types of title were created in order to administratively convert titles from the unregistered system into the registered system. During this conversion titles were automatically entered into the title register as part of the implementation of eRegistration. No application was required by the owner. Teranet[172] converted these titles into qualified titles called Land Titles Conversion Qualified (LTCQ) and such titles can be upgraded to Land Titles Plus (LT Plus). An LT Plus title "is the best of all titles."[173] If these types of registered title in Ontario were graded against an absolute title according to the benefits they offered the land owner they would be listed in the following order:

1. LT Plus
2. LTCQ
3. Absolute title

This is in contrast with most other title registration systems, including Ireland's, where the absolute title remains the highest quality title on offer. Lyall says that absolute title "suggests a title absolutely guaranteed against interests not appearing on the register, but this is far from the case and the description is in fact quite misleading. A better description would be "least qualified title"."[174]

Title registration and the types of registered title in Ireland and Ontario is explored further in Chap. 4.

Purchase Monies

The amount paid by the transferee to the transferor to purchase the title to land.

[171] See sections 33 and 40 of the 1964 Act as substituted by sections 56 and 57 of the 2006 Act.

[172] Teranet operates Teraview which delivers the electronic system under contract from the Ontario Ministry.

[173] Moore and Globe (2003), pp. 18 and 219.

[174] Lyall (2010), p. 938.

Conclusion
This chapter explored the methodology and defined the neutral vocabulary to be used in the creation of the abstracted model of the conveyancing process. Before developing that model the next two chapters explore eConveyancing and title registration in more detail.

References

Akhtar, Z. (2014). Land registry, electronic conveyancing and harmonisation: A review of current practice. *The Conveyancer and Property Lawyer*.

Arruñada, B. (2010). Leaky title syndrome? *New Zealand Law Journal*.

Battersby, G. (1998). Informally created interests in land. In S. Bright & J. Dewar (Eds.), *Land law themes and perspectives*. Great Britain: Oxford University Press.

Birks, P. (1998). Before we begin: Five keys to land law. In S. Bright & J. Dewar (Eds.), *Land law themes and perspectives*. Great Britain: Oxford University Press.

Brennan, G., & Casey, N. (Eds.). (2014). *Conveyancing* (7th ed.). Oxford: Oxford University Press.

Calabresi, G., & Melamed, A. D. (1972). Property rules, liability rules, and inalienability: One view of the cathedral. *Harvard Law Review, 85*(6).

Canada Mortgage and Housing Corporation. (2014). *Housing now Ontario region*. http://www.cmhc-schl.gc.ca/odpub/esub/64143/64143_2014_Q02.pdf?fr=1400081037361. Accessed 14 May 2014.

Chodosh, H. (1998–1999). Comparing comparisons: In search of methodology. *Iowa Law Review, 84*.

Clancy, D. (2007). *Benchmarking land registration*. In Registering the World Conference, Dublin, 26–28 September 2007. http://www.prai.ie/uploadedfiles/conference20071/papers/s5p4.pdf. Accessed 14 May 2014.

Connolly, F. (2007, October). *E-conveyancing: Who will benefit?* (B.Sc. Hons Dissertation). Dublin Institute of Technology and Irish Auctioneers and Valuers Institute.

Dale, P., Mahoney, R., & McLaren, R. (2006). Land markets and the modern economy. *Royal Institution of Chartered Surveyors*. http://www.knowedge.co.uk/Papers/Land_markets.pdf. Accessed 23 June 2014.

Deeney, J. (2014). *Registration of deeds and title in Ireland*. Great Britain: Bloomsbury.

Dol, K., & Haffner, M. (Eds.). (2010). *Housing statistics in the European Union 2010*. In Ministry of Interior and Kingdom Relations, The Hague. http://www.iut.nu/Literature/2010/HousingStatistics_InTheEU_2010.pdf. Accessed 14 May 2014.

Donahue, D. J., Quinn, P. D., & Grandilli, D. C. (2003). *Real estate practice in Ontario* (6th ed.). Canada: LexisNexis Butterworths.

Engle, E. (2010). Taking the right seriously: Hohfeldian semiotics and rights discourse. *The Crit, 3* (1). http://papers.ssrn.com/sol3/papers.cfm?abstract_id=1424691 and http://thecritui.com/2010/01/volume-3-issue-1-winter-edition-2010/. Accessed 13 June 2014.

Ewald, W. (1995). Comparative jurisprudence (II): The logic of legal transplants. *American Journal of Comparative Law, 43*(4).

Ferlan, M., Šumrada, R., & Mattsson, H. (2007). Modelling property transactions. In J. Zevenbergen, A. Frank, & E. Stubkjær (Eds.), *Real property transactions: Procedures, transaction costs and models*. Amsterdam: IOS.

Flaws, J. (2003). Compensation for loss under the Torrens system – Extending state compensation with private insurance. In D. Grinlinton (Ed.), *Torrens in the twenty-first century*. Wellington: LexisNexis.

Gray, K., & Gray, S. F. (1998). The idea of property in land. In S. Bright & J. Dewar (Eds.), *Land law themes and perspectives*. Great Britain: Oxford University Press.
Hage, J., & Verheij, B. (1999). The law as a dynamic interconnected system of states of affairs: A legal top ontology. *International Journal of Human-Computer Studies, 51*.
Hohfeld, W. N. (1913). Some fundamental legal conceptions as applied in judicial reasoning. *Yale Law Journal, 23*(1).
Irish Banking Federation/PriceWaterhouseCoopers Mortgage Market Profile Quarter 1. (2014). http://www.ibf.ie/gns/publications/research/researchmortgagemarket.aspx. Accessed 14 May 2014.
Kahn-Freund, O. (1974). On uses and misuses of comparative law. *Modern Law Review, 37*(1).
Killilea, M. (2010, April). *eRegistration in Ireland – An assessment of the transferability of the Queensland model* (Dissertation). Dublin Institute of Public Administration.
Lawson, F. H., & Rudden, B. (1982). *The law of property* (2nd ed.). Oxford: Clarendon.
Legrand, P. (1997). The impossibility of 'Legal Transplants'. *Maastricht Journal of European and Comparative Law, 4*(2).
Lemmen, C., van der Molen, P., Van Oosterom, P., Zevenbergen, J., & Quak, W. (2005). *Further progress in the development of the core Cadastral Domain model*. In International Federation of Surveyors (FIG) Working Week 2005 and 8th International Conference on the Global Spatial Data Infrastructure (GSDI – 8) Cairo, Egypt, 16–21 April 2005. http://www.fig.net/pub/cairo/ppt/ts_11/ts11_01_lemmen_etal_ppt.pdf. Accessed 13 June 2014.
Lepaulle, P. (1921–1922). The function of comparative law with a critique of sociological jurisprudence. *Harvard Law Review, 35*.
Lyall, A. (2010). *Land law in Ireland* (3rd ed.). England: Round Hall.
Meadows, J., & Griffin, M. (2007). *Introducing land title registration to Bermuda: Another world?* In Registering the World Conference, Dublin, 26–28 September 2007. http://www.prai.ie/uploadedfiles/conference20071/papers/s2p3.pdf. Accessed 14 May 2014.
Miceli, T. J., et al. (2002). Title systems and land values. *Journal of Law and Economics, 45*.
Moore, M. E., & Globe, J. M. (2003). *Title searching and conveyancing in Ontario* (5th ed.). Canada: LexisNexis.
Neave, M. (1976). Indefeasibility of title in the Canadian context. *University of Toronto Law Journal, 26*.
O'Connor, P. (2003). Registration of title in England and Australia: A theoretical and comparative analysis. In E. Cooke (Ed.), *Modern studies in property law* (Vol. II). Oxford: Hart.
O'Connor, P. (2006). *Electronic conveyancing: Who benefits?* Public lecture Monash Centre for Regulatory Studies at Monash Law Chambers, 6 June 2006. http://www.law.monash.edu.au/regstudies/pamspaper.pdf. Accessed 1 Dec 2010.
O'Sullivan, J. (2007). *eRegistration and eConveyancing in Ireland – The story so far....* In Registering the World Conference, Dublin, 26–28 September 2007. http://www.prai.ie/uploadedfiles/conference20071/papers/s3p6.pdf. Accessed 14 May 2014.
Ottens, M., & Stubkjær, E. (2007). A socio-technical analysis of cadastral systems. In J. Zevenbergen et al. (Eds.), *Real property transactions: Procedures, transaction costs and models*. Amsterdam: IOS.
Paasch, J. M. (2007). Real property transactions. In J. Zevenbergen et al. (Eds.), *Real property transactions: Procedures, transaction costs and models*. Amsterdam: IOS.
Pienaar, G. (2008, May). The inclusivity of communal land tenure: A redefinition of ownership in Canada and South Africa? *Electronic Journal of Comparative Law, 12.1*. http://www.ejcl.org/121/abs121-19.html. Accessed 23 June 2014.
Property Registration Authority. (2013). *Annual report 2012*. Property Registration Authority http://www.prai.ie/eng/Publications/Annual_Reports/PRA_Annual_Reports_.html. Accessed 5 June 2014.
Rätsep, H. (2008). *Estonian land registration and experiences in electronic conveyancing*. In CINDER XVI International Congress on Registration Law, Valencia, Spain, 20–22 May 2008.

http://www.cinder2008.com/ingles/detalle_ponencia.cfm?id_ponencia=297. Accessed 26 Aug 2010.

Registering the World Conference Dublin. (2007). *Conference papers*, 26–28 September 2007. http://www.prai.ie/eng/Publications/Other_Publications/Conference_2007_Papers.html. Accessed 14 May 2014.

Ruoff, T. (1952). An Englishman looks at the Torrens system: Part 1: The mirror principle. *Australian Law Journal, 26.*

Sen, A. (2009). *The idea of justice*. London: Allen Lane.

Statistics Canada. (2011). *Canada at a glance 2011*. http://www.iut.nu/Facts%20and%20figures/Canada/CanadaAtGlance_2011.pdf. Accessed 14 May 2014.

Stubkjær, E. (2003). Modelling units of real property rights. In K. Virrantaus & H. Tveite (Eds.), *The 9th Scandinavian research conference on Geographical Information Science (GIS)*, 4–6 June 2003, Espoo, Finland – Proceedings. http://www.scangis.org/scangis2003/papers/. Accessed 3 Feb 2011.

Stubkjær, E., Frank, A., & Zevenbergen, J. (2007). Modelling real property transactions. In J. Zevenbergen, A. Frank, & E. Stubkjær (Eds.), *Real property transactions: Procedures, transaction costs and models*. Amsterdam: IOS.

Teubner, G. (1998). Legal irritants: Good faith in British law or how unifying law ends up in new divergences. *Modern Law Review, 61.*

The Food and Agriculture Organization of the United Nations. (2003). *Multilingual thesaurus on land tenure*. In G. Ciparisse (Ed.). http://www.fao.org/DOCREP/005/X203s8E/X2038E00.HTM. Accessed 13 June 2014.

The Law Reform Commission. (2006). *eConveyancing: Modelling of the Irish conveyancing system*. In The Law Reform Commission (LRC 79-2006). http://www.lawreform.ie/Reports_Published/Default.135.html.

The Law Society of Upper Canada. (2002). *Practice guidelines for electronic registration of title documents*, 28 June 2002. http://rc.lsuc.on.ca/pdf/eReg/july08_eregguidelines.pdf. Accessed 13 June 2014.

United Nations Economic and Social Council. (2007). *Report on the Dublin conference "Registered the World"*, United Nations. http://www.unece.org/fileadmin/DAM/hlm/documents/2007/ece/hbp/wp7/ece.hbp.wp.7.2007.9.e.pdf. Accessed 13 June 2014.

United Nations Economic Commission for Europe. (2004). *Guidelines on real property units and identifiers*. Geneva: United Nations. http://www.unece.org/fileadmin/DAM/env/documents/2005/wpla/Guidelines_On_Real_Property_Identifiers.pdf. Accessed 13 June 2014.

United Nations Economic Commission for Europe Working Party on Land Administration. (2005). *Inventory of land administration systems in Europe and North America* (4th ed.). http://www.unece.org/hlm/documents/Publications/landadminsystems.inventory.ed4.pdf. Accessed 13 June 2014.

United Nations Economic Commission for Europe Working Party on Land Administration. (2014). *Survey on land administration systems (draft)*, United Nations. http://www.unece.org/fileadmin/DAM/hlm/documents/Publications/Benchmarking_41.pdf. Accessed 23 June 2014.

Van Erp, S. (2002). Different degrees of convergence: A comparison of tort law (Example: Fairchild v. Glenhaven Funeral Services) and property law. *Electronic Journal of Comparative Law, 6.3*. http://www.ejcl.org/63/abs63-4.html. Accessed 13 June 2014.

Van Erp, S. (2003a). A Numerus Quasi-Clausus of property rights as a constitutive element of a future European property law? *Electronic Journal of Comparative Law, 7.2*. http://www.ejcl.org/72/art72-2.doc. Accessed 13 June 2014.

Van Erp, S. (2003b). Linguistic diversity and a European legal discourse. *Electronic Journal of Comparative Law Editorial, 7.3*. http://www.ejcl.org/73/editor73.html. Accessed 13 June 2014.

Van Oosterom, P., Lemmen, C., Ingvarsson, T., van der Molen, P., Ploeger, H., & Quak, W., et al. (2006). The core cadastral domain model. *Computers, Environment and Urban Systems, 30*. http://www.eurocadastre.org/pdf/the_core_cadastral_domain.pdf. Accessed 13 June 2014.

Visser, P., & Bench-Capon, T. (1998). A comparison of four ontologies for the design of legal knowledge systems. *Artificial Intelligence and Law, 6*.

Visser, U., & Schlieder, C. (2003). Modelling real estate transactions: The potential role of ontologies. In H. Stuckenschmidt, E. Stubkjær, & C. Schlieder (Eds.), *The ontology and modelling of real estate transactions*. England: Ashgate.

Watson, A. (1996). Aspects of reception of law. *American Journal of Comparative Law, 44*(2).

Wilsch, H. (2008). *Legality checks in the attributing of real rights*. In CINDER XVI International Congress on Registration Law, Valencia, Spain, 20–22 May 2008. http://www.cinder2008.com/ingles/detalle_ponencia.cfm?id_ponencia=303. Accessed 26 Aug 2010.

Zevenbergen, J., et al. (Eds.). (2007). *Real property transactions: Procedures, transaction costs and models*. Amsterdam: IOS.

Zweigert, K., & Kötz, H. (1998). *Introduction to comparative law* (3rd ed.). Oxford: Clarendon.

Chapter 3
Defining Econveyancing

3.1 What Is Conveyancing?

In order to understand eConveyancing it is first necessary to ask; what is conveyancing? To the layman it is the purchase or sale of property. For example number 15 Royal Road, Ontario. The vendor owns the property and wishes to sell and the purchaser wishes to buy the property.

As set out in Chap. 2, in legal terms what is owned is not the property but an estate or an interest in land. Sometimes this is also referred to as title. Thus, to the lawyer, conveyancing is the process whereby title is passed from one party to another. In our neutral vocabulary the transferor sells title to the transferee and the donor gifts title to the donee.

There is no universal conveyancing process. Many jurisdictions do have similar steps in their conveyancing process though these may not occur in the same order. Ontario and Ireland, as two common law jurisdictions whose foundations go back to a common source, the English legal system, have a large degree of commonality in their conveyancing processes. While the name of the key documentation may differ the function is often the same. Similarly steps in the process may sometimes be carried out by different parties or in a different sequence but the main tasks in the process are the same.

These include:

(a) obtaining initial mortgage approval from the lender[1]
(b) making an offer to purchase[2]
(c) doing a home inspection[3]

[1] In Ireland this is known as a loan offer while in Ontario it is referred to as pre-approval.

[2] In both jurisdictions this will usually be subject to conditions.

[3] In Ireland this is usually done prior to the formal agreement but in Ontario the formal agreement is usually signed subject to a satisfactory home inspection by a professional home inspector.

G. Brennan, *The Impact of eConveyancing on Title Registration*,
DOI 10.1007/978-3-319-10341-9_3

(d) searches of public registers[4]
(e) negotiation of main terms and conditions such as purchase monies and conditions of the sale
(f) agreeing key terms and conditions
(g) acceptance of the main terms and conditions[5]
(h) final approval of mortgage[6]
(i) completion of mortgage documentation
(j) formalities for completion including signing of the assurance
(k) release of loan funds
(l) purchase monies being held on trust
(m) statement of disbursements to be delivered[7]
(n) key and possession handed over
(o) assurance and charge delivered to registering authority
(p) legal formalities completed including registration of the assurance

The usual steps in an Irish conveyancing transaction as set out in Brennan and Casey[8] can be compared with the steps in the Ontario system as set out by Donahue.[9]

3.2 What Is eConveyancing?

There is a broad spectrum of electronic conveyancing systems. Harpum refers to the different models of eConveyancing[10] and there is no doubt that there are many variations on the same theme in existence. Sneddon also 'scopes' this spectrum.[11] Some jurisdictions claim to have eConveyancing but only have an electronic

[4] Examples include searching of records held by the registering authority, planning and environmental bodies and court records. Additional queries may also be raised with the transferor about private information which is not available in a public register. An example would be information about any tax liability which might impact on the sale. See Appendix 6 of Moore and Globe (2003) for examples of searches to be done in Ontario. See also Donahue et al. (2003), pp. 312–315 for an explanation of how to do electronic searching in the Teraview system.

[5] In Ireland this is by way of a Contract for Sale. In Ontario it is by way of an Offer to Purchase. Both are standard documents which contain the key terms and conditions of the transaction such as payment of deposit, amount of purchase monies, particulars of the property, date of completion and details of any issues that need to be addressed as part of the transaction.

[6] This generally occurs before execution of the contract. It involves formal confirmation based on the specific transaction in question.

[7] In Ireland this is called an Apportionment Account. In Ontario it is a Statement of Adjustments.

[8] Brennan and Casey (2014), chapter 2.

[9] Donahue et al. (2003), chapter 12.

[10] Harpum (2004), p. 5.

[11] Sneddon (2007), pp. 2–3.

registration system or an electronic lodgement system. One example is the Automated Registration of Title to Land (ARTL) system in Scotland.

eConveyancing moves the conveyancing process from being a paper-based process to an electronic process via the creation of electronic communications networks. This includes not just the system of recording transactions in the registering authority but also all the other steps in the conveyancing process. The Law Society of Ireland has described it as a secure, paperless, electronic, end to end, pre-sale to post-completion, conveyancing process.[12]

As Sneddon has demonstrated eConveyancing does not have a precise meaning but encompasses a range of activities in the process of recording, searching and transferring interests in land which may be effected using electronic (or digital) communications and/or electronic (or digital) processing.[13] For the purposes of this research the term means the integration of technology into most or all of the conveyancing process from pre-sale to post completion of the transaction.[14] This includes the contract stage, electronic transfer, completion and title registration. The term eConveyancing is used though other terms may be used in quotations from commentators and other researchers.

Thus eConveyancing can be broadly defined as the placing of all conveyancing systems and processes on a secure electronic platform usually available through an online portal or hub. This platform, portal or hub is the creation of an electronic communication network which facilitates system to system exchange of data. In essence it allows one computer to "speak" to another. Information only has to be typed in once for each user to have access to it. The security of the platform is important due to the sensitive and confidential nature of the information being transmitted and different groups of users may have different levels of access. The England and Wales Law Society has recognised that there are consequences to the development of electronic initiatives. These include "the dangers of electronic attack and threats to the confidentiality, integrity and availability of electronic services and personal data. . .electronic privacy, online security and access to online services."[15]

Libbis explains the move towards eConveyancing as follows:

> From the early 1980s jurisdictions have been converting their manual title records to electronic systems. Late in the 1980s some jurisdictions introduced remote electronic searches of their electronic title records. From the early 1990s there were proposals for a fully electronic process to prepare and lodge instruments affecting title records. Through the 1990s, deregulation of financial markets and increasing competition in the mortgage industry together with development of the internet, electronic payment systems and

[12] Law Society of Ireland (2008a), p. 1. This is similar to the broad scope of the eConveyancing project initially proposed in England and Wales. Harpum offers a brief practical guide showing how domestic conveyancing might work in this context while Butt provides additional detail for a typical transaction in that jurisdiction. See Harpum (2000), pp. 5–7 and Butt (2006), pp. 7–22.

[13] Sneddon (2007), p. 2.

[14] O'Sullivan (2007), p. 5.

[15] The Law Society (2005), p. 16.

> electronic commerce generally led to interest in a more convenient and efficient way of completing property conveyances. With the new century, it was only a matter of when electronic conveyancing would be come (sic) a reality and how it would be achieved.[16]

Many jurisdictions began the move towards eConveyancing without even realising it when paper registers were computerised and converted to electronic format. Making that information available electronically to users was the next inevitable step. Sometimes this involved scanning material into an electronic database[17] and in other jurisdictions they converted the information into data sets that could be manipulated electronically. An electronically scanned version of a document can be accessed and viewed but it cannot be digitally manipulated and thus this is not truly eRegistration or eConveyancing.[18] A full eConveyancing system requires documents to be capable of being created, manipulated, transmitted and signed electronically.

Thus there are a number of change processes required before eConveyancing is feasible. The first is the conversion of all data into an electronic format to be held in central databases. This includes not just all information on the register but all contractual forms. The second process is the linking of the stakeholders via an online portal or hub. This second process requires co-ordination by multiple stakeholders in order to link the individual databases or systems into an electronic communication network.

Within the overall eConveyancing theme there are different levels of sophistication. These range from making title registration information available online to facilitating differing levels of interaction between stakeholders to a full conveyancing transaction done electronically. The increasing integration of information technology (IT) into the conveyancing process, leading towards eConveyancing, generally follows this sequence:

1. Conversion of paper records held by the registering authority to an electronic format. These paper records are converted to electronic data sets that are capable of being manipulated.
2. Electronic access to data held by the registering authority.
3. Electronic access to data held by the registering authority and authorised users permitted to lodge electronic applications. Initially these will be followed by the paper documents.
4. Electronic access to data held by the registering authority and authorised users permitted to lodge electronic applications with no requirement to lodge the paper documents.
5. Electronic access to data held by the registering authority, authorised users permitted to make electronic applications and manipulation of the data sets by

[16] Libbis (2007), p. 3. Libbis doesn't specifically identify what will be more convenient and efficient about eConveyancing.

[17] This model is used in Queensland. See Killilea (2010).

[18] See Killilea (2010) for an alternate view. Killilea has no difficulty labelling the Queensland method of scanning paper documents as an eRegistration system.

authorised users leading to a change in the register. The information provided electronically by the authorised user will automatically fill in i.e. pre populate the register. In this sense the process is automated. This manipulation may or may not require sign off by staff in the registering authority. If it does not require confirmation by staff in the registering authority the changes are automatic.
6. Other stakeholders in the conveyancing process begin multiple electronic interaction through the online portal or hub.
7. The entire end to end conveyancing process is completed electronically. This includes not just the initial stages of drafting and execution of the contract but also the final stages of completion of the transaction and registration.

Phase 1 above can be labeled eRecords. Phases 2 and 3 come under the heading of eLodgement or eApplication. Phases 4 and 5 are part of the development of eRegistration and phases 6 and 7 come into the realm of eConveyancing. Thus there are four distinct phases in the development of eConveyancing; eRecords, eApplication, eRegistration and eConveyancing itself. These are explained in further detail later in this chapter.

Some of the key changes that occur during these phases which lead to eConveyancing are;

(a) standardisation of documentation[19]
(b) standardisation of process
(c) increased access to data online
(d) dematerialisation[20]
(e) extension of title registration
(f) digital signatures
(g) standard format of data[21]
(h) EFT

[19] Common registration documents have been introduced in Ontario for both registered and unregistered titles. See Donahue et al. (2003), p. 1. The standard transfer deed has been reduced to three pages and the standard charge to two pages. This is in line with other advances whereby the contract between the transferor and transferee has been reduced to four pages.

[20] Dematerialisation is the process of replacing paper with an electronic process or no process at all. Many jurisdictions have removed the need for paper certificates of title which mirrored the ownership record details recorded in the registry. This paper was required to be produced on each sale of the land and thus would prove to be an impediment to an electronic system. Examples include Ontario which did this in 1979 (section 32, The Land Titles Amendment Act, 1979, S.O. 1979, c. 93), New Zealand which did this in 2002 (section 18, Land Transfer (Computer Registers and Electronic Lodgement) Amendment Act 2002) and Ireland which did this in 2006 (section 73, Registration of Deeds and Title Act 2006). Harpum (2000), p. 3 notes that the "mechanisms by which property is transferred are undergoing a revolution, namely, the move from paper-based to dematerialised dealings." Treacy (2007), p. 29 sees the removal of paper certificates as "a far-reaching and necessary milestone on the road towards implementation of a full e-conveyancing system in Ireland."

[21] Common data standards are particularly important for eConveyancing projects that straddle jurisdictions. For example the NECS (now PEXA) system in Australia will involve eight jurisdictions. See Libbis (2007), p. 8.

(i) electronic instruments[22]

Dematerialisation involves the transformation of the information or data to electronic information stored on a computer which is capable of being electronically manipulated.[23] It means a move from paper based processes to information based processes.[24] Information migrates from the physical world to the electronic world heralding the arrival of the paperless office.[25]

Electronic service delivery heralds a move towards simplification, standardisation and dematerialisation. Initially key paper documents are reviewed and fixed into a standard text and format which is adopted by all the stakeholders in the conveyancing process. Once this standardisation is completed the paper documents can then be dropped in favour of an electronic version that is completed, executed and transmitted by computers in a secure electronic system. This dematerialisation of paper documents into data sets that are capable of electronic manipulation is a core tenet of eConveyancing.

Many of these changes require legislative reform which will enable, authorise and structure the key developments above.

3.2.1 *What Is Not Included?*

There is no doubt that an eConveyancing system can facilitate the electronic transformation of the conveyancing process however there are certain elements of the process that cannot, or it could be argued, should not, be made electronic. It may also exclude other parts of the conveyancing process that cannot be replicated by an electronic application. Examples may include the verification of the client's identity[26] in order to meet the requirements of anti-money laundering legislation and the client's authorisation for the transaction.

The formalities of a conveyancing transaction can be made electronic but any physical act that is intrinsic or substantive must be either dropped or kept in an eConveyancing environment.

The most obvious of these is the role of a physical inspection of the property. Land is a physical entity but title to it cannot be dug up and handed over in person

---

[22] See Christensen et al. (2003).

[23] No jurisdiction has yet succeeded in making the process entirely paperless. In many instances the client's authority must still be given by a wet signature on a paper document. In Ontario the client must sign an Acknowledgement and Direction authorising the lawyer to enter into a DRA and to electronically sign and register the documents.

[24] Kelly (2010).

[25] Widdison (1997), p. 144. Note however that on occasion the electronic world may instead add to the paper environment. In the Irish eStamping system Revenue replaced a physical stamp on the deed with an electronic return but lawyers must now print that return for their file.

[26] Though in England solicitors often do this via electronic identity verification providers.

on a sale. It is not like a car, table or phone. The transferee must ensure that the property actually exists, where it's located and check who is in occupation, the physical condition and if there are any obvious factors which would impact on the purchase such as a right of way. These enquiries could or should not be done remotely.

In Ontario some of the enquiries that would take place during a physical inspection have been replaced by title insurance.[27] Moore and Globe note that title insurance in Ontario has been held out and accepted as a potentially less expensive alternative to a boundary survey.[28] However there is a danger in this. Title insurance will only offer compensation. It will not return the property to someone who has lost it. The shift from 'buyer beware' to 'buyer insure' has socialised the risk presumably on the grounds that it is cheaper to take the risk and buy title insurance on the assumption that in most instances no claim will need to be made. Thus there is a risk shift from the buyer to the insurance company. The impact of title insurance is explored further in Chap. 9.[29]

In America and Canada lenders use electronic valuation systems to check the level of risk in relation to the amount of funds being advanced on the purchase. These are called automated valuation mechanisms (AVMs). Lenders use these to determine an approximation of fair market value for the property as part of the loan underwriting process. In other jurisdictions lenders retain valuers to inspect the property and to provide a valuation. This replacement of a personal inspection and valuation with electronic valuation systems has drawn some comment and blame for the sub-prime crises in America and the global financial crisis.[30] While lenders in other jurisdictions also use electronic valuation systems they use them as an additional check on the value of the property. It appears that lenders in some jurisdictions do not want to bear the expense of a physical check as they are not concerned with the land as such but only want to know the value and if the borrower is willing and able to pay.

The question of mortgage fraud is also relevant in this context as bogus valuations of property are more easily maintained when dealing with a computer. Fraudsters can sell the property between themselves at artificially inflated prices which will fool a computer and thus lull a lender into advancing more money than the property is actually worth.[31]

Making all physical acts electronic may thus lead to increased risk and a potential loss on the part of a lender or transferee. Sneddon having carried out a detailed risk assessment over 5 months of the proposed Australian system expressed

---

[27] A contract for insuring and indemnifying against loss or damage. In conveyancing transactions it may compensate the land owner if a title defect arises.

[28] Moore and Globe (2003), pp. 40–41.

[29] See Sect. 9.6.

[30] See O'Connor (2009), pp. 133–159 for an examination of the lowering of lending standards including the omission of physical inspection of the property at p. 139.

[31] For types of mortgage fraud see Pierson (2007).

the view that eConveyancing systems "may have more concentrated points of failure than paper based systems, for the same reasons that they generate greater efficiencies."[32] These risks and the necessity and desire of the transferee to have some physical acts remain as part of the process mitigates the ultimate reach of an eConveyancing system.

3.2.2 *Phases of eConveyancing*

As noted already four distinct phases can be identified within the overall development of eConveyancing. Each phase is a precursor to the development of the next more sophisticated phase.

The first is the most basic. This requires the registering authority to convert all its paper records to an electronic format. These paper records are converted to electronic data sets that are capable of being manipulated on a computer. This phase can be called 'eRecords' as it involves the creation of electronic records. This phase becomes subsumed into the second phase and is a subset of eApplication and eRegistration.

The focus of the second phase of eConveyancing, called 'eApplication', has the objective of allowing the lawyer to lodge an application electronically with the Land Registry.

The information in the electronic application is pre-populated into the register but the transaction will only proceed once the paper documents have been received and approved by staff in the registering authority. Pre-populated means that the data entry is filled in (typed) on the register in 'draft' form as the electronic application is completed and this draft is then verified when the paper application is received. The staff in the registering authority do not need to type the information again but only need to amend the data if there is any error.

Pre-population can also occur in another way in that the electronic system can pull information already on the title register into the creation of the electronic document.[33] This avoids the need for entering information already contained in the register and may be the reason why many commentators believe that an electronic system will lead to less errors.[34] This, however, will only be the case if the information already in the register is correct. If the error is already on the register,

---

[32] Sneddon (2007), p. 9. See also National Electronic Conveyancing Office *Risk Assessment of the National Electronic Conveyancing System*, 9 February 2007. http://www.necs.gov.au/ArticleDocuments/FinalReportOfClaytonUtz_RiskAssessment.pdf. Accessed 23 June 2014.

[33] In Ontario title information already stored in the POLARIS (Province of Ontario Land Registration Information System) database will automatically be brought forward and entered into the electronic document. See Moore and Globe (2003), p. 425.

[34] Moore and Globe (2003), p. 267 state that all necessary Family Law Act statements are preprogrammed into the electronic document and this reduces clerical errors while simplifying document drafting.

staff in the registering authority may approve the new application based on that incorrect information. If the register is definitive then the information on it will be deemed to be correct.

In eApplication the process is automated but not automatic as input is required from staff in the registering authority before the information can affect the register. In one sense this phase could not really be called part of an eConveyancing system since it is dependent on the paper documents being lodged before the information can be acted upon.

Thus this phase retains the ultimate authenticative status of the paper documents. The electronic lodgment is a provisional stage contingent for its effects upon the lodgment of the effective papers. The application only has provisional status until the paper documents are lodged and these are required before the registering authority staff can amend the register. A fundamental tenet of a complete eConveyancing system is the replacement of paper with electronic information however in eApplication the transaction only gains priority upon receipt of the paper documents.

Where no input from staff in the registering authority is required before a change is effected in the title register the system may be labelled automatic. The eConveyancing process is automated because it occurs immediately via electronic channels but it may also be automatic if no 'human' input is required from the registering authority. Arruñada calls this agency registration where conveyancers alter the register after automatic controls by an "electronic registrar" but without manual intervention by the registry staff and notes that this has generally been rejected or only applied to simple transactions.[35]

The ARTL[36] system in Scotland is an automatic registration system[37] as no input from staff in the registering authority is required to effect a change in registration on the basis of the electronic application. England and Wales also proposed to adopt automatic registration.[38]

The New Zealand e-dealing system is also automatic.[39] The lawyer for the transferee submits the dealing online for registration and provided it passes the necessary business rules the transaction is registered. These business rules are built into the system as compliance checks. There is no manual intervention by registry staff before registration.[40]

35 Arruñada (2010), p. 115.

36 ARTL stands for Automated Registration of Title to Land but the system is both automated and automatic.

37 Traynor (2008).

38 The proposal was to allow solicitors and licensed conveyancers to make alterations to the register by registering dispositions at the same time as they are made. See Law Commission and HM Land Registry (2001), p. 287. The report states that this is the only practicable way to have simultaneous disposition and registration. See also Butt (2006), p. 10.

39 See Muir (2003) for an explanation of how this system operates.

40 Greenwood and Jones (2003), pp. 325 and 330.

Arruñada states that this provides the paradigm of agency registration.[41] He warns of associated dangers and the implications of the transfer of risk, costs and liability between registries and conveyancers.[42] Though presumably it is the registry who set the business rules and built them into the system. The transaction is rejected if it does not meet the requirements of those rules.

It appears that Arruñada is not convinced that such rules can entirely replace intervention by the registry staff. This appears to be the prevailing view though it may be difficult to see what is added by registry staff signing off on the application except that the government accepts liability for the error or fraud of the applicant or land owner. This liability will depend on the extent to which the system provides for rectification.

If the system supports dynamic security there will be no rectification even if the registration is based on fraud, force or deceit in the electronic application. Dynamic security is often referred to as indefeasibility[43] and the principle of indefeasibility is frequently advanced to justify the upholding of the register. If a mistake is made then compensation, and not rectification, will be the remedy for those deprived of their interest in land. By contrast if the system supports static security there will be rectification whenever it is deemed fair.

This conflict can also be expressed as a dispute between the principles of certainty and fairness. Certainty of the register will benefit transferees and acquisition lenders but this may be at the expense of a prior registered owner who is blameless but is now being offered a sum of money instead of title to his home as if they were "perfect substitutes".[44] The competing claims that may arise and how these are dealt with in Ireland and Ontario is examined in Chap. 7.[45]

In a system with automatic registration it appears that there can be a reduction in land registration staffing levels. The checking function and the associated expense is transferred to the conveyancer, usually a lawyer, and hence the house owner.[46] It could be argued that agency registration reduces the role of the registering authority as the arbitrator of 'good title' and redefines it as an auditor which ensures compliance[47] with the business rules. The registering authority thus develops a new role in authorising lawyers to conduct electronic conveyancing and an audit function to ensure compliance with the specified requirements.[48] The two new

---

[41] Arruñada (2010), p. 115. He notes at p. 116 that staff do perform some checks and audits after registration but by then it is too late to change anything as the registrar's powers of correction are limited.

[42] Arruñada (2010), p. 119.

[43] The particular legislative sections that provide for indefeasibility are often called "paramountcy" provisions. See the use of this term in Cooke and O'Connor (2004), p. 645.

[44] Miceli and Sirmans (1995), p. 83.

[45] See also Sect. 4.4.

[46] Perry (2003b), p. 1696.

[47] For further details in relation to the New Zealand system see Muir (2007), p. 5.

[48] See Greenwood and Jones (2003) for details of how the post-registration audit function operates in New Zealand.

functions would be to license users and then to promulgate and enforce practice rules on those users. It would also have an obligation to maintain and update the system.[49]

In Ontario the Director of Land Registration has the power to suspend the authorisation of an applicant if (a) there is reasonable grounds to believe that the person has submitted an electronic document that is not authorised by the registered owner or is not otherwise authorised at law or (b) considers it in the public interest to do so.[50] This would be a serious sanction as it would prevent the lawyer from practicing conveyancing. A new set of criteria were developed for the authorisation of account holders in Ontario as part of the Real Estate Fraud Action Plan. These included criteria about identity, financial resources adequate to compensate victims of fraud and good character/accountability.[51] In effect all users were required to re authenticate themselves as a fraud prevention measure.

In England and Wales it was proposed that entries on the register be made directly by the lawyer and not by the registering authority[52] however lawyers were reluctant to take on this function.[53] Lawyers, as professional users of the system, are reluctant to be able to make changes to the register. They do not wish to be liable for error or fraud and to be sued by the consumers who directly suffer the system failure. Lawyers and other users do not want to become registrants. The same concerns do not appear to have arisen in relation to simpler transactions which are seen as presenting a lower risk and thus automated electronic discharge of a charge by a lender has been implemented in England and Wales without the same difficulties.

In Ireland it has been generally agreed between the stakeholders that "[i]n order to ensure that the PRA's responsibility for maintaining the register is not diminished, PRA officials will continue to have input into applications for changes to the register before the register is updated."[54] Thus the aim is to make the process automated but not automatic.[55] The registrar or staff in the registering authority will need to act upon the electronic message or data transfer before a change in the title register can take place. Kostova is of the view that the Irish choice to keep registration automated rather than automatic should be welcomed.[56] Keating notes that this retention of the registering authority as the "ultimate decision maker will play a crucial role in the balancing of risk in any proposed electronic

---

[49] It is difficult to see how the registrar would not also have a role in registration particularly where rectification of the title or boundaries is required.

[50] See Murray (2007), p. 7. Section 23.1 Land Registration Reform Act R.S.O. 1990 CHAPTER L. 4.

[51] Murray (2007), pp. 10–13.

[52] Harpum (2000), p. 6.

[53] Lawyers in Victoria also rejected the possibility of agency registration because of the transfer of risk. See Arruñada (2010), p. 118.

[54] O'Sullivan (2007), p. 7.

[55] McHugh (2010). See also Deeney (2014), p. 369.

[56] Kostova (2010), p. 59.

conveyancing model."[57] Automation delivers most of the benefits that the registering authority tends to seek, allowing it to keep the state guarantee intact. Whereas automatic registration would change its role to that of an enforcement and validation authority.

This is also the position in Ontario where the registry staff manually review documents for compliance before registering or rejecting them. Section 23 of the Land Registration Reform Act[58] (hereafter the LRRA)[59] stipulates that an electronic document delivered to the electronic land registration database by direct electronic transmission is not registered until the land registrar registers it in the prescribed manner. Similarly in British Columbia the registering authority reviews applications to check compliance with legal requirements.[60]

However, many jurisdictions have built some of the simple checks that would previously have been done by registry staff, into the electronic system in order to generate efficiencies and reduce the level of manual input.[61] They have also adopted a "tell me, don't show me" approach[62] to the supporting documentation that would previously have been required. The question arises as to whether these two developments of themselves have led to the possibility of more errors appearing in the title register and thus a balance is to be achieved between efficiency and risk.

This eApplication phase becomes obsolete and subsumed into the next phase of eConveyancing. Clancy calls this phase eLodgement of Applications for Registration and identifies its key features as allowing professional customers to pay fees on-line, build and track applications.[63] Also key data is validated on-line and pre-populates the register with drafts of the registration. He is of the view that this "is the precursor to full eRegistration and, other than electronic supporting documents, it contains most of the elements of full eRegistration."[64]

O'Sullivan has divided this phase into two distinct parts; eApplication and eLodgement.[65] eApplication being the ordering of documents and services online and eLodgement relating to the lodgement of applications resulting in changes to

---

[57] Keating (2012), pp. 8–9.

[58] Land Registration Reform Act R.S.O. 1990 CHAPTER L. 4.

[59] The aim of the LRRA was to computerise, modernise and combine the unregistered and registered systems.

[60] Low (2005), p. 8. See also BC OnLine.

[61] For example the system may automatically calculate the fee payable or force the applicant, or registrant, to choose options from a predetermined list. In Ontario the system will not allow the application to be lodged until certain required elements are completed. Similarly the ARTL system requires all questions relevant to the application to be completed before it allows the application to be submitted for registration.

[62] This approach means that supporting documentation is not lodged in the registry. Instead the applicant, or registrant, certifies that such documentation has been executed and is held by them. This approach can cause concern among lawyers who, rather than lodging such documentation in the registry, now have to certify the existence of same while bearing the cost of storage.

[63] Clancy (2008), p. 5.

[64] Clancy (2008), p. 5.

[65] O'Sullivan (2007), p. 5.

the register. These two parts are linked. Together they form the second phase of eConveyancing and the term eApplication will be used to denote this phase.

eRegistration is the third more sophisticated phase. This is truly part of an eConveyancing system as the paper is now replaced with an electronic process and this is the primary focus of eRegistration. The aim is to change the register solely on the basis of electronic information without the need for paper documents to be lodged. In the eApplication phase the electronic entry is ineffective unless it mirrors the paper. The electronic application is a shadow of the paper application and only has a provisional status.

By contrast in the eRegistration phase the electronic entry is the legal act that leads to a change in the register. The data input has independent legal effectiveness and is not dependent on a paper application. It may however be subject to a number of factors. Firstly the electronic act must conform with the data that's already on the register. Second it must meet the business rules or other formalities laid down by the registering authority for the electronic entry and thirdly, in most instances, it must be signed off by staff in the registering authority.

In eConveyancing the implementation of the eRegistration phase generally begins with the electronic discharge of registered charges by authorised users (may be lawyers or lenders) and then moves on to electronic charges and finally transfers.

British Columbia is an example of an eRegistration system. The Land Title and Survey Authority (LTSA) operates an electronic filing system (EFS)[66] which enables authorised persons such as lawyers and conveyancers to electronically sign and submit documents to the authority. EFS operates through a web portal known as BC Online. By the end of August 2013 the LTSA maintained a record of over 2 million land titles with over 2.2 million active registered charges on those titles.[67]

The fourth, most extensive and most sophisticated phase is eConveyancing itself. The aim is to electronify not just the registration aspects of conveyancing but the entire end to end process from pre-sale to post completion. Some physical acts may however be excluded.[68]

Arruñada suggests that there is no need for a physical closing act at all as digital signatures allow consent to be given without a physical presence at closing.[69] However this will only work if the client has a digital signature that meets the needs for identity verification. In most systems it is the lawyer, and not the client, who has the digital signature.[70] This may lead to additional risk and liability for the

[66] BC OnLine.

[67] BC OnLine.

[68] For example physical inspection of the property by the transferee, verification of identity in order to meet anti-money laundering legislation and authorisation for the transaction.

[69] Arruñada (2010), p. 119.

[70] Examples include Scotland, New Zealand, British Columbia and Ontario. For an examination of the potential for fraud and security issues arising from the use of digital signatures in eConveyancing see Kostova (2010), pp. 21–32. See also Keating (2012).

lawyer and thus a rise in professional indemnity insurance[71] premiums.[72] Griggs and Low highlight in respect of the national Australian system

> that it is entirely possible that under an electronic system the allocation of risk and liability will fall on the stakeholders involved in consummating the transaction, rather than the landowner. The tension between these stakeholders (including conveyancers, lawyers, registry offices, issuers of identity and the government) as to this allocation of risk is palpable and will demand sensitive negotiation and much introspection and examination as we embrace the efficiency, advantages, and complexity of the national electronic conveyancing system.[73]

Kostova similarly warns that the impact of such an increased risk of liability on the success of any Irish system should not be underestimated.[74]

Perry takes the view that the central objective of eConveyancing is the elimination of the paper documents but the restriction of digital signatures to legal representatives results in his view in its failure to achieve this objective.[75] The requirement to ensure that the client gives authority for the signing of the electronic document has resulted in practices whereby the client applies a wet signature[76] to a paper copy of the electronic document or executes some other form of paper authority.

In both Ontario and Scotland wet signatures are required from the client in order to authorise the transaction. In Ontario this authority is kept on the lawyers file. In Scotland it is lodged with the registering authority. The lawyer then uses his or her digital signature on the basis of that paper authority. For Perry the "difficulty with this solution is that a major part of the rationale behind e-conveyancing is destroyed in the process."[77] He quotes an Ontario real-estate lawyer as noting that there seems to be more paper rather than less in lawyers' files as a result of the changes in Ontario.[78]

In New Zealand a paper authorisation is executed and retained for 10 years. In Scotland the paper authorisation is scanned and lodged with the registry. Instead of removing paper documents from the process you now have an additional document added to the conveyancing process and this document must be preserved for a considerable length of time. This is problematic if you accept Perry's view that dematerialisation is the major driver of eConveyancing. Even if you do not accept his view, the objective of reform is to generate efficiencies, not to add further complexity and paper to the process.

---

[71] See Law PRO Magazine Supplement Fall (2011) for the requirements in different jurisdictions.

[72] Kostova (2010), p. 26.

[73] Griggs and Low (2011), pp. 285–308.

[74] Kostova (2010), p. 27.

[75] Perry (2003a), p. 29.

[76] The stroke of a pen.

[77] Perry (2003a), p. 27.

[78] Perry (2003b), p. 1696.

These difficulties and risks can however be avoided by ensuring that the land owner has his or her own digital signature and there is no interference with the role of each stakeholder in the process i.e. land owners execute contracts and transfers as normal, lawyers advise and witness, lenders lend and so on.

The eRecords, eApplication or eRegistration phases are sometimes referred to as eConveyancing and there is no doubt that any eConveyancing system must also include these. The development of these electronic processes are stepping stones on the path towards full eConveyancing. Many jurisdictions have chosen to stop at eRecords, eApplication or eRegistration and not proceed further. By contrast other jurisdictions are planning to move forward to convert the entire conveyancing process to an electronic platform by developing complete systems of eConveyancing. This would include that part of the conveyancing process prior to registration i.e. drafting of the contract and assurance, execution of the contract and assurance together with completion involving EFT of the purchase monies.

3.2.3 *Relationship Between eRecords, eApplication, eRegistration and eConveyancing*

The relationship between the four phases of an overall eConveyancing system can be represented by Fig. 3.1.

eRecords and eApplication are subsets of eRegistration and become subsumed into eRegistration once the system moves into this phase. By contrast eRegistration is retained as a distinct subset of eConveyancing as it relates solely to the registration element of the conveyancing process.[79] It is the element of eConveyancing involving direct participation by the registering authority.[80] The final phase is eConveyancing itself which expands the electronic interaction to stakeholders and other parts of the process separate from the registration element.

eRegistration involves electronic interaction between the registering authority and users, usually lawyers, to facilitate electronic registration. eConveyancing expands this interaction to other stakeholders such as lenders, surveyors and auctioneers and it facilitates virtually all the phases of the conveyancing process from pre sale to post completion.

eRegistration necessarily involves automated electronic communication between the users and registrar but it may not be automatic. In Ireland eRegistration is taken to mean an automated but not an automatic system.

Figure 3.2 represents the same process but as a sequential timeline. Some of these phases may run in parallel for periods of time until the next phase is fully implemented.

[79] Deeney (2014), p. 365.

[80] Property Registration Authority 'Strategic Plan 2013–2015' (2013), p. 37.

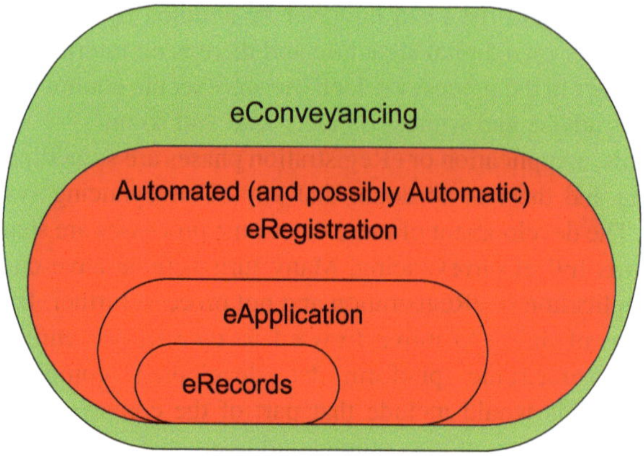

Fig. 3.1 Four phases of an eConveyancing system

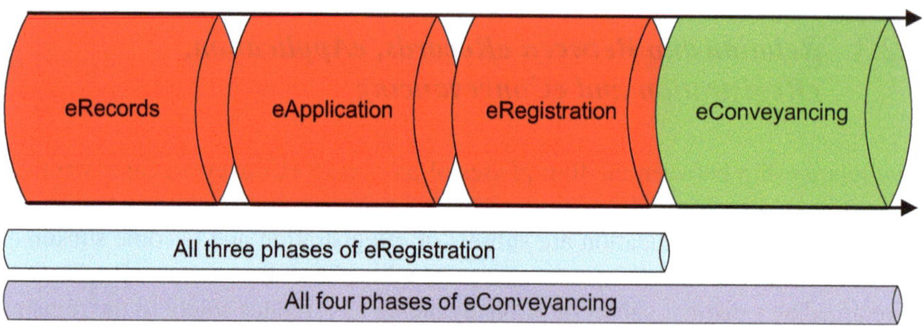

Fig. 3.2 Sequential timeline

Traditionally the conveyancing process is seen as being very paper based, lacking transparency and with many inherent delays.[81] This provides potential for reform, transformation and process improvements. The case for reform may be compelling but whether this reform should embrace eConveyancing is the subject of much discussion and debate. Even if the conveyancing process requires reform does this necessarily mean that eConveyancing will solve all its ills? Does eConveyancing provide a realistic solution to difficulties in the process or is it a mirage never to be achieved?

Paper based transactions are seen as been outdated and traditional and often the existence of such paper is blamed for delays. The immediacy of email versus post which can take one, two or more days to be delivered is seen as self-evident proof that paper causes delay. While no one likes unnecessary delays, is the difference between paper and electronic forms the source of delays in the conveyancing process? Much rhetoric espouses the paper based process as being out of date,

[81] The Law Reform Commission (2006), p. 5.

traditional and 'bad' and the new modern electronic systems as being new, better and 'good'. But what exactly about paper based transactions is seen as being outdated and traditional and where is the evidence for this?

Perhaps the delay is due to other factors such as the formalities associated with completing a conveyancing transaction. There is a value in the formalities associated with executing a contract or deed so as to ensure that the client's authority cannot be questioned and the contract or deed subsequently set aside. The person cannot deny their own signature and its witnessing. It is for this reason that many jurisdictions, despite other advances towards dematerialisation, have still retained a paper authority to be signed by the client with a wet signature.[82]

There is much written about the legal reasons for these formalities but little has been written about their symbolic ceremonial purpose. This change of formalisation has echoes with the past with the move from memory and storytelling to written records. Such change in ritual is a field of study in its own right and was explored by Clanchy in his book *From Memory to Written Record, England 1066–1307*.[83] He explores the growth of practical literacy and the move from living memory to written records. This can be seen as a continuum[84] whereby society is now moving from those written records to electronic data sets. This further change moves us away from the formal symbolism of a physical document with its feudal connotations towards dematerialisation.

All these changes can be seen as part of the information technology movement even though it is now computers facilitating the change rather than the printing press and the word IT was unknown in the twelfth century. Previous transformations show how technology can affect process, sometimes in unforeseen ways.[85]

When it comes to conveyancing many citizens and particularly land owners like paper deeds.[86] They like having paper 'proof' of ownership that they can hold. It is a familiar concept and the holder may feel a sense of security that by holding the paper deed, title to the land cannot be taken away. Of course a paper deed may be burnt or destroyed just as a computer record can be deleted or infected by a virus.

In referring to the UK CREST system Micheler notes that electronic share transfer has been very popular with institutional investors but there has been less success with some private investors.[87] She notes that this may be due to doubts about the reliability of information technology in general and while owners of paper

[82] E.g. Scotland. See Christensen (2004) for an example of the paper documents that are retained in a number of jurisdictions.

[83] Clanchy (1993).

[84] For example Ruoff, writing in 1952, was encouraging title registrars to use cash registers for recording fees paid and photography for copying plans and documents. Ruoff (1952), p. 163.

[85] Keating examines the development of signatures and seals in looking at the form and function of signatures in conveyancing and how these have developed due to technological innovations. See Keating (2012), pp. 26–28 and also p. 34.

[86] In writing about eRegistration Muir notes the symbolic value of the paper title as a tangible representation of a land owners legal title and ownership. See Muir (2003), p. 316.

[87] Micheler (2002), p. 12.

certificates can personally ensure that they are stored securely the "owner of uncertificated securities has no comparable means of ensuring that the electronic records are properly maintained."[88]

Despite fears and doubts the conveyancing process cannot remain immune to the march towards eCommerce and eGovernment. Furlong is of the view that it is no longer sufficient to provide access to data. He believes that end users who regularly book airline tickets or cinema tickets will also demand the same level of interactive service online from government departments and agencies.[89] "Those who prevaricate and ignore these changes will be neither digital natives nor digital immigrants, but will be set to lose out – as digital dinosaurs."[90]

3.2.4 eConveyancing in the Context of eCommerce and eGovernment: Towards an Information Age

As land registration is under government control the delivery of registration services electronically will focus a spotlight on the entire conveyancing process.

> E-conveyancing is the single most significant e-government initiative for the [legal] profession. In stimulating legal e-business, the [England and Wales] Land Registry's e-conveyancing plans will affect all practitioners, not just conveyancers. New technology and the Internet are already fuelling the dynamism of the conveyancing market.[91]

As this quote demonstrates in some jurisdictions the registering authority have taken ownership of not just eRegistration but also eConveyancing as part of its mandate to deliver eCommerce and eGovernment.[92]

eConveyancing can be seen as a subset of eCommerce and eGovernment. The danger of eConveyancing however being confined within eGovernment or being delivered by the registering authority is that the parts of the process that relate to a private transaction between the buyer and seller (the negotiation and contract) can become blurred with the public transaction (completion and registration) and state intervention (payment of tax). Government and state agencies should ensure that, in engaging with eConveyancing, they do not stray into areas of private interaction between citizens. Instead eConveyancing should be seen as overlapping with eCommerce and eGovernment (Fig. 3.3).

---

88 Micheler (2002), pp. 12–13.

89 Furlong (2008), pp. 44–47.

90 Furlong (2008), p. 47.

91 The Law Society (2005), p. 10.

92 This was the original proposal in England and Wales. See Law Commission and HM Land Registry (2001). See also Howell (2006), p. 569.

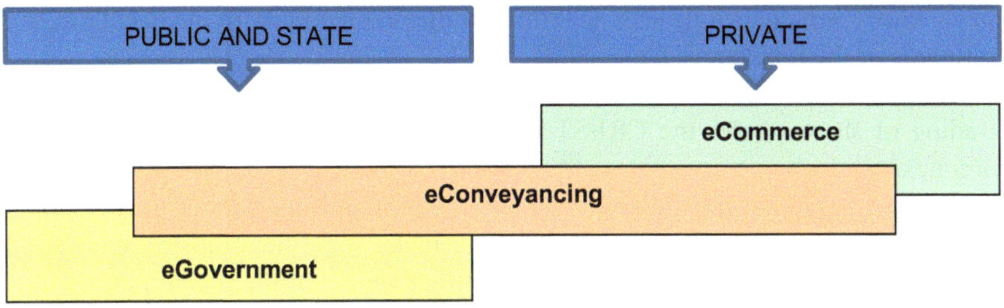

Fig. 3.3 eConveyancing in the context of eCommerce and eGovernment

eGovernment has been

> defined as electronic interaction between government and the private sector or the citizen. The possibilities for eGovernment have been enormously increased by the availability of personal computers and the increasing penetration of the internet.[93]

It has also been defined as the placing of existing government services online.[94]

Globalisation demands shared and reusable knowledge in all sectors of the economy including the property market.[95] The transformation of conveyancing by the application of technological advances to a previously paper based process is part of a wider move towards the values and technologies of the information age.[96] The term information society is also used to refer to "the increasing contemporary significance of information and communication technologies (ICTS)."[97] Castells refers to this new society as the network society and one of the key dimensions of this new social structure is "the material transformation of our social fabric, as new information technologies allow the formation of new forms of social organization and social interaction along electronically based information networks."[98] He refers to this as a socially embedded process and not as an exogenous factor affecting society.[99]

Other commentators are of the view that we have already moved on. Brande-Lavridsen is of the view that we are leaving the network society and entering the mobile society.[100] In referring to the move from paper-based to dematerialised dealings Harpum refers to a revolution.[101] The extent of this change has been compared with other significant events in the past. "The unfolding influence of these technologies across all areas of economic and social activity in the twenty-

93 Gahan (2008), p. 15.

94 McDonagh and White (2008), p. 21.

95 Hess and Vaskovich (2007), p. 183.

96 Castells (2000), p. 693.

97 Irish Government (2002), Foreword.

98 Castells (2000), p. 693.

99 Castells (2000), p. 693.

100 Brande-Lavridsen (2002), p. 10.

101 Harpum (2000), p. 3.

first century is increasingly seen in terms parallel to electricity in the twentieth, and railroads in the nineteenth."[102]

Harpum notes that this process has already occurred in other spheres such as the trading of shares under the CREST system and this has attracted little attention amongst academic commentators.[103] This electronic trading system is operated by the London Stock Exchange and allows a share broker to carry out the settlement process electronically. The objective was to make securities transfer as safe and efficient as possible and thus increase the attractiveness of the marketplace.[104]

> The CREST system has reduced the time that lapses between trade and settlement. It has also caused transfers of uncertificated shares to be carried out almost simultaneously with payment of the purchase price. This has significantly reduced the transactional risk investors in shares are exposed to.[105]

CREST is just one example of the way information technology and online service channels through computerisation have completely transformed the way in which products and services are delivered.

It is perceived that those in charge of delivering such products and services are under pressure from ordinary citizens to meet the full potential of this information age by better service by way of more information and greater transparency.[106]

> The rapid development of modern information and communications technologies is having a dramatic impact on all aspects of life, including government. It is creating an environment characterised by demands for timely delivery of information and services.[107]

The increase of uptake in broadband[108] would suggest that businesses are recognising that electronic communication systems are a key component in maintaining competitiveness but in relation to citizens there is a question as to whether they are driving online services or are online services driving demand? For example the cheap flights offered by Ryanair, which can only be booked online, may have enticed many people on to the internet, including some who would not otherwise seek electronic access to services.[109]

Many governments, including the Irish government, have increasingly committed themselves to the use of computer technology in the delivery of public services.[110] "[S]uccessful eGovernment systems send a signal to the rest of the world that the economy is at the forefront of technology and that the business environment

---

102 Irish Government (2002), Foreword.

103 Harpum (2000), p. 3.

104 Micheler (2002), p. 9.

105 Davies (2008), p. 952.

106 Brande-Lavridsen (2002), p. 1.

107 Forfás (2008), p. 5.

108 ComReg.

109 Van Oosterom et al. refer to a *technology push* and a *market pull*. Van Oosterom et al. (2006), p. 629.

110 Department of Public Expenditure and Reform.

is conducive to high-technology applications."[111] Various action plans have been published about the potential of the information society,

> raising expectations on the part of the general public...[which] have an evitable (sic) impact on the legal profession and the service it provides...the day is surely rapidly approaching when members of the public will not understand why in the age of the computer a conveyancing transaction seems bedevilled with uncertainties, involves a huge paper chase and seems to take an extraordinary time to complete.[112]

In 2008 McDonagh and White carried out an evaluation of eGovernment in Ireland and found that "[o]verall the roll-out of eGovernment in Ireland, while initially very promising, appears to have stalled somewhat."[113] They refer to a number of very successful initiatives including motor tax online (www.motortax.ie), etenders (www.etenders.gov.ie/), companies registration office filing (www.cro.ie) and the PRA electronic access service (www.landregistry.ie/eng/landdirect_ie/).[114]

Despite these successes there have, however, been a number of notable and high profile failures. These failures include www.reachservices.ie[115] which was intended to act as a single point of access to online public services in Ireland. This public service broker project was a key eGovernment infrastructure project in that it aimed to make all public services accessible online. The Comptroller and Auditor General criticised the reach project. He found that "the feasibility of the project was not examined early on and planning was weak. As a result, expectations for the project were unrealistic, and implementation has been far slower and more costly than anticipated."[116] The only transactions service provided was the Revenue online service. Reach did not deliver the mandated integrated social services system and responsibility has now been transferred.[117]

The progress of many projects was slower than planned and a substantial number did not proceed or were abandoned after starting. Examples of abandoned projects include on-line applications for passports, driving licences and registration on the electoral register.[118] Other examples of failed projects include the electronic voting project[119] and PPARS.[120] On an examination the Comptroller and Auditor General

[111] Gahan (2008), p. 15.

[112] Wylie (2004), pp. 10–11.

[113] McDonagh and White (2008), p. 45. See also Gahan (2008), p. 15; and Forfás (2008), p. 5.

[114] McDonagh and White (2008), pp. 19–55.

[115] This weblink has now been closed.

[116] Comptroller and Auditor General *eGovernment* Special Report (2007), p. 10.

[117] Comptroller and Auditor General *eGovernment* Special Report (2007), p. 11. See also Comptroller and Auditor General *Accounts of the Public Services 2008* Annual Report (2009), p. 76.

[118] Comptroller and Auditor General *eGovernment* Special Report (2007), p. 28.

[119] Comptroller and Auditor General *Accounts of the Public Services 2008* Annual Report (2009), p. 74.

[120] See Comptroller and Auditor General *Development of Human Resource Management System for the Health Service (PPARS)* Report on Value for Money Examination (2005).

found that while many department and agencies claimed to have achieved efficiencies arising from the implementation of eGovernment projects, only a few provided hard evidence of substantial savings.[121]

The European Commission has also found Ireland's information society performance to be a "mixed picture, with some indicators (like eGovernment and eCommerce) above the EU [European Union] average and others (like internet access for citizens and businesses) below or close to the EU average."[122] In 2014 the Commission noted that Ireland's Point of Single Contact remains underdeveloped as it "is essentially only an information portal that does not provide e-services or enable online applications and completion of procedures....and the absence of this capability negatively affects the free circulation of services."[123]

The OECD also identified the necessity for Ireland to improve its performance in this arena. Its 2008 public management review stated that

> E-Government, and the development of a more integrated ICT interface, provides a major opportunity to deliver faster, more readily accessible services and secure internal data sharing to simplify contact with the Public Service. While Ireland has had many successes in developing internal e-government systems, co-operation across different Public Service bodies is not widespread. Fragmentation of responsibility for different elements of e-government has meant that the full potential of ICT is not being realized by public sector organizations for citizens.[124]

McDonagh and While are of the view that Ireland's record is weakest in terms of the delivery of the more sophisticated levels of eGovernment and they cite numerous international benchmarking reports in support of this.[125] There is however some evidence of a regeneration of the government commitment to electronic service delivery.

While eRegistration remains a flagship project[126] other recent initiatives include the availability of planning documentation online by local authorities and http://www.myplan.ie/en/index.html which provides information directly to citizens about development and local area plans. The aim of this website is to create a one stop shop for information relevant to planning decision making (such as census records, heritage sites and patterns of housing development). It brings together information from all planning authorities and is a clear demonstration of integrated information delivery that can be of considerable benefit not just to citizens but also to public service providers. Another example is http://www.fixyourstreet.ie/ which allows citizens to report problems with public facilities such as roads, lighting, illegal dumping or water leaks directly to their local council.

---

[121] Comptroller and Auditor General *Press Release*: *Report on eGovernment* (2007).

[122] European Commission (2010), p. 32.

[123] European Commission (2014), p. 32.

[124] OECD (2008), p. 14.

[125] McDonagh and White (2008), pp. 46–47.

[126] See Sect. 3.4.

While these initiatives are a one way flow of information and not sophisticated digital transactional hubs they do demonstrate a commitment by government to spend money on online projects and to allow citizens to engage online with public services.

http://e.gov.ie/reporting/ also provides details of other projects. This website facilitates reporting by public bodies to the eGovernment Policy Unit in the Department of Public Expenditure and Reform. This forms the basis for progress reports on the 44 actions included in the current eGovernment strategy.[127] Hopefully the success of these developments along with the benefits of eRegistration[128] will encourage the Irish government to move further and accelerate its penetration into the digital arena.

While the term eConveyancing is not mentioned in the eGovernment strategy[129] there are many aspects of eConveyancing that will assist in delivering the objectives of this strategy. These include[130]:

- providing a reduction in the administrative burden for citizens and businesses;
- implementing digital delivery of applications for registration to the PRA;
- ensuring greater interoperability of government services;
- facilitating increased data sharing in relation to the property sector;
- providing an electronic collaboration tool to empower citizens and businesses;
- implementing business process improvements which deliver gains to all stakeholders in the conveyancing process;
- group transactional services around the life event of buying and selling property and allows for this to be integrated across organisational boundaries;
- incentivise take up of electronic services with the potential to link to ePlanning and many other online eGovernment services; and
- provide scope for gathering necessary statistical data about the property sector.

eConveyancing is included in the more recent Construction Strategy 2020 published by the government in May 2014.[131] This strategy acknowledges that conveyancing remains largely paper based and takes a disproportionate amount of time

> [t]herefore, a system of eConveyancing which harnesses modern technology to assist in the timely transfer of property ownership would provide a more modern, efficient, cost effective and secure system to support transactions in the property market in the future. Moving to a full eConveyancing system will require a number of further elements over and above existing and planned developments to be put in place to provide for the secure transmission of communications, the management and disbursement of funds between parties and the creation and management of digital signatures.[132]

127 Department of Public Expenditure and Reform.

128 See Sect. 3.4.1.

129 Department of Public Expenditure and Reform.

130 Department of Public Expenditure and Reform, pp. 2, 7, 9–13 and 17.

131 Government Publications.

132 Government Publications, p. 58.

All of these developments fit within the context of eCommerce and eGovernment. This strategy adds to the compelling case for reform of the current conveyancing system.

3.3 The Case for Reform

> With the ever-increasing reliance of our society on information technology, it is perhaps not surprising that information technology has been chosen as the means by which it is hoped to modernise conveyancing – hence, *electronic* conveyancing.[133]

Many commentators have advocated eConveyancing as a means of achieving this modernisation.[134] In 2005 the then Irish Taoiseach, Bertie Ahern, acknowledged that modernisation, simplification and reform of land law and conveyancing was long overdue and that eConveyancing would bring this process into the twenty-first century.[135]

> No one could possibly argue against that as being a highly desirable and indeed, essential goal. With all aspects of Irish life enjoying unprecedented modernisation – transport, infrastructure, communications – why should the legal profession allow itself…to, remain in the past.[136]

The application of technology is seen as a means of standardising and simplifying the conveyancing process, improving efficiency and providing transparency. The development of eConveyancing has been advocated as a 'cure all' solution to the difficulties presented by a centuries old, paper based, traditional process that on the face of it appears to no longer fit the twenty-first century. In moving towards eConveyancing there is the opportunity to redefine and re-engineer processes as part of the reform programme to take maximum advantage of available technologies.[137] Kostova applauds this determination to make conveyancing easier, cheaper and more efficient, noting that "great hopes have been invested in the development of an end-to-end fully electronic system of conveyancing."[138]

To some extent the case for reform has been predicated on the need to be seen to be making advances in line with other related jurisdictions rather than a comprehensive cost benefit analysis.[139] The complexity of such an analysis has meant that

---

[133] Kostova (2010), p. 1.

[134] Wylie for example. See Wylie (2004).

[135] Ahern (2005).

[136] Jamieson (2006), p. 75.

[137] The Law Society of Ireland (2008a) insists that it would be a fundamental mistake to digitise the current paper based system. It advocates that the whole process be re-designed and simplified to suit the online environment.

[138] Kostova (2010), p. 3.

[139] Kostova (2010), p. 33 notes that it is difficult to measure the potential savings, be it less clerical time, volume of paper or some other feature of the solution. However see ConsultingWhere

jurisdictions have chosen to rely on other evidence to advocate eConveyancing. The Irish Law Reform Commission is of the view that the "experience in other jurisdictions has shown that a business case does exist for undertaking an eConveyancing initiative of this nature."[140] The experience drawn upon is that of Ontario, England and Wales, New Zealand, Australia and South Africa.

Many commentators have however relied upon perceived benefits rather than empirical data. This process whereby 'perceived' innovation is adopted is reflected in innovation-diffusion literature. Abrahamson looks at the diffusion literature and divides it into two types.

> The first claims that fads or fashions facilitate the diffusion of technically inefficient administrative technologies....A second type of account claims that fads or fashions harm organizations' economic performances because they prompt rejections of administrative technologies that had the potential to become technically efficient for their adopters.[141]

Do organisations imitate other organisations in order to appear legitimate by conforming to emergent norms that sanction these innovations?[142] Is this the case with eConveyancing? Is it the new fad or fashion?

While Abrahamson has focused on the literature from an organisational point of view other commentators look at it from the perspective of social systems. Levi-Faur has defined:

> diffusion as the process by which the adoption of innovation by member(s) of a social system is communicated through certain channels and over time and triggers mechanisms that increase the probability of its adoption by other members who have not yet adopted it....Their own particularistic order is then "exported" or "projected" globally as a "universal rationality"[143]

He points out that new sources of change have emerged since the 1980s and these sources include technological innovations.[144] While looking in particular at the spread of regulatory approaches across jurisdictions, his comments are of equal interest in the context of legal processes which would require the backing of new regulation.

Rogers points out that the internet has created increased interest in the study of diffusion and particularly in the role of communication networks in the diffusion process.[145] This according to Levi-Faur is a reflection of an increasingly interdependent world.[146] Hence when change is sought or demanded it is not

---

Limited and ACIL Allen Consulting for LINZ 'Better Property Services' Final Report (2013) which looks at the potential economic benefits of easier access to government property and building services and information in New Zealand.

[140] The Law Reform Commission (2006), p. 2, Appendix.

[141] Abrahamson (1991), pp. 588–589.

[142] Abrahamson (1991), p. 597.

[143] Levi-Faur (2005), pp. 23–24.

[144] Levi-Faur (2005), p. 23.

[145] Rogers (2003), p. 348.

[146] Levi-Faur (2005), p. 28.

surprising that decision makers look to advances made in other jurisdictions in order to benchmark their own organisation or system. What is surprising is that decision makers so readily accept the perceived benefits articulated by adopters of change in other jurisdictions, who themselves have a vested interest in their new systems being perceived to be a success.[147] Relying on such a weak rationale for expensive systems, it is then not surprising when they often fail to be a success.

Few jurisdictions appear to have carried out a detailed risk assessment before advancing eConveyancing or if they have these results are not in the public domain. The exception to this is Australia which carried out a risk assessment of NECS (now PEXA) with the final report published on the 9 February 2007.[148] This risk assessment focused primarily on possible system failures.[149]

Despite this there is a considerable amount of literature advocating the advantages of eConveyancing. Gahan lists them as including[150]:

(a) round the clock availability (presumably for authorised users);
(b) clearer and quicker interaction with quicker responses (again presumably for authorised users in getting information from the electronic system);
(c) reduced administrative burden on the customer side (presumably he is referring to the customer not having to complete and post paper documents);
(d) higher productivity on the government side because the data can be processed more quickly compared to paper-based forms (this is likely a reference to the pre-population of data that can occur in a computer based system);
(e) facilitating information-sharing and analysis of trends; and
(f) improved national competitiveness.

As Connolly points out:

> Even the most superficial examination of the conveyancing process reveals the potential for the use of ICT, the retrieval of information being the most obvious, as the kernel of a conveyancing transaction is the retrieval of information about the property and those who claim an interest in it.[151]

---

[147] Rogers criticizes the pro-innovation bias of diffusion research and says this is a serious shortcoming caused by the research being funded by change agencies and a rejected and/or discontinued innovation is less likely to be investigated by a researcher. The implication is that either researchers are biased because they have been 'bought' or only successful innovations receive publicity and kudos. Of course researchers may be biased and it is possible that unsuccessful innovations are more likely to be covered up but it is cynical to taint all diffusion research with these shortcomings. See Rogers (2003), pp. 106 and 110.

[148] National Electronic Conveyancing Office (2007). This report is in three volumes and was carried out by the law firm Clayton Utz (contact Mark Sneddon).

[149] Risks 34, 77, 78 and 81 relate to land registry errors. These are of interest but are not of direct relevance to this research. See 10.1 of volume 1 and also volume 3.

[150] Gahan (2008), p. 15. Similar type benefits have been articulated by McDermott. See McDermott (2006), p. 68.

[151] Connolly (2007), p. 11.

It will be possible to update ownership on the land register as soon as completion of the transaction has taken place and to immediately have this information available to all stakeholders. The availability of this information in real time has the potential to remove risk and cut out delay.[152]

The benefits of eConveyancing and eRegistration were also discussed at the UNECE WPLA Workshop on the Influence of Land Administration on People and Business held in Croatia on the 2nd and 3rd October 2008. These benefits were identified as including the prevention of multiple registration which is time consuming and as the registration takes less time it meets the need of the market; reducing the risk of incorrect data[153]; and increasing the possibility of transparency and the opportunity to "[m]ake all necessary information available to the players of the real estate market internal and external users (professionals, buyers and sellers) at one place at the Internet."[154]

The prevention of multiple registration could mean a move from several registers to one register and the expansion of that one register to reflect all the required information.[155] Locke explains an approach that is being explored in Australia whereby the land registry would continue to maintain the title register but would also be an online portal to information maintained by other agencies.[156] This idea of an electronic hub for all information relating to land has been adopted in many jurisdictions.[157] In some the land registry is taking on this role[158] and in others it is private enterprise[159] or a public private partnership.[160]

For Perry the thrust of the electronic communications revolution[161] or evolution, including eConveyancing, is towards greater connectivity.[162] Currently the information about property is stored by a variety of bodies. For example the lawyer has to retrieve information about planning from the local authority. Information about any tax liability has to be sought from Revenue. A variety of registers have to be searched for details of any encumbrances on the property. Wylie, states that it would be much easier if this information was stored in computer databases which were interlinked and easily accessible.[163]

---

[152] See Sect. 6.2 for a more detailed analysis.

[153] This may only be true if there is some means of the data being validated as it is entered into the system.

[154] Conclusions of the sessions 'Conclusions of the sessions' United Nations Economic Commission for Europe's Working Party (2008).

[155] In Ireland it is proposed to merge the PRA with Ordnance Survey Ireland (OSi) and the Valuation Office. See Property Registration Authority 'Strategic Plan 2013–2015' (2013), p. 3.

[156] Locke (2007), p. 5.

[157] Dale et al. (2006) refer at p. 15 to a 'one-stop-shop' method of access to land registration.

[158] For example in England and Wales.

[159] Teranet in Ontario.

[160] Teranet started as a public private enterprise.

[161] Widdison refers to an information revolution. See Widdison (1997), p. 144.

[162] Perry (2003a), p. 29.

[163] Wylie (2004), p. 11.

This would benefit not just the lawyer but other stakeholders in locating the information required to complete the legal and procedural formalities to complete a conveyancing transaction. For the land owner it is likely to mean that the transaction time and cost is reduced.

An example of this is the setting up of the Land and Property Services Agency in Northern Ireland in 2008. This brought together the Rate Collection Agency, the Valuation and Lands Agency, Ordnance Survey and the Land Registers with the aim of delivering integrated mapping, registration, valuation and rating services. Similarly Ireland plans to amalgamate the PRA, Ordnance Survey Ireland (OSi) and the Valuation Office.[164] These changes are in line with the UNECE guidelines for land administration which recommend that a single agency be responsible for land administration.[165]

This may mean the expansion of the title register beyond its traditional role[166] and possibly, by implication, the creation of new registered titles in land. This aspect and its implications are explored further in Chap. 8.

The Australian States appear to have embraced the possibilities afforded by these changes. In Australia water licences which previously attached to specific land parcels are now being converted to water allocations which can be bought, sold, mortgaged and sub-divided.[167] They do not have the benefit of a government guarantee or statutory indefeasibility but do "benefit from the same principles of priority and certainty in resource ownership that applies to interests recorded in the freehold land register."[168] Queensland is also examining how it might register sub-terrain storage areas and Western Australia has created a new interest in land called a carbon right which is the right to the benefits and risks arising from carbon sequestration and release on a parcel of land.[169] There is an argument however that these new registered interests are created to meet the demands of a changing society and have nothing intrinsically to do with eRegistration.[170] In Ireland the registering authority is similarly looking at extending its scope through the development of synergies with other state agencies such as providing a link to planning data.[171] The registering authority has already agreed to supply land parcel data to the

[164] Deeney (2014), p. 426.

[165] Stanley and Adlington (2007), p. 3.

[166] Deeney notes that eConveyancing will require a fundamental review of the present functionality of the Irish land register. Deeney (2014), p. 365.

[167] Dale et al. (2006), p. 5 note the increasing concern to see land from a three-dimensional perspective so as to record various horizontal layers of information.

[168] Locke (2007), pp. 8–9.

[169] Locke (2007), pp. 9–10. See also Gray and Gray (2009), p. 139.

[170] Locke does not make a direct causal link between the new interests in Australia and the development of eRegistration. Instead he examines them in the context of the challenges and opportunities faces by the land registries and the use of the land titling system to support efficient operation of markets which are of significant value to the economy. See Locke (2007), pp. 3 and 8.

[171] Property Registration Authority 'Strategic Plan 2013–2015' (2013), p. 31 which states that it is in the public interest that the authority pursue an active approach in relation to such collaborations.

Department of the Environment, Community and Local Government for the new planning portal.[172]

Alternatively the reference to a prevention of multiple registration by the UNECE WPLA[173] may mean a move from registration several times in the one register to a necessity to only register once.[174] The UNECE WPLA noted that a balance must be achieved between transparency and data protection to maintain confidence in the system and combat new ways of fraud[175] but session 4 concluded that land administration authorities should improve by making new services based on eGovernment and electronic signatures, following the one stop-shop principle.[176]

Sabaliauskas and Mikuta explain this principle as meaning that as:

> information [in electronic documents] is entered and examined only once, [the] probability of errors is minimised. [And with an] [i]ntegrated environment all actions are performed within the framework of one system.[177]

The potential is for the data entered into the system by authorised users to be automatically verified by the system and checked against data already validated and this presents the opportunity to minimise any errors.

Data amendment however is likely to be much more difficult than data entry. Any errors already in the system are likely to be replicated in future entries and thus verification and validation of the initial data entry is a key requirement. Limiting access to the system to authorised users and retaining a final sign off before registration to staff of the registering authority are some of the means of retaining control over the data. The design of the system is also a key factor so as to minimise input errors.

While single entry will likely decrease entry errors the likelihood of any errors already in the system being discovered is reduced. The data already in the system will only be checked once instead of multiple times. Input errors may be minimised

[172] Property Registration Authority 'Annual Report 2012' (2013), p. 11. This new portal called MyPlan.ie provides information about development plans and planning decision-making. See http://www.myplan.ie/en/index.html.

[173] Conclusions of the sessions 'Conclusions of the sessions' United Nations Economic Commission for Europe's Working Party (2008).

[174] This could mean a move from several registers e.g. tax, planning, title, to one register and the expansion of that one register to reflect all the required information about the property.

[175] For an examination of the move from a closed to an open register in England and Wales see Timothy (2007). The Irish title register is also an open register but the original title documents on which the register is based are only available to authorised persons. See Deeney (2014), p. 73.

[176] An example of this principle is the National Land Information System (NLIS) in England and Wales which provides a hub or channel for conveyancing searches. This is a commercial service licensed and regulated by government. For a recent review of this service see ConsultingWhere Limited and ACIL Allen Consulting for LINZ (Land Information New Zealand) (2013), p. 64 and Annex A to that report.

[177] Sabaliauskas and Mikuta (2008).

but process errors may be maintained as they may not be detected if there is no double checking.[178]

However, there is potential to limit further errors entering the system. McDermott notes that due to in-built system prompts and automatic calculation of registration fees the on-line form completion in the Irish landdirect.ie system is leading to a significantly lower incidence of errors in the documentation presented for registration.[179] According to Deeney eRegistration will address to a large degree the common administrative errors such as payment of the incorrect fee, inadequate completion of forms and use of the wrong folio reference.[180] In Ontario the e-reg system automatically warns the user when a draft registration is incomplete so that signing and registration are only allowed after all mandatory information has been submitted.[181]

Treacy and O'Sullivan also list some of the major benefits to users of the Irish Land Registry's Electronic Access Service.[182] These include improved timeliness and speed of service, improved convenience, on-line data is far more usable and flexible, improved service through local offices and improved business processes in other government departments and agencies.[183]

In Ontario Moore and Globe set out the goals of land registration reform as including to simplify conveyancing law and procedure, reduce the costs of conveyancing and standardise law, terminology and procedure.[184] While remaining concerned about digital signatures, Kostova acknowledges that eConveyancing could remove some of the risks and delays.[185]

Other benefits of eConveyancing were articulated at the CINDER XVI International Congress on Registration Law held in Valencia, Spain from the 20th to 22nd May 2008. At that forum Rätsep set out the following reasons for eConveyancing being much easier:

> activities are half-automated which means registration is more efficient and ... routine work can be done without human intervention. Texts of entries are composed automatically as they base (sic) on templates. Thanks to digital structured data exchange there are fewer mistakes and less paper. Information system is sustainable and can be easily developed further. It is easy to get statistics. You can get land register information everywhere you have internet connection, it is possible to build new online services according to clients' needs. And information you get from the register has legal power electronically[186]

[178] See Arruñada (2010), pp. 116–117 for an analysis of the incidence of errors in the New Zealand system.

[179] McDermott (2006), p. 69.

[180] Deeney (2014), p. 53.

[181] Moore and Globe (2003), p. 425.

[182] Treacy and O'Sullivan (2004).

[183] Treacy and O'Sullivan (2004), p. 6.

[184] Moore and Globe (2003), p. 12.

[185] Kostova (2010), p. 56.

[186] Rätsep (2008), p. 3.

Takács, in referring to Hungary, sees a different change in land registration. He points out that the changing function of real estate from being "only a property" to being a tool of investment and a source of income increases the importance of land registration.[187] This 'commodity-isation' of land ownership is a recurring theme. It is reflected in the conflict between use value and exchange value which has become more evident in the development of the complex commodities market.[188] Use value reflects the value an occupier will put on having possession and use of a property and this aspect is particularly important in the context of the family home. By contrast, exchange value focuses on the monetary value of the property, as a commodity or asset, the value of which can be realised by sale, lease, exchange or mortgage.

Land registration must provide prompt case management, reliability, simplicity, elasticity and legal security.[189] For many registries the move to eRegistration provides the opportunity to fulfill this brief. While acknowledging it is:

> axiomatic that reducing the number of procedures generates simplicity and efficiency... [Clancy is of the view that] there is a limit to the level of simplification that is effective.... Obviously, if a figure lower then one [procedure] is achieved, then there is no system. As a corollary, on what basis do we then presume that a number greater than one is a weakness? Is there a risk that a disproportionate emphasis on reducing the number of procedures could lead to an erosion of the integrity and security of registration?[190]

Similarly Arruñada warns that some solutions do not achieve real simplification but instead lead to a mere transfer of paperwork and that standardisation can lead to a more abstract register which forces the parties to rely on contract documents.[191] Gaining access to these documents can then constrain the transaction as they will be held by individual stakeholders.[192]

There are, however, few dissenting voices among the overwhelming support expressed for eConveyancing. Perry says there has been widespread acceptance by lawyers that eConveyancing would be a change for the better partly due to their reluctance to be seen as backward looking and partly due to feeling that the introduction of new technology is inevitable.[193] He is of the view that these facts tend to stifle any opposition to the introduction of eConveyancing and such unquestioning acceptance often results in a lack of any real scrutiny.[194] Given that the implementation of any new system is a challenging process and failures are not uncommon, "it is unwise to assume that the introduction of e-conveyancing is, at a practical level, in any way inevitable, as is often asserted."[195] His views are

---

[187] Takács (2008), p. 5.

[188] See Sect. 4.3.

[189] Takács (2008), p. 5.

[190] Clancy (2007), p. 11.

[191] Arruñada (2010), p. 119.

[192] Arruñada (2010), p. 119.

[193] Perry (2003a), p. 26.

[194] Perry (2003c), p. 215.

[195] Perry (2003a), p. 26.

very much aligned with some of those expressed in the diffusion-innovation literature referred to earlier.

One of the main benefits of eConveyancing is often cited as cost savings. Perry takes the view that the absence of cost savings, or even a substantial increase in costs, are not necessarily by themselves reasons not to adopt eConveyancing if the new system is more efficient than the old system.[196] He points out that the economic benefit in the long term of IT investment is a difficult area and generates a lot of disagreement. It is rare that the effects of different systems are compared.[197] Perry cites Mähring as evidence of research that suggests the risks of large IT projects are not properly appreciated by those who end up bearing the consequences should things go wrong.[198]

As noted previously Sneddon having carried out a detailed risk assessment over 5 months of the Australian NECS (now PEXA) system expressed the view that eConveyancing systems "may have more concentrated points of failure than paper based systems, for the same reasons that they generate greater efficiencies."[199] Griggs argues that eConveyancing will have many advantages but also questions if it will allow those committing fraud to offend on a wider scale.[200]

Having looked at the limited information on costing available for a number of systems Perry takes the view that "the argument that the introduction of e-conveyancing will make conveyancing cheaper is almost certainly incorrect" but qualifies this to the extent that costs for land registration may be reduced as the process of updating the register is automated.[201] His conclusion is that claims made about the cost advantages of eConveyancing do not usually withstand detailed scrutiny and the costs are usually substantially underestimated.[202] He notes that in New Zealand and Ontario project costs were more than originally anticipated.[203] These costs ultimately have to be paid by the consumer.[204] Butt also notes that the many criticisms leveled at eConveyancing is how much the system will cost and the problem is we just don't know.[205]

---

196 Perry (2003a), p. 29. While an increase in costs might be justified for other benefits it would be difficult to justify any substantial increase in costs even if short term.

197 For one example see Miceli et al. (2002), pp. 565–582.

198 Perry (2003a), p. 29.

199 Sneddon (2007), p. 9.

200 Griggs (2001).

201 Perry (2003a), p. 29.

202 For example in Australia an audit was called for after it was alleged that the Victorian government spent an estimated $50 million to build its state based eConveyancing system which had been used for only one completed property transaction; see Merritt (2009).

203 Perry (2003b), p. 1696.

204 Perry (2003a), p. 29. One of the additional costs is software licensing fees.

205 Butt (2006), p. 5.

Brown notes that inevitably there will be a fee for the operating licence and premiums on indemnity insurance may increase[206] but this will be offset by efficiency savings. However in Ontario LawPRO the insurer for lawyers

> changed their requirements in order to take into consideration the changes to real estate practice from electronic registration. . ..[and] waived certain deductibles related to electronically registered documents provided certain protocols have been followed.[207]

Thus it may be possible, given the increased certainty in the system, to negotiate savings with the professional insurers.[208]

Arruñada is also critical of eConveyancing advances.[209] He looks at some of the tradeoffs involved in substituting tasks performed by humans with computers and expresses concern about the risk of transferring costs and risks instead of reducing them.[210] He is also of the view that the benefit of immediacy of results may be illusory because eConveyancing makes indefeasibility unsustainable in the long term due to a greater incidence of fraud[211] and thus will debase the registry into a mere recording of rights.[212] His perspective is, however, on the basis of the New Zealand automatic system and as Kostova puts it so articulately "if solicitors are not commonly forging their clients' signatures in the paper-based system, the introduction of digital signatures is not likely to lure them over to the dark side of fraud."[213]

Arruñada gives the example of the Victoria system which cost $40–50 million but only registered a single pilot transaction in its first 18 months of operation

---

[206] Brown (2003), p. 626.

[207] Murray (2004), p. 20.

[208] For an example of how the property market can impact on lawyers professional indemnity insurance see Elliot (2014).

[209] Arruñada (2010), pp. 115–120.

[210] Arruñada (2010), p. 118. Grinlinton (2003), p. 218 notes that transactions remotely registered by conveyancers may not be subject to the same scrutiny and there is a strong possibility that a substantial number of errors may infect the system and sit latent on the register possibly for many years.

[211] Thomas is also critical of the New Zealand system on the basis that it makes the title less secure due to the removal of the paper title document and non-intervention of registry staff. Also the new system transfers more risk to conveyancers for fraudulent and incorrect transactions. See Thomas (2003), pp. 366–367.

[212] Arruñada (2010), p. 118.

[213] Kostova (2010), p. 28. Two recent cases where solicitor fraud did occur in the paper environment relate to Michael Lynn and Thomas Byrne. Both engaged in mortgage fraud causing losses to financial institutions of amounts estimated to be in excess of 100 million euro. See Law Society of Ireland (2008b), p. 12. See also Keating (2012), pp. 20–21. Deeney refers at p. 373 to two serious cases of fraud coming to the attention of the Irish registering authority in October 2007, "one of which related to the fraudulent registration of the ownership of a large number of investment properties and the registration of multiple fraudulent mortgages." It is likely that this is a reference to the fraud perpetuated by Lynn and Byrne. See Deeney (2014). It is surprising that there have been no reported court cases arising from these frauds.

because both banks and conveyancers refused to participate.[214] Under pressure from the banks a National Electronic Conveyancing System (NECS) was under consideration and in 2010 NECS was replaced by National E-Conveyancing Development Limited (NECDL). From 3 March 2014 NECDL became known as PEXA.[215] In 2013 the four major banks all joined the project[216] as part of release 1 and began doing single party transactions such as new mortgages, discharges and refinancing online.[217] An ambitious roll out schedule is now in place with transfer and financial settlement functionality to be deployed in New South Wales and Victoria in autumn 2014 and other territories coming on stream during 2015.[218] The first practitioner to use the platform did so in June 2014 by lodging a caveat on a Victorian title.[219] After a rocky start it appears that this huge project appears to be well on its way to success.

The experience in England and Wales however provides a stark warning to any jurisdiction tempted to view eConveyancing as an easy task. The chain matrix project and Home Information Pack (HIP) initiatives were both shelved after a considerable amount of money had been expended[220] and more recently the move to etransfers has been put on hold.[221] Land Registry consultation with stakeholders showed that the majority of respondents were not persuaded that etransfers were desirable or achievable, they felt that the echarge solution did not meet their needs and significant concern was expressed that the process for creating and applying electronic signatures was too complicated.[222] Only 20 or so echarges were done between 2009 and 2011.[223]

Thus in 2011 £6.4 million of development costs attributable to electronic charges, signatures and transfers was written off with the Land Registry making the decision to focus on electronic lodgement and dispatch whereby customers can use electronic channels to send in paper documents.[224] More recently in January 2014 the Department for Business, Innovation and Skills published a consultation document re the introduction of a Land Registry service delivery company.[225] This company would take over responsibility for processing land and property

[214] Arruñada (2010), p. 118. See ConsultingWhere Limited and ACIL Allen Consulting for LINZ (Land Information New Zealand) (2013) and Annex C for details of the advances in the different Australian states and territories.

[215] Short for property exchange Australia. PEXA 'NECDL Name Change' email 3 March 2014.

[216] This has now extended to seven transacting banks and financial institutions.

[217] PEXA 'NECDL Name Change' email 3 March 2014.

[218] PEXA 'An Update on the PEXA Release Schedule' email 22 May 2014.

[219] PEXA 'First Practitioners Start Transacting on PEXA' email 17 June 2014.

[220] Cross (2009) and Department for Communities and Local Government.

[221] HM Land Registry Press Release (2011).

[222] HM Land Registry.

[223] HM Land Registry Press Release (2011).

[224] HM Land Registry Press Release (2011).

[225] Department for Business, Innovation and Skills (2014).

registration under the oversight of a government Chief Land Registrar. This proposal has not been well received by key stakeholders.[226] It begs the question of what went wrong and is outsourcing to the private sector 'punishment' for the failure to deliver eConveyancing?[227] This experience presents a warning to registering authorities not to stray into areas of private interaction between citizens particularly if there is not clear stakeholder support.[228] Keating refers to 'a cautionary tale' noting that the halt to full eConveyancing in England and Wales reflects the multi-dimensional challenges that regulators and policy makers face when considering the introduction of eConveyancing.[229]

Kostova notes that initial plans are often ambitious, with consideration given to full end-to-end eConveyancing, but "after some deliberation and consultation, a slightly more modest solution is usually introduced instead."[230] England and Wales provides a timely example of this.[231] Australia has also struggled but is now moving forward swiftly with PEXA. Given that this project encompasses the multiple states and territories in Australia, each with its own laws and registering authority, it is an admirable feat and provides inspiration for other jurisdictions.

The critical viewpoints expressed by Perry and Arruñada have failed to find widespread support.[232] Perry's opinion that there is a lack of real scrutiny and unquestioning acceptance of eConveyancing advances,[233] is certainly evident in the lack of empirical data put forward by commentators advocating eConveyancing.[234] Connolly expresses the view that Irish house purchasers could save as much as 40 million euro per year in transaction costs through efficiency savings[235] but she does not explain the basis for this figure.

---

[226] Cross (2014).

[227] Outsourcing or the involvement of private sector finance is not new in the delivery of land information services. In England and Wales NLIS is a commercial service licensed and regulated by government. For a recent review of this service see ConsultingWhere Limited and ACIL Allen Consulting for LINZ (Land Information New Zealand) (2013), pp. 64–72 and Annex A to that report. See also p. 81 of the final report which notes that Landweb Direct in Northern Ireland was one of the first financially free-standing information technology projects in the Private Finance Initiative (PFI) field. The model in Ontario is also one where the government has outsourced operation of the land registry to private enterprise. See Annex B to the report. The role of Public Private Partnerships in Australia is also addressed in Annex C. With this report New Zealand is examining the benefits to be gained by moving in this direction.

[228] See Sect. 3.2.4.

[229] Keating (2012), pp. 83 and 87.

[230] Kostova (2010), p. 39.

[231] HM Land Registry acknowledging the move away from etransfers towards electronic applications with scanned transfers.

[232] Browning provides another dissenting voice. He has been vocal in his prediction that England's eConveyancing project will crash and burn. See Browning.

[233] Perry (2003a), p. 26.

[234] ConsultingWhere Limited and ACIL Allen Consulting for LINZ (Land Information New Zealand) (2013), Annex C, p. 21 notes the lack of a strong evidence base for the development of a national eConveyancing system in Australia.

[235] Connolly (2007), p. 20.

Many commentators and politicians see eConveyancing as a panacea to solve all ills. In commenting on the reform of land law in Ireland in 2006 the then Tánaiste and Minister for Justice, Equality and Law Reform expressed the view that "eConveyancing has, I believe, the capacity to simplify the conveyancing process and reduce costs for all those involved in property transactions and it is, therefore, a prize worth striving for."[236] More recently the European Commission in its 2014 Assessment of Ireland's national reform and stability programme recognises the moves to extend title registration and notes that this "should facilitate a complete e-Conveyancing system and reduce delays."[237]

There is certainly the potential for significant improvement in the Irish conveyancing process and many of these have been articulated in interviews with representatives from stakeholder groups.[238] Whether eConveyancing can deliver all these improvements has yet to be determined and much depends on the system design.

The skepticism expressed by a minority of commentators has failed to halt the ongoing advance of IT into the conveyancing process and surely a regulated, organised, communal system has to provide more security for property transactions over and above that offered by ordinary email. Even if property owners are not demanding change, is it not incumbent upon key stakeholders to deliver improvements in the process whenever possible in the public interest? Obviously what is in the public interest may be a matter of debate and more research is needed to contribute to that dialogue.

It is important to note that the failures, and much of the critical commentary, relate to jurisdictions that have implemented, or attempted to implement, automatic eRegistration, those that have attempted to deliver initiatives without stakeholder consultation and agreement or where the government, through its state agencies, has attempted to move outside eRegistration into the wider eConveyancing process. It can be seen from developments to date that Ireland is not likely to encounter these pitfalls.

Ireland does not propose to implement automatic eRegistration. There has been considerable stakeholder consultation since publication of the Law Reform Commission report in 2006 and the registering authority is focusing its remit on delivering eRegistration and not eConveyancing. Thus provided the system design is robust and based on a sound business case there is every reason to be optimistic for the success of the Irish eConveyancing project.

---

236 McDowell (2006).

237 European Commission (2014), p. 33.

238 Connolly (2007), pp. 36–51. See also Killilea (2010).

3.4 Development of eConveyancing in Ireland and Ontario

The development of eConveyancing to date in Ireland and Ontario is set out under the headings of eRecords, eApplication, eRegistration and eConveyancing. The initiatives in each jurisdiction are examined based on the degree to which they meet the criteria of each phase as defined in the neutral vocabulary and as set out earlier in this chapter.

3.4.1 eConveyancing in Ireland

Background

The Irish Law Reform Commission published its report entitled eConveyancing: Modelling of the Irish Conveyancing System[239] in 2006. BearingPoint were hired as consultants and their report is published as an appendix to the Law Reform Commission's Report. Together they have become known as the BearingPoint report.

The Law Reform Commission identified three workstreams as setting out a roadmap for eConveyancing; a development workstream, process improvement workstream and legislative changes workstream.[240] While there has been much legislative reform, to date there has been less progress on the other workstreams. However even before the BearingPoint report the Irish Land Registry was engaged in modernisation that fell within the remit of eRegistration.

eRecords

Initially the registration authority commenced a major programme of data capture of existing paper documents in tandem with the development of a new system for extensive on-line searching and retrieval of title records. This new system, introduced in 1999, was called the Electronic Access Service (EAS) and then renamed as landdirect.ie in April 2006. This service is the public interface of an internal Land Registry project entitled Integrated Title Registration Information System (ITRIS). ITRIS provides support for staff throughout the registration process including electronic storage and retrieval of ownership records, tracking and processing of applications, generation and transmission of electronic correspondence and provision of key statistics.[241] The title records are called folios[242] and title plans. Title

[239] The Law Reform Commission (2006).

[240] The Law Reform Commission (2006), p. 11.

[241] Treacy and O'Sullivan (2004), p. 5.

[242] In Ontario the title record is called the parcel register. For an example see Moore and Globe (2003), p. 166.

plans are the maps attached to the folios and they were previously known as filed plans. Folios set out details of the registration and any burdens thereon.

Part of the registration authorities' strategy to deliver its services electronically required the conversion of all paper title records into electronic records. This conversion programme commenced early in 2002 and was completed in 2004. The conversion of these paper records into electronic format involved the scanning and indexing of 6.4 million pages of official records and this data capture led to improved timeliness and speed of service with instantaneous inspections of title records, automated copying services and a reduction in time taken to process certain applications.[243]

EAS and subsequently landdirect.ie is an internet based service delivery system. It was the first eGovernment project to 'go live' in the Irish civil service.[244] The main objective was to simplify access to records and improve the timeliness of information thus providing a better quality and more responsive service.[245] Authorised users can do on-line searches, view and print ownership records, view and track the progress of pending applications, apply for copies of records and prepare and complete applications for registration. Initially those who are not authorised users could access some of this information but only by contacting the registering authority in person or by post. In 2011 however the registration authority started to make the searching, viewing and printing of ownership records available online to the general public on a trial basis. This was 'very well received' and by the end of 2012 map and folio data for all counties was available online to non-account holders.[246]

The legislation to support these changes was introduced in 2006. Section 50 of the Registration of Deeds and Title Act 2006[247] (hereafter the 2006 Act) amended the definitions in the 1964 Act by providing that record would include information in electronic or other non-legible form and register would include and be deemed to always have included any register kept in electronic or other non-legible form.

By 2008 over 95 % of all searches and applications for certified copy documents were conducted on-line through landdirect.ie.[248] Full access to all maps via a digital mapping project was completed in August 2010. This involved the conversion into digital format of approximately 2.5 million land parcel boundaries[249] and brought to an end a 10 year programme of converting the national title register into digital format.[250] This completed the eRecords phase of eRegistration.

[243] Treacy (2006), pp. 33–34.

[244] Treacy (2006), p. 34.

[245] Treacy and O'Sullivan (2004), p. 5.

[246] Property Registration Authority 'Annual Report 2012' (2013), p. 16.

[247] No. 12 of 2006.

[248] Clancy (2008), p. 6.

[249] Treacy (2007), p. 31.

[250] Deeney (2014), pp. 368–369.

eApplication

The registration authority has also moved into eApplication. It developed an electronic application form called eForm 17 that can be lodged using landdirect.ie. This form

> interacts dynamically with the Land Registry database, facilitating accurate input of information and calculation of the fee to be paid. . ..The effect is to considerably reduce the common errors which arose in applications made in the manual system. It validates key data online and pre-populates the register with drafts of the appropriate registrations leading to significant improvements in efficiency.[251]

Upon lodging the form there is also the advantage that users receive a dealing reference number instantaneously and can then track the application through the registration process.

As eApplication retains the paper documents any errors come to light when the paper is lodged. In the case of a conflict between the electronic application and the paper, the paper document prevails as this is the legally effective application.

This eApplication element of eRegistration was introduced in late 2002 and by 2007 this facility had grown to represent over 32 % of all applications for registration and over 98 % of some services were conducted online exclusively.[252] During 2012 almost three million searching and certification transactions were processed through the landdirect.ie portal.[253]

The growth of landdirect.ie has been a tremendous success for the Irish registering authority as represented by Table 3.1.[254]

While anyone can apply to be a registered user of the service the vast bulk are solicitors and law searchers.[255] Other users include lenders, government departments, surveyors and law enforcement agencies.

As at 1 June 2014 67 % of applicants used the online application form,[256] 59 % used the eDischarge facility[257] and 95 % of applications for certified copy documents were done online.[258] Taking into account the fact that the eDischarge system does not facilitate partial discharges 59 % is a high percentage of take up. The PRA confirms that there has been a 99.9 % accuracy rate in these applications.[259] This compares very favourably with overall rejection rates as set out in Table 3.2.[260]

---

[251] Deeney (2014), p. 369.

[252] O'Sullivan (2007), p. 4.

[253] Property Registration Authority 'Annual Report 2012' (2013), p. 15.

[254] James O'Boyle Financial Controller Property Registration Authority by email 13 June 2014.

[255] Interview with Greg McDermott ICT Manager Property Registration Authority 1 March 2012 confirmed that solicitors and law searchers account for in excess of 90 % of users.

[256] eForm 17.

[257] This facility was the first phase of eRegistration and it provides for the electronic release of registered charges.

[258] James O'Boyle Financial Controller Property Registration Authority by email 13 June 2014.

[259] James O'Boyle Financial Controller Property Registration Authority by email 13 June 2014.

[260] James O'Boyle Financial Controller Property Registration Authority by email 13 June 2014. See Deeney (2014), pp. 54–55 for common reasons for rejection of applications.

Table 3.1 Growth of online services Ireland: landdirect.ie portal

Year	2000	2006	2007	2008	2009	2010	2011	2012	2013
No. of registered users	1,700	10,900	12,741	13,872	14,837	15,775	16,565	17,657	19,829
No. of online transactions (million)	0.2	2.2	2.3	2.5	2.6	2.5	2.5	2.9	2.9

Table 3.2 Overall rejection rates Ireland

Year	2007	2008	2009	2010	2011	2012	2013
Rejections (%)	17.6	12	9	12	14	13	12

There have been productivity gains as a result of the move towards electronic services particularly the folio data capture completed in 2009 and digital mapping project completed in 2010.[261] In relation to eDischarges the PRA estimates that there has been about an 85 % reduction in manual staff input as a result of the initiative.[262] The growth of electronic services has meant that the PRA has delivered instantaneous access to information to its customers and also maintained ongoing services despite significant reductions in staff.[263]

The 2012 Annual Report confirms that all electronic applications for eDischarge and eNursing Home charges[264] were completed within 2 days.[265] 75 % of mainstream cases for registration are completed within 10 working days and 80 % of online applications for folios and title plans are issued within 24 h.[266] In addition during 2010 there was a 32 % reduction in the backlog of casework in the Land Registry.[267] This was further reduced by 33 % in 2011[268] and 11 % in 2012.[269] Thus eApplication has proved to be a successful initiative and provides a framework for eRegistration.

eRegistration

The third strategic objective of the PRA is to contribute to the eConveyancing programme[270] and this will be done by the roll out of eRegistration services. The key principles of the eRegistration project are standardised forms, no lodgment of paper documents, registrations relating to registered land only, voluntary usage incentivised by differential fees and payment of registration fees by EFT.[271]

[261] Property Registration Authority 'Strategic Plan 2010–2012' (2010), p. 24.

[262] Interview with Greg McDermott ICT Manager Property Registration Authority 1 March 2012.

[263] Property Registration Authority 'Strategic Plan 2010–2012' (2010), p. 24. See also Property Registration Authority 'Annual Report 2010' (2011), p. 22.

[264] This was the second phase of eRegistration and allows the Health Services Executive to electronically register charges created under the Nursing Homes Support Scheme.

[265] Property Registration Authority 'Annual Report 2012' (2013), p. 14.

[266] Property Registration Authority 'Annual Report 2012' (2013), p. 14.

[267] Property Registration Authority 'Annual Report 2010' (2011), p. 15.

[268] Property Registration Authority 'Annual Report 2011' (2012), p. 15.

[269] Property Registration Authority 'Annual Report 2012' (2013), p. 14.

[270] Property Registration Authority 'Annual Report 2012' (2013), p. 12.

[271] O'Sullivan (2008). See also O'Sullivan (2007), p. 7.

The first element of eRegistration went live in March 2009.[272] This was eDischarges with a new system for electronic release of registered charges.[273] This project developed a secure system for releasing registered charges where no paper is lodged, issued or stored.[274] The electronic discharge is lodged by the lender and in order to facilitate this there is no fee.[275] The system is automated not automatic as the registrar continues to sign off on the cancellation of charges from the register. This system won the state body category at the Public Sector Times 2010 eGovernment Awards[276] and usage of the eDischarge system has exceeded the land registry's expectations.[277] Approximately 90 % of the lending market is signed up to use the system.

Some of the reasons for this may include the fact that the system is subsidised in order to incentivise take up.[278] There is no fee charged to the lender. The lender is acting directly in respect of its own charges so there is no agency problem. Also it could be said that lenders are used to the need for secure systems and thus there may have been less of a familiarisation issue. The project board also engaged in extensive consultation with the lenders to ensure that the system addressed their security concerns.

The registering authority also developed an online portal, eRegistration.ie, for the electronic registration of all transactions affecting the title register.[279] The second eRegistration service was added to this portal in January 2010. This allows the Health Services Executive to electronically register charges (eCharging Orders) created under the Nursing Homes Support Scheme. The signature of the chargee is not required and thus the power to create the charge rests solely with the Health Services Executive.

Based on the success[280] of eDischarges and eCharging Orders the PRA rolled out a further development in April 2013.[281] This allows a lawyer to generate the documentation for registration (transfers) and have them approved by the lawyer for the other party to the transaction. Thus registered users can collaborate in generating the documentation for registration. The final documents are based on data submitted to and retrieved from the system and the format of such documents

[272] See Law Society of Ireland (2009). See also the Land Registration Rules 2008 (SI 326/2008) now incorporated into the Land Registration Rules 2012 (SI 483/2012).

[273] See www.edischarges.ie/login.aspx.

[274] See Clancy (2008), p. 5.

[275] Land Registration (Fees Relating to Discharges Lodged by Electronic Means) Order 2009 (SI 52/2009).

[276] See www.irishegovernmentawards.ie/winners-2010.html.

[277] McHugh (2010).

[278] There is a mandate to incentivise electronic delivery through reduced fees. See Department of Public Expenditure and Reform, p. 10.

[279] www.eregistration.ie.

[280] Property Registration Authority 'Annual Report 2012' (2013), p. 12.

[281] See Law Society of Ireland (2013).

are in compliance with the relevant rules. This pre-population and automatic formatting of documentation reduces the risk of error and the possibility of the application for registration being rejected. Multiple data entry is avoided thus minimising the potential for errors. The system also facilitates electronic correspondence between the lawyers and the acquisition lender. Notices of lodgement and completion issue electronically and fees are paid electronically by variable direct debit.[282]

A dealing number can be made available at an earlier stage in the transaction and while this will confer no priority, it will facilitate collaboration based on a single identifier. There is also potential, in the future, for draft entries on the register to be displayed prior to finalisation of the application for registration so the applicant can be sure that the registration will accurately effect the agreed transaction. There is also the possibility for further notifications to be built into the system which may increase transparency and visibility for all parties.

The PRA have also provided a landdirect.ie service for members of the public that allows for payment of the appropriate fee. This provides wider access and transparency as citizens can directly access the title register online. Additional web services have been implemented which allows for direct interaction between the register and case management systems. Other electronic registration of title services will be developed through the eRegistration portal in the coming years. The plan is to include charges, transmissions and priority entries during 2014. Standard forms of charge have already been introduced as of 1 March 2012 thus facilitating the electronic registration of charges.[283] These are one page forms specifically designed to facilitate the introduction of eRegistration.[284]

The project board includes *inter alia* representatives from the Revenue Commissioners, Law Society, Irish Mortgage Council and the Companies Registration Office thus providing a broad base of engagement with consumers of land registry data. The objective is to extend incrementally the range of applications which can be registered without the presentation of paper documents.[285] To date paper documents are still required for all transactions save those falling under the eDischarge system and the Nursing Homes Support Scheme. It should be noted however that while a specific paper discharge may not be required in each transaction those lenders who sign up to the eDischarge system are required to execute formal one off documentation. This still needs to be printed, signed with a wet or manuscript signature and sign up to the service will only proceed based on this initial paper application to the registry.

McDonagh and White refer to the PRA electronic access service (www.landregistry.ie/eng/landdirect_ie/) as one of a number of very successful Irish

[282] See Deeney (2014), p. 370 for other features.

[283] Land Registration Rules 2011 (SI 559/2011) now incorporated into the Land Registration Rules 2012 (SI 483/2012).

[284] Deeney (2014), p. 413.

[285] O'Sullivan (2007), p. 6.

eGovernment initiatives.[286] This service along with other PRA eRegistration initiatives have won numerous awards.[287] Kostova points out that no award is in itself a guarantee of a successful operation but that take up of the system is impressive.[288] The PRA itself notes that the continued development of eRegistration services in consultation with its main stakeholders is fundamental to any future system of eConveyancing in Ireland.[289] It is to be hoped that Ireland's eConveyancing project will be one of its successes and the progress of eRegistration to date augurs well for the success of a wider eConveyancing project.

eConveyancing

eRegistration is seen by the registration authority:

> as a distinct subset of activities but also as a critical element within the wider eConveyancing process....[thus] all plans and activities arising from the eRegistration project are carefully designed to advance, complement and integrate with the wider national eConveyancing agenda.[290]

Thus while the PRA has not taken responsibility for the wider eConveyancing project it is working with other stakeholder groups to advance that agenda. This co-operation is vital so that eRegistration and eConveyancing do not conflict and also much of eConveyancing is based on legislative reform that impacts on title registration.

In tandem with these eRegistration developments some eConveyancing type initiatives have also been implemented. One such initiative is the introduction of a new streamlined procedure, called the QeD (Quick electronic Discharge), to provide a standardised approach for communications between lenders and solicitors.[291] The Irish Institution of Surveyors has established an Inter-Professional Task Force to look at property boundaries and how boundary information is reflected by state bodies and this has provided an opportunity for stakeholder groups to collaborate on reform proposals.[292]

While there have been no significant eConveyancing advances there has been much dialogue and debate about the path that Ireland should take and a clear vision is emerging of how eConveyancing would operate in Ireland. The proposals put

[286] McDonagh and White (2008), pp. 19–55. Note that in the United Nations Global E-Government Survey of 2012 Ireland was ranked 34th as against Canada's 11th place. See United Nations (2012).

[287] The Property Registration Authority 'Annual Report 2010' (2011), p. 8.

[288] Kostova (2010), pp. 17–18.

[289] Property Registration Authority 'Annual Report 2012' (2013), p. 12.

[290] O'Sullivan (2007), p. 5.

[291] This can be accessed at www.ibf.ie/qed.asp See also the Law Society of Ireland (2009).

[292] http://www.tfpb.ie/index.html accessed 23 June 2014. The final report of this Task Force was published in April 2014. See Brennan et al. (2014).

forward by the Law Reform Commission and Law Society have been universally supported by stakeholder groups and have formed a benchmark for reform.[293]

Thus to date eRecords and eApplication have been achieved in Ireland. Only a limited eRegistration service is in operation but new initiatives are anticipated. No specific eConveyancing advances have been launched though there is a mandate and platform for reform agreed by the main stakeholder groups.

The governments Construction Strategy 2020 acknowledges that the steps to eConveyancing will require the representatives of the legal profession, the banking sector and the relevant statutory agencies to work together closely building on work already completed on this issue under the aegis of the Law Society.[294] It identifies the Department of Justice and Equality as the lead responsible body for reviewing and reporting on the steps required to deliver a system of eConveyancing in Ireland, including the resource implications and timeframes for delivery.[295]

3.4.2 eConveyancing in Ontario

Background

In 1968 the Ontario provincial government asked the Law Reform Commission to study the land registration system and make recommendations.[296] This examination led to the publication of a report in 1971 that recommended sweeping reforms including the conversion of unregistered titles (Registry records) to registered titles (Land Titles), automation of records and electronic searching and registration. While the government accepted the recommendations it was not until the late 1980s that the process of reform began. Murray notes that the Ontario government decided "that the paper-based system of recording interests in land should be automated and services needed to be delivered electronically."[297]

This reform accelerated when:

> in the early 1990's the Ministry, in conjunction with a private sector consortium, established Teranet...The Ministry owns the land registration data and develops the business rules. Teranet owns and operates the electronic system.[298]

This partnership allowed the province to accelerate the computerisation of the land registration system[299] and thus deliver the first eRegistration system in the

[293] Law Society of Ireland (2008a) and The Law Reform Commission (2006).

[294] Government Publications, p. 58.

[295] Government Publications, pp. 58–59.

[296] Donahue et al. (2003), p. 5.

[297] Murray (2004), p. 1.

[298] Murray (2004), p. 1.

[299] Donahue et al. (2003), p. 6.

world.[300] To quote from a recent assessment of the Ontario system by New Zealand:

> [i]t can be argued that the public private partnership and subsequent contractual arrangement have been a success. It enabled the development of a fully functioning electronic land registration system by the late nineties. The land registration process is now virtually all electronic, all records have been converted and there is an effective electronic land registration system readily accessible to the property business and the citizen.[301]

Christensen refers to the Ontario system as an example of the reformist approach[302] where all dealings are required to be undertaken electronically, information is prescribed rather than the forms and dealings are no longer in writing.

Ontario is on the cutting edge internationally[303] in relation to eRegistration. It is widely acknowledged to be the first jurisdiction in the world to introduce full electronic document registration.[304] This includes the eRecords, eApplication and eRegistration elements of eConveyancing.

Ontario moved quickly from eRecords directly to eRegistration and thus there was no eApplication phase.

eRecords

The reform process started in the late 1980s with the automation of records i.e. the eRecords phase of eConveyancing. Paper records were converted into electronic information to be stored on databases so that all information relating to registered titles would become electronically accessible.[305]

During this automation process unregistered titles were converted to registered titles. The full automation of land registration records and the conversion process was completed on 31 March 2011.[306] Approximately 36,000 unregistered properties remain because it was determined that these titles could not be converted to registered parcels due to planning act issues, description issues, easement and water issues, conflicts of ownership and inability to establish owners or breaks in the chain of title.[307]

---

[300] Murray (2004), p. 21.

[301] ConsultingWhere Limited and ACIL Allen Consulting for LINZ (2013), Annex B, p. 18.

[302] Christensen (2004). She contrasts this with the system in British Columbia which operates a dual paper and electronic system with voluntary opt in.

[303] Moore and Globe (2003), Foreword.

[304] Murray (2004), p. 21.

[305] Donahue et al. (2003), p. 6.

[306] Alex Radley Legal and Technical Officer Service Ontario by email 7 June 2012.

[307] Alex Radley Legal and Technical Officer Service Ontario by email 7 June 2012.

eRegistration

The Ontario Ministry began by building POLARIS (the Province of Ontario Land Registration Information System)[308] with the objective of automating Ontario's land registration system. Following this automation the Ministry introduced electronic remote search facilities and then electronic registration of land title documents through software called Teraview. This eRegistration system was developed by Teranet[309] in conjunction with the Ministry. It was launched as a pilot project in 1999 and subsequently implemented gradually across the province on a county by county basis. The first electronic land registration took place on 25 January 1999 at London in the County of Middlesex and in "less than five years, the majority of land titles searches and land registrations. . .moved from an archaic paper-based records system to the most sophisticated fully electronic registration system in the world."[310]

The land registration system is the responsibility of the Ministry and Teranet under contract facilitates the delivery of this service through Teraview.[311] The system provides an automated land registration database and web based gateway for registration.[312] Users must be registered with Teranet in order to lodge dealings electronically. The system allows for the creation and lodgement of registration documents. Pertinent information is automatically populated from the POLARIS database into the draft documents which are then shared electronically between the lawyers. Once certified by the lawyer for each party with an electronic signature the documents are lodged for registration.[313]

The documents are created in an electronic format and are also transmitted and filed electronically. "The result is an all-electronic, paperless system, where documents are created, submitted and maintained in electronic format."[314]

Murray expresses the view that Ontario used:

> existing legislative provisions to offer a better guarantee of title to consumers and users of the land registration system. The automation of the paper records and the conversion of Registry records [unregistered titles] to Land Titles [registered titles] set the stage for the introduction of electronic registration.[315]

Thus title to land was moved from the deeds register to the title register prior to electronic processes being introduced.[316] However this did not apply universally

---

[308] Donahue et al. (2003), p. 6.

[309] Teranet Enterprises Inc. See http://www.teranet.ca/ Teranet also offers a range of property related services across Canada. One example is AVMs to lenders called Purview/Reavs.

[310] Moore and Globe (2003), p. 455.

[311] Alex Radley Legal and Technical Officer Service Ontario by email 7 June 2012.

[312] Christensen (2004).

[313] For the Law Society guidelines see The Law Society of Upper Canada (2002).

[314] Donahue et al. (2003), p. 7.

[315] Murray (2004), p. 8.

[316] This refers to the creation of LTCQ and LT Plus as noted in Chap. 2 under registrable interests.

with some land being automated in POLARIS but not being converted to registered title.[317]

Some commentators have taken issue with the benefits of reform. Moore and Globe are of the view that while the length of many searches has reduced POLARIS has not reduced the legal complexity of the title search.[318] Because POLARIS contains titles from both registers

> lawyers and title searchers are now confronted with more title search scenarios than ever before, each with different legal requirements and administrative procedures. From a risk management point of view, it is arguably more difficult today than in the past for lawyers to review the title search notes carefully.[319]

The LRRA and its Regulations and Orders set out the framework for the eRegistration initiative.[320] The LRRA Part 1 dealt with the modernisation of record keeping and forms. For example a common form of transfer, charge and discharge was introduced for both the unregistered and registered systems.[321] Part II introduced automation and part III introduced electronic registration. Together they form the basis for a complete system of eRegistration.

Thus the first phase of Ontario's eConveyancing initiative was the automation of land registration records (eRecords) and conversion of unregistered titles to registered titles. The second phase involved electronic remote search facilities and, beginning in 1999, electronic registration of registered titles, both delivered through the Teranet gateway software known as Teraview. This software provides access to POLARIS and is administered and controlled by Teranet. The eRegistration system is known as e-reg.

E-reg is described by Moore and Globe as:

> a mandatory, fully electronic or paperless registration system that will allow documents in electronic format with digital signature to be registered online from a remote location, such as a lawyer's office, instead of actual attendance for closing and registration at a Registry office.[322]

In order to introduce e-reg some legislative changes were required. These included the removal of the requirement that a document be in writing and signed,[323] authority for direct electronic transmission of documents to the registered titles database,[324] the fact that the electronic document will prevail over a

---

[317] There are approximately 36,000 unregistered titles.

[318] Moore and Globe (2003), p. 16.

[319] Moore and Globe (2003), p. 16.

[320] This Act became applicable to all land in Ontario on 1 April 1985 by O. Reg. 35/85.

[321] Donahue et al. (2003), p. 4.

[322] Moore and Globe (2003), p. 13.

[323] Section 21 LRRA provides that an electronic document that deals with an interest in land is not required to be in writing or to be signed by the parties thereto and has the same effect for all purposes as a document that is in writing and is signed by the parties.

[324] Section 2 Electronic Registration Act (Ministry of Consumer and Business Services Statutes) 1991 S.O. 1991 c. 44.

written document[325] and the introduction of law statements[326] which the registrar may rely on thus replacing the need for evidence to be provided by the lawyer.[327] It is the information required in a document that is prescribed and not the form.[328]

Law statements are based on the principle of "tell me, don't show me". This means that lawyers are authorised to confirm certain facts without the need to provide supporting evidence.[329] Only lawyers can register transfers or charges which include law statements and these account for the vast majority of such registrations.[330] This principle allows certain paper documents to be removed from the process as the lawyer can confirm that perhaps a certain enquiry was made but the search result does not have to be submitted in hard copy.[331] The purpose of these statements is to reduce the amount of paper filed in the registered title system.[332] However while this paper may have been removed from the application to the registrar, it has not been removed from the process as all compliance with law statements must be supported by evidence retained in the file.[333] This removes paper from the registry but may add to the lawyers costs.

"A Law Statement may only be made by a person who is entitled to practice law in Ontario as a solicitor."[334] The system will only allow users with the proper authority and an active Law Society of Upper Canada (LSUC) number to sign a document for completeness when these statements are included. The system receives a daily file from the LSUC database and verifies the lawyer is in good standing. If the user is not, the system switches the user type to "non-lawyer" and they are not able to sign a document containing law compliance statements, including transfers. Authority can only be gained by purchasing a license from Teranet and all users are authenticated. Applicants for a license must provide one piece of photographic identification or two pieces of non-photographic identification. Since 2008 users apply to Teranet for an account and if they meet the requirements Teranet will provide search access only. If the ability to register is

325 Section 22 LRRA.

326 Section 24 LRRA.

327 Murray (2004), pp. 9–10.

328 Murray (2004), p. 10.

329 For examples of the type of statements that may be made see Donahue et al. (2003), p. 336.

330 These law statements could be seen as similar to the statement of title in Form 3 that a lawyer may give in Ireland upon first registration of a title.

331 Section 24 of the LRRA is the statutory basis for law statements. Under section 24(2) evidence in an electronic format made in accordance with the section is deemed to comply with any requirement under a statute to provide written evidence in the form of an affidavit, declaration, statement or other written evidence despite the fact that the evidence is not in writing or signed by the parties required to provide the evidence.

332 Moore and Globe (2003), p. 424.

333 Moore and Globe (2003), p. 424. See also http://rc.lsuc.on.ca/jsp/eReg/practiceIssues.jsp and The Law Society of Upper Canada (2002).

334 Murray (2004), p. 14. See also The Law Society of Upper Canada (2002).

required, users must additionally apply to the Ministry providing information about their identity, financial status and good character.[335]

Non lawyers may lodge documents but only those that do not require compliance with a law statement. They may also do searches in the system however effectively lawyers have a monopoly on conveyancing.

In practical terms authorised users of the system create and register documents from their PC using Teraview.[336] The system allows users to select the appropriate document type from a list and through a series of prompts to create the document, including all necessary statements. Some information, such as property description and current owner, are pre-populated in the document from the title database. This reduces the risk of errors in this information. When a document is sent for registration the system automatically checks the information against the existing automated record. Fields and statements are programmed into the system for each document type and thus ensure that the requirements for electronic registration are met. The system will check that all mandatory fields have been completed and that inconsistent information is not provided.

There is however always the danger that unauthorised users gain access to the system. The system will have no idea who is at the keyboard and will accept anyone logged on with the required passwords. In Ontario each user is given a personalised profile, that can be stored on a diskette or USB device, that must be used to gain access to the system. This requires the user to insert their password when logging in. This identifies the user to the system and records their identity for each registration and each law statement. Thus Teranet can trace each registration and statement to an individual.[337]

The registry report no real changes in the reporting of errors or applications to the compensation fund noting that the pre-population of data into registration documents has improved the quality of the data.[338]

Registry staff continue to review the documentation and complete the registration through the normal certification process. This "two-step registration process existed in the legislation prior to the introduction of electronic registration"[339] and has been maintained in the e-reg system. Thus the electronic registration is automated but not automatic. Registration of an instrument is only complete when the entry is certified by the registrar.[340] The first step is the making of the application by the user of the system and the second step is the authorisation of that application by

[335] See http://www.ontario.ca/en/information_bundle/land_registration/content/ONT06_018594.html.

[336] See Donahue et al. (2003), pp. 335–336.

[337] A lawyer is prohibited from allowing any other person to use his or his diskette or password. The lawyer is also responsible for ensuring that any non-lawyers in their office who have access do not allow unauthorised persons access to the system via their diskettes. See rule 5.01 of the Law Society of Upper Canada (2013).

[338] Alex Radley Legal and Technical Officer Service Ontario by email 7 June 2012.

[339] Murray (2004), p. 15.

[340] See Donahue et al. (2003), p. 35.

the registry staff before any change is made to the register. There is no paper lodged.

The system allows documents to be electronically shared by their creator with other users for review, amendment or approval and all communications are encrypted using Entrust technology.[341] All documents are digitally signed but any subsequent modification invalidates the signature and the document must then be signed again before registration.

Registration documents are prepared simply by inputting information into the system and once each document is complete it can be digitally signed by the lawyer. The system does not rely on the signatures of the parties to the transaction and instead restricts use to authorised users so as to maintain the integrity of the system. These users must get authority from their clients before they proceed with registration. This authority to the lawyer to do the electronic registration is given by way of a direction[342] which is a paper document that is physically signed with a wet signature by the client.

The system was introduced in a phased manner both in terms of functionality and geographical spread. Initially e-reg was introduced on an optional basis and after a transitional period it became compulsory. It ensures that all lawyers can run their real estate practices electronically. Murray takes the view that electronic registration has:

> provided the users of the system with a more efficient method of dealing with interests in land. It has provided the Ministry with opportunities to streamline its operations. It has increased security of the records and improved the data integrity.[343]

As 99 % of all applications for registration are now submitted electronically there has been a reduction in manual registry staff input.[344] Table 3.3 demonstrates the growth in electronic applications and the corresponding drop in paper.[345]

Table 3.4 represents the same information in approximate percentages.

The number of system users[346] demonstrates the same growth pattern as set out in Table 3.5.[347]

On 18 June 2014 8,023 of these users were active lawyers in the system.[348]

As of November 2010 electronic registration has been mandatory in all 54 land registry offices throughout Ontario.[349] There is no doubt but that Ontario has

---

[341] Murray (2004), p. 15.

[342] Donahue et al. (2003), p. 336.

[343] Murray (2004), p. 21.

[344] Alex Radley Legal and Technical Officer Service Ontario by email 7 June 2012.

[345] Alex Radley Legal and Technical Officer Service Ontario by email 27 June 2014 and Ken Crawford Sr. Legal and Technical Analyst Service Ontario by email 27 June 2014.

[346] As of January each year.

[347] Vicki McArthur Teranet by email 18 June 2014.

[348] Vicki McArthur Teranet by email 18 June 2014.

[349] Alex Radley Legal and Technical Officer Service Ontario by email 7 June 2012. There are a number of limited exceptions where a paper document may be accepted. For example where the number of properties exceeds the system limits.

Table 3.3 Growth of electronic applications for registration Ontario

Year end	2000	2003	2004	2007	2008	2011	2013
Electronic	41,797	1,316,490	1,641,693	1,949,943	1,905,669	1,843,437	1,670,357
Paper	1,413,985	643,138	495,139	203,170	115,264	21,377	24,263

Table 3.4 Growth in percentages Ontario

Year end	2000	2003	2004	2007	2008	2011	2013
Electronic (%)	2	67	76	90	94	99	99
Paper (%)	97	32	23	9	5	1	1

Table 3.5 Growth in users Ontario

Year	2000	2004	2008	2012	2013
Number of users	5,374	17,082	27,595	35,781	37,638

implemented a full eRegistration system however there is some debate as to whether this system could be labeled eConveyancing.

eConveyancing

eConveyancing requires a number of elements as follows[350]:

(a) the application of information technology
(b) transmission of digital data
(c) move from paper to electronic system
(d) online portal or hub
(e) electronic communication network
(f) system to system exchange of data
(g) information only to be typed in once
(h) integration of technology into most or all of the conveyancing process from pre sale to post completion of the transaction

The elements from (a)–(g) are all features of the Ontario system so the only question remains in relation to (h). Does the Ontario system electronify not just the registration aspects of conveyancing but also the entire end to end process from pre-sale to post completion? Though as noted earlier in the chapter some elements are excluded such as the physical inspection and verification of the client's identity.

A major part of any conveyancing process is the searches that have to be done. These include searches of the title register, deeds register, judgments, known in Ontario as executions, and other registers to establish encumbrances on the title. In Ontario most of this searching is done through the Teraview system. There is a remote-access, online program for searching POLARIS and for searching writs of execution. The system offers electronic data interchange, EFT for search and registration costs and land transfer tax payments which is equivalent to the Irish stamp duty.

[350] See Sneddon (2007), pp. 1–3, Law Society of Ireland (2008a) and The Law Reform Commission (2006), p. 10 and Exhibits B and C.

Moore and Globe have set out the services available.[351] These are:

1. automated title searching
2. writ searching
3. subsearching (this is a facility to update earlier search results)
4. creation of both draft and registerable documents
5. automatic electronic calculation and payment of land transfer taxes
6. communication between lawyers throughout the document production and registration process
7. review, amendment and approval of draft documents by lawyers
8. electronic submission and registration of documents
9. transfer of funds for registration and land transfer tax fees
10. secure private communication network for authorised users
11. docket summary, Acknowledgement and Direction, document preparation, registration and land transfer tax, and deposit account and activity reports, and
12. confidentiality, security and an electronic audit trail traceable to the user.

Item 11 appears at first glance to be a repetition of the earlier services but it also includes access to standard documentation and also the printing of reports for the client file.

This is an impressive list but in considering whether the system fulfils the requirements for eConveyancing the following should be noted.

Firstly, there are a considerable number of searches that must be done outside the system. Examples include bankruptcy, zoning, realty taxes and services.[352]

Secondly, the system does not facilitate electronic communication between all the stakeholders in the conveyancing process. The primary authorised users are lawyers and staff in the registering authority.

Thirdly, the purchase monies are not included as part of the electronic exchange.

Finally, and most importantly, the system does not include the contract stage. Part of the reason for this is likely due to the fact that it is often the real estate broker who gets this Agreement of Purchase and Sale signed by the parties. In other jurisdictions this stage in the process is done by the lawyer. Donahue and his colleagues[353] note that these agreements are almost always prepared by real estate agents.

> Apparently, because it is printed, most people sign before consulting a lawyer and, in many cases, without even reading it. The purchase or sale of a house is the biggest transaction most people ever enter into, yet an amazing number blithely sign the agreement without ever calling on their lawyer for advice.[354]

Thus Ontario has not made the offer to purchase electronic. This forms the binding contract between the transferor and transferee. It has however been reduced

[351] Moore and Globe (2003), p. 413.

[352] See Moore and Globe (2003), pp. 474–478.

[353] Donahue et al. (2003), p. 207.

[354] Donahue et al. (2003), p. 206.

to a standard four pages. This is in line with other advances whereby the standard transfer has been reduced to three pages and the standard charge to two pages.

The absence of the binding contract stage and electronic fund transfer of the purchase monies means that the Ontario system is closer to eRegistration than eConveyancing.

However, this is subject to legislative change. Currently there is a prohibition on electronic contracts for interests in land contained in the Electronic Commerce Act 2000.[355] This Act gives legal recognition to electronic documents but in section 31 (1) excludes documents, including agreements of purchase and sale, that create or transfer interests in land and require registration to be effective against third parties. There appears to be a contradiction between this and section 21 of the LRRA which provides that an electronic document that creates, transfers or otherwise disposes of an estate or interest in land is not required to be in writing or to be signed by the parties and has the same effect for all purposes as a document that is in writing and is signed by the parties. The Electronic Commerce Amendment Act 2013[356] proposes to amend this provision to remove the exemption and permit digital signature on such agreements. If passed this has the potential to pave the way for Ontario to move into eConveyancing.

Conclusion

At its most advanced eConveyancing is the integration of information technology into the entire conveyancing process including the contract stage, transfer and registration. Thus each jurisdiction can be placed on a scale of movement towards eConveyancing based on the extent to which it facilitates system to system exchange of data without the necessity for paper documentation. This scale ranges, at one end, from the basic system that can facilitate electronic applications for registration followed by the paper (eApplication) to the more complex systems that make electronic parts or all of the registration process (eRegistration) and finally those that make electronic the entire conveyancing process (eConveyancing).

There is a broad range of different models and systems[357] however each jurisdiction has generally followed the same pattern of development; eRecords, eApplication, then eRegistration and finally eConveyancing. Phases of eRegistration have also tended to follow similar lines with the discharge of mortgages introduced first, followed by the creation of charges and then transfers and other forms of registration.

(continued)

[355] Section 31 Electronic Commerce Act 2000 S.O. 2000, CHAPTER 17.

[356] Bill 28 of 2013. See http://www.ontla.on.ca/web/bills/bills_detail.do?locale=en&BillID=2745&detailPage=bills_detail_the_bill.

[357] Harpum (2004), p. 5.

It can be difficult to grasp to what degree systems have evolved along this continuum. In particular it can be difficult to determine to what degree systems are electronic systems of title registration as opposed to merely being a system of electronic communication of dealings to the registry. For example the system may only provide for scanned paper documents to be transmitted. This was the view expressed by Harpum in relation to the Ontario system as the rationale for England seeking to develop its own system of eConveyancing from first principles.[358]

While Ontario was the first jurisdiction to introduce full electronic document registration[359] recently developments in other jurisdictions challenge the perception that it is by far the most developed eConveyancing system in the world. Even if it was accepted that Ontario has eConveyancing, rather than just eRegistration, it is clear that some other jurisdictions are rapidly catching up. In particular Australia's PEXA system is rapidly gaining momentum.[360]

Also as of November 2014 Scotland will have the potential to move to eConveyancing with the implementation of the Land Registration etc. (Scotland) Act 2012[361] which will enable electronic contracts (called e-missives).[362] Part 10 of the Act amends the Requirements of Writing (Scotland) Act 1995[363] and e-enables all documents referred to in section 1 (2)(a) of that Act. The 1995 Act required a written document for the constitution of a contract or unilateral obligation for the creation, transfer, variation or extinction of an interest in land.

This will enable fully electronic conveyancing transactions. Rennie and Brymer note however that the full effects of the change will not be harnessed until a secure electronic document exchange facility is available and this is "a natural progression for conveyancing and the sale/purchase of heritable property generally."[364] The full effects of the change are also hindered in other respects. Scotland does not have standard formats of common conveyancing documents and does not have a single standard missive for all transactions. Despite these limitations Scotland may become the first jurisdiction to venture from eRegistration into eConveyancing.

(continued)

358 Harpum (2004), p. 3.

359 Murray (2004), p. 21.

360 See Sect. 3.3.

361 2012 asp 5. See http://www.legislation.gov.uk/asp/2012/5/contents.

362 Rennie and Brymer (2014).

363 1995 c. 7.

364 Rennie and Brymer (2014).

While England and Wales has given digital signatures the same legal standing as those written with a pen in the Electronic Communications Act 2000,[365] thus paving the way for eConveyancing, the registering authority has taken the decision to only allow electronic applications based on scanned images of original paper documents. As noted earlier the wider eConveyancing project has now stalled and it is not proposed to extend the Electronic Document Registration Service (eDRS) to etransfers and echarges.

The main focus of eConveyancing initiatives to date have been on eRecords, eApplication and eRegistration. There has been little attention paid to the pre completion and non registration aspects of conveyancing transactions and the contract stage has been entirely neglected.[366] Despite this many jurisdictions freely claim to be on the march towards eConveyancing. Connolly is of the view that "[w]hile several international countries claim the success of their implementation of e-conveyancing sys-tem (sic), the correct term of reference should be, in default of a pre-contract process,. . .an "E-Registration" system."[367]

There is no doubting that Ontario was the first jurisdiction to introduce full electronic document registration[368] however commentators often cite it as the most developed eConveyancing system in the world. This may be due to a misunderstanding of the terminology and a lack of research that sets out clear boundaries between eRegistration and eConveyancing.

When examined in detail it is clear that the Ontario e-reg system is one of eRegistration and is missing some vital elements that would move it into the realm of eConveyancing. This is also true of advances in other jurisdictions. "For the time being, e-conveyancing solutions in most jurisdictions are closer to e-registration than to end-to-end e-conveyancing."[369] Though the Ontario system seems to be a major success and it is the widely considered to be the most advanced.[370] Forthcoming legislative reform may pave the way for it to move further into the electronic realm and along the spectrum towards eConveyancing.

Ireland appears to have embarked on the road to eConveyancing success-fully[371] with the modernisation of the law,[372] extension of compulsory

(continued)

[365] 2000 CHAPTER 7.

[366] See Christensen (2004); and Low (2005), pp. 155–178. Note however that changes have been implemented since 2004/2005.

[367] Connolly (2007), p. 53 (emphasis removed from quote).

[368] Murray (2004), p. 21.

[369] Kostova (2010), p. 53.

[370] Kostova (2010), p. 54. See also Butt (2006), p. 1.

[371] Kostova (2010), p. 56.

[372] The 2006 Act and the 2009 Act.

registration[373] and digitisation of registry information however it has some way to go before it moves from eApplication fully into eRegistration. "The successful operation of eDischarge, the first instalment of eRegistration, and the soaring numbers of users availing of the PRA's online services should be a source of encouragement for all stakeholders".[374]

However in implementing eConveyancing we must not lose sight of the purpose of conveyancing and that technology can be adapted to meet the needs of different types of policies. Computers will not decide how the land market should operate. It is the policy makers who design the system and who have to balance risks and rewards, costs and efficiency that will dictate how eConveyancing is to be implemented.

> Conveyancing practice is no longer severable from technology. As with any new technology, it is important to remember that technology is a tool, and that the primary focus and value of the real estate transactions must remain the investigation of all aspects of title and the acquisition and protection of property rights.[375]

The next chapter explores the property rights currently protected by registration and in particular focuses on what rights and interests have been deemed worthy of protection by policy makers in Ontario and Ireland. It also looks at where changes have occurred as a result of the move towards technology and anticipates further developments in implementing eConveyancing.

References

Abrahamson, E. (1991). Managerial fads and fashions: The diffusion and rejection of innovations. *The Academy of Management Review, 16*(3).

Ahern, B. (2005). *Speech on the occasion of the 30th Anniversary of the Law Reform Commission*. Dublin: Law Reform Commission. http://www.lawreform.ie/_fileupload/Speeches/30th%20Anniversary%20Taoiseach%20speech%20final%2023%20June%202005.pdf. Accessed 14 May 2014.

Arruñada, B. (2010). Leaky title syndrome? *New Zealand Law Journal*.

BC OnLine. Land Title and Survey Authority (LTSA) Electronic Services. https://www.bconline.gov.bc.ca/land_titles.html. Accessed 18 June 2014.

BC OnLine. Land title registration process. http://www.ltsa.ca/cms/land-title-registration-process. Accessed 18 June 2014.

[373] Since 1 June 2011 all areas are subject to compulsory first registration in the case of freehold land upon conveyance on sale and in the case of a leasehold interest on the grant or assignment on sale of such an interest. See sections 23 and 24 of 1964 Act. 'On sale' means for money or money's worth and accordingly would not apply to a voluntary transfer of title by way of gift or a title transferred on death.

[374] Kostova (2010), p. 56.

[375] Moore and Globe (2003), Preface.

BC OnLine. Title security in BC. http://www.ltsa.ca/cms/title-security-in-bc. Accessed 18 June 2014.

Brande-Lavridsen, H. (2002). *The spatial information market in Denmark*. In GSDI 6 Conference – From Global to Local Budapest, Hungary, 16–19 September 2002. http://www.gsdidocs.org/gsdiconf/GSDI-6/Stream2/Wednesday_11hr/Hanne_Brande_Lavridsen/Paper-Hanne%20Brande-Lavridsen.pdf. Accessed 14 May 2014.

Brennan, G., & Casey, N. (Eds.). (2014). *Conveyancing* (7th ed.). Oxford: Oxford University Press.

Brennan, G., de Buitléir, M., & Prendergast, W. P. (Eds). (2014). *Towards the registration of defined property boundaries in Ireland*. Inter-Professional Task Force on Property Boundaries.

Brown, D. (2003). Electronic conveyancing – Beware and prepare. *New Law Journal, 153*.

Browning, B. E-conveyancing – it will crash and burn. http://www.textor.com/e-conveyancing-updated.html. Accessed 9 Mar 2012.

Butt, P. (2006). *Electronic conveyancing: A practical guide*. London: Thomson Sweet & Maxwell.

Castells, M. (2000). Toward a sociology of the network society. *Contemporary Sociology, 29*(5).

Christensen, S. (2004). Electronic land dealings in Canada, New Zealand and the United Kingdom: Lessons for Australia. *Murdoch University Electronic Journal of Law, 11*(4). http://www.murdoch.edu.au/elaw/issues/v11n4/christensen114_text.html. Accessed 14 May 2014.

Christensen, S., Duncan, W., & Low, R. (2003). The requirements of writing for electronic land contracts – The Queensland experience compared with other jurisdictions. *Murdoch University Electronic Journal of Law, 10*(3). http://www.murdoch.edu.au/elaw/issues/v10n3/christensen103_text.html. Accessed 14 May 2014.

Clanchy, M. T. (1993). *From memory to written record, England 1066–1307* (2nd ed.). Oxford: Blackwell.

Clancy, D. (2007). *Benchmarking land registration*. In Registering the World Conference, Dublin, 26–28 September 2007. http://www.prai.ie/uploadedfiles/conference20071/papers/s5p4.pdf. Accessed 14 May 2014.

Clancy, D. (2008). *From caveat emptor towards full disclosure – Developments in Ireland*. In United Nations Economic Commission for Europe's Working Party on Land Administration Workshop on the Influence of Land Administration on People and Business. http://wpla.uredjenazemlja.hr/prezentacije/Presentation%20Caveat%20Emptor%20to%20Vendor%20Disclosure%208-9-08.pdf. Accessed 14 May 2014.

Comptroller and Auditor General *Accounts of the Public Services 2008* Annual Report. (2009, September). http://www.audgen.gov.ie/documents/annualreports/2008/Appropriation_Account_2008Rev.pdf. Accessed 13 June 2014.

Comptroller and Auditor General *Development of Human Resource Management System for the Health Service* (*PPARS*) Report on Value for Money Examination. (2005, December). http://www.audgen.gov.ie/documents/vfmreports/VFM_51_PPARS_Report.pdf. Accessed 13 June 2014.

Comptroller and Auditor General *eGovernment* Special Report. (2007, October). http://www.audgen.gov.ie/documents/vfmreports/58_eGovernment.pdf. Accessed 13 June 2014.

Comptroller and Auditor General *Press Release*: *Report on eGovernment*. (2007, October). http://www.audgen.gov.ie/viewdoc.asp?DocID=1081. Accessed 13 June 2014.

ComReg. *Statistical information on the Irish electronic communications market*. http://www.comstat.ie/data/data.472.1267.data.html. Accessed 13 June 2014.

Connolly, F. (2007). *E-Conveyancing: Who will benefit?* (B.Sc. Hons Dissertation).

ConsultingWhere Limited and ACIL Allen Consulting for LINZ. (2013). *Better property services*. Final Report. http://www.linz.govt.nz/about-linz/news-publications-and-consultations/consultation-projects-and-reviews/better-property-services. Accessed 23 June 2014.

Cooke, E., & O'Connor, P. (2004). Purchaser liability to third parties in the English land registration system: A comparative perspective. *The Law Quarterly Review, 120*.

Cross, M. (2009, February 19). Land registry climbdown is welcome sign of change. *The Guardian.* http://www.guardian.co.uk/technology/2009/feb/19/land-registry-data. Accessed 13 June 2014

Cross, M. (2014, January 27). Land registry is not for meddling. *Law Society Gazette.* http://www.lawgazette.co.uk/5039590.article. Accessed 19 June 2014.

Dale, P., Mahoney, R., & McLaren, R. (2006). Land markets and the modern economy. *Royal Institution of Chartered Surveyors.* http://www.knowedge.co.uk/Papers/Land_markets.pdf. Accessed 23 June 2014

Davies, P. L. (2008). *Gower and Davies principles of modern company law* (8th ed.). London: Thomson Sweet and Maxwell.

Deeney, J. (2014). *Registration of Deeds and Title in Ireland.* Great Britain: Bloomsbury.

Department for Business, Innovation and Skills. (2014, January). *Introduction of a land registry service delivery company.* https://www.gov.uk/government/consultations/land-registry-new-service-delivery-company. Accessed 19 June 2014.

Department for Communities and Local Government. *HIPs are history: Pickles suspends Home Information Packs with immediate effect* Press release 20 May 2010. http://www.communities.gov.uk/news/newsroom/1591783. Accessed 13 June 2014.

Department of Public Expenditure and Reform. Supporting Public Service Reform eGovernment 2012–2015. http://egovstrategy.gov.ie/. Accessed 19 June 2014.

Donahue, D. J., Quinn, P. D., & Grandilli, D. C. (2003). *Real estate practice in Ontario* (6th ed.). Canada: LexisNexis Butterworths.

Elliot, J. (2014, June 16). Irish lessons. *The Law Society Gazette, 19.* http://www.lawgazette.co.uk/law/practice-points/irish-lessons-on-pii/5041660.article. Accessed 1 July 2014.

European Commission. (2010). 'Europe's Digital Competitiveness Report' Vol II (2010) Brussels SEC (2010) 627. http://ec.europa.eu/digital-agenda/en/news/digital-agenda-investment-digital-economy-holds-key-europes-future-prosperity-says-commission. Accessed 19 June 2014.

European Commission. (2014). Assessment of the 2014 national reform programme and stability programme for Ireland. Brussels SWD (2014) 408 final. http://ec.europa.eu/europe2020/pdf/csr2014/swd2014_ireland_en.pdf. Accessed 19 June 2014.

Forfás. (2008, September). *eGovernment: International best practices.* http://www.forfas.ie/media/forfas080916_eGovernment.pdf. Accessed 13 June 2014.

Furlong, J. (2008, July). Going native. *Law Society Gazette, 102*(6).

Gahan, E. (2008). Taking full advantage of the possibilities of eGovernment. *Public Affairs Ireland, 51.*

Government Publications. Construction strategy 2020. http://www.merrionstreet.ie/wp-content/uploads/2014/05/Construction-Strategy-14-May-20141.pdf. Accessed 19 June 2014.

Gray, K., & Gray, S. F. (2009). *Elements of land law* (5th ed.). Great Britain: Oxford University Press.

Greenwood, J., & Jones, T. (2003). Automation of the register: Issues impacting on the integrity of title. In D. Grinlinton (Ed.), *Torrens in the twenty-first century.* Wellington: LexisNexis.

Griggs, L. (2001). Torrens title in a digital world. *Murdoch University Electronic Journal of Law, 8*(3). http://www.murdoch.edu.au/elaw/issues/v8n3/griggs83_text.html. Accessed 13 June 2014.

Griggs, L., & Low, R. (2011). Identity fraud and land registration systems: An Australian perspective. *The Conveyancer and Property Lawyer, 4.* http://eprints.qut.edu.au/46059/1/45749.pdf. Accessed 24 June 2014.

Grinlinton, D. (2003). The registrar's powers of correction. In D. Grinlinton (Ed.), *Torrens in the twenty-first century.* Wellington: LexisNexis.

Harpum, C. (2000). *Property in an electronic age* (Modern studies in property law, Vol. 1). Oxford: Hart.

Harpum, C. (2004). *English experience: Title by registration – Preparation for e-conveyancing.* In Law Reform Commission Annual Conference. http://www.lawreform.ie/Annual%20Conference%202004.PDF. Accessed 18 Feb 2009.

Hess, C., & Vaskovich, M. (2007). Ontology engineering for comparing property transactions. In J. Zevenbergen et al. (Eds.), *Real property transactions: Procedures, transaction costs and models*. Amsterdam: IOS.

HM Land Registry Press Release. (2011, June 20). *Land registry maintains focus on transformation programme despite a challenging year*. http://www.landregistry.gov.uk/media/all-releases/press-releases/2011/annual-report-201011. Accessed 19 June 2014.

HM Land Registry. *Report on responses to e-conveyancing secondary legislation part 3*. http://www.landregistry.gov.uk/__data/assets/pdf_file/0006/3102/econveyancing_cons.pdf. Accessed 19 June 2014.

Howell, J. (2006). Land law in an E-conveyancing world. *The Conveyancer and Property Lawyer*.

Irish Government. (2002, March). *New connections*. http://www.taoiseach.gov.ie/upload/publications/1153.pdf. Accessed 13 June 2014.

Jamieson, D. (2006). *Implications of eConveyancing for the Irish conveyancer*. In First Law Land Law and Conveyancing Law Reform Conference, Dublin.

Keating, S. (2012). *Digital signatures and electronic conveyancing* (LL.M. thesis). National University of Ireland, Galway.

Kelly, M. (2010). *Back to the future? A view on a possible future model for mortgage security perfection*. In Irish Banking Federation and The Institute of Bankers in Ireland Property Conveyancing Seminar, Dublin, 11 March 2010.

Killilea, M. (2010, April 17). *eRegistration in Ireland – An assessment of the transferability of the Queensland model* (Dissertation). Dublin Institute of Public Administration.

Kostova, T. (2010). *Moving towards eConveyancing in Ireland: An analysis* (LL.M. thesis). University College Cork.

Law Commission and HM Land Registry. (2001). Land registration for the twenty-first century: A conveyancing revolution (Report) (2001) EWLC 271. http://www.bailii.org/ew/other/EWLC/2001/271.html. Accessed 18 June 2014.

Law PRO Magazine Supplement Fall. (2011). Professional indemnity insurance around the world. http://www.practicepro.ca/lawpromag/default.asp. Accessed 13 June 2014.

Law Society of Ireland. (2008a). *eConveyancing: Back to basic principles. Vision of an Electronic System of Conveyancing ('eVision')*.

Law Society of Ireland. (2008b). Annual Report and Accounts 2007/2008. Law Society of Ireland. http://www.lawsociety.ie/Global/About%20Us/Annual%20Reports/AR0708.pdf. Accessed 29 June 2014.

Law Society of Ireland. (2009). New conveyancing initiatives – eDischarge and QED Form. *Law Society Gazette, 103*(2).

Law Society of Ireland. (2013, March). PRA – eRegistration Phase 2 Roll-Out. Legal eZine for Members Issue 46.

Law Society of Upper Canada. (2013). Rules of professional conduct (current to 24 January 2013). http://www.lsuc.on.ca/WorkArea/DownloadAsset.aspx?id=2147489377. Accessed 23 June 2014.

Levi-Faur, D. (2005). The global diffusion of regulatory capitalism. *Annals of the American Academy of Political and Social Science, 598*.

Libbis, S. (2007). *E-conveyancing sans frontieres; The development of an electronic conveyancing system for Australia*. In Registering the World Conference, Dublin, 26–28 September 2007. http://www.prai.ie/uploadedfiles/conference20071/papers/s3p1.pdf. Accessed 14 May 2014.

Locke, M. (2007). *Challenges facing land registries into the 21st century – An Australian perspective*. In Registering the World Conference, Dublin, 26–28 September 2007. http://www.prai.ie/uploadedfiles/conference20071/papers/s5p2.pdf. Accessed 14 May 2014.

Low, R. (2005). Maintaining the integrity of the Torrens system in a digital environment: A comparative overview of the safeguards used within the electronic land systems in Canada, New Zealand, United Kingdom and Singapore. *Australian Property Law Journal, 11*(2).

McDermott, G. (2006). *Background to the land registry use of technology to improve customer service*. In First Law Land Law and Conveyancing Law Reform Conference, Dublin.

McDonagh, M., & White, F. (2008). eGovernment in Ireland: An evaluation of the legal and policy framework. *Administration, 56*(1).

McDowell, M. (2006). *Opening address*. In First Law Land Law and Conveyancing Law Reform Conference, Dublin. http://www.justice.ie/en/JELR/Pages/Speech_on_land_law_and_conveyancing. Accessed 3 Sept 2010.

McHugh, P. (2010, April 30). eRegistration; The story so far and next steps. *Presentation to Law Society*.

Merritt, C. (2009, June 19). E-conveyancing plan thrown a $2m lifeline. *The Australian*.

Miceli, T. J., & Sirmans, C. F. (1995). The economics of land transfer and title insurance. *Journal of Real Estate Finance and Economics, 10*(1).

Miceli, T. J., Munneke, H. J., Sirmans, C. F., & Turnbull, G. K. (2002). Title systems and land values. *Journal of Law and Economics, 45*.

Micheler, E. (2002). Modernising securities settlement in the U.K. *The Company Lawyer, 23*(1).

Moore, M. E., & Globe, J. M. (2003). *Title searching and conveyancing in Ontario* (5th ed.). Canada: LexisNexis.

Muir, R. (2003). Electronic registration: The legislative scheme and implications for the Torrens system in New Zealand. In D. Grinlinton (Ed.), *Torrens in the twenty-first century*. Wellington: LexisNexis.

Muir, R. (2007). *E-conveyancing in New Zealand: Progress to date and future developments*. In Registering the World Conference, Dublin, 26–28 September 2007. http://www.landregistry.ie/eng/Dublin_Conference_2007/Conference_Papers/. Accessed 9 Sept 2010.

Murray, K. (2004). *Electronic registration and other modernization initiatives in Ontario's land registration system*. In Law Reform Commission Annual Conference. http://www.lawreform.ie/Annual%20Conference%202004.PDF. Accessed 18 Feb 2009.

Murray, K. (2007). *Legislative amendments relating to real estate fraud and the Ministry of Government Services Real Estate Fraud Action Plan*. In Registering the World Conference, Dublin, 26–28 September 2007. http://www.landregistry.ie/eng/Dublin_Conference_2007/Conference_Papers/. Accessed 9 Sept 2010.

National Electronic Conveyancing Office. (2007, February 9). *Risk assessment of the national electronic conveyancing system*. http://www.necs.gov.au/ArticleDocuments/FinalReportOfClaytonUtz_RiskAssessment.pdf. Accessed 23 June 2014.

O'Connor, P. (2009). Immediate indefeasibility for mortgagees: A moral hazard? *Bond Law Review, 21*(2).

O'Sullivan, J. (2007). *eRegistration and eConveyancing in Ireland – The story so far....* In Registering the World Conference, Dublin, 26–28 September 2007. http://www.prai.ie/uploadedfiles/conference20071/papers/s3p6.pdf. Accessed 14 May 2014.

O'Sullivan, J. (2008, November 7). *The introduction of e-Discharges*. In Virtual reality – Towards the Electronic Conveyance Law Society of Ireland Technology Committee Conference, Dublin.

OECD. (2008). Ireland towards an integrated public service. http://www.oecd-ilibrary.org/governance/oecd-public-management-reviews-ireland-2008_9789264043268-en. Accessed 19 June 2014.

Perry, R. (2003a). E-conveyancing – A critical view. *Conveyancing & Property Law Journal, 8*(2).

Perry, R. (2003b). E-conveyancing: Costs to the user. *New Law Journal, 153*.

Perry, R. (2003c). E-conveyancing: Problems ahead? *The Conveyancer and Property Lawyer*.

Pierson, H. (2007). Mortgage fraud boot camp: Basic training on defending a criminal mortgage fraud case (September/October 2007). The Champion 14–23. http://www.nacdl.org/public.nsf/698c98dd101a846085256eb400500c01/80920782c7de80808525738e005fafe2?OpenDocument. Accessed 5 May 2010.

Property Registration Authority 'Strategic Plan 2010–2012'. (2010). Property Registration Authority. http://www.prai.ie/eng/Publications/Strategic_Plan/. Accessed 5 June 2014.

Property Registration Authority 'Annual Report 2010'. (2011). Property Registration Authority. http://www.prai.ie/eng/Publications/Annual_Reports/PRA_Annual_Reports_.html. Accessed 5 June 2014.

Property Registration Authority 'Annual Report 2011'. (2012). Property Registration Authority. http://www.prai.ie/eng/Publications/Annual_Reports/PRA_Annual_Reports_.html. Accessed 18 June 2014.

Property Registration Authority 'Annual Report 2012'. (2013). Property Registration Authority. http://www.prai.ie/eng/Publications/Annual_Reports/PRA_Annual_Reports_.html. Accessed 5 June 2014

Property Registration Authority 'Strategic Plan 2013–2015'. (2013). Property Registration Authority. http://www.prai.ie/eng/Publications/Strategic_Plan/. Accessed 5 June 2014.

Rätsep, H. (2008). *Estonian land registration and experiences in electronic conveyancing*. In CINDER XVI International Congress on Registration Law, Valencia, Spain, 20–22 May 2008. http://www.cinder2008.com/ingles/detalle_ponencia.cfm?id_ponencia=297. Accessed 26 Aug 2010.

Rennie, R., & Brymer, S. (2014, January). E-missives. What now? *The Journal of the Law Society of Scotland*. http://www.journalonline.co.uk/Magazine/59-1/1013511.aspx. Accessed 19 June 2014.

Rogers, E. M. (2003). *Diffusion of innovations* (5th ed.). London: Free Press.

Ruoff, T. (1952). An Englishman looks at the Torrens system: Part II: Simplicity and the curtain principle. *Australian Law Journal, 26*.

Sabaliauskas, K., & Mikuta, B. (2008). *Land administration in Lithuania: Challenges and perspectives*. In United Nations Economic Commission for Europe's Working Party on Land Administration Workshop on the Influence of Land Administration on People and Business. http://wpla.uredjenazemlja.hr/prezentacije/22_K.%20Sabaliauskas_%20B.%20Mikuta_Land%20Administration%20in%20Lithuan.pdf. Accessed 13 June 2014.

Sneddon, M. (2007). *Risk assessment and management in electronic conveyancing*. In Registering the World Conference, Dublin, 26–28 September 2007. http://www.prai.ie/uploadedfiles/conference20071/papers/s4p1.pdf. Accessed 14 May 2014.

Stanley, V., & Adlington, G. (2007). *World Bank experience in land administration in the transition economies of Eastern Europe and Central Asia*. In Registering the World Conference, Dublin, 26–28 September 2007. http://www.prai.ie/uploadedfiles/conference20071/papers/s2p4.pdf. Accessed 14 May 2014.

Takács, E. (2008). Land registration in Hungary, legal effects of registration, legal guarantees, legality checks. In CINDER XVI International Congress on Registration Law, Valencia, Spain, 20–22 May 2008. http://www.cinder2008.com/ingles/detalle_ponencia.cfm?id_ponencia=302. Accessed 26 Aug 2010.

The Law Reform Commission. (2006). eConveyancing: Modelling of the Irish conveyancing system. The Law Reform Commission (LRC 79 – 2006).

The Law Society. (2005). *An e-strategy for the law society*. The Law Society.

The Law Society of Upper Canada. (2002, June 18). Practice guidelines for electronic registration of title documents. http://rc.lsuc.on.ca/pdf/eReg/july08_eregguidelines.pdf. Accessed 13 June 2014.

Thomas, R. (2003). Fraud, risk and the automated register. In D. Grinlinton (Ed.), *Torrens in the twenty-first century*. Wellington: LexisNexis.

Timothy, J. (2007). *The open register*. In Registering the World Conference, Dublin, 26–28 September 2007. http://www.prai.ie/uploadedfiles/conference20071/papers/s4p3.pdf. Accessed 14 May 2014.

Traynor, M. (2008). *Working with business communities to enable digital land registration for the 21st century*. In United Nations Economic Commission for Europe's Working Party on Land Administration Workshop on the Influence of Land Administration on People and Business. http://wpla.uredjenazemlja.hr/prezentacije/19_M.%20Traynor_Working%20with%20Business%20Communities%20to%20Enable%20Di.pdf. Accessed 13 June 2014.

Treacy, C. (2006). *The Property Registration Authority – Building on progress to date.* In First Law Land Law and Conveyancing Law Reform Conference, Dublin.

Treacy, C. (2007, March). Doing the deed. *Law Society Gazette, 101*(2):29.

Treacy, C., & O'Sullivan, J. (2004). *Land registration in Ireland – Current position and future developments.* In Law Reform Commission Annual Conference. http://www.lawreform.ie/Annual%20Conference%202004.PDF. Accessed 10 March 2009.

United Nations. (2012). 2012 global E-government survey. United Nations http://www.unpan.org/egovkb/global_reports/08report.htm. Accessed 13 June 2014.

United Nations Economic Commission for Europe's Working Party. (2008). Land Administration Workshop on the Influence of Land Administration on People and Business. http://wpla.uredjenazemlja.hr/zapisnik.pdf. Accessed 13 June 2014.

Van Oosterom, P., Lemmen, C., Ingvarsson, T., van der Molen, P., Ploeger, H., & Quak, W., et al. (2006). The core cadastral domain model. *Computers, Environment and Urban Systems, 30.* http://www.eurocadastre.org/pdf/the_core_cadastral_domain.pdf. Accessed 13 June 2014.

Widdison, R. (1997). Electronic law practice: An exercise in legal futurology. *Modern Law Review, 60.*

Wylie, J. (2004). *Keynote address: Need for a modern legislative framework.* In Law Reform Commission Annual Conference. http://www.lawreform.ie/Annual%20Conference%202004.PDF. Accessed 29 Jan 2009.

Chapter 4
Defining Title Registration

4.1 What Is Land Registration?

Land registration is the system under which titles to land are recorded. As outlined in Chap. 2 there are two basic divisions; deeds registration and title registration, and these have co-existed in many jurisdictions for decades.[1]

Many researchers and commentators ascribe very lofty aims to land registration systems. For example Manthorpe claims that "the essential purpose of land registration world-wide: [is] to promote the social stability and the economic well being of all but especially the landless poor and disadvantaged."[2] Lawson and Rudden say that "[r]egistration is a familiar device for preserving evidence and guaranteeing its truth".[3] De Soto sees land registration as part of a process of capital formation and points out the difficulties that arise when property rights are not formalised.[4]

> The absence of an efficient, trustworthy and transparent property rights infrastructure – and thereby access to modern financial services enjoyed by all citizens – constitutes one of the most important obstacles for economic growth in developing and transition countries in general.[5]

If the poor cannot participate in an expanding market because they do not have access to a legal property rights system that would allow them to realise the value of their assets then their assets are dead capital stuck in the extralegal sector.[6]

In order to turn land into capital owners need a formal system that provides a representation of their ownership which can be easily combined, divided, mobilised

---

[1] See Yavuz (2005), p. 8.

[2] Manthorpe (2007), p. 1.

[3] Lawson and Rudden (1982), p. 213.

[4] De Soto (1994).

[5] Roić et al. (2008).

[6] De Soto (2001), pp. 23 and 30.

G. Brennan, *The Impact of eConveyancing on Title Registration*,
DOI 10.1007/978-3-319-10341-9_4

and used to stimulate business deals.[7] This formal representational system allows "the fully capitalized assets to enjoy a multiple existence; namely, a physical existence, a legal existence, an economic existence, a political existence, and so forth."[8] In practical terms it could be said that while conveyancing deals with the passing of the asset (land, estates, interests or title to land) from one person or entity to another, land registration is the system that represents the same asset on a formal record. Any change in ownership of the asset through a conveyancing transaction will be reflected by a change in the record. This formal record can be used for multiple purposes and in a multitude of ways.

Zaibert and Smith have identified some of these ways.[9] For example land has a physical existence as it can be dug up, ploughed and planted. In terms of its legal existence it can be sold, sub divided or mortgaged. In its economic existence it can be leased or be the subject for payment of a grant or subsidy. It can have a political existence in that the franchise may be confined to land owners. Zaibert and Smith refer to it as being fully capitalized indicating the commercial nature of land as an asset.[10] As it can be mortgaged its value can be realised and translated into cash. This is an important feature of land which can only be fully utilised in an effective land registration system.

The key features of land registration systems are set out clearly in the Inventory of Land Administration Systems in Europe and North America produced by the English Land Registry on behalf of the UNECE WPLA.[11] This inventory includes information from 50 separate jurisdictions including Ireland and Canada. 100 % of respondents had land ownership and legal rights recorded on the land register. 90 % had mortgages and secured loans on the register and displayed the land purchase price. 85 % of land registers were backed by state guarantee, 86 % were wholly or partly computerised and 81 % had a system to protect priority of registrations.

Land registration often sits alongside a cadastre.[12] This is the official record that enables the boundaries of land properties to be reliably located.[13] Together cadastre and land registration can be defined as the land administration system (LAS).[14]

---

[7] De Soto (2001), chapter 3.

[8] Zaibert and Smith (2003), p. 40.

[9] Zaibert and Smith (2003), p. 40.

[10] Zaibert and Smith (2003), p. 40.

[11] HM Land Registry on behalf of the United Nations Economic Commission for Europe Working Party on Land Administration (2005), p. 10. For more up to date information in draft see the United Nations Economic Commission for Europe Working Party on Land Administration (2014).

[12] King recommends that where suitable for a country or jurisdiction one organisation should have overall responsibility for registration and cadastre. King (2008), p. 9.

[13] ConsultingWhere Limited and ACIL Allen Consulting for LINZ (2013).

[14] Roić et al. (2008). See also United Nations Economic Commission for Europe (2004), p. 5 which defines land administration as the management of information about the ownership, value and use of land and its associated resources. Dale et al. (2006), p. 19 that a sound land administration system, good land policy and a legal framework must be in place to underpin a thriving and efficient land market.

Another related term is land management which is the process of managing the use and development of land resources.[15] Sometimes the terms 'land administration' and 'cadastral system' are used interchangeably however this does not reflect the complexity of the position in many countries. Alternatively the term 'cadastre' is sometimes used to also include land registration.

Stubkjaer notes that this definition rather reflects the situation in Anglo-American countries and he notes that in continental Europe cadastre and legal land registers were born separately.[16] He goes on, however, to suggest that "[r]ecent definitions show an agreement on the concept of a cadastral system, namely the combination of a cadastre – with its spatial focus – and a land register – with its legal focus"[17] and he credits this development to Silva and Stubkjaer.[18]

The confusion arises because in some countries the cadastre office may maintain the title and/or deeds register[19] and in others this is a separate body.[20] In many parts of Europe, the cadastre evolved as a support for land taxation, while land registration was dealt with separately by lawyers. This resulted in dual systems.

The cadastre which exists in Norway and many other west-European countries, once under the command of Napoleon, generally deals with mapping, land use and land values for taxation.[21] In other countries these tasks often fall within the remit of local authorities or may be split into several registers, each maintained by different entities. "Basically cadastral tasks are associated with the creation, maintenance and dissemination of data about real property units, while registration undertakes the responsibility to record, make known and guarantee property rights".[22]

Silva and Stubkjaer do acknowledge that the terms 'cadastre' and 'cadastral system' are "unsatisfactorily close"[23] and they relate this to the different conceptualisations of the cadastral institution in countries with different administrative traditions. They explain that no satisfactory alternatives have been found.[24]

However adopting this overarching term 'cadastral system' as also including land registration does not fit neatly with those jurisdictions that do not have a cadastre. The basis for a cadastre is usually ground surveys[25] however the mapping in some jurisdictions does not provide a similar level of detail.

---

[15] International Federation of Surveyors (FIG) (1995).

[16] Stubkjær (2003), pp. 227–238.

[17] Stubkjær (2003), pp. 227–238.

[18] Silva and Stubkjær (2002), pp. 403–423.

[19] Dale et al. (2006), p. 14 that many countries are evolving their registration of ownership rights and fiscal and planning data into integrated institutional arrangements.

[20] In New Zealand for example LINZ is the government agency responsible for the administration of the cadastre and the title register.

[21] For more information on cadastres and in particular the German cadastre, see Sperling (2008).

[22] Roić et al. (2008).

[23] Silva and Stubkjær (2002), p. 411.

[24] Silva and Stubkjær (2002), p. 411.

[25] International Federation of Surveyors (FIG) (1995).

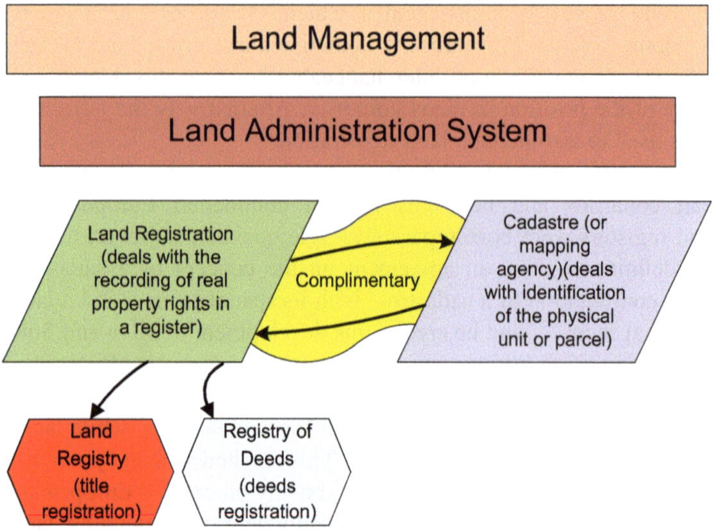

Fig. 4.1 Land management and land administration system

Prendergast *et al.* note that in Ireland "[l]arge scale topographic maps from Ordnance Survey Ireland (OSi) were used to record property boundaries rather than creating a cadastre."[26] They make the distinction between the (non-conclusive) general boundary system in Ireland and the fixed boundary system available from a cadastre "which is supported with measurements, descriptions and coordinates of markers, which define boundaries on the ground".[27]

Thus in jurisdictions such as Ireland Fig. 4.1 provides a more accurate way of classifying the arrangement between land registration and mapping.

This is however subject to change with the proposal to merge the PRA, OSi and the Valuation Office.[28] Deeney refers to the fact that such a fully integrated land, property and spatial information services organisation would provide "an opportunity for more efficient and cost-effective delivery of land, spatial data and property administration services."[29]

---

[26] Prendergast et al. (2009), p. 2.

[27] Prendergast et al. (2009), p. 2. He calls for a gradual migration towards conclusive boundaries over a number of decades. See p. 1. See also the Irish Institution of Surveyors (2008). The Land Registry has rejected this move as being unnecessary as it would add little to the title registration system and may not be justified on cost grounds. See Deeney et al. (2011), pp. 34–37 and 36–39. See also Deeney (2014), pp. 63 and 65. An Inter Professional Task Force was set up to look at the issue and its report was launched in April 2014. See Brennan et al. (2014).

[28] Property Registration Authority 'Strategic Plan 2013–2015' (2013), p. 3.

[29] Deeney (2014), p. 426.

Often the title registration element is further categorised under headings such as European, Torrens and English.[30] Much debate arises as to where particular jurisdictions fall within these categories[31] and what exactly determines how a system should be classified. Cooke and O'Connor classify the Irish and Ontario systems together as being modeled on the English system.[32] It may be that these distinctions are becoming blurred with the advance of globalisation, the integration of systems through computerisation and the development of more modern land information systems and processes. However there will always be a need for clarity in categorising and classifying systems in order to provide a firm basis for benchmarking and comparability.

One method of categorising and classifying is according to what type of title registration is in operation. This will regulate not just what can be owned but to what extent that ownership is protected by the state.

4.2 What Is Title Registration?

Some commentators use alternative, and in some instances confusing, terminology to mark the division between deeds registration and title registration. For example Miceli refers to the title registration system as the Torrens system and the deeds registration system as the recording title system.[33] He, along with many commentators, marks the division on the basis of the role of government in guaranteeing land title. Moore and Globe also refer to Ontario's registered title system (called Land Titles) as a form of "Torrens" or government guaranteed land registration system.[34]

---

[30] Cooke (2004) divides title registration systems into three main families; Torrens, English and German. O'Connor suggests that it would not be surprising if the English and Torrens systems were the offspring of a common but unacknowledged German parent. See O'Connor (2003b), p. 98.

[31] Ruoff and his colleagues believe Torrens titles are infinitely simpler than English titles as the latter are freely rectifiable but Torrens titles are "so relatively sacrosanct that, save, to some degree, for fraud, duress and illegality, even the highest courts in Australia have claimed no more than a half-hearted jurisdiction over them. And yet, strangely enough, the Torrens system produces far more litigation than the English system." See Ruoff et al. (1986), p. 13. See also Cooke (2003b), p. 100.

[32] Noting that the Ontario Land Titles Act is based on the English Land Transfer Act of 1875 but pointing out that it is not easy to state the essential points of difference between the Torrens and English systems. See Cooke and O'Connor (2004), p. 643. For Murphy the distinction is that the Torrens system has conclusive state guaranteed boundaries but in the English system the boundaries are not conclusive. See Murphy (2013), p. 52. Lyall is of the view that the Irish system is basically the same as the English system but has some features typical of the Torrens system. See Lyall (2010), p. 931.

[33] Miceli et al. (2002), p. 565.

[34] Moore and Globe (2003), p. 11.

In a deeds registration system only the existence of the deed is registered and not the ownership or title. Whereas in a title registration system the ownership or title is registered. Under the deeds registration system the title must be investigated *de novo* every time the property is transferred whereas in the title registration system only the authentication of the transferor's title need be investigated as the accuracy of the register and thus the title is guaranteed.

This is important for the authentication of a transferor's title which can be investigated through a title search against the register. No further enquires may be required as the accuracy of the register and the guarantee of the title will protect a transferee. This guarantee of the title based on the register leads to a concern about giving power to amend or change the register to anyone other than the registrar.

Other commentators refer to positive and negative systems of land registration.[35] In a negative system registration does not confer or guarantee the title. This is the system of deeds registration. In contrast title registration is a positive system of land registration in that it may confer or guarantee the title or both. This may however be subject to rectification. Thus in a positive system "even an unauthorised registration is legally effective to create or terminate an interest, unless and until the register is rectified to restore title to the person previously entitled."[36] A void title will in fact become voidable and the validity or otherwise of the underlying title will be ignored unless challenged as the fact of registration will take precedence.

Cooke also makes the distinction between bijuralism and monojuralism. "While a negative system operates within the normal rules of property law (because a void transfer does not confer ownership even if registered), and is thus monojural, a positive system superimposes its own rules, and can be called bijural."[37] In the case of a forged transfer from A to B, A will remain the owner in a negative system however, in a positive system B will remain the owner "although according to the ordinary rules of property law A *ought* to be."[38] Such is the importance of registration. This is explored further in Chap. 7.

The Torrens system of title registration developed and implemented by Robert Torrens was introduced first in Australia by the Real Property Act 1858 (SA). This system was quickly adopted in Western Canada[39] and many other countries.[40] It is often seen as being similar, if not identical, to the systems of title registration in operation in other common law countries. However on an examination of the individual systems differences can be distinguished.

Bradbrook et al.[41] argue that the Australian system has fundamental differences from British real property law. "The [Australian] system is one where title to land is

[35] See O'Connor (2009a), pp. 194–195.

[36] O'Connor (2005), p. 46.

[37] Cooke (2004), p. 402.

[38] Cooke (2004), p. 402.

[39] Coffin and Pierre (2005), p. 4.

[40] See O'Connor (2009a), p. 198.

[41] Bradbrook et al. (2002), p. 1 cited in Libbis (2007), p. 2.

derived from registration – it is a system of title by registration and not one of registration of title."[42] A title by registration system means that entry on the land or title register is required before the estate or interest is created. The act of recording the ownership on the register creates the interest. Thus a party must apply for this registration before they have legal title. Whereas registration of title is merely that, registration of title that already exists.

In Ireland the legal effect of non-registration where registration is compulsory[43] is set out in section 25 of the 1964 Act.[44] All such conveyances and assignments must be registered within 6 months, or such later date as the registrar, or, in the case of its refusal, the court may allow. If such conveyance, grant or assignment is not registered, no title vests in the party holding under such a conveyance or assignment. The section provides that the person shall not acquire the estate or interest purported to be conveyed, granted or assigned. On registration the title relates back to the date of execution of the conveyance, grant or assignment and any dealings with the land before the registration have effect accordingly.

Section 51(2) is the corresponding provision for land already registered. It provides that until a transferee is registered as owner of the land transferred, that instrument shall not operate to transfer the land. There is however no 6 month time limit. Thus the transfer does not vest title in the transferee. It only confers, as against the transferor, an equity to be registered though the entire beneficial interest passed with the signing of the contract. A purchaser of registered land will only have an equitable interest in the land until registration occurs[45] even though they have parted with the purchase monies and the transaction is completed. Thus Ireland operates a title by registration system. There are no comparable provisions in Ontario which operates a registration of title system.

There is an argument that title by registration puts the purchaser in a worse position for a period of time than a purchaser of an unregistered interest as that purchaser gets the legal estate with delivery of the deed. The protection given that legal estate is not as great as that conferred by registration but it is conferred immediately on completion.[46] In advance of registration of a registered title a purchaser only has an equitable interest. Thus the registering authority grants legal title. It is the fact of registration that gives title and nothing else. By contrast in a registration of title system the registering authority records the title that is already granted by a land owner and guarantees that title.

---

[42] Bradbrook et al. (2002), p. 1 cited in Libbis (2007), p. 2.

[43] Under both sections 23 and 24.

[44] As substituted by section 128 of the 2009 Act.

[45] See *Coffey v. Brunel Construction Co. Ltd.* [1983] IR 36.

[46] Torrens apparently failed to consider how the race system would apply in a two-stage land transaction where the contract and completion represent two distinct stages separated by a time interval. See O'Connor (2003a), p. 261. She describes the race system of registration as one where priority is awarded to the interest-holder that wins the race to the register; see p. 254.

Again many commentators use different terminology to distinguish between systems that require title by registration and those that offer registration of title. For example Estonia has a system of title by registration referred to as a "title based electronic register. The right has to be entered in the land register in order to be valid."[47] Regardless of the terminology used and the points of difference identified the term title registration is used here to identify those systems that have two fundamental characteristics. Firstly the title is registered and not the deed as in a deeds register, regardless of whether registration is required for the interest to be created, and secondly the register is guaranteed by the state.

It is interesting to note that despite the lofty aims of Robert Torrens all title registration systems have been diluted to a greater or lesser extent. "Establishing a trusted land register remains as the compelling yet elusive priority".[48] Locke points out that while:

> the Torrens system was designed and introduced to simplify and streamline the process of buying and selling land.... over time, the introduction of different pieces of legislation...has effectively unbundled information about the range of rights, obligations and restrictions...which attach to land.[49]

Legislation about matters such as planning, family situation and tax requires transferees to search multiple registers and systems held by numerous authorities and agencies and this "increases the chance of pertinent information being inadvertently missed, overlooked or incorrectly disregarded."[50] Frank argues that land registration is burdened by legal procedural connections to multiple tax laws, planning laws, family law, social laws and law about agrarian reform and he makes a case for simple laws.[51] This aspect of title registration is examined further in Chap. 8.

No jurisdiction has, it appears, attempted to devise a true paperless eConveyancing system except in respect of registered land.[52] Wylie says that the reason is clear. While it may be possible to capture information held by public bodies, including the Land Registry, on computer databases it is difficult to see how this could be done in relation to title deeds for unregistered land held by private land owners and lending institutions. The "logistics of such an exercise would seem to be insurmountable and the costs involved barely worth thinking about, never mind considering who should bear them."[53]

---

[47] Rätsep (2008), p. 2.

[48] Manthorpe (2007), p. 2.

[49] Locke (2007), p. 3.

[50] Locke (2007), p. 4.

[51] Frank (2003).

[52] Wylie (2004), p. 13.

[53] Wylie (2004), p. 13.

In Ontario it was felt that maintaining two separate land registration systems created costly public and private resource duplication and a legal complexity that increased the risk of error.[54] Land registration reform aimed to convert to one registered title system and to integrate fully all land related information and databases into one centralised, automated, online land information system.[55]

Thus the development of eConveyancing can provide an impetus for deeds registers to be closed down,[56] title registers to be extended and also for a move towards title by registration. In addition to extending the title register to incorporate all land in the State, with the consequent closing of the deeds register, the emphasis of registration changes. Wylie notes that instead of a:

> *registration of title* system, where the process of registration is viewed largely as an attempt to reflect the title or ownership as it would exist in unregistered land, we would increasingly have a system of *title by registration*, where it is the act of registration which confers the title or ownership.[57]

Gray and Gray refer to the changing nature of modern title which marks the transition from a world in which title originates in physical possession towards a different world in which the source of title is an administrative act of registration.[58]

The extension of the title register does not just relate to geographical area. It may also mean the extension of registration to encompass interests which were previously kept off the register. This approach has been endorsed by the Law Society of Ireland[59] and it is explored further in Chap. 8.

4.3 Why Title Registration?

Title registration is seen as being an important tool in the development of land markets and the growth of economic wealth.[60]

> The State guaranteed system of title to property, as administered by the Land Registry, is an invaluable instrument for the protection of rights and interests in property and makes possible the numerous financial transactions which are the hallmark of a thriving, modern market economy.[61]

---

[54] Moore and Globe (2003), p. 12.

[55] Moore and Globe (2003), p. 12.

[56] McDowell (2006).

[57] Wylie (2004), p. 15.

[58] Gray and Gray (2009), p. 180.

[59] Law Society of Ireland (2008), p. 1.

[60] See Dale et al. (2006), p. 10 for the connection between good title and prosperity.

[61] Treacy and O'Sullivan (2004), p. 2. See also Property Registration Authority 'Strategic Plan 2013 – 2015' (2013), p. 6.

In Ireland the value of housing alone indemnified under the registration of title system has been estimated to exceed €500 billion, with well over €80 billion worth of mortgages registered.[62] Property transactions are a key driver of wealth and property is a popular investment vehicle and thus generates substantial wealth.

The efficiency, transparency and justice of how these transactions are conducted is a fundamental consideration that effects the level of activity in the marketplace. In order for land-related financial activity to be sustained the title registration system must provide transparency of ownership and security of title. De Soto points out that where real ownership of assets exists outside the official registry system the result is that:

> people's resources are commercially and financially invisible. Nobody really knows who owns what and where, who is accountable for the performance of obligations, who is responsible for losses and fraud, and what mechanisms are available to enforce payment for services and goods delivered.[63]

In effect there is no transparency. Title registration is seen as an effective means of providing this transparency which facilitates investment in land.

The United Nations has recognised the social and economic benefits of good land administration.[64] The World Bank has financed more than 30 land administration projects in the Europe and Central Asia region.[65] The reason for this investment is because throughout the region "insecure and uncertain property rights have been and in many countries continue to be a barrier to investment and a constraint on economic development."[66]

Barriers preventing such investment are seen as being negative. In the context of Ireland, Clancy has asserted that "[b]arriers to trading in land are excessive relative to other areas of investment and this discourages investment in property to the detriment of economic activity and tax receipts."[67] Although it is only one source of impediment the transactions costs of dealing in land are seen to be relatively high and legal costs are often seen as a significant part of these transaction costs. Title registration offers a potential lowering of legal costs and the possibility for a stronger and more certain title that can provide security to investors.

Though the barriers may be there for very good reasons. Barriers may arise as land is a finite and scarce resource and an important source of wealth. Onerous legislative provisions may be a means to protect the social value of home ownership, to collect tax or to protect against unfair bargain or oppressive use of remedies. Registration ensures certainty of title and ownership and provides the guarantee that

[62] O'Sullivan (2007), p. 1.

[63] De Soto (2001), p. 29.

[64] United Nations Economic Commission for Europe Working Party on Land Administration (2005).

[65] Stanley (2008), p. 2.

[66] Stanley (2008), p. 4.

[67] Clancy (2008), p. 7.

underpins the considerable financial investment involved in purchasing property. Given this perspective, of course it is going to be onerous and expensive.

Wallace and Williamson set out five land market stages in the move towards wealth acceleration.[68] They are

1. Land
2. Land Rights
3. Land Trading
4. Land Market
5. Complex Commodities Market

Stage 5 features dynamic trading in complex commodities, secondary securitisation and corporatisation of land ownership which gives a multiplier effect leading to wealth acceleration and a mature property market. They are of the view that the land administration system must be flexible enough to accommodate stage 5 and the fact that these complex commodities will not necessarily be physical objects. However the development of such complex financial instruments that few understood has been identified as one of the features of inadequate regulation of the real estate and financial markets that led to the current global financial crisis.[69]

Rapaczynski gives the example of the more "propertied classes" of modern America where:

> the intangibles become ever more prevalent and ever more esoteric: patents, futures, financial derivatives, tax shelters, mortgage-backed securities, junk bonds and instruments that only a few wizards understand. The problem with most of these sophisticated forms of property is that the law of even the most powerful, rational and benevolent states cannot fully define or protect them.[70]

A complex commodities market is often referred to as 'sweating' the assets. The principle is that the asset (title to land) can be used as security for a loan that can be traded in the lending market. Thus title to land can be used by the land owner to raise cash for investment and wealth generation. The lender in advancing the loan funds can make interest on the loan but can also repackage the loan and sell its title or interest on to another investor. From this perspective dynamic security will be dominant so as to encourage new loans on property.

Dynamic security facilitates exchange by reducing or eliminating the risk that the transferees's title and the lender's interest will be subject to unknown prior claims and title defects. It is suggested that this lowers transaction costs by limiting the enquiries that need to be made. The shift from static to dynamic security is

---

[68] Wallace and Williamson (2004).

[69] United Nations Economic Commission for Europe Working Party on Land Administration (2010).

[70] Rapaczynski (1996), p. 89.

reflected in the move towards market capitalism and the trade of land for its economic value rather than its use.[71]

4.4 Dynamic Versus Static Security

The principle of dynamic security provides that the transferee's title and right will be protected where there is a conflict between that interest and the title of the transferor. Thus even where the transfer occurred due to fraud, force or deceit and there is an innocent transferor title will still pass to the transferee. The innocent transferor will not be able to recover his prior title as there will be no rectification of the register but instead may be able to claim compensation.

In our schematic this would have the effect of removing the risk to some participants but not others. A and X would lose their title as there will be no rectification and they will have to rely on claiming compensation from the registering authority or from the party who did the wrongful act. However as the register is upheld there would be no risk to B, Y or C. They would have their title and right protected. This is explored further in Chap. 7.

Thus

> a good faith third party for value acquires a property right if the purchase is based on the information provided by the register. If the seller's right is later shown to be defective, the buyer keeps the property right and the original owner gets contract rights against the seller and the register.[72]

Static security is the opposing principle. Static security will allow rectification of the register whenever it's fair. Static security will preserve the existing allocation of property rights. It determines that owners should not be deprived of their rights by the act of another without their consent. The register would be rectified to protect the interest of the transferor in the event that the transaction was based on force, fraud or deceit. In our schematic this would remove the risk to the transferor A. Instead the risk is passed to B, Y and C. B, Y can C would lose their title however they may be able to claim compensation from the registering authority or from the party who did the wrongful act. The title held by one party is upheld at the expense of another party.

Third parties and property claimants who claim against the property rights of the transferor also value static security as their claim may disappear as a result of a transfer. Dynamic security may have the effect of causing a transfer to destroy their rights. The transaction itself may be the event that destroys or damages their right

[71] This dichotomy reflects the many uses of land; as a physical space, for food and shelter, as an economic resource, to create rights and obligations, as an expression of cultural heritage or to generate a land market. The United Nations Economic Commission for Europe (2004), pp. 1–2 sets out some of these perspectives.

[72] Arruñada (2011), p. 9.

thus protecting the dynamic property rights of the transferee. The destructive effects of a registered transaction are explored in Chap. 8.

Transferors value static security more and dynamic security less. Transferees value dynamic security more and static security less. The prior lender with an undischarged charge will also value static security but the acquisition lender will value dynamic security.

This conflict can be expressed as a dispute between the principles of certainty and fairness or flexibility of the register. Certainty of the register will benefit transferees and acquisition lenders. This may be at the expense of the transferor who is blameless but is now being offered a sum of money instead of title to his home as if they were "perfect substitutes".[73] This conflict between certainty and flexibility of the register is explored further in Chap. 8.

O'Connor notes that both static and dynamic security are:

> essential to the enterprise of land title registration. For land assets to be used productively, existing owners must be sure that they will not be deprived of the property without their consent. Without static security, there would be little incentive to invest in improving land or bringing it into production. [In the alternative] [p]urchasers need to be sure that the law will uphold their reasonable expectations that they are acquiring a sound title free of hidden claims. If they are to invest in the productive use of land, they need to be sure that no challenger will step forward in the future to assert a prior claim. Long after acquisition, purchasers and owners continue to require dynamic security. The dilemma for the law is that it is sometimes impossible to provide both forms of security when the rights of a prior owner conflict with those of a good faith purchaser.[74]

As there is only one property "[t]he law must provide an adjudication rule to determine which of the two innocent parties gets the disputed property interest.... The law must create a winner and a loser."[75] This dilemma is referred to by O'Connor as "perhaps the most vexed legal problem in land title registration systems."[76]

While transferees are more interested in dynamic security, once they have acquired registered title they are then less supportive of dynamic security and more keen on static security. As a transferee they wish to promote ease of transfer but as a registered owner they are more interested in maintaining the security of their title.

A system that provides for no rectification of the register under any circumstances favours dynamic security. Under this principle "[r]egistration of title is designed to protect purchasers rather than owners."[77] This does not include owners of third party property rights or property claimants as only new owners or transferees are protected.

---

[73] Miceli and Sirmans (1995), p. 83.

[74] O'Connor (2005), p. 48.

[75] O'Connor (2005), p. 46.

[76] O'Connor (2005), p. 47.

[77] Clancy (2007), p. 11.

Dynamic security is often referred to as indefeasibility.[78] This principle of indefeasibility is frequently advanced to justify the upholding of the register. If a mistake is made then compensation, and not rectification, will be the remedy for those deprived of their interest in land.

A distinction may be made between immediate and deferred indefeasibility.[79] Immediate indefeasibility provides that a transferee is protected from any defect or problem with the title or transaction and no rectification will take place subsequent to the transaction. The transferee must have acted without fraud and given valuable consideration for the transfer. Deferred indefeasibility means that the transferee is not protected from a defect or problem but if that transferee sells on then the subsequent purchaser is protected.[80] The operation of the positive system is deferred until the next register entry.[81]

With deferred indefeasibility a title obtained fraudulently can be defeated until it is perfected by the sale to a subsequent *bona fide* purchaser for value. With immediate indefeasibility registration immediately validates a transfer even if it is forged or otherwise is void or voidable. Both, to different degrees, offend the *nemo dat* principle of property law.[82]

With immediate indefeasibility the innocent transferee becomes the registered owner even if the transfer was made fraudulently. Deferred indefeasibility provides that the innocent transferee will not be protected in this circumstance but any innocent other part who deals with that transferee will be protected. This would include a subsequent transferee and may include the lender. Immediate indefeasibility is a manifestation of dynamic security while deferred indefeasibility seeks to balance dynamic and static security. "The compromise is that static security is not affected by the registration of a forged instrument, but yields to dynamic security only when a supervening purchaser transacts in reliance on the registration."[83]

O'Connor notes the tendency of the terms to confuse as the term deferred indefeasibility "directs attention to a subsequent register entry, whereas the

[78] The particular legislative sections that provide for indefeasibility are often called "paramountcy" provisions. See the use of this term in Cooke and O'Connor (2004), p. 645.

[79] Mason (2003), p. 5. Mason notes the criticism of immediate indefeasibility is that it is too rigid and deferred or even discretionary indefeasibility might deliver fairer results. See p. 17. O'Connor notes that it was in Australia and New Zealand that the debate over deferred and immediate indefeasibility first erupted. See O'Connor (2009a), p. 199 with the case of *Frazer v. Walker* [1967] 1 AC 569 giving the first unequivocal endorsement of immediate indefeasibility. For details of the position prior to this case and its applicability in the Canadian context at that time see Neave (1976), pp. 173–192.

[80] Cooke provides a more simplistic definition of indefeasibility in stating that in England it takes the form of a guarantee of indemnity when title is upset, rather than any principle that registered title is unassailable. See Cooke (2003a), p. 281.

[81] O'Connor (2009a), p. 197.

[82] *Nemo dat quod non habet*; one cannot give what one does not have.

[83] O'Connor (2009a), p. 221.

difference between the two positions actually relates to the effect of the registered interest that results "immediately" from the forgery."[84]

"Indefeasibility confers registered titles with immunity from attack but a degree of ambiguity arises in relation to the origin of the attack."[85] Woods notes that some view the principle as preventing the defeasance of a registered title by unregistered rights arising subsequent to registration (the prohibition or veto rule) while others view the principle as only operating to protect a registered owner from unregistered rights arising prior to registration (the refresh rule).[86] "[F]or some it performs a continuing prospective protective function in relation to the registered owner while for others the principle performs a retrospective cleansing of the title for purchasers who rely on the register."[87]

So indefeasibility can apply in different ways. It can provide retrospective cleansing of the title and thus protect from rights arising prior to first registration. What Woods calls the refresh rule means that

> registration cleanses the title allowing a purchaser to rely on the register as conclusive evidence of ownership and a shield against any prior claims. The static security of the owners of interests which are not reflected on the register must be sacrificed in order to simplify the investigation of title and promote the dynamic security of purchasers and the marketability of land.[88]

Indefeasibility can also provide a continuing prospective function to protect from unregistered rights arising subsequent to registration. This is the prohibition or veto rule referred to above.

Thus the type of indefeasibility sets out the extent of the protection or immunity from attack afforded by registration. Indefeasibility "measures the security of title that registration confers."[89] It can be

(a) immediate; or
(b) deferred; and it can
(c) protect from rights arising prior to first registration; and/or
(d) protect from unregistered rights arising after first registration; and
(e) be absolute; or
(f) qualified.[90]

---

84 O'Connor (2009a), p. 200.

85 Woods (2009), p. 32.

86 Woods (2009), p. 32.

87 Woods (2009), p. 32.

88 Woods (2009), p. 33.

89 O'Connor (2005), p. 47.

90 O'Connor (2005), p. 47 refers to absolute or presumptive. Absolute as providing no discretion and presumptive as giving the court discretion to vary the rule in circumstances where it would cause hardship. Other commentators have referred to the latter as discretionary indefeasibility. See Mason (2003).

How the system is classified under these headings will determine who is at risk from an error in the register, whose interest is protected and who gets compensation instead.[91]

Torrens registration systems are strong on dynamic and weak on static security and some favour immediate indefeasibility.[92] This principle has been the subject of vast literature and much litigation in Torrens registration systems but has attracted less notice and provoked very few cases in England[93] and Ireland. In particular it has been much debated and litigated in Australia and New Zealand both of which favour immediate indefeasibility.[94]

In England and Wales the principle of qualified indefeasibility was adopted in the Land Registration Act 2002. Harpum describes this principle as follows:

> [i]f there is a mistake in the register, a person affected by that mistake can seek to have the register altered to correct that mistake. However, where the correction of that mistake prejudicially affects the title of a registered proprietor who is, or is deemed to be in physical possession of the land in question, the register will not be rectified against him or her unless he/she has caused or substantially contributed to the mistake by fraud or lack of proper care or it would for some other reason be unjust for the alteration not to be made. . .A wide range of proprietors are treated as being in physical possession of land. If, in such circumstances, the register is not rectified, the party suffering loss as a result of the mistaken registration is entitled to the payment of an indemnity from the Registry.[95]

This Act also provides that if a person is registered as proprietor of a legal estate in circumstances where that legal estate would not otherwise have been vested in him, it is deemed to be vested in him as a result of the registration. Harpum stated that if "therefore, the transfer to him/her was a forgery, the transferee is, nonetheless, the registered proprietor of the legal estate."[96] Thus the principle of qualified indefeasibility is intended to provide safeguards to the transferee. It does not provide any safeguard to the land owner who was registered before forgery shifted the ownership.

Griggs argues that immediate indefeasibility in the Torrens system maximises the welfare of society as a whole, but in individual cases, effects a grievous injustice upon the 'formal' legal owner: that being the loss of the property.[97] This 'formal' legal owner presumably being the person who would be entitled if it were not for the error in the register, rather than the person actually registered in error. Which is the 'true' or 'formal' legal owner? It would be more accurate to refer to the displaced owner, whose ownership is displaced by the error, or the innocent prior registered owner.

---

[91] For a graphical analysis see Miceli and Sirmans (1995), pp. 81–88.

[92] See O'Connor (2005), pp. 45–64. See also Cooke (2003b), p. 100.

[93] Cooke and O'Connor (2004), p. 641.

[94] Cooke (2003b), p. 102.

[95] Harpum (2004), pp. 10–11.

[96] Harpum (2004), p. 11.

[97] Griggs (2001).

She refers to this as a liability based solution in that the property interest is not paramount, the right of the 'formal' legal owner can be infringed but that it is ultimately cheaper to allow that infringement and pay compensation (i.e. accept the liability), rather than enforce the proprietary rights of the formal legal owner.[98] Thus certainty of title (the joint welfare maximising solution) is valued more highly than the protection of the individual property interest. The system permits the infringement to occur and the interest of the 'formal' legal owner to be extinguished.[99] This enhances the marketability of land and provides an impetus to use land for investment. Thus dynamic security provides an incentive to acquire assets as it will protect transferees so that they acquire title free from unknown claims and defects. For this reason dynamic security is also known as market security.

O'Connor cites Ontario as an example of the evaporation of public acceptance of immediate indefeasibility where the rule was perceived as contributing to a rising incidence of losses through identity fraud.[100] She explores the position in Australia referring to changes in the mortgage lending industry as unleashing the moral hazard inherent in immediate indefeasibility.[101] This is a reference to immediately indefeasibility shifting fraud risk to a person external to the loan transaction thus relieving the lender from the necessity to ensure they are dealing with the land owner and to carry out identity checks.[102]

"In a world where information is not perfect, we can protect a later owner's interest fully, or we can protect the earlier owner's interest fully. But we cannot do both."[103] If an error arises then there are a number of responses to it. The system may provide that if registration ignores or contradicts what would have been your property right then your right is gone but you are entitled to compensation. Or alternatively the register may be rectified to correct the error and thus your right is protected. If static security takes priority over dynamic security then the register will be rectified whenever it is fair. The continual tension between these claims and the rights of land owners is reflected in every conveyancing transaction.

O'Connor explains

---

[98] Griggs (2001).

[99] Griggs makes reference to the Tragedy of the Commons and the Prisoners' Dilemma, two perspectives that demonstrate the conflict between a joint welfare maximising solution (community welfare) and the maximisation of individual welfare. See Griggs (2001). Both individual welfare and community welfare is highest if co-operation can be enforced. The selfish behaviour of individuals erodes everyone's welfare.

[100] O'Connor (2009a), p. 222. See Griggs and Low (2011) for another perspective on identity fraud.

[101] O'Connor (2009b), p. 158. Moral hazard is referred to at p. 133 as the tendency of a party to take less care to avoid a loss-producing event if the loss is borne by someone else. See also Griggs and Low (2011), p. 291.

[102] O'Connor (2009b), p. 158. See also Tuffin (2009).

[103] Baird and Jackson (1984), p. 300.

> [i]n this terminology there is "static" security to the extent that the law prevents deprivation of property other than by consensual transfer, and there is "dynamic" security (or security of transaction) to the extent that the law upholds the expectation that *bona fide* purchasers will acquire a good title to an asset, free of unknown claims. Static security allows assets to be securely held, while dynamic security allows assets to pass securely to new owners. The dilemma is that while both conceptions of security are desirable, they are to some extent antithetical. Rules that promote static security tend to derogate from dynamic security and vice versa.[104]

Registration will thus protect but may also restrict property rights. It may add to the transaction cost and the drive towards registration of interests may enhance dynamic security as registration will protect one class of interests at the expense of others.

Lawson and Rudden express this conflict as one between different elements of the community noting that while a

> French or Irish peasant will cling to his land at all costs; a business man engaged in land speculation will sell out at what seems to him the most propitious moment and will regard as absurdly old-fashioned any restrictions which prevent the present holder of land from selling to him. The law does not indeed always conform to what is desired by one group or another, or even express the balance of power between groups.[105]

Traditionally the law of private conveyancing was based on the principle of static security.[106] This was achieved through rules such as *nemo dat quod non habet*, the priority for interests first in time and the doctrine of notice. "Equity's preference for the 'bona fide purchaser for value without notice', was an attempt to balance static security against the reasonable expectations of purchasers in good faith".[107] O'Connor is of the view that this suited a society where land ownership was confined to the privileged few and was rarely traded[108] but with the move to registration of title conveyancing law shifted towards rules that protect the transferee and facilitate exchange.[109]

This move towards exchange value rather than use value can be seen in the development of the complex commodities market which many commentators blame for the current collapse of the global economy. These arguments come to the fore when we look at the nature of title registration and its role in our society.

If due to an error there is a dispute about who owns and that error is due to some fraud or fault of a stranger then innocent transferees could be pitted against innocent transferors or prior owners. In this situation the question arises as to whether money can compensate one party for the loss of title. The answer may be 'no' where the property in question is a home and a disposed owner is to be compensated. O'Connor notes that there has been a failure by the courts who adopt immediate

---

[104] O'Connor (2009a), p. 198 (footnotes removed from quote).

[105] Lawson and Rudden (1982), p. 227.

[106] O'Connor (2003b), p. 85.

[107] O'Connor (2003b), p. 85.

[108] O'Connor (2003b), p. 85.

[109] O'Connor (2003b), pp. 85–86.

indefeasibility to "acknowledge the loss of static security and the hardship to owners evicted from their homes as a result of a fraud."[110]

> The question needs to be asked whether or not it is time to reward the real victim in the scheme of things, that is, the original registered proprietor. Is it not more sensible to offer compensation, albeit in limited defined circumstance, to innocent purchasers and mortgagees.[111]

This is a valid argument. Should the transferor who lived in the property all their life and who came back from holiday to find that fraudsters had sold the property not regain ownership and the new owner get compensation instead of being able to retain the property?

4.5 Indefeasibility Outside Land Registration

It is not only in the context of land registration systems that this debate is being waged.

As Davies points out in relation to the CREST system there are

> obvious risks that either an unauthorised person obtains access to the system or a person with authorised access uses the system in an unauthorised way, in both cases sending an instruction to transfer shares not belonging to him or her to an innocent third party. Can the former holder of the shares secure the restoration of his or her name to the. . .register to the detriment of the third party?[112]

If the unauthorised instruction is sent in accordance with the rules, the recipient is entitled, with few exceptions, to act on it and the person by whom or on whose behalf it was purportedly sent may not deny that it was sent with property authority. Thus a legal owner who was in no way to blame for the fraud may find that title to the shares has been lost.[113] The owner may have a case against the agent whose equipment was used to send the unauthorised instruction or against the system operator if the instruction was not sent from a system computer or the instruction should not have been acted upon.[114]

In general the CREST system favours dynamic security as the liability of the system operator is capped and falls away entirely if the operator identifies the person responsible, even if the owner is not able to recover any compensation from that person.[115] The definition of 'forged dematerialised instruction' means that the operator is liable for security defects in its system but not for unauthorised use of

[110] O'Connor (2009a), p. 222.

[111] Greenwood and Jones (2003), p. 346.

[112] Davies (2008), pp. 952–953.

[113] Davies (2008), p. 953.

[114] Davies (2008), p. 953.

[115] Davies (2008), p. 953, fn 84.

the system.[116] Thus transferees are protected at the expense of the transferor and not at the expense of the company.

Micheler is of the view that investors in the system are protected to a lesser extent against unauthorised transactions than investors who hold paper securities.[117] "[T]he legal owner of certificated securities is better protected against unauthorised transfers than the owner of uncertificated securities."[118] If a paper certificate is stolen and the thief or a purchaser from the thief obtains registration, the legal owner has a right to have his or her name restored on the register. This will also apply if the legal owner entrusts an employee or broker with the paper certificate. However in the case of uncertificated securities the owner is bound by an instruction that is send with his or her password from his or her access terminal even if the person accesses the system without his or her authority.

> The same principle applies to an investor who accesses the system through a sponsor. He or she is bound by unauthorised instructions sent by the sponsor on his or her behalf. In both cases, the owner does not have a claim against the system operator because the instructions sent were not forged. They were sent from a system terminal by a person who used the correct password.[119]

Micheler does not suggest that these transactions should be unwound as this would "seriously disrupt the system" but she does recommend that the position of these investors could be significantly improved by the implementation of a guarantee scheme similar to the scheme in place for bank deposits.[120]

4.6 Exceptions to Indefeasibility

Any formal elimination of indefeasibility would in Arruñada's view transform a system from a Torrens registration of rights to a mere recording of deeds.[121] However in New Zealand Greenwood and Jones argue that indefeasibility may already be a myth from a practical point of view as there are a wide range of exceptions which serve to undermine or seriously erode indefeasibility.[122]

---

116 See Uncertificated Securities Regulation 2001 SI 2001/3755 and Davies (2008), p. 953.

117 Micheler (2002), p. 9.

118 Micheler (2002), p. 13.

119 Micheler (2002), p. 13.

120 Micheler (2002), p. 13.

121 Arruñada (2010), p. 117.

122 Greenwood and Jones (2003), p. 345.

Fraud is the common exception to indefeasibility.[123] The principal other exceptions are overriding interests, *in personam* claims,[124] the position of volunteers, interests incapable of registration or excluded by statute e.g. statute of limitations,[125] and the registrar's power of rectification.[126] The exceptions can be divided into statutory[127] and non statutory.[128]

In personam claims, often referred to as personal equities,[129] allow a plaintiff to bring an action against a registered owner, founded in law or equity, for such relief as a court may grant. Low comments on the inappropriateness of both the *in personam* and personal equity labels; the former because it implies that such claims necessarily have no proprietary effect and the latter because it implies that "only claims originating in equity fall within its embrace."[130]

Many commentators do not consider *in personam* claims to be a true exception to indefeasibility as the claim is against the registered owner personally and not a proprietary claim against the land though the result of a successful claim may be to create a "de facto proprietary interest, but not one that amounts to a legal interest in the land, as a true proprietary claim would ordinarily do."[131] Low argues that personal equities do not actually form an exception to indefeasibility but instead the two concepts operate on completely different planes.[132] Cooke and O'Connor also point out that indefeasibility relates to the survival and priority of prior unregistered interests as opposed to the creation of new ones.[133] The "vital

[123] See Cooke and O'Connor (2004), pp. 645–666 for a comparison of the 'so called' Torrens systems [Australasia, Canada (excluding Ontario) and elsewhere in the Commonwealth] with the English system. The definition of 'Torrens' fraud is behaviour on the part of the purchaser that will nullify the indefeasibility protection; see p. 646.

[124] A registered owner should not be allowed to refuse to perform contracts he had made and anyone who entered into such a contract should be entitled to claim such relief in law or in equity as a Court may grant. This includes specific performance or enforcement of a trust and may result in the Court ordering the registered owner to part with his title. For an examination of these claims and whether they detract from the principle of indefeasibility see Wu (2008), pp. 672–697. See also Stevens and O'Donnell (2003) and Hughson et al. (1997), pp. 490–496.

[125] Allowing for adverse possession.

[126] See Deeney (2014), p. 340 for other examples.

[127] Ruoff notes that many inconvenient breaches of indefeasibility occur primarily due to inconsistent legislation. See Ruoff (1952), p. 119. This causes loss of faith in the register and "unhappily, each fresh breach made by a heedless or a ruthless legislature facilitates the making of future breaches." See p. 121.

[128] Murphy notes that the register has always been qualified and thus the "principle of a mirror is a good analogy because just as a mirror is only capable of reflecting what is physically present before it so too…the register is limited in what can be reflected in it." Murphy (2013), p. 9.

[129] Low (2009).

[130] Low (2009).

[131] Tipping (2003), p. 23.

[132] Low (2009).

[133] Cooke and O'Connor (2004), p. 649.

characteristic of this liability" i.e. *in personam* claims is that it arises anew from the purchaser's conduct.[134]

Mason is of the view that indefeasibility does not mean, and has never meant, absolute indefeasibility[135] and that some of the problems with the Torrens system were "unreal expectations of what the system of registered title would deliver, engendered by the notion of indefeasible registered title."[136] In support of this perspective he notes that when introduced in Australia registration under the Torrens system was voluntary and that equitable unregistered interests can be created in respect of registered land.[137]

These exceptions to indefeasibility and their impact on land owners are explored further in Chaps. 7 and 8.

4.7 Title Registration System in Ontario

Similar to Ireland there are two systems of recording information relevant to property interests in Ontario. The older Registry system introduced in 1795 and now governed by the Registry Act R.S.O. 1990[138] (hereafter the Registry Act) and the Land Titles system introduced in 1885 now governed by the Land Titles Act.

Like the Registry of Deeds in Ireland, the Registry system in Ontario offers no statement of ownership or guarantee of title.[139] It warrants only that the register is properly created and that the documents are properly recorded. In both jurisdictions, if the documents comply in form when lodged, the registrar has no authority to refuse them for registration. The term deeds registration or unregistered title is used to describe deeds registered in the Registry of Deeds in Ireland and deeds registered in the Registry system in Ontario. The record held is the deeds register.

In the Land Titles system the records are organised and maintained as parcels based on ownership. The government makes a statement of ownership and guarantees the state of the title with some exceptions.[140] The Ontario Land Titles system is comparable to Ireland's Land Registry system and the term title registration or registered title is used to describe titles in this system. The title register is the record held by the registering authority. The title register in Ontario is called a parcel whereas in Ireland it is referred to as a folio.

134 Cooke and O'Connor (2004), p. 649.

135 Mason (2003), p. 4.

136 Mason (2003), p. 3.

137 Mason (2003), p. 3.

138 Registry Act R.S.O. 1990 CHAPTER R. 20.

139 Murray (2004), p. 2. Note however that the Registry system does have a limited compensation scheme available under section 116.2.

140 Murray (2004), p. 2.

Both jurisdictions are in the process of converting titles from the unregistered to the registered system. In Ontario this process is done by 'title automation' i.e. conversion is done by the registry without the owners being aware that their properties have been converted. Conversion is not triggered by a transaction with the property but instead "is part of a systematic master conversion plan."[141] However in Ireland conversion is triggered by a transaction.

The World Bank has developed a league table on registering property in different countries which is based on three criteria: the number of procedures involved, the time taken and the cost. This table on registering property feeds into the World Bank economy rankings for ease of doing business.[142] It is one of eleven factors which together determine the rankings for ease of doing business.

In the 2010 report[143] Ireland and Canada were placed side by side at seventh and eighth position respectively under the rankings for ease of doing business. By contrast under the registering property rankings they were placed poles apart. Ireland was ranked 79th and Canada 35th. The overall rankings up to June 2013 were poorer but show an improvement in Ireland's ranking for registering property. The scores are 15th and 19th respectively for the ease of doing business and 57th and 55th for registering property. When Ontario was ranked separately from the other Canadian provinces in 2005/2006 it was ranked first.[144]

While these rankings have been subject to criticism[145] and "[l]ike most international comparisons, the results have to be treated with a certain amount of caution",[146] they are one measure of how effective the systems are perceived to be.

4.8 Estates and Interests Protected by the Title Register in Ontario

Similar to other jurisdictions the Ontario title register mirrors and guarantees all interests pertaining to the ownership of a parcel of land.[147] Subject to some exceptions a land owner can rely on the register and need not enquire about prior transactions on the title. This is in stark contrast to the unregistered title system which is not guaranteed by the state and where each time the property is sold a 40 year search of the prior title must be completed.[148]

---

141 Coffin and Saunders (2007), p. 6.

142 http://www.doingbusiness.org/rankings.

143 The World Bank (2009), Table 1.3, p. 4.

144 Cited in Law Reform Commission (2006), p. 20.

145 See Clancy (2007), pp. 9–13. See also Arruñada (2011), note 38, p. 30.

146 Ferris (2008), p. 5.

147 Moore and Globe (2003), p. 9.

148 See chapter 4, Moore and Globe (2003).

Land owners may apply to have their title entered into the registered title system. Alternatively the title may have been automatically entered into that system as part of the implementation of eRegistration. Thus some titles are administratively converted from the unregistered system into the registered system. This is not done by the owner but is done automatically by the conversion of the title into the registered title system. Teranet converts these titles into qualified titles called Land Titles Conversion Qualified (LTCQ).

This is one of a number of titles that can be registered in this jurisdiction. Section 32(2) of the Land Titles Act provides that land may be registered with an absolute, possessory, qualified or leasehold title.[149]

The first title is an absolute title. This title is subject to section 44(1) title qualifiers and any encumbrances entered on the register.[150] First registration of an estate in fee simple will be registered as an absolute title.[151]

The second type of registered title is the LTCQ. These titles have been converted from unregistered titles and they are subject to the title qualifiers set out in section 44(1). For example they are subject to mature claims for adverse possession, misdescription and some short term unregistered leases.[152] This qualification for short term unregistered leases is to reconcile the differences in the length of term required before registration is required. This is 7 years for unregistered title and 3 years for registered title.

Donahue *et al.* note that one of the standard qualifications[153] on an LTCQ title is that the title is subject to the rights of a person who would, but for the Land Titles Act, be entitled to the land or any part of it through length of adverse possession,[154] prescription, misdescription or boundaries settled by convention i.e. agreement. This will arises where the Teranet searchers have not been able to satisfy themselves as to inconsistencies in the description of the property and adjoining properties. As it is a form of qualified title it may also be subject to some other estate, right or interest that is excepted.

However some of the section 44(1) qualifiers do not apply. For example is it unnecessary to check for succession duties, dower rights,[155] planning act contraventions, spousal rights, railway interests and escheats to the Crown prior to the

[149] See also sections 36–38 Land Titles Act.

[150] Section 71 of the Land Titles Act provides a mechanism whereby those with unregistered interests may register a notice of such rights on the registered title in order to protect them.

[151] Section 45 Land Titles Act.

[152] Moore and Globe (2003), p. 18 and for a detailed list of the qualifications see pp. 217–218.

[153] Donahue et al. (2003), p. 29.

[154] A declaration of possession will be given on closing to assist in rebutting any such third party claims. See Donahue et al. (2003), p. 259.

[155] Prior to 1978, under the Dower Acts, a widow had a right to tarry in her husband's main house for 60 days following his death. This right is now enshrined in section 26(2) of the Family Law Act. A widow was also entitled to a one third possessory life interest however such rights, which had not already vested by 31 March 1978, were abolished by the Family Law Reform Act, 1978, S.O. 1978, c. 2.

date of conversion.[156] Moore and Globe note that except for the uncertainty of mature adverse possession and easement by prescription rights a LTCQ title provides a title guarantee superior to an absolute registered title.[157] Donahue *et al.* also state that the LTCQ title created under section 46 may be superior to the absolute title referred to in section 45.[158]

During the automation process issues such as adverse possession could not be dealt with so additional qualifiers are added to the parcel but other additional guarantees to the title can be given due to the searches performed during the conversion process.[159] These additional guarantees, which apply as of the date of conversion, include a guarantee against planning contravention, dower, succession duty and previous corporate escheats or forfeitures to the Crown.[160] Unlike the previous system, the automation and conversion process does not include notifying all the interested parties and thus it cannot guarantee against adverse possession, survey issues and unregistered Registry leases. In the deeds system an unregistered lease of 7 years or less is protected whereas in the title system an unregistered lease of 3 years or less is protected.[161] The additional qualifiers can be removed by application.

The reason LTCQ titles are seen as superior is that these titles are not subject to the following exceptions that would otherwise apply pursuant to section 44:

1. dower and spousal rights
2. succession duty liens
3. planning act contraventions prior to the date of transfer to registered title
4. provincial succession duties; and
5. escheats to the Crown following dissolution of a corporate registered owner.

The title is not subject to any of these arising before the date of registration in the registered title system but may be subject to any that arise thereafter. Hence it will not be necessary to search before the date of conversion but will be necessary to search after that date, save in respect of dower and succession duty liens as these have been abolished.[162]

This is an unusual anomaly whereby pre-existing absolute registered titles are now, in effect, downgraded, to make way for a better class of new registered titles that are based on the conversion of previous unregistered titles. This anomaly is

---

[156] Moore and Globe (2003), p. 18.

[157] Moore and Globe (2003), p. 18.

[158] Donahue et al. (2003), p. 30.

[159] Murray (2004), p. 5.

[160] Murray (2004), p. 7.

[161] Murray (2004), p. 7.

[162] See Moore and Globe (2003), pp. 217–218 for a more detailed explanation of the LTCQ qualifications.

even more unusual in that the award of this title is not based on any application by the land owner but instead is done automatically as part of the reform agenda.[163] Teranet transfers these properties from the unregistered to the registered title system pursuant to section 32 of the Land Titles Act.[164] The owner does not initiate this transfer and is not even notified.[165]

A land owner may apply to have a LTCQ title upgraded[166] to Land Titles Plus (LT Plus). The effect of this is to remove the qualifiers of mature adverse possession, easements by prescription, misdescription and pre-conversion unregistered leases. Thus a LT Plus title has different title qualifications from both LTCQ and absolute title parcels. Only the land owner can deal with these issues and thus the prior automatic conversion was unable to address these qualifiers. Notice is served on adjoining land owners so that they may raise objections if they wish. Once this LT Plus title is awarded no claim for adverse possession can subsequently be made in relation to the land. In addition the exceptions to the qualifications contained in section 44(1) relating to dower, succession duties, planning act contraventions and escheats found on the LTCQ parcel are carried forward into the LT Plus parcel. Thus the parcel is free of these qualifications.

Thus an LT Plus title has "both the advantages of an LTCQ title and no adverse possession rights. It is the best of all titles."[167] It can be "considered an upgrade as the resulting title is superior to both an absolute title and LTCQ title as there are fewer qualifications affecting it and a corresponding greater guarantee afforded by the Act."[168]

As noted already in Chap. 2 if these three types of registered title in Ontario were graded according to the benefits they offered the land owner they would be listed in the following order:

1. LT Plus
2. LTCQ
3. Absolute title

This is in contrast with most other title registration systems, including Ireland's, where the absolute title remains the highest quality title on offer.

The LTCQ title and LT Plus title are both a product of the reform agenda in Ontario however other forms of registered title have been and continue to be

---

163 See Moore and Globe (2003), p. 216 for more details of how unregistered titles are converted to LTCQ titles.

164 Note that if material title problems are found the practice is not to convert that parcel to LTCQ but to leave the title in the unregistered system. See Donahue et al. (2003), p. 30. Moore and Globe (2003), p. 217 note that if the title deficiency is serious, while the title record will still be automated, the title will be classified as a "non-convert".

165 Donahue et al. (2003), p. 29.

166 Pursuant to section 46(2) Land Titles Act.

167 Moore and Globe (2003), pp. 18 and 219.

168 Donahue et al. (2003), p. 31.

available on an application for first registration. The first is the absolute title mentioned previously. The second is a leasehold title.

The registrar provides a separate leasehold register for long term leasehold titles.[169] This register contains leasehold land held under a lease for a life or lives, or determinable on a life or lives, or for a term of years of which at least 21 are unexpired.[170]

The third type of title is a qualified title which is the same as the absolute title except for any qualifier or limitation entered on the register. LTCQ is a form of qualified title.[171]

The registrar may also grant possessory title and this can be upgraded after 10 years. This can be granted on an application for first registration.[172] The registrar could also register this title as an absolute title. Moore and Globe note that those who go to the time and expense of making an application invariably choose to be registered with absolute title and thus possessory registered title is extremely rare.[173] This is compounded by the fact that acquiring ownership rights through possession is prohibited[174] in respect of registered titles. Once a title is registered in the registered title system no new possessory rights can be acquired.[175] Thus adverse possession or easements by prescription do not arise in respect of registered land. LTCQ title is only subject to such claims arising before first registration.

The complexity of the qualifiers that apply to the different types of registered titles appear to have made title searching incredibly complex. Moore and Globe note that it is relatively simple as compared to the 40 year search in the unregistered system[176] however with each class of registered title it is still necessary to search behind the register to some degree.

Section 66 of the Land Titles Act provides that every transfer or charge shall, until cut out by a conflicting registration, confer upon the person a right to be registered as the owner of the land or charge. Section 72 provides that no person other than the parties thereto shall be deemed to have notice of the contents of any instruments other than those on the register or those in the course of entry.

Under section 78(5) of the Land Titles Act priority is determined according to the order in which instruments are registered. Instruments will be registered in the order each is received unless withdrawn, or containing a material error, omission or deficiency, or there is evidence lacking, or the registrar declines registration for any other reason. In those instances the registrar must under section 78(2) notify the

---

[169] Section 38 Land Titles Act.

[170] Where the remaining term of the lease is less than 21 years section 111 permits the registration of a notice of lease against the freehold parcel.

[171] Section 46 Land Titles Act.

[172] Section 47 Land Titles Act.

[173] Moore and Globe (2003), p. 147.

[174] Moore and Globe (2003), p. 142.

[175] Section 51 Land Titles Act.

[176] Moore and Globe (2003), p. 156.

parties or their lawyer within 21 days and must allow a period of at least 7 and not more than 30 days for the application to be corrected. If it is corrected within this time period priority will be retained but otherwise priority is lost.

Under section 78(3) registration is only complete when the entry is certified by the registrar. Instruments gain priority according to the order in which they are entered on the register and not according to the order in which they were created.[177] This is despite any express, implied or constructive notice. Under section 78 (4) when registered an instrument is deemed to be effective according to its nature and intent i.e. to create, transfer, charge or discharge as the case requires except in the case of a fraudulent instrument. Section 78 (4.2) provides that this does not invalidate the effect of a registered instrument registered subsequent to such a fraudulent instrument (provided of course that the second instrument is not itself fraudulent).[178]

Under section 71(1) any person entitled to or interested in any unregistered estates, rights, interests or equities in registered land may protect same by entering a notice, caution, inhibition or other restriction on the register. Where this is done every registered owner and every person deriving title through the registered owner, except prior owners, are bound by notice.

So the position in Ontario is straight forward. Instruments get priority according to the date of registration except in the case of a fraudulent instrument. Transferees are bound by notice of anything on the register and overriding interests[179] but are not otherwise bound.

4.9 Title Registration System in Ireland

In Ireland land registration is under the control of the PRA which was established on 4 November 2006 under the provisions[180] of the 2006 Act. The PRA is divided into the Registry of Deeds which has operated since 1707[181] and the Land Registry which has operated since 1891.[182]

The Land Registry was founded in 1891 to provide a secure and reliable title registration system for recording transactions. Its mission as expressed in the 2012

---

[177] Section 78(5).

[178] See MacInnes and Pinnington (2010), pp. 19–22 for the common types of real estate frauds in operation in Ontario.

[179] See Chap. 2 for details of the overriding interests in Ontario and Ireland.

[180] Section 9.

[181] Registration of Deeds (Ireland) Act, 1707. This was repealed by the Registration of Deeds and Title Act 2006.

[182] Local Registration of Title Act, 1891. Prior to that there was the Record of Title Act, 1865. This earlier Act, however, provided only for a voluntary registration system and no more than 700–800 titles were registered under it. For the first time under the 1891 Act registration in the Land Registry was compulsory in certain cases.

Annual Report is "[t]o promote and safeguard the legal, societal and economic framework of property ownership in Ireland."[183] The 1891 Act was replaced by a modern statute which is the 1964 Act which came into effect on 1 January 1967.[184]

> One of the main priorities for the Property Registration Authority is to complete the register and to close the Registry of Deeds system. There is general agreement that this is a pre-requisite to the full implementation of a system of eConveyancing in Ireland...The registration of title system has a number of advantages over the deeds system:
>
> - State guarantee of title
> - Elimination of repetitious and time-consuming investigations of title
> - Transparent register showing property, ownership and interests
> - Curative effect on minor defects in title or descriptions
> - Accurate and up-to-date digital map
> - Advanced searching and indexing facilities
> - Supports eConveyancing.[185]

Since 1 June 2011 all areas are subject to compulsory first registration (CFR) in the case of freehold land upon conveyance on sale and in the case of a leasehold interest on the grant or assignment on sale of such an interest.[186] 'On sale' means for money or money's worth and accordingly would not apply to a voluntary transfer of title by way of gift or a title transferred on death.[187]

Section 25 of the 1964 Act[188] provides that where registration becomes compulsory it must be carried out within 6 months of the relevant document becoming operative, otherwise no title passes to the transferee. The registrar has power to extend this period of 6 months. The section does not clarify where ownership of the title goes after the 6-month period has expired without an application being made for registration. The registrar will generally extend the 6-month period for registration but if for any reason they should refuse then the court has power to do so. Thus while all land is now subject to compulsory first registration this only applies where there is a sale at arms length. Gifts and transmissions[189] are excluded.

The first strategic objective of the PRA is to complete the Irish land register.[190] Ultimately this will lead to the closing of the Registry of Deeds.[191] "The ultimate goal is to have a unified system of title registration supportive of government

[183] Property Registration Authority 'Annual Report 2012' (2013), p. 3.

[184] For a more detailed historical account of registration of title see Deeney (2014).

[185] Clancy (2008), pp. 6–7.

[186] Sections 23 and 24 of 1964 Act.

[187] Section 24(3).

[188] As substituted by section 54 of the 2006 Act.

[189] Inheritance on death.

[190] Property Registration Authority 'Annual Report 2012' (2013), p. 10. See also Property Registration Authority 'Strategic Plan 2013–2015' (2013), pp. 10 and 13.

[191] This could be facilitated by increasing the triggers for first registration, closing the deeds register from a specified date or the PRA moving to register titles even where there is no application for first registration by the owner. See Deeney (2014), p. 426. He notes at p. 425 that the deeds register is entirely incompatible with eConveyancing. Registering in the absence of

Table 4.1 First registration applications Ireland

Year	2008	2009	2010	2011	2012	2013
Number	3,857	3,856	4,139	5,294	10,286	7,719

policies on land administration, including electronic registration, electronic conveyancing and the emerging Irish spatial data infrastructure."[192]

At present approximately 96 % of the land mass of the State and about 92 % of legal titles are registered in the Land Registry.[193] As of 1 June 2014 there are 2.14 million folios on the register[194] and there are approximately 200,000–250,000 unregistered titles.[195] While first registration applications have been growing as per Table 4.1,[196] increased activity in the market and the extension of first registration triggers is required in order to speedily move all titles onto the register.[197]

The Authority is looking at proposals relating to the extension of the triggers but these are subject to authority and ultimately ministerial decision.[198]

4.10 Estates and Interests Protected by the Title Register in Ireland

The Land Registry in Ireland maintains three registers. The first register deals with freehold interests, the second with leasehold interests and the third with subsidiary interests. The subsidiary register deals with matters such as rentcharges, fee farm rents, fishing rights and some charges. The title to other interests may not be registrable by themselves but may be registered as burdens against the title of other interests or estates.

The Land Registry can register a person with two different classes of ownership; full freehold owner or full leasehold owner.

a request by the owner would follow the Ontario model and be against the 'principle of request'. See González Garcia (2008).

192 Treacy (2007), p. 29.

193 Deeney (2014), pp. 3 and 193.

194 James O'Boyle Financial Controller Property Registration Authority by email 13 June 2014. See The Property Registration Authority 'Annual Report 2010' (2011), p. 10 for the growth in numbers of registered parcels since 2006.

195 James O'Boyle Financial Controller Property Registration Authority by email 13 June 2014.

196 James O'Boyle Financial Controller Property Registration Authority by email 13 June 2014.

197 Based on 5,000 first registration applications per year it would take circa 50 years to move all unregistered titles onto the land register. James O'Boyle Financial Controller Property Registration Authority by email 22 February 2012. See Deeney (2014), pp. 211–213 for suggestions as to possible new triggers for first registration.

198 Consultation with Greg McDermott ICT Manager Property Registration Authority 1 March 2012.

The register sets out different classes of titles which may be registered.[199] Thus within the classes of ownership are classes of title which identify the quality of the title registered. There are seven classes of title:

1. Absolute freehold.
2. Possessory/subject to equities freehold.
3. Qualified freehold.
4. Absolute leasehold.
5. Possessory/subject to equities leasehold.
6. Qualified leasehold.
7. Good leasehold.

The best class of title is an absolute title. This can be given where the title is approved by the Land Registry and the effect of registration is to vest in the registered owner an estate in fee simple or the leasehold interest together with all implied or express rights, privileges and appurtenances belonging or appurtenant thereto.

A qualified title is the same as an absolute title but subject to qualifications affecting the land at first registration. Thus title is registered subject to specific limitations. This limitation will except from the effect of registration any right arising before a specified date, arising under a specified instrument or otherwise as described in the register.

Possessory title, good leasehold title and qualified title may be converted into a better class of title after a period of time and once various conditions are met.[200] Good leasehold title will be granted where the title to the leasehold interest is approved by the Land Registry but the lessor's title has not been established. With a good leasehold folio the State guarantee does not extend to the title of the lessor. Possessory title will be granted where the Land Registry is not satisfied that an absolute or qualified title is warranted. Previously these titles were referred to as being subject to equities.

Section 52(1) of the 1964 Act provides that a transferee is vested with an estate in fee simple on registration as full owner with an absolute title of freehold land and this is only subject to registered burdens and section 72 burdens. Otherwise the estate is free from all other rights, including rights of the state.

Section 31(1) of the 1964 Act provides that the register shall be conclusive evidence of the title of the owner to the land as appearing on the register and of any right, privilege, appurtenance or burden[201] as appearing thereon; and such title shall not, in the absence of actual fraud, be in any way affected in consequence of such owner having notice of any deed, document or matter relating to the land. It goes on to say that nothing in the 1964 Act shall interfere with the jurisdiction of the court

---

[199] See sections 33 and 40 of the 1964 Act as substituted by sections 56 and 57 of the 2006 Act.

[200] Section 50 1964 Act.

[201] Affirmed by McGovern J. in a dispute about title to a right of way in *Byrnes & Anor v. Meakstown Construction Ltd.* [2009] IEHC 123.

based on the ground of actual fraud or mistake and the court may upon such ground make an order directing the register to be rectified.

This is the guarantee given by the State and is the basis for the integrity of the register.[202] The section also states that the doctrine of notice does not apply to registered land. In effect it abrogates the equitable doctrine of notice.[203] A transferee for value who becomes registered as new owner is not affected by anything that does not appear on the register. However a volunteer has no protection under the Act. Also the protection offered by section 31 is limited. While the register is conclusive evidence of the title and any right, privilege, appurtenance or burden appearing therein this is subject to section 72 interests which bind without registration[204] and the register being rectified for fraud or mistake.[205] Section 30(1) provides that any disposition which if unregistered would be fraudulent and void shall, notwithstanding registration, be fraudulent and void.

Also the description and map are not conclusive. Section 85 of the 1964 Act as substituted by section 62 of the 2006 Act provides that the description of land on the register shall not be conclusive as to its boundaries or extent. Registered boundaries are thus often referred to as general boundaries.[206]

Section 72 burdens are binding even if the purchaser has no notice, actual or constructive, of them. Lyall notes that this replaces the doctrine of notice and places "an additional imposition on purchasers which is not found in unregistered conveyancing."[207] These overriding interests affect all classes of title in the register. In addition the Statute of Limitations 1957 applies to registered land and thus a registered title may be lost by adverse possession.[208] Even before an adverse possessor becomes a registered owner his or her interest is protected by section 72(1)(p). Thus the registered title is not guaranteed against all comers.

In relation to burdens section 69(1) sets out the class of burdens that may be registered as affecting registered land.[209] This includes *inter alia* any incumbrance on the land existing at the time of the first registration of the land, any charge

---

[202] Fitzgerald (1995), p. 443. See also Deeney (2014), p. 339.

[203] Brennan and Casey (2014), p. 451.

[204] See Chap. 2 for details of the overriding interests in Ontario and Ireland.

[205] Section 32 1964 Act.

[206] Ontario and Ireland both operate general boundaries. Note however the decision in *Boyle v. Connaughton* [2000] IEHC 28 (21 March 2000) where Laffoy, J. agreed that section 85 is only intended to cover minor errors in calculation and it should not be taken that the provisions in the Act as to the extent and boundaries of registered land not being conclusive extend to substantial discrepancies in areas. Hence the Connaughton's were entitled to succeed in their claim for rectification of the land registry map. See also *Persian Properties Ltd v. The Registrar of Titles and the Minister for Finance* [2003] IESC 12. This general boundaries 'rule' means that other evidence is admissible to determine the correct boundary and extent of the land. See Deeney (2014), p. 34.

[207] Lyall (2010), p. 937.

[208] See section 49 1964 Act.

[209] For a detailed description of these burdens see Deeney (2014), chapter 18.

created after first registration, any judgement or order of the Court, any judgment mortgage or lis pendens, any easement or *profit à prendre* created by express grant or reservation after the first registration of the land or any easement or *profit à prendre* where the Land Registry is satisfied, pursuant to section 49A, that there is an entitlement to such an easement or *profit à prendre*.[210] Some, but not all of these, are V and U type claims. For example an easement is such a claim but C's charge is also a section 69 burden.

Conclusion
It is the protection, or lack thereof, that this registration offers to land owners, third parties and property claimants that is the primary focus of this research and how, in particular, this is impacted by the move towards eConveyancing.

Having articulated the methodology and neutral vocabulary in Chap. 2 and explored eConveyancing and title registration in Chap. 3 and this chapter, the background and framework for the modelling process has been set out. The next chapter, Chap. 5, explains the model, identifies the abstract participants, the risks that they bear and categorises the pertinent risks.

Chapter 5 also looks at the distinction between a *bona fide* purchaser for value and a volunteer, the categorisation of rights and the sequential nature of the conveyancing process as these have a bearing on the overall examination of risk and also on the degree to which the conveyancing process can be reformed to minimise or eliminate risk.

References

Arruñada, B. (2010). Leaky title syndrome? *New Zealand Law Journal.*

Arruñada, B. (2011). Property titling and conveyancing. In K. Ayotte & H. E. Smith (Eds.), *Research handbook on the economics of property law*. UK: Edward Elgar. http://www.econ.upf.edu/docs/papers/downloads/1177.pdf. Accessed 14 May 2014.

Baird, D., & Jackson, T. (1984). Information, uncertainty, and the transfer of property. *Journal of Legal Studies, 13.*

Bradbrook, A., Moore, A. P., & MacCallum, S. V. (2002). *Australian real property law* (3rd ed.). Lawbook Co.

Brennan, G., & Casey, N. (Eds.). (2014). *Conveyancing* (7th ed.). Oxford: Oxford University Press.

Brennan, G., de Buitléir, M., & Prendergast, W. P. (Eds.). (2014). *Towards the registration of defined property boundaries in Ireland.* InterProfessional Task Force on Property Boundaries.

Clancy, D. (2007). *Benchmarking land registration.* In Registering the World Conference, Dublin, 26–28 September 2007. http://www.prai.ie/uploadedfiles/conference20071/papers/s5p4.pdf. Accessed 14 May 2014.

Clancy, D. (2008). *From caveat emptor towards full disclosure – Developments in Ireland.* In United Nations Economic Commission for Europe's Working Party on Land Administration Workshop on the Influence of Land Administration on People and Business. http://wpla.

[210] Inserted by Section 42 of the Civil Law (Miscellaneous Provisions) Act 2011.

uredjenazemlja.hr/prezentacije/Presentation%20Caveat%20Emptor%20to%20Vendor%20Disclosure%208-9-08.pdf. Accessed 14 May 2014.

Coffin, M., & Pierre, K. (2005). *Land registration: The Nova Scotia experience*. Mapping a Seamless Society, Caris. http://www.caris.com/conferences/caris2005/proceedings/papers/11.pdf. Accessed 29 Jan 2009.

Coffin, M., & Saunders, N. (2007). *E-submission of land documents in Nova Scotia: The government perspective*. In Registering the World Conference, Dublin, 26–28 September 2007. http://www.prai.ie/uploadedfiles/conference20071/papers/Nova_Scotia_Paper.pdf. Accessed 14 May 2014.

ConsultingWhere Limited and ACIL Allen Consulting for LINZ. (2013). *Better property services*, Final Report. http://www.linz.govt.nz/about-linz/news-publications-and-consultations/consultation-projects-and-reviews/better-property-services. Accessed 23 June 2014.

Cooke, E. (2003a). E-conveyancing in England: Enthusiasms and reluctance. In D. Grinlinton (Ed.), *Torrens in the twenty-first century*. Wellington: LexisNexis.

Cooke, E. (2003b). *The new law of land registration*. Oxford: Hart.

Cooke, E. (2004). Land registration: Void and voidable titles. *Edinburgh Law Review, 8*.

Cooke, E., & O'Connor, P. (2004). Purchaser liability to third parties in the English land registration system: A comparative perspective. *Law Quarterly Review, 120*.

Dale, P., Mahoney, R., & McLaren, R. (2006). Land markets and the modern economy. *Royal Institution of Chartered Surveyors*. http://www.knowedge.co.uk/Papers/Land_markets.pdf. Accessed 23 June 2014.

Davies, P. L. (2008). *Gower and Davies principles of modern company law* (8th ed.). London: Thomson Sweet and Maxwell.

De Soto, H. (1994, June). The Missing Ingredient what poor countries will need to make their markets work. *Housing Finance International*. http://www.housingfinance.org/uploads/Publicationsmanager/9406_Dev.pdf. Accessed 13 June 2014.

De Soto, H. (2001). *The mystery of capital*. London: Black Swan.

Deeney, J. (2014). *Registration of Deeds and Title in Ireland*. Great Britain: Bloomsbury.

Deeney, J., O'Sullivan, J., & Arthur, S. (2011). Here be Dragons. *Law Society Gazette, 105*(8, 9), 34–37 and 36–39.

Donahue, D. J., Quinn, P. D., & Grandilli, D. C. (2003). *Real estate practice in Ontario* (6th ed.). Canada: LexisNexis Butterworths.

Ferris, T. (2008). The effect of regulation on business activity. *Public Affairs Ireland, 53*.

Fitzgerald, B. (1995). *Land registry practice* (2nd ed.). Dublin: Round Hall Press.

Frank, A. (2003). *A case for simple laws*. In The Mystery of Capital and the Construction of Social Reality Multi-disciplinary Workshop with Hernando De Soto Institute for Liberty and Democracy and John Searle University of California. http://ontology.buffalo.edu/03/moccsr/Frank. Accessed 13 June 2014.

González Garcia, I. (2008). *Land registry and the security of tenure in Spain*. In United Nations Economic Commission for Europe's Working Party on Land Administration Workshop on the Influence of Land Administration on People and Business. http://wpla.uredjenazemlja.hr/prezentacije/4_I.%20Gonzalez%20Garcia_Land%20Registry%20and%20the%20Security%20of%20Tenur.pdf. Accessed 13 June 2014.

Gray, K., & Gray, S. F. (2009). *Elements of land law* (5th ed.). Great Britain: Oxford University Press.

Greenwood, J., & Jones, T. (2003). Automation of the register: Issues impacting on the integrity of title. In D. Grinlinton (Ed.), *Torrens in the twenty-first century*. Wellington: LexisNexis.

Griggs, L. (2001). Torrens title in a digital world. *Murdoch University Electronic Journal of Law, 8*(3). http://www.murdoch.edu.au/elaw/issues/v8n3/griggs83_text.html. Accessed 13 June 2014.

Griggs, L., & Low, R. (2011). Identity fraud and land registration systems: An Australian perspective. *The Conveyancer and Property Lawyer*, 4. http://eprints.qut.edu.au/46059/1/45749.pdf. Accessed 24 June 2014.

Harpum, C. (2004). *English experience: Title by registration – Preparation for e-conveyancing*. In Law Reform Commission Annual Conference. http://www.lawreform.ie/Annual%20Conference%202004.PDF. Accessed 18 Feb 2009.

HM Land Registry on behalf of the United Nations Economic Commission for Europe Working Party on Land Administration. (2005). *Inventory of land administration systems in Europe and North America* (4th ed.). http://www.unece.org/hlm/documents/Publications/landadminsystems.inventory.ed4.pdf. Accessed 13 June 2014.

Hughson, M., Neave, M., & O'Connor, P. (1997). Reflections on the mirror of title: Resolving the conflict between purchasers and prior interest holders. *Melbourne University Law Review, 21*.

International Federation of Surveyors (FIG). (1995). *FIG statement on the cadastre*. http://www.fig.net/commission7/reports/cadastre/statement_on_cadastre.html. Accessed 13 June 2014.

Irish Institution of Surveyors. (2008). *Green paper proposing reform of boundary surveys in Ireland*. http://www.irish-surveyors.ie/downloads/best_practice_guidelines_for_boundary_surveys_final_2.pdf. Accessed 13 June 2014.

King, N. (2008). *Fees & charges in cadastre and registration: Proposals for best practice*. In United Nations Economic Commission for Europe's Working Party on Land Administration Workshop on the Influence of Land Administration on People and Business. http://wpla.uredjenazemlja.hr/prezentacije/6_N.%20King_WPLA%20Fees%20and%20Charges%20in%20Cadastre%20and%20Registration.pdf. Accessed 13 June 2014.

Law Reform Commission. (2006). *eConveyancing: Modelling of the Irish Conveyancing System*. The Law Reform Commission (LRC 79 – 2006).

Law Society of Ireland. (2008). *eConveyancing: Back to basic principles. Vision of an Electronic System of Conveyancing ('eVision')*.

Lawson, F. H., & Rudden, B. (1982). *The law of property* (2nd ed.). Oxford: Clarendon.

Libbis, S. (2007). *E-conveyancing Sans Frontieres; The development of an electronic conveyancing system for Australia*. In Registering the World Conference, Dublin, 26–28 September 2007. http://www.prai.ie/uploadedfiles/conference20071/papers/s3p1.pdf. Accessed 14 May 2014.

Locke, M. (2007). *Challenges facing land registries into the 21st century – An Australian perspective*. In Registering the World Conference, Dublin, 26–28 September 2007. http://www.prai.ie/uploadedfiles/conference20071/papers/s5p2.pdf. Accessed 14 May 2014.

Low, K. (2009). The nature of Torrens indefeasibility: Understanding the limits of personal equities. *Melbourne University Law Review, 7*. http://www.mulr.com.au/issues/33_1/33_1_7.pdf. Accessed 23 June 2014.

Lyall, A. (2010). *Land law in Ireland* (3rd ed.). England: Round Hall.

MacInnes, N., & Pinnington, D. (2010, December). Real estate claims trends. *LawPRO Magazine*. http://www.practicepro.ca/lawpromag/default.asp. Accessed 23 June 2014.

Manthorpe, J. (2007). *Land registration – A health check*. In Registering the World Conference, Dublin, 26–28 September 2007. http://www.prai.ie/uploadedfiles/conference20071/papers/keynote%281%29.pdf. Accessed 14 May 2014.

Mason, A. (2003). Indefeasibility – Logic or legend? In D. Grinlinton (Ed.), *Torrens in the twenty-first century*. Wellington: LexisNexis.

McDowell, M. (2006). *Opening address*. In First Law Land Law and Conveyancing Law Reform Conference, Dublin. http://www.justice.ie/en/JELR/Pages/Speech_on_land_law_and_conveyancing. Accessed 3 Sept 2010.

Miceli, T. J., & Sirmans, C. F. (1995). The economics of land transfer and title insurance. *Journal of Real Estate Finance and Economics, 10*(1).

Miceli, T. J., Munneke, H. J., Sirmans, C. F., & Turnbull, G. K. (2002). Title systems and land values. *Journal of Law and Economics, 45*.

Micheler, E. (2002). Modernising securities settlement in the U.K. *The Company Lawyer, 23*(1).

Moore, M. E., & Globe, J. M. (2003). *Title searching and conveyancing in Ontario* (5th ed.). Canada: LexisNexis.

Murphy, S. (2013). *An examination of eConveyancing: A comparison of the treatment of overriding interests in the context of eConveyancing: Ireland with England and Wales* (Master of Law thesis). National University of Ireland, Galway.

Murray, K. (2004). *Electronic registration and other modernization initiatives in Ontario's land registration system*. In Law Reform Commission Annual Conference. http://www.lawreform.ie/Annual%20Conference%202004.PDF. Accessed 18 Feb 2009.
Neave, M. (1976). Indefeasibility of title in the Canadian context. *University of Toronto Law Journal*, 26.
O'Connor, P. (2003a). Information, automation and the conclusive land register. In D. Grinlinton (Ed.), *Torrens in the twenty-first century*. Wellington: LexisNexis.
O'Connor, P. (2003b). Registration of title in England and Australia: A theoretical and comparative analysis. In E. Cooke (Ed.), *Modern studies in property law* (Vol. II). Oxford: Hart.
O'Connor, P. (2005). Registration of invalid dispositions: Who gets the property? In E. Cooke (Ed.), *Modern studies in property law* (Vol. III). Oxford: Hart.
O'Connor, P. (2009a). Deferred and immediate indefeasibility: Bijural ambiguity in registered land title systems. *Edinburgh Law Review, 13*.
O'Connor, P. (2009b). Immediate indefeasibility for mortgagees: A moral hazard? *Bond Law Review, 21*(2).
O'Sullivan, J. (2007). *eRegistration and eConveyancing in Ireland – the story so far....* In Registering the World Conference, Dublin, 26–28 September 2007. http://www.prai.ie/uploadedfiles/conference20071/papers/s3p6.pdf. Accessed 14 May 2014.
Property Registration Authority 'Strategic Plan 2013–2015'. (2013). Property registration authority. http://www.prai.ie/eng/Publications/Strategic_Plan/. Accessed 5 June 2014.
Prendergast, P., Flynn, M., Corrigan, P., Sweeny, B., Martin, Á., & Moran, P. (2009). *Progress report on the green paper proposing reform of boundary surveys in Ireland*. In The Council of European Geodetic Surveyors Boundary Seminar. http://www.theboundary.no/ep_tmp/files/19417028654a0721218075f.pdf. Accessed 13 June 2014.
Rapaczynski, A. (1996). The roles of the state and the market in establishing property rights. *Journal of Economic Perspectives, 10*(2).
Rätsep, H. (2008). *Estonian land registration and experiences in electronic conveyancing*. In CINDER XVI International Congress on Registration Law, Valencia, Spain, 20–22 May 2008. http://www.cinder2008.com/ingles/detalle_ponencia.cfm?id_ponencia=297. Accessed 26 Aug 2010.
Property Registration Authority 'Annual Report 2010'. (2011). Property Registration Authority. http://www.prai.ie/eng/Publications/Annual_Reports/PRA_Annual_Reports_.html accessed 5 June 2014.
Property Registration Authority 'Annual Report 2012'. (2013). Property Registration Authority. http://www.prai.ie/eng/Publications/Annual_Reports/PRA_Annual_Reports_.html. Accessed 5 June 2014.
Roić, M., Fjalestad, J. B., & Steiwer, F. (2008) *Regional cadastral study reforms in the region*. In United Nations Economic Commission for Europe's Working Party on Land Administration Workshop on the Influence of Land Administration on People and Business, Croatia. http://wpla.uredjenazemlja.hr/prezentacije/26_M.%20Roic_%20F.%20Steiwer_%20J.B.%20Fjalestad_Regional%20Cadastral%20St.pdf. Accessed 13 June 2014.
Ruoff, T. (1952). An Englishman looks at the Torrens system: Part 1: The mirror principle. *Australian Law Journal, 26*.
Ruoff, T. B. F., & Roper, R. B. (1986). *Ruoff & Roper on the law and practice of registered conveyancing* (5th ed.). London: Stevens and Sons.
Silva, M. A., & Stubkjær, E. (2002). A review of methodologies used in research on cadastral development. *Computers, Environment and Urban Systems, 26*.
Sperling, D. (2008). *Property registration in Ireland: The role of the state guarantee*. Dublin Institute of Technology.
Stanley, V. (2008). *Results from the ECA Region: World Bank financed projects supporting land administration reform*. In United Nations Economic Commission for Europe's Working Party on Land Administration Workshop on the Influence of Land Administration on People and Business. http://wpla.uredjenazemlja.hr/prezentacije/25_V.%20Stanley_Results%20From%20ECA%20Region_World%20Bank%20Financed%20Pr.pdf. Accessed 13 June 2014.

Stevens, L., & O'Donnell, K. (2003). Indefeasibility in decline: The in personam remedies. In D. Grinlinton (Ed.), *Torrens in the twenty-first century*. Wellington: LexisNexis.

Stubkjær, E. (2003). Modelling units of real property rights. In K. Virrantaus & H. Tveite (Eds.), *Proceedings of the 9th Scandinavian Research Conference on Geographical Information Science (GIS)*, Espoo, Finland, 4–6 June 2003. http://www.scangis.org/scangis2003/papers/. Accessed 3 Feb 2011.

The World Bank. (2009). *Doing business 2010; Reforming through difficult times*. The World Bank, IFC and Palgrave MacMillan. http://www.doingbusiness.org/documents/fullreport/2010/DB10-full-report.pdf. Accessed 13 June 2014.

Tipping, A. (2003). Commentary on Sir Anthony Mason's address. In D. Grinlinton (Ed.), *Torrens in the twenty-first century*. Wellington: LexisNexis.

Treacy, C. (2007, March). Doing the deed. *Law Society Gazette, 101*(2).

Treacy, C., & O'Sullivan, J. (2004). *Land registration in Ireland – Current position and future developments*. In Law Reform Commission Annual Conference. http://www.lawreform.ie/Annual%20Conference%202004.PDF. Accessed 10 Mar 2009.

Tuffin, J. (2009). Responsible lending laws: Essential development or overreaction? *Queensland University of Technology Law & Justice Journal, 9*(2), 280–310. https://lr.law.qut.edu.au/article/view/32. Accessed 23 June 2014.

United Nations Economic Commission for Europe. (2004). *Guidelines on real property units and identifiers*. Geneva: United Nations. http://www.unece.org/fileadmin/DAM/env/documents/2005/wpla/Guidelines_On_Real_Property_Identifiers.pdf. Accessed 13 June 2014.

United Nations Economic Commission for Europe Working Party on Land Administration (2010) Policy *Framework for sustainable real estate markets*, Real Estate Market Advisory Group, United Nations. http://www.unece.org/hlm/documents/Publications/policy.framework.e.pdf. Accessed 13 June 2014.

United Nations Economic Commission for Europe Working Party on Land Administration. (2014). Survey on land administration systems (draft), United Nations. http://www.unece.org/fileadmin/DAM/hlm/documents/Publications/Benchmarking_41.pdf. Accessed 23 June 2014.

United Nations Economic Commission for Europe Working Party on Land Administration 'Social and Economic Benefits of Good Land Administration' (2005) 2nd Edition HM Land Registry on behalf of United Nations. http://www.unece.org/hlm/documents/Publications/benefits.landadmin.pdf. Accessed 13 June 2014.

Wallace, J., & Williamson, I. (2004). *Developing cadastres to service complex property markets*. In FIG Conference on Standardization in the Cadastral Domain. http://www.fig.net/commission7/bamberg_2004/papers/ts_03_04_wallace_williamson.pdf. Accessed 13 June 2014 (PowerPoint presentation).

Woods, U. (2009). The English law on adverse possession: A tale of two systems. *Common Law World Review, 38*.

Wu, T. H. (2008). Beyond the Torrens mirror: A framework of the in personam exception to indefeasibility. *Melbourne University Law Review,* 32.

Wylie, J. (2004). *Keynote address: Need for a modern legislative framework*. In Law Reform Commission Annual Conference. http://www.lawreform.ie/Annual%20Conference%202004.PDF. Accessed 29 January.

Yavuz, A. (2005). *A comparative analysis of cadastral systems in the EU countries according to basic selected criteria*. In International Federation of Surveyors (FIG) Working Week 2005 and 8th International Conference on the Global Spatial Data Infrastructure (GSDI), Cairo, Egypt, 16–21 April 2005. http://www.fig.net/pub/cairo/papers/ts_18/ts18_03_yavuz.pdf. Accessed 23 June 2014.

Zaibert, L., & Smith, B. (2003). Real estate: Foundations of the ontology of property. In H. Stuckenschmidt, E. Stubkjær, & C. Schlieder (Eds.), *The ontology and modelling of real estate transactions*. England: Ashgate.

Chapter 5
Identification of Risks

5.1 Modelling

As already stated in Chap. 1, given the broad nature of the conveyancing process, it is not possible to deal with all the potential risks that might lead to loss in the course of the operation of a conveyancing system (whether electronic or not). Thus this analysis focuses on risk solely in the context of title registration.

In order to identify any relevant risks a transaction analysis is done through the use of a model or abstracted process. This involves the creation of abstracted conveyancing transactions and the allocation of risk to the parties to those transactions. This type of model is an 'idealised' form of social reality.

In comparing law and economics Commons refers to the individualism of economic theory, focused solely around the selfishness of the individual rather than the interests of others.[1] Thus some economists have borrowed from law the method of approach adopted by the courts of deciding conflict between a plaintiff and defendant "as representatives of two opposing classes of people.... The court begins with a transaction.... Thus the method of approach is both individualistic and socialistic."[2] This balance between the rights of the individual and the common good can be explored by the use of a transactional analysis expressed through the ideal model.

Schelling looks at some of the families of models that are widely used in the social sciences.[3] They are less commonly used in humanities. He advocates being aware of applications outside one's own field as this can enhance appreciation of a model and often the use one can make of it.[4] In the case of his thermostat system the model can be agreed without reference to any specific house. In the same way the

[1] Commons (1924–1925), p. 374.
[2] Commons (1924–1925), pp. 374–375.
[3] Schelling (2006), p. 90.
[4] Schelling (2006), p. 90.

G. Brennan, *The Impact of eConveyancing on Title Registration*,
DOI 10.1007/978-3-319-10341-9_5

model here can be created without reference to any specific conveyancing transaction.

Calabresi and Melamed warn of two shortcomings of model building; that models can be mistaken for the total view of the phenomena and that models:

> generate boxes into which one then feels compelled to force situations which do not truly fit. There are, however, compensating advantages. Legal scholars, precisely because they have tended to eschew model building, have often proceeded in an ad hoc way....But this approach.…may neglect some relationships among the problems involved in the cases which model building can perceive, precisely because it does generate boxes, or categories.[5]

Schelling notes that "[c]yclical behavior is one of those kinds of social behavior for which it can be helpful to have a set of familiar models"[6] and the conveyancing process would certainly fall into this category. Each transaction follows the same pattern. Schelling warns however of creating simple models for simple events as they are so simple that no model is needed. In reverse he also warns of complicated models as they may be too specialised to fit any events except the particular events from which the model was derived.[7]

Thus there is a balance to be achieved. "Models tend to be useful when they are simultaneously simple enough to fit a variety of behaviors and complex enough to fit behaviors that need the help of an explanatory model."[8]

The use of theoretical models in property law is not new but has rarely been done expressly. As noted above legal scholars tend to avoid model building. One example is given by Miceli[9] and his colleagues who developed a theoretical model to determine how expected title risk and transaction costs affect land values across two alternative title[10] systems in Cook County, Illinois. This model identified the relevant attributes of the two systems and their individual effects on land prices. This attempt to compare the effects of two different systems is novel and it is rarely done by the use of theoretical models, particularly not in property law.

Tiainen gives an example of semantic modeling in the property law field[11] while an example of an object oriented approach is given by Paasch.[12] Each approach demonstrates the difficulties associated with capturing and exchanging knowledge and information about specific aspects of property law.

Stuckenschmidt and his colleagues note that the significant differences between legal systems make conventional comparison approaches difficult to apply and thus they turned to modeling techniques from computer sciences in an attempt to

[5] Calabresi and Melamed (1972), pp. 1127–1128.

[6] Schelling (2006), p. 87.

[7] Schelling (2006), p. 89.

[8] Schelling (2006), p. 89.

[9] Miceli et al. (2002), pp. 565–582.

[10] He calls the two systems the Torrens (registration) system and the recording title system.

[11] Tiainen (2004).

[12] Paasch (2005), pp. 117–136.

compare property rights in Europe.[13] Their research aimed firstly to provide a comprehensive and comparable description of real property transactions across European countries and secondly, to assess and compare the costs related to these transactions.[14] A modeling approach for transactions in land and other real property was elaborated and tested primarily by researchers in land surveying, real estate management, geo-information sciences and knowledge engineering. The model was developed using computer language called Unified Modelling Language (UML). This language is often used for the analysis and design of information systems.[15] The aim was to use this language to provide transparency and allow comparison[16] however "the influence of the national and social contexts, and the different perspectives that can be taken, prevent a simple ranking of the studied procedures.... the book eventually warns of simplification in this field full of complex, national institutional arrangements."[17]

Stubkjær and his colleagues point out that the focus was on describing a single realistic case and thus avoid getting lost in differentiations particular to a single country.[18] However, "a straightforward comparison of the cost of comparable steps in property transactions in different countries is tantamount to comparing apples with oranges and reveals only half the truth."[19] After 4 years of research, by multiple researchers in different jurisdictions, a tried and tested modelling tool, when applied to real property transactions, only provided limited comparable data on the costs involved.

This study makes evident the differences and thus the difficulties with eliciting a common set of concepts and models across even neighbouring countries. The real value in the research was in its articulation of the process which can be used for improving efficiency, inspiring improvement and increasing transparency across jurisdictions.

Zevenbergen notes that while those working on projects to introduce or improve land registration "have gained considerable working expertise, there has been relatively little attention for describing land registration in a theoretically sound conceptual model."[20] He is of the view that such a model is needed for both academic and practical reasons. Thus he presents a static model and a dynamic

---

[13] Stuckenschmidt et al. (2003). This book is the opening book for research conducted between 2001 and 2005. The concluding book is Zevenbergen et al. (2007). Available at http://repository.tudelft.nl/view/ir/uuid%3Ace45bcf6-2cc8-46a3-9305-8526df914887/. See also http://costg9.plan.aau.dk/ for further details of this study and ongoing commentary and research.

[14] Stubkjær et al. (2007), p. 3.

[15] Stubkjær et al. (2007), p. 9.

[16] Stubkjær et al. (2007), p. 4.

[17] Zevenbergen et al. (2007) back cover. Available at http://repository.tudelft.nl/view/ir/uuid%3Ace45bcf6-2cc8-46a3-9305-8526df914887/.

[18] Stubkjær et al. (2007), p. 8.

[19] Stubkjær et al. (2007), p. 4.

[20] Zevenbergen (1998), p. 2.

model of land administration systems.[21] The static model answers the questions of who, where, how much and how i.e. the owner, parcel and the right or title. These are represented diagrammatically as a mushroom. However this model on its own "falls short when trying to understand for instance the interaction between LASs [land administration systems] and land markets, the reasons for unregistered transactions, and the trustworthiness of the whole."[22] For this reason he also presents the dynamic model which addresses the functions of adjudication (first registration), transfer and subdivision.

Thus while the use of models in property law is not new it has rarely been done expressly and as such it provides a novel approach for analysing risk in conveyancing transactions. The model here involves the creation of abstracted conveyancing transactions and the allocation of risk to the parties to that transaction. The use of abstracted transactions with abstract participants generalises the problematic and allowed the risks to be identified and allocated. This approach removed the difficulties associated with using live empirical data.[23]

The two most common conveyancing transactions are modeled; an arms length transaction for value and a gift i.e. transaction not for value. While land owners generally purchase their homes it is common in Ireland for family members to gift each other land to build upon. Thus the schematic includes a gift.

The second reason for this inclusion is that the law provides less protection to a volunteer as set out later in this chapter. This means that the risk profile of the transferee and donee are different and these differences merit examination particularly given the move towards eConveyancing.

The abstract participants for the arms length transaction are the transferor, transferee, prior lender and acquisition lender. The abstract participants for the gift transaction are the donor and donee. The acquisition lender is removed for the gift transaction as financing would not be required. Both transactions could be impacted by third parties or property claimants. The risks in conveyancing transactions are identified, analysed and allocated to these participants. This requires an examination of which of the abstract participants suffers if the risk leads to a loss.

As the focus is on risk solely in the context of title registration both titles are registered.

5.2 Schematic

The schematic at Figs. 5.1 and 5.2 is based on the definitions contained in the neutral vocabulary set out in Chap. 2.

---

[21] Zevenbergen (2006).

[22] Zevenbergen (2006).

[23] Miceli et al. (2002), n. 18 acknowledged these difficulties when admitting that they would like to include a measure of parcel-specific title risk in their model but appropriate measures of title risk were not available.

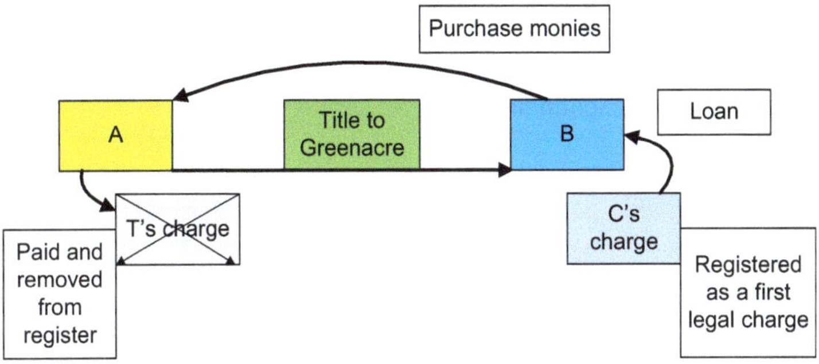

Fig. 5.1 Transaction for value

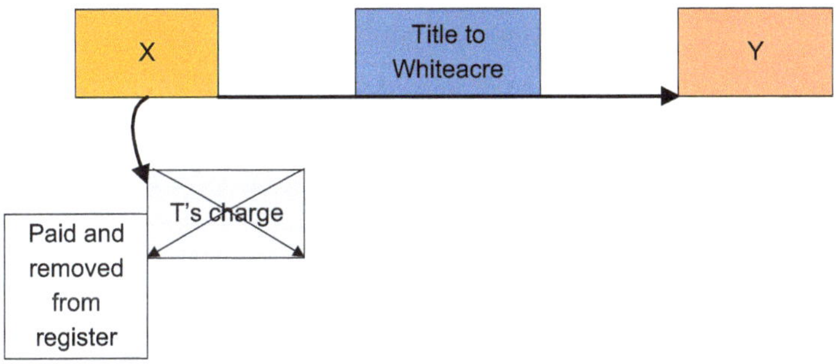

Fig. 5.2 Transaction not for value

5.2.1 Transaction for Value

The parties to this transaction are:

A—transferor
B—transferee
T—prior lender
C—acquisition lender

The name of the property is "Greenacre".

A sells the freehold title to Greenacre to B. B makes this purchase with loan funds advanced by C and this loan is secured by a charge on the title. A's title is unencumbered save for the charge in favour of T. This charge held by T will be paid in full from the purchase monies and will then be removed from the title register. This will allow C's new charge to be registered as a first legal charge on B's title to the property.

5.2.2 Transaction Not for Value i.e. a Gift

The parties to this transaction are:

X—donor
Y—donee
T—prior lender

The name of the property is "Whiteacre".
X gifts the freehold title to Whiteacre to Y.

The additional parties that might arise in both transactions are:

U—third party
V—property claimant
D—subsequent purchaser (purchasing from B or Y)

The position of D will only be examined where it differs from that of B.

5.2.3 Distinction Between U and V

When V is successful in asserting a property claim against the land, he becomes U, the third party. Thus V is only of relevance when exploring the effect of a claim that changes or matures. For example V may have an equitable remedy that matures and as a result he obtains a remedy against another party. That remedy is only of interest when, and if, it becomes a proprietary interest in the land i.e. the point at which V becomes U. This may be due to a court order or some factor such as occupation of the property or the passing of a time period e.g. 12 years adverse possession.

V is also of significance when looking at rights that are not recognised and not capable of registration. V may have a claim but it may not be sufficiently mature to affect the land or it may be a personal claim that is not capable of becoming a property claim. V may be able to register a note on the register temporarily but when his claim is defeated this note will be removed.

V is also of relevance in the context of a land owner's freedom of contractual action. If A or X grant new rights to V and those are upheld by the courts then V becomes U.

The role of V will be referred to separately to illustrate these particular aspects but otherwise U, the third party, should be taken to include V when he is successful in a claim against the land.

Having identified the participants to the model transactions the next step is to look at the perspective of each individual participant so as to determine the liability each bears for risk. Thus this examination looks at the conveyancing process from the standpoint of each abstract participant and examines how risk is distributed between those participants.

5.3 Standpoints

Standpoint in this context is defined in terms of role of each participant expressed as personifications.[24] Thus a specific person is of no interest. These roles or players in the conveyancing process are transferor, transferee, donor, donee and lender. The role of the lender may be divided into the prior lender and the acquisition lender. Other participants are the third party and property claimant who may be a spouse, neighbour or other party seeking to protect an existing right or assert a new right in relation to the property. More detailed explanations of these players are set out in Chap. 2.

This meaning of standpoint:

> implies some *criteria of relevance* determined by the conception of the task or role or objective in question. Thus, "the standpoint of the judge" assumes some more or less clearly defined notion of "the judge's role" which provides, *inter alia*, a basis for determining what the judge needs to know and to understand in order to do his job, as he or as others conceive it.[25]

An individual player or participant is of no concern e.g. a transferor in a real life transaction. Instead we are focused on the standpoint of all similar type participants i.e. all transferors in the conveyancing process. The collective of these objectives, viewpoint or interests allows each role in the conveyancing process to be expressed over indefinite repetitions i.e. all conveyancing transactions.

Taking the viewpoint of each player or role in the conveyancing process and identifying the desires and interests of that role provides a tool for evaluating the process. This evaluation is expressly based on a restricted view of the conveyancing process as anything the abstracted participants are not concerned with or about is excluded from the analysis.

Thus standpoint allows us to take an integrated substantive law and institutional process approach as the abstract participant is trying to achieve something from the law, and is not a disinterested expositor of it. Each abstract participant or personification has some objective that they wish to achieve from the conveyancing process. This objective is shared across all real life parties fulfilling the same role.

In terms of the debate between use value and exchange value all participants will be interested in the property maintaining its exchange value but only those who wish to occupy will be interested in its use value.

The key objective for each participant is summarised in Table 5.1.

The objectives are depersonalised in this model as we are dealing with abstract participants rather than real people who by their nature will exhibit personal characteristics such as greed and dishonesty or engage in fraud or sharp practice. A real life seller would likely push for the highest possible purchase price, negotiate the lowest possible professional fees and push for the purchase monies to be paid

[24] Twining (1972–1973), p. 286.

[25] Twining (1972–1973), p. 286.

Table 5.1 Participant's key objective

Participant	Key objective	Heading
Transferor and donor	No liability in relation to the property after completion	Security of transaction (complete)
Transferee and donee	Immediately acquire occupation and registered title at completion and these are not subject to challenge	Use and title
Lender	Priority over and above all other interests	Security
Third party and property claimant	Can claim and protect the right	Resilience

over to them immediately on completion in a spendable form. Our abstract participants display none of these personal characteristics. Thus risks arising from fraud or dishonesty are excluded except where the threat is posed by someone other than the abstract participants. Our abstract 'pure' participants are deemed to have acted correctly at all time.

The standpoint and criteria of relevance of each abstract participant in this model are set out below. This standpoint provides a basis for identifying the threats or risks to that role in the conveyancing transaction.

Each participant is open to numerous risks. The focus is on risk solely in the context of its impact on title registration and the security, protection or lack thereof that this registration offers to land owners, third parties and property claimants. Other risks that challenge the key objective of each abstract participant fall outside the remit of this analysis.

Each participant is examined according to their standpoint and the risks are identified. Those in *italics* are to be examined and those in normal text are excluded as they fall outside the remit.

5.3.1 Standpoint of Transferor

An objective of the transferor will be the desire to have sole and uncontested right of disposition. The transferor will wish to have an absolute right to sell the property and for this right to be uncontested so that no one else can prevent the sale.

The transferor wishes to sell his interest for the purchase monies and have no further liability in relation to the property after completion. Such liability might arise from:

(a) A lender enforcing the terms of a secured charge that has not been discharged by the sale
(b) The assurance does not deal with the transferors entire interest in the property
(c) Liability arises on foot of ancillary documentation furnished to the transferee at the time of completion

(d) The terms of the contract or assurance not being fulfilled so that the transferor is subject to a claim for

- Breach of contract
- Misrepresentation
- Deceit
- Breach of covenants of title[26]

(e) A claim of prior ownership from someone seeking

- *Maintenance*
- *Occupation*
- *Damages*

(f) Proceedings in relation to the property such as

- *A claim by a third party or property claimant*
- A claim in tort e.g. for an injury on the property
- A claim for unpaid tax
- Liability to maintain the property or to pay outgoings relating to the property such as rent or service payments

(g)The consideration (purchase monies) not being received in a disposable form on completion and subsequently being withheld

(h) An unauthorised or illegitimate alteration of the register

5.3.2 Standpoint of Transferee

The transferee wishes to pay the purchase monies at completion and immediately acquire occupation and registered title that is not subject to challenge. Such challenges might arise from the following:

(a) Some other party is in occupation of the property

(b) An unknown or undisclosed claim by a third party or property claimant arises that binds the transferee

(c) The property is subject to restricted use

(d) There has been a breach of the terms of the contract or assurance e.g. the nature and quality of the title has been misrepresented

(e) There is a prior encumbrance on the title that has not been cleared e.g. a secured loan

(f) The transaction cannot be registered as the transferor did not have title

(g) There is a delay in registration and some other intervening interest is registered during this delay

---

[26] Sections 5 of the LRRA and section 80 of the 2009 Act.

(h) Some other event or formality is required for registration to take place
(i) There was a prior breach of legislation that impacts on the property e.g. a breach of planning which requires the buildings to be demolished
(j) Registration is subject to a post registration claim which leads to rectification
(k) An unauthorised or illegitimate alteration of the register

5.3.3 Standpoint of Lender

The acquisition lender wishes to advance money for the purchase so as to make a profit and immediately have a registered first legal charge on the title until the full amount of the loan is paid. The prior lender wishes to have the loan plus interest and any other fees arising on foot of the charge repaid before or at completion of the sale of the property. During the term of the loan a lender may wish to enforce the terms of the charge if there is a breach by the mortgagor. The following risks may arise:

(a) Delay in registration and some other intervening interest is registered
(b) Prior encumbrance on the title that has not been cleared e.g. another charge takes priority
(c) The charge cannot be registered as the mortgagor did not have title to grant the charge
(d) Some other event or formality is required for registration to take place
(e) The charge is not effective and cannot be enforced due to some breach of the required formalities
(f) The charge is not repaid before or at completion
(g) The charge cannot be enforced against a third party who is interested in the land and therefore has little or no value as security
(h) The charge is ineffective due to a substantive wrong or defect and rescission is available e.g. undue influence or unconscionable bargain
(i) An unauthorised or illegitimate alteration of the register

These risks will be examined primarily from the perspective of the acquisition lender who is advancing money to the transferee to finance the conveyancing transaction. This party is the provider of secured finance for the purchase. This role includes where the transferee re-mortgages after the purchase as this lender will be stepping into the shoes of the acquisition lender and will be seeking to have a first legal charge registered against the title.

In any particular conveyancing transaction the aims of the prior lender and acquisition lender will differ but over a series of transactions, as set out in the model, the role will be the same. On a subsequent transaction the acquisition lender becomes the prior lender.

5.3.4 Standpoint of Donor

The donor wishes to gift his interest and have no further liability in relation to the property after completion. Such liability might arise from:

(a) A lender enforcing the terms of a secured charge that has not been discharged at the time of the gift
(b) The terms of the assurance not being fulfilled so that the donor is subject to a claim for

- Misrepresentation
- Deceit
- Breach of covenants of title

As the transaction is a gift the donor will be subject to a lesser duty than a transferor.

(c) A claim of prior ownership from someone seeking

- *Maintenance*
- *Occupation*
- *Damages*

(d) Proceedings in relation to the property such as

- *A claim by a third party or property claimant*
- A claim in tort e.g. for an injury on the property
- A claim for unpaid tax
- Liability to maintain the property or to pay outgoings relating to the property such as rent or service payments

(e) An unauthorised or illegitimate alteration of the register

5.3.5 Standpoint of Donee

The donee wishes to accept the gift and immediately acquire registered title that is not subject to challenge. Such challenges might arise from the following:

(a) Some other party is in occupation of the property
(b) An unknown or undisclosed claim by a third party or property claimant arises that binds the donee
(c) The property is subject to restricted use
(d) There has been a breach of the terms of the assurance e.g. the nature and quality of the title has been misrepresented
(e) There is a prior encumbrance on the title that has not been cleared e.g. a secured loan
(f) The transaction cannot be registered as the donor did not have title

(g) There is a delay in registration and some other intervening interest is registered during this delay
(h) Some other event or formality is required for registration to take place
(i) There was a prior breach of legislation that impacts on the property e.g. a breach of planning which requires the buildings to be demolished
(j) Registration is subject to a post registration claim which leads to rectification
(k) An unauthorised or illegitimate alteration of the register

5.3.6 Standpoint of Third Party

The third party wishes to protect their existing right in relation to land such as an easement or an equitable interest. The risk for the third party is that they will not be able to protect the right because:

(a) some other right has priority and destroys the third party right
(b) some other right has priority and makes their right less valuable
(c) the right is not protected by the registering authority as it is not recognised as a right capable of registration by the legislation
(d) An unauthorised or illegitimate alteration of the register

5.3.7 Standpoint of Property Claimant

The property claimant wishes to claim or assert a new right in relation to land. The risk for the property claimant is that they will not be able to claim or assert the right because:

(a) some other right has priority and destroys their right
(b) some other right has priority and makes their right less valuable
(c) the right is not protected by the registering authority as it is not recognised as a right capable of registration by the legislation
(d) An unauthorised or illegitimate alteration of the register

In respect of both the third party and property claimant the right that has priority and destroys their right might in fact be the right of the parties to the transaction. The transfer or charge might itself be the event that destroys or damages their right thus protecting the dynamic property rights of the transferee or chargee at the expense of the right of the third party or property claimant.

5.4 Risk Matrix

These risks, which can undermine the key objective of each abstract participant, and the events that can create them are grouped into categories as indicated by the colour coding on the matrix at Table 5.2. This matrix provides an overview of all

Table 5.2 Risk matrix

Participant whose interest is at risk	Risk	Circumstance that can create this risk	Risk from
Transferor A and Donor X	Claim of prior ownership	Error in register	Prior registered owner
		Interests off the register which affect title	Prior registered owner
	Claim by a third party or property claimant	Interests off the register which affect title	U the third party or V the property claimant
	Unauthorised or illegitimate alteration of the register	Error in register	All other parties and/or the registrar
Transferee B and Donee Y	Claim by a third party or property claimant	Interests off the register which affect title	U the third party or V the property claimant
	Prior encumbrance on the title that has not been cleared	Registration gap	T the prior lender, U the third party or V the property claimant
	Transferor/Donor did not have title	Error in register	A the transferor/X the donor
		Interests off the register which affect title	A the transferor/X the donor

(continued)

Table 5.2 (continued)

	Delay in registration and some other intervening interest is registered	Registration gap	U the third party or V the property claimant
	Some other event or formality is required for registration	Formalities for registration	A the transferor/X the donor and/or the registrar
	Registration is subject to a post registration claim which leads to rectification	Interests off the register which affect title	U the third party or V the property claimant
	Unauthorised or illegitimate alteration of the register	Error in register	All other parties and/or the registrar
Acquisition Lender C	Delay in registration and some other intervening interest is registered.	Registration gap	U the third party or V the property claimant
	Prior encumbrance on the title that has not been cleared e.g. another charge takes priority	Registration gap	T the prior lender, U the third party or V the property claimant
	Mortgagor did not have title to grant the charge	Error in register	B the transferee
		Interests off the register which affect title	B the transferee
	Some other event or formality is required for registration	Formalities for registration	B the transferee and/or the registrar

(continued)

Table 5.2 (continued)

	The charge cannot be enforced against a third party who is interested in the land and therefore has little or no value as security	Interests off the register which affect title	U the third party or V the property claimant
	Unauthorised or illegitimate alteration of the register	Error in register	All other parties and/or the registrar
Third Party U and Property Claimant V	Some other right has priority and makes their right less valuable	Destructive effects of a registered transaction	B the transferee, C the acquisition lender or Y the donee
	The right is not protected by the registering authority as it is not recognised as a right capable of registration by the legislation	Right not recognised and not capable of registration	The state acting through the registrar
	Unauthorised or illegitimate alteration of the register	Error in register	All other parties and/or the registrar
	Some other right has priority and destroys the third party right or property claim	Destructive effects of a registered transaction	B the transferee, C the acquisition lender or Y the donee

the risks to be examined and also sets out a structure for allowing similar type risks to be dealt with together. It establishes six categories of risk.

The transferor and donor share the same risks as do the transferee and donee. Similarly the third party and property claimant share the same risks but the acquisition lender has to be dealt with separately. However, while some parties do share the same risk heading, each party must be examined individually as the impact of that risk will not be the same.

Thus while the matrix at Table 5.2 groups the participants, for the purposes of identifying the key risks to be examined, they will be unbundled in the following chapters which look at the specific impact on each individual participant. Some participants may be affected by risk in terms of a monetary loss in their investment whereas for other participants the loss may be a loss of use or a loss of enrichment.

Thus the key risks to be examined, and their associated colours in the matrix at Table 5.2, are:

1. Registration gap: time lag between transfer and registration (blue)
2. Formalities for registration: some other event required before registration (pink)
3. Error in the register (green)
4. Interests off the register which affect title (purple)
5. Interests not recognised and not capable of registration (orange)
6. Destructive effects of a registered transaction (brown)

From the examination above it can be seen that conveyancing transactions inherently bring risks to the participants and eConveyancing is not some magic formula that can dissipate risk in its entirety. That said there is the potential for risk to be mitigated for some participants though this may result in increased risk for other participants.

The law treats some of these abstract participants more favorably than others. In particular it makes a clear distinction between the protection afforded to a *bona fide* purchaser for value and a volunteer.[27] In the schematic the transferee B, and subsequent purchaser D, are *bona fide* purchasers for value. C will usually be treated in a similar manner as a lender for value. By contrast as Y is obtaining a gift the law provides less protection to this participant and thus Y is subject to increased risk in the conveyancing process. Y is a volunteer.

O'Connor notes that all reform bodies in Australia and Canada who have examined voluntary transfers in recent years have concluded that volunteers should be afforded the same registration protection as purchasers for value, to facilitate the generation of new wealth, as "[i]t is not in the interests of general economic welfare

[27] See sections 52(2) and 55(2) of the 1964 Act which provide that where the transfer is made without valuable consideration, to a volunteer, then the transferee is subject to all unregistered rights subject to which the transferor held the land transferred. Similarly in Ontario under sections 90 and 109 of the Land Titles Act a volunteer is subject to any unregistered estates, rights, interests or equities subject to which the transferor held the land. It is irrelevant that the unregistered right was unregistrable or could have been protected by a note on the register or could have been registered itself but no such registration was made.

to allow the titles of volunteers to remain clouded."[28] However given the spate of voluntary dispositions to spouses occurring as a result of the property crash, this approach is unlikely to be adopted in Ireland.

As Lyall has pointed out "[t]he law assists the buyer of commodities in the market, but not those who take, even innocently, outside the market."[29] Thus B and C are afforded a greater degree of protection than Y in conveyancing transactions.

5.5 Distinction Between *Bona Fide* Purchaser for Value and Volunteer

It is a well-settled principle of common law that a *bona fide* purchaser for value without notice[30] acquires a good title to property unaffected by matters of which they had no notice.[31] The question of notice may arise either by some matter arising from the title or replies to enquiries or may be apparent from an inspection of the premises.

If the purchaser is fixed with notice then he will take subject to the rights and interests which reasonable enquiries and searches would have revealed. The question as to what is reasonable may be difficult to determine as it will depend on the facts of a particular case.

The law will protect the transferee as a *bona fide* purchaser for value provided he is not on notice of the matter prejudicial to his interest. If he is on notice then his interest will be subject to it. In order to avail of this protection the transferee must carry out reasonable enquiries and searches so he is not fixed with constructive notice of some matter that would have come to his attention, but did not, because he failed to carry out such enquiries and searches. Standardised enquiries and searches have thus become a major part of any conveyancing transaction.

For unregistered land this doctrine of notice still applies to fix a person with knowledge and to determine priorities between interests. After the title is registered it still has a role to play in fixing a purchaser with notice of the contents of the register and to fix a land owner with knowledge of fraud.

Otherwise in the case of registered land the equitable doctrine of notice is replaced by the principle of registration.[32] The purchaser is deemed to have notice of any matter on the register but what about matters off the register? The idea of the register being a mirror of the title implies that it is only the register that needs to be consulted. Certainly the original vision of title registration was that it would replace

[28] O'Connor (2003), p. 91. In relation to Canada see Joint Land Titles Committee (1990), pp. 36–37.

[29] Lyall (2010), p. 960.

[30] Often called 'Equity's Darling'. See Gray and Gray (2009), p. 83.

[31] See section 86 of the 2009 Act and section 72 of the Land Titles Act.

[32] Lyall (2010), p. 936.

the need for the detailed investigation of title and of prior transactions required by conveyancing of unregistered land. The register would be all. This was seen as one of the major benefits in moving to title registration.

However this simplistic vision has not borne fruit. Instead there has been an extensive growth[33] in the interests and charges affecting land which are not reflected on the register and which are not easily discoverable by an inspection of the property.[34] The majority are created by statute and are burdens on the land which affect successive owners.[35] To add to this difficulty they are generally not registered in any central searchable register and can only be determined by making written enquiries to numerous different bodies.

Overriding interests affect title without registration but, in a situation where there are no such interests, an owner of registered land acquired for value is not affected by any unregistered right in or over the land. In the schematic B, C and, on a subsequent transaction, D will acquire registered title unaffected by any prior unregistered interests. This is subject to any such interests not having been protected by a notice on the register or having gained priority by registration.

Searches and enquiries will be required to establish whether there are any interests noted on the register, any pending registrations, overriding interests or *in personam* claims such as pending litigation or judgments about to be registered against the title. The existence of such claims raises the specter of some other interest being registered in the registration gap ahead of B or C's interest. A prudent purchaser and lender would require such claims to be dealt with before completion.

The position of Y as a volunteer is very different.[36] A voluntary conveyance is usually between related parties where the donor transfers to the donee for 'natural love and affection'. No purchase monies are paid.[37] The law takes the view that a donee will 'not look a gift horse in the mouth' and will take the gift regardless of any title defects. Thus a donee is unlikely to carry out the usual enquiries in relation to the property or title. In addition the law tries to avoid the situation where a donor transfers to a spouse, sibling or other related person in order to avoid the title being claimed by creditors or someone else who has an interest in the property.[38] Thus the transaction is more likely to be set aside.

For these reasons a volunteer is not given the same protection as a *bona fide* purchaser for value. The donee is deemed to take his interest subject to all prior interests, whether registered or not.

---

[33] Wylie and Woods (2005), p. 99.

[34] Murphy refers to the extensive list of overriding interests. See Murphy (2013), p. 21.

[35] Wylie and Woods note the public health and housing legislation, roads and highways legislation and planning and environmental legislation as being examples. See Wylie and Woods (2005), p. 99.

[36] Deeney notes that the distinction between purchasers and volunteers is fundamental as a volunteer take the registered title 'warts and all'. See Deeney (2014), p. 340.

[37] A judgment mortgagee is a volunteer. See *ACC Bank plc. v. Markham* [2007] 3 IR 533.

[38] See section 74 of the 2009 Act. The usual practice in Ireland is to obtain a declaration of solvency from the donor and to carry out a bankruptcy search.

Section 52(2) of the 1964 Act provides that where the transfer is made without valuable consideration, to a volunteer, then the transferee is subject to all unregistered rights subject to which the transferor held the land transferred. Section 55(2) is the corresponding provision in relation to a leasehold interest which is also subject to the implied and express covenants, obligations and liabilities incident to the leasehold interest being transferred. A similar effect arises in relation to the other classes of registered titles save and except that these classes of registered titles have additional qualifications as denoted by their labelling i.e. possessory title, qualified title and good leasehold title. Similarly in Ontario under sections 90 and 109 of the Land Titles Act a volunteer is subject to any unregistered estates, rights, interests or equities subject to which the transferor held the land.

It is irrelevant that the unregistered right was unregistrable or could have been protected by a note on the register or could have been registered itself but no such registration was made.

Thus while B and C will be able to take title free of such unregistered rights, Y will not. He will be bound by all unregistered rights to which X held the land. However if Y sells the land to D, D will take title free of such unregistered rights.

5.6 Categorisation of Rights

Generally rights can be divided into a number of categories however it should be acknowledged that some rights fall into more than one category.

> We take trouble in our legislation to ensure that the rights are codified and that the systems of rights transfer will work effectively. We ensure that third party rights are recorded so that all with a stake in the land parcel are protected under the law.[39]

Thus this categorisation of rights demonstrates what society values as being important. It determines which rights are deemed as being more vital than others and this in turn illustrates whose standpoint is valued.

A simplistic view would divide rights into two categories; property rights which bind land and personal rights, incorporating all other rights, but this division does not reflect the true complexity. Some property rights may be capable of binding land but may not do so because they are not registered or can be defeated. Some rights may be property rights but not in the land. Instead the property may be a trust fund.

The rights capable of substantive registration have already been examined in Chap. 4.

There are also property rights that are capable of affecting title but which cannot be registered directly. They may be rights capable of registration but only as

[39] Manthorpe (2007), p. 2.

burdens on the registered title e.g. a charge. These rights need to be registered to gain priority. These rights may be destroyed by a transaction to a *bona fide* purchaser for value. The risks to the idealised participants presented by these rights are examined in Chap. 8.

Some rights are protected as overriding interests. This category of rights can be divided into two specific types; those that are overriding by their nature and those that are overriding by occupation. They affect title without registration and bind the world. There is no distinction between how they affect *bona fide* purchasers for value and volunteers. The specific risks these overriding interests present to the idealised participants are also examined in Chap. 8.

There are also purely personal rights that are not capable of registration and are not recognised as being capable of affecting title to land.

> Only those rights which are conventionally classified as *proprietary* have the potential to bind a purchaser of the land. Personal rights can never do so, although they may sometimes retain a limited enforceability (usually by way of a remedy in damages) against their grantor, the former owner of the estate now transferred. In effect, those claims or interests which appear low in the calibrated scale of 'property' value. . .will simply not make the grade. Even though they relate in some way to the land, they lack a sufficient intensity of 'property' content to merit general or long-term protection. Consequently they do not rank, in the relevant conveyancing sense, as *proprietary* rights in land and cannot survive dispositions of the estate to which they refer.[40]

Some of these rights always remain personal whereas others may be considered hybrid rights as they are capable of being converted into a property right that is recognised. An example is a debt that is converted into a judgment mortgage that is then registered against the title. Purely personal rights fall outside the remit of this analysis. Hybrid rights are however of relevance i.e. when V makes a successful property claim and becomes U. This aspect is also examined in Chap. 8.

From time to time rights may move from one category to another based on how they are treated by the legislature and courts.

Gray and Gray present a figure representing rights in land.[41] This figure divides registered title into four categories; registered estates which can be substantively registered, registered charges which are non-substantively registrable; registrable (minor) interests which can be protected by entry of notice and overriding interests which are automatically binding unless overreached.

The interest being sold by A to B and transferred from X to Y in the schematic is a registered freehold title. This is a right capable of substantive registration in the title register as a registered estate. By contrast C's right is only capable of registration as a burden on the registered title as a registered charge. The freehold title can be substantively registered under its own unique folio number and the charge held by C will be registered by entry against that freehold folio.

[40] Gray and Gray (2009), p. 137 (footnotes removed from quote).

[41] Gray and Gray (2009), p. 141.

B, C and Y will be attempting to complete the transaction and attain registration free from the interests of U and V. U and V may hold a registrable (minor) interest or an overriding interest capable of being overreached.

The transaction may provide an opportunity for U and V to interpose their right or interest ahead of B, C and Y or may defeat the right or interest held by U and V. Thus it is necessary to consider briefly the nature of the conveyancing process itself before undertaking a detailed examination of the specific risks.

5.7 Conveyancing as a Process

Conveyancing is a continual series of steps occurring over a period of weeks, months and in the occasional instance over years. It is not a fixed point in time though many of the formal stages can be linked to a fixed point such as the execution of the contract or assurance, completion and registration.

Much of the tension between the, often competing, interests of the participants can be addressed by effective management and co-ordination of this process. For example if the process allows for the time of completion to correspond exactly with:

(a) the payment of the purchase monies in a disposable form;
(b) the taking of occupation;
(c) discharge of any prior registered charge;
(d) the registration of the transferee's title; and
(e) the registration of the acquisition lender's charge

then a number of the risks set about above can be avoided.

For example the following risks would be minimised and possibly even eliminated:

(a) the prior lender enforcing the terms of a secured charge that has not been discharged by the sale;
(b) the purchase monies being withheld;
(c) some other party being in occupation of the property;
(d) the transaction not being registered as the transferor did not have title;
(e) a delay in registration allowing some other intervening interest to be registered;
(f) some other event or formality being required for registration to take place;
(g) the new charge not being registered as a first legal charge as some other intervening interest arose e.g. another charge takes priority;

The delay between stages in the paper process occurs while the paper, and often the money, has to be transmitted from one physical location to another. After completion occurs in the paper process:

(a) the cheque or bank draft has to be lodged with the lender and it may take 3–5 days to clear. In the interim it may be lost, stolen or withdrawn.
(b) the transferee or donee may not be able to collect the keys immediately in order to take occupation.
(c) it may take a few days for the paper to arrive in the registering authority and it will then have to join the queue. In the interim the title may be transferred elsewhere or an intervening interest may be registered.

Thus the timeline of the conveyancing process has a significant impact on the level of risk.

In order to mitigate these risks lawyers have adapted the process in various ways. The purchase monies may be paid in advance of completion and held in trust by the transferor's lawyer. A priority period may be used to protect the application pending registration though this is rarely used in Ireland.[42] Carrying out searches against the title provides reassurance to the transferee that there is no other application that might take priority. The transfer might also be executed in advance and held in escrow pending completion so as to avoid the necessity to simultaneously co-ordinate physical execution and completion. However these adaptations do not eliminate the risks entirely.

Each step in the current process is conditional upon satisfaction of other steps being completed or certain conditions being met so by its very nature conveyancing is sequential. The question arises as to what extent technology might shorten this sequence or even eliminate parts of it entirely. Can parts be done simultaneously or does the process by necessity require certain delays to be built in and one step to be done in advance of another?

The argument may be made that it takes time to resolve the competing interests of the parties and any delay in the process allows the opportunity for this to be done. It may also be argued that consumers need that time to consider what is possibly the most important investment in their lives. However a similar argument cannot be used in respect of investors for whom the property is merely another commodity to be used or traded for profit. Their interest will likely be to complete the transaction in as quick and simple a manner as possible.

Transformation of the process by the elimination of paper and its replacement with instant electronic communication has the potential to impact significantly on risk. One of the gaps in this timeline is the time lag between transfer and registration. This is known as the registration gap and is the first key risk to be examined.

[42] Cooke notes that in England where priority searches are used, the registered title is frozen and a purchaser can proceed with confidence as to the state of the register however overriding interests are not frozen. The danger of them coming into being during the registration gap is a "significant hazard". See Cooke (2003), p. 289.

Conclusion
Having examined the nature of eConveyancing and title registration and identified the risks borne by each participant, it remains to determine how each risk is impacted by the move to eConveyancing, how each party might be protected, is such protection desirable and feasible and if not, what other party should bear the risk. Chapters 6–8 examine these in the context of each risk category.

Chapter 6 looks at two risk categories i.e. the registration gap and the formalities for registration thus examining the situation before registration of the title. The risk arising from the interface of the registration system with those participants who seek registration is examined.

Chapter 7 examines the impact of the register itself. The participant has made a successful application for registration but due to some error in the transaction or by the registering authority their interest is at risk.

Chapter 8 explores the remaining risk categories. These are interests off the register which affect title, the destructive effects of a registered transaction and where interests are not recognised and are not capable of registration. Each demonstrates how third party rights are impacted by the operation of the registration system and the effect of those rights on the other participants.

The concluding chapter, Chap. 9, takes an overarching view of the impact of eConveyancing on risk and determines if there can be risk mitigation. It also makes some recommendations for further research and reform of the conveyancing process in Ireland.

References

Calabresi, G., & Melamed, A. D. (1972). Property rules, liability rules, and inalienability: One view of the cathedral. *Harvard Law Review, 85*(6).

Commons, J. R. (1924–1925). Law and economics. *Yale Law Journal, 34*.

Cooke, E. (2003). E-conveyancing in England: Enthusiasms and reluctance. In D. Grinlinton (Ed.), *Torrens in the twenty-first century*. Wellington: LexisNexis.

Deeney, J. (2014). *Registration of Deeds and Title in Ireland*. Great Britain: Bloomsbury.

Gray, K., & Gray, S. F. (2009). *Elements of land law* (5th ed.). Great Britain: Oxford University Press.

Joint Land Titles Committee. (1990). *Renovating the foundation: Proposals for a model land recording and registration act for the provinces and territories of Canada*. http://www.law.ualberta.ca/alri/docs/Model%20Land%20Recording%20Act.pdf. Accessed 13 June 2014.

Lyall, A. (2010). *Land law in Ireland* (3rd ed.). England: Round Hall.

Manthorpe, J. (2007). *Land registration – A health check*. In Registering the World Conference, Dublin, 26–28 September 2007. http://www.prai.ie/uploadedfiles/conference20071/papers/keynote%281%29.pdf. Accessed 14 May 2014.

Miceli, T. J., Munneke, H. J., Sirmans, C. F., & Turnbull, G. K. (2002). Title systems and land values. *Journal of Law and Economics, 45*.

Murphy, S. (2013). *An examination of eConveyancing: A comparison of the treatment of overriding interests in the context of eConveyancing: Ireland with England and Wales* (Master of Law thesis). National University of Ireland, Galway.
O'Connor, P. (2003). Registration of title in England and Australia: A theoretical and comparative analysis. In E. Cooke (Ed.), *Modern studies in property law* (Vol. II). Oxford: Hart.
Paasch, J. (2005). Legal cadastral domain model – An object-oriented approach. *Nordic Journal of Surveying and Real Estate Research, 2*. http://ojs.tsv.fi/index.php/njs/article/viewFile/1679/1526. Accessed 28 Oct 2010.
Schelling, T. C. (2006). *Micromotives and macrobehavior*. New York: Norton and Company Inc.
Stubkjær, E., Frank, A., & Zevenbergen, J. (2007). Modelling real property transactions. In J. Zevenbergen, A. Frank, & E. Stubkjær (Eds.), *Real property transactions: Procedures, transaction costs and models*. Amsterdam: IOS.
Stuckenschmidt, H., Stubkjær, E., & Schlieder, C. (Eds.). (2003). *The ontology and modelling of real estate transactions*. England: Ashgate.
Tiainen, E. (2004). *Directions in modeling land registration and cadastre domain – Aspects of EULIS glossary approach, semantics and information services*. In FIG Conference on Standardization in the Cadastral Domain. http://www.fig.net/commission7/bamberg_2004/papers/ts_03_01_tiainen.pdf. Accessed 13 June 2014.
Twining, W. (1972–1973). The bad man revisited. *Cornell Law Review, 58*.
Wylie, J. C. W., & Woods, U. (2005). *Irish Conveyancing Law* (3rd ed.). Great Britain: Tottel.
Zevenbergen, J. (1998). *The interrelated influence of the technical, legal and organisational aspects on the functioning of land registrations (cadastres)*. In International Federation of Surveyors (FIG) Proceedings of XXI International Congress Commission, 7, Brighton. http://www.oicrf.org/document.asp?ID=2995. Accessed 23 June 2014.
Zevenbergen, J. (2006). Trustworthiness of land records – The basis of land administration systems. *GIS Asia Pacific, 10*(6). http://www.geospatialworld.net/uploads/magazine/925d04_apJune2006.pdf. Accessed 13 June 2014.
Zevenbergen, J., et al. (Eds.). (2007). *Real property transactions: Procedures, transaction costs and models*. Amsterdam: IOS.

Chapter 6
Before Registration

6.1 Introduction

This chapter examines two risk categories; the registration gap and the formalities for registration. Thus it explores risk arising before registration of the transfer of Greenacre and Whiteacre. The risk to those participants who seek registration on foot of the idealised transactions is considered. These participants are the transferee B, donee Y and acquisition lender C.

6.2 Registration Gap

The registration gap is the time lag between transfer and registration. It is the "hiatus between the date of the making of the disposition and the date of its registration".[1] Registration could occur some considerable time after the disposition. This gap poses a risk to those who buy registered land or who wish to acquire some right or interest over the land.[2]

This time gap between transfer and registration is seen as a presenting a period of risk for the transferee and acquisition lender. The transferee has parted with the full purchase monies, part or all of which will comprise the monies advanced by the acquisition lender, but neither will yet have the protection of registration. Thus the interests of B and C are at risk.

Y's interest is also at risk but since he has not paid any monies and is a volunteer, his loss is of a different nature. Y's exposure is as great as B's in that both are in danger of losing the entire value of the property. However, Y's risk is not of loss, but of no gain. He may lose an enrichment but will not be impoverished in the same

[1] Harpum (2004), p. 6.

[2] Harpum (2004), p. 6.

G. Brennan, *The Impact of eConveyancing on Title Registration*,
DOI 10.1007/978-3-319-10341-9_6

way that B and C might. Both B and C are at risk of suffering a monetary loss. B is further exposed in that he may have given up the right to occupy elsewhere but still may not have the use value of Greenacre. Thus the nature of each idealised participant's exposure to risk during the registration gap is different.

However there is not the same level of risk exposure during the entire period. In Ireland there is less risk after the application for registration is lodged. Provided such an application is successful registration will be backdated to the date of lodgement and priority will arise from that date. Anyone dealing with the title after the application is lodged but before the registering authority staff process the application will be on notice as a pending dealing will be noted on the folio. However if the application is not successful and is rejected then the registration gap is extended as priority will be lost. Any subsequently pending applications will be processed and priority will be lost until a successful application is lodged.

Presuming any application for registration is successful the exposure to risk really arises during the period between completion of the transaction and lodgement of the application for registration. C has released the loan funds, B has paid over the purchase monies but there is the danger of another interest getting registered in advance of theirs. The gap between contract and completion does not present the same exposure to risk as no funds have been released to A.[3]

The risk period is extended if registration is denied due to some fault or error in the transaction or the registering authority mistakenly rejects the application. Presuming that the application is a successful application for registration the risk arises if some event occurs after completion and before the application for registration. The vulnerability to that risk is a product of the conveyancing process.

So the risk period may be divided into two. The gap between completion and the application for registration. This is not produced by the registration system but instead is a feature of the conveyancing process and will be compounded if there is some neglect by the lawyer and hence delay in applying for registration. The second period arises between the application for registration and actual completion of registration and this is a feature of the registration process.

A priority period mechanism could reduce the likelihood of an intervening event having a detrimental effect on the transaction but this would similarly be dependent on the subsequent application for registration being successful. If for any reason the application for registration was rejected priority would be lost.

In some jurisdictions the registration gap is a limited problem because it is standard practice to have a priority period whereby no other registration is allowed. The transfer receives priority once it is registered within the appropriate time period. This is the practice in England and Wales where there is a system of priority

[3] The contract deposit is held pending completion.

searches[4] and outline applications[5] however Harpum has expressed the view that these measures are "contrived and imperfect...also bureaucratic and add to the costs of conveyancing".[6]

In Ireland a priority search[7] has the added advantage that when the registrar issues the search he puts an inhibition on the folio.[8] This inhibits all dealings for a period of 44 days,[9] save the dealing by the party on whose behalf the search was made. Nothing can be registered after the search until registration of the transaction. After the 44 days a further priority search may be applied for however, this does not continue the previous period. This search is available to someone who has contracted to buy the property or the lender who has lent money for the purchase.

In Ireland the paper application must be submitted within 44 days of completing the eForm 17 (the electronic application form) and on average the application is received within 10 days.[10] The average time between the paper application being lodged and registration of a full transfer of title where no queries arise is 10 days.[11] Thus the time between the electronic application and lodgment for registration is generally 10 days however it is impossible to determine the general time period between completion of the transaction and registration. The eForm 17 may not be completed until some considerable time after completion of the transaction. The longer the time lag the greater the risk that some other intervening interest will gain priority. This situation leaves B, Y and C open to risk.

As a result of the eDischarge system the registration gap has shortened somewhat but where the lender is not part of this system or the property needs to be mapped, the registration gap in Ireland can extend into months or even years. There is no requirement to register within a certain time limit.[12]

The risks for B, Y and C are that a prior encumbrance on the title has not been cleared or due to the delay in registration some other intervening interest is

---

[4] Cooke notes that where priority searches are used, the registered title is frozen and a purchaser can proceed with confidence as to the state of the register however overriding interests are not frozen and the danger of them coming into being during the registration gap is a "significant hazard". See Cooke (2003), p. 289.

[5] Harpum (2004), p. 6.

[6] Harpum (2004), p. 6.

[7] Section 108 of the 1964 Act, as substituted by section 66 of the 2006 Act, provides for priority searches.

[8] This inhibition is called a priority entry.

[9] The period was previously 21 days but this was deemed to be too short. It was extended to 44 days by the Land Registration Rules 2012 (SI 483/2012). These rules also allow the application to be made by electronic means and the intention of the Land Registry is to introduce an electronic priority entry facility, as part of eRegistration, in the latter half of 2014.

[10] Interview with Greg McDermott ICT Manager Property Registration Authority 1 March 2012.

[11] Interview with Greg McDermott ICT Manager Property Registration Authority 1 March 2012. Transfers of part take longer to process as these involve mapping changes and the opening of a new folio. First registrations applications where there is a full investigation of the title also take longer.

[12] There is a 6 month time period for first registration but not for subsequent dealings with registered land.

registered. Loan monies have already been released by C but its interest is not yet secured by registration of a charge on the title. If another charge takes priority, the lenders charge cannot be registered as a first legal charge. Similarly if another interest is registered ahead of B and Y's title then it will take priority.

> Title registration relieves the duty of inquiry upon purchasers, in order to reduce transaction costs; the priority rules that apply during the registration gap re-impose the duty. Purchasers must either search for prior interests as if the land were unregistered, or assume the risk of losing priority to an undiscovered prior interest during the registration gap. The loss will not be compensated by the statutory indemnity scheme, unless it arises from a registry error or omission such as an error in a search certificate.[13]

The reason for this danger period is as a result of the nature of the right held by B, Y or C during the gap. It is not a registered right and thus must compete with other unregistered rights for priority. Wylie expresses the view that the purchaser has an equity to be registered as owner and has an unregistered right to the land valid against his vendor and all other persons except a registered transferee for value.[14] This equity will survive against a volunteer but will be defeated by a registered transaction for value.

This is supported by section 68(2) of the 1964 Act which provides that nothing in the Act shall prevent a person from creating any right in or over any registered land or registered charge, but all such rights shall be subject to the provisions of the Act with respect to registered transfers of land or charges for valuable consideration. Similarly section 68(3) provides that an unregistered right in or over registered land, not being a section 72 burden, is not to affect the registered owner of a charge created for valuable consideration.

Thus a transferees right or interest during the registration gap is vulnerable in that it will be defeated if the transferor transfers to another party for value and that second transfer is registered first. The first transferees unregistered right can only be protected by a note on the folio or by a priority period.

In *Coffey v. Brunel Construction Co. Ltd*[15] the defendant registered a *lis pendens* as a burden pursuant to section 69 of the 1964 Act. This occurred after the plaintiffs had purchased the land but before registration of their title. The plaintiffs were registered subject to that burden and obtained an order from the High Court directing the registrar to cancel the burden but the defendant appealed to the Supreme Court. The Court held that the plaintiffs' right arising from the contract and payment of the purchase monies would not survive against the rights of a registered transferee 'but the defendants are not such' or a charge for valuable consideration 'but a *lis pendens* is not such'. O'Higgins C.J. found that section 74 only related to the priority as between registered or unregistered burdens[16] and the plaintiffs' right was not a "burden". The plaintiffs held the entire beneficial

[13] O'Connor (2003), p. 263.

[14] Wylie (1996), p. 369. See p. 370 for supporting case law.

[15] *Coffey v. Brunel Construction Co. Ltd.* [1983] IR 36.

[16] Burdens rank according to the order in which they are entered on the register.

estate in the lands from the time of the contract and the Court ordered that the registration of the *lis pendens* be vacated.

During the registration gap B and C are at risk in the purchase of Greenacre and Y is at risk in the transfer of Whiteacre. They are at risk from:

(a) T: the prior lender whose charge has not been discharged;
(b) U: the third party who wishes to protect their existing right in relation to the land; and
(c) V: the property claimant who is successful in asserting a new right in relation to the land.

6.2.1 Risk from T

Even in the most efficient of conveyancing transactions there will be a slight delay before the prior charge on the title is discharged. This delay can only be avoided if the discharge is done in advance of or at the point of completion.

T will not want to provide a discharge in advance of completion unless it has already been paid the redemption monies in full. This is unlikely to occur as the redemption monies will form part of the purchase monies to be paid on completion. Thus A will not be in a position to redeem the charge until the property has actually been sold.[17]

The other option is that the discharge is done at the point of completion. In order for this to occur three elements are required. Firstly that the redemption monies are paid to T at that point; secondly that T is in a position to immediately discharge the charge and thirdly the discharge is registered immediately.

Immediate Payment of Redemption Monies

In a typical Irish paper conveyancing transaction a bank draft or cheque is handed over on completion and subsequently the transferor's lawyer lodges this with the prior lender in order to clear the prior charge on title. The obligation to lodge these funds and clear the prior charge arises from an undertaking given to the transferee's lawyer on completion. The terms of the contract between the parties will also have provided for an unencumbered title to be furnished on completion though, strictly speaking, this is not possible unless the discharge is done simultaneously or in advance.

Further delay may arise if the transferor is in negative equity and additional monies need to be added to the purchase monies in order to clear the prior charge. Also difficulties may arise in establishing the exact amount required to clear the

[17] There are some instances where a discharge may be provided in advance of completion such as in a scheme of development however these fall outside the scope of this research.

prior charge and a discharge will prove impossible until the exact amount is confirmed and paid in full.

During this time period the acquisition lender C is at risk. Completion has taken place and the purchase monies have been released by the transferee's lawyer to the transferor's lawyer in order to purchase the property. Despite advancing the loan funds, and those funds passing out of C's control, C does not have a legal charge on the title and will not have a first legal charge until the prior charge is discharged in full and its charge is registered.

B and Y are also at risk as they will not obtain unencumbered title until any prior loan secured on the property is discharged. In particular B has paid over the purchase monies in order to purchase Greenacre but Greenacre remains subject to T's charge. B has completed the purchase on foot of loan funds from C subject to the requirement that C's charge be registered on the title as a first legal charge. While A's (the transferor's) charge, held by T, remains on the title, B is unable to comply with this requirement.

As a volunteer Y does not have a lender's requirements to satisfy but Y would find it very difficult to sell the property or to raise finance on it while the prior charge remains on the title.

Provided the monies owned to T on foot of its charge have been paid in full, A and X will have an equity of redemption.[18] A and X would be in a position to call for T to release the charge. However, if there is any dispute about the amount owed or the redemption figure furnished for completion was incorrect, then it may take some time for the discharge. Meanwhile T's charge will remain registered against the title.

The delay may provide the opportunity for some event to occur which prevents the prior charge from being discharged. For example the prior charge might provide cross security for monies advanced on other properties and the lender may refuse to release the prior charge until those monies are repaid. The bank draft or cheque may be lost or stolen or the funds may be misappropriated. If there are monies outstanding which A and X refuse to pay then B and Y may be liable to dispossession and sale of the property on the basis of A and X's default.

A dispute about the amount to be repaid to order to obtain a discharge can be avoided by obtaining accurate unequivocal redemption figures from the prior lender. However, it is more difficult to avoid the risk of negligence, theft or fraud.

In Ontario the usual practice is for the transferor's lawyer to give the transferee's lawyer a statement of the amount owning on the mortgage as issued by the prior lender, together with a direction by the transferor to his lawyer to pay that amount directly to the prior lender and an undertaking by the transferor's lawyer to obtain and register the discharge.[19] The Irish practice is also to rely on an undertaking by the transferor's lawyer.

---

[18] Under section 121 of the Irish Consumer Credit Act 1995. This relates to housing loans which are acquisition loans or the refinancing of acquisition loans.

[19] Donahue et al. (2003), p. 247.

Thus in both jurisdictions the purchase monies are paid by the transferee's lawyer to the transferor's lawyer and the transferor's lawyer then redeems the charge held by the prior lender. Both rely on the lawyer's undertaking.[20] It would be more straightforward for the redemption monies to be paid directly by the transferee to the prior lender with the balance of the monies paid to the transferor.

This system of undertaking has dangers associated with it[21] including the risk of lawyer fraud. Connolly notes that "elimination of the "*registration gap*" as a fraud prevention tool in today's climate has to be seriously considered."[22]

The use of EFT has the potential to move the money faster and thus reduce part of the gap. This means the money can transfer in hours or minutes rather than days. Also an eConveyancing system provides the potential for the prior charge to be paid off at the time of completion. In Ireland at the moment cheques and bank drafts are typically taking 3–5 days to clear. EFT generally takes up to 24 h. Contrast this with Ontario were the money can be transferred in a matter of minutes.

Ensuring that the money moves quicker will however only go some way towards eliminating this risk. Paying the amount due on foot of the prior charge allows the discharge to occur however a formal discharge must also take place and then this must be registered with the registering authority.

Immediate Discharge of the Prior Charge

Once T has received the redemption monies it must be in a position to immediately discharge the prior charge. In Ireland some moves have been made towards this position with the launch of the eDischarge facility. Prior to the launch of this facility a formal paper discharge could take 6–12 months to issue due to inefficiencies in the lender's process. The eDischarge facility now allows a lender to confirm the discharge of a charge directly with the registering authority via an electronic message. Both the discharge and the registration of same are taking place within 1 month.

In the Ontario e-reg system registration of the discharge occurs as part of the same application for registration of the transfer and new charge.

[20] According to Law Society of Ireland (2013) an undertaking is any unequivocal declaration of intention addressed to someone who reasonably places reliance on it which is made by a solicitor in the course of his practice, either personally or by a member of the solicitor's staff, whereby the solicitor, or in the case of a member of his staff, his employer, becomes personally bound. See paragraph 6.5.

[21] Donahue et al. (2003) p. 253.

[22] Connolly (2007), p. 24.

Simultaneous Registration of Discharge

Once the redemption monies are paid and the discharge issued then the discharge must be registered with the registering authority. If all of these steps can occur during completion then there is no risk of a prior charge remaining on title. B and Y take unencumbered title and C can register a first legal charge.

As noted already the eDischarge facility has considerably shortened the time period between completion and registration of the discharge of the prior charge however this time lacuna has not been eliminated entirely. Thus there remains a risk to B, Y and C.

In both Ireland and Ontario staff in the registration authority must sign off on the discharge and thus the registration is not simultaneous. However in the absence of any problem with the application, registration of the discharge will be back dated to the date of application.

Until the discharge is registered the new charge cannot be registered as a first legal charge leaving C exposed and both B and Y are exposed as they own a property encumbered with a prior charge. Unless any prior charge on title can be discharged in advance of, or simultaneously with completion of the sale, B, C and Y remain exposed to risk.

A similar risk arises in relation to other prior encumbrances on the title register. This might include a judgment mortgage that has not been paid. A wise transferee will require that any such encumbrances are cleared from the title in advance of completion so as to avoid the risk of their title being burdened.

In addition to interests on the register there may be others off the register that create a risk during the registration gap. These overriding interests are dealt with separately in Chap. 8.

Apart from these overriding interests there may be other interests that are not on the title register but which make their way on to the register during the registration gap. These interests are often called minor interests and they need to be registered to be binding. This risk will arise from U the third party or V the property claimant. During the registration gap an intervening interest held by U or V may be registered and thus gain priority over the transaction.

6.2.2 Risk from U

During the registration gap there is a danger that some third party may act to protect their existing right in relation to the land. An example would be someone with an option to purchase or holding a contract for the same land.

This right will pose a risk to B and C in the purchase of Greenacre. If the right was not disclosed by A and should have been under the terms of the contract, B may have a case for breach of contract, misrepresentation, deceit or breach of covenant of title.[23] B may be able to rely on a number of different remedies such as rescission, restitution or damages. If B was successful in applying to the Court for an order of rescission the parties would be restored to their original position before the contract was entered into. B would be entitled to recover not only the deposit with interest but also any legal expenses incurred in investigating title. This remedy is not available post completion.

The risk is that the interest held by U would be registered in advance of B and C's interest during the registration gap. The longer the gap the higher the likelihood that U will register its right thus increasing the level of risk for B and C. If this occurs B and C will lose priority to U. Thus B and C will be keen to have their interests registered as soon as possible.

If U succeeds in having his interest registered first the title of B will be subject to such a right though, as already noted, B may have a remedy against A if the right should have been disclosed and was not.

The registration gap will also increase the level of risk for C as the quality of its security may be compromised. The value of the property may have decreased though this will only have an impact if C is required to repossess and sell the property. In Ireland the borrower B remains liable for the balance of the loan funds even if the property sells for less than the amount due and thus in the long term C may recover the shortfall anyway. Ideally C would recover all the loan funds plus interest and penalties on a sale of the property but this is subject to market conditions.

If the quality of C's security is compromised C may have a remedy against B on the basis that the right should have been discovered and disclosed by B or B's lawyer during the transaction.[24] The chances of such an action being successful will be strengthened if B or B's lawyer did not carry out the appropriate enquires during the transaction and as a result of this lack of enquiry U's right remained undiscovered.

Y is also at risk in the gift of Whiteacre. As a volunteer Y will not be in a position to sue unless X gave guarantees that the property was not subject to such a right. As Y is a volunteer and takes subject to all unregistered rights to which X held the land he will not be concerned about prior unregistered rights. He takes subject to any such right held by U regardless of whether or not his title is registered. Y will, however, be concerned with new rights coming into existence during the registration gap. If this gap is reduced there is less opportunity for this new right to be registered in advance of Y.

Any rights on the register would have come to light during the transaction so, subject to any error of the registry in executing searches, the risk from U only arises in relation to rights not already on the register. The registration gap has no effect on

[23] Note that these risks to A are excluded from the remit of this research.

[24] In a residential conveyancing transaction B's lawyer will have certified title to the lender. Any qualifications on title need to be disclosed to the lender in advance.

overriding interests as they will bind both transferor and transferee regardless of when the transfer is registered.

6.2.3 Risk from V

During the registration gap there is the possibility of a new right being asserted in relation to the land. As this is a new right that has matured since completion B will likely have no remedy against A and C may not have a remedy against B. This is subject to the right not having been granted by A or B.

This new right may be capable of protection by registration or by occupation or some other factor and this protection may be secured during the registration gap. V then becomes U a successful property claimant who is now the third party in the schematic. For example V may have been successful in asserting a personal right which the court finds is a property right during this period. Alternatively V may have a right that becomes overriding through occupation. If the occupation is post-completion but pre-registration then the registration gap could allow a new overriding interest to come into existence. This will be examined further in Chap. 8.

6.2.4 Removal of the Registration Gap

Is it possible to remove the registration gap entirely? Surely one element has to occur first. The possible combinations for sequencing in a paper environment are listed in Table 6.1.

Completion encompasses closing of the transaction with the redemption of T's charge, discharge of that charge and registration of the discharge. This must take place prior to the registration of the transaction from A to B and X to Y. Where there is no prior charge on the title then the registration gap can automatically be reduced as there is no necessity to wait for registration of the discharge. B and Y can immediately apply to be registered as owner.

Sequences B, E and F do not occur because passing of the title by completion has to occur before registration of the fact. The registration reflects the fact that completion has already taken place. These two steps could however be amalgamated whereby registration is completion. This is difficult to achieve where staff in the registering authority are required to sign off on the application before registration occurs.

There is also a difficulty with sequence D as the formalities for registration often require that the money will already have changed hands i.e. the transfer will acknowledge that the purchase monies have been paid. C also presents a difficulty in that completion cannot be said to have occurred without the passing of the purchase monies.

Table 6.1 Sequencing for completion

	A	B	C	D	E	F
1	Money	Money	Completion	Completion	Registration	Registration
2	Completion	Registration	Money	Registration	Completion	Money
3	Registration	Completion	Registration	Money	Money	Completion

Thus most, if not all, jurisdictions including Ireland adopt sequence A. The money generally changes hands at the same time as completion. It may also be paid by B's lawyer to A's lawyer in advance on the understanding that it is held in trust until completion. Completion then takes place followed by subsequent registration of B's title and C's charge.

In Ontario the purchase monies are paid but are held in escrow pending completion and registration. In effect the money is paid, completion occurs and then registration. So sequence A has not changed in this electronic environment.

Lawyers often separate in time and space the physical and financial actions associated with completion from the legal act of completion. By the use of escrow and the holding of monies or documents on trust lawyers can co-ordinate the legal act of completion so that the intent of the transaction is fulfilled at the right time. Thus the legal act of completion is centred more on the status of the transaction than on actual physical events that need to occur.

It would be almost impossible to design an eConveyancing system whereby the money, completion and registration all occur simultaneously unless completion became the fact of registration and at the same time as registration occurs the money passes.[25] Unless the final sign off by the registering authority staff is removed there will always remain at least a small registration gap in the conveyancing process. This is one reason why some jurisdictions have chosen to make their systems both automated and automatic.

6.2.5 *Effect of eConveyancing*

The expectation is that eConveyancing will lead to a reduction of or perhaps even removal of the registration gap. "Completion and registration will be completed electronically, the main advantage here will be the removal of the '*registration gap*' between completion and entry on the Register of the new owner, therefore minimising the risk of conflicting or illegal rights".[26]

This abolition of the registration gap would involve changes to the register taking place at the same time as electronic completion of the transaction. In effect

[25] See the charts in the Law Society of Ireland (2008).

[26] Connolly (2007), p. 52.

this would be "completion by registration".[27] In an electronic system "the making of a disposition and its registration, although in theory different acts, can in fact occur simultaneously."[28] "The threefold process of execution, lodgement and registration of deeds would be replaced by a single act of "execution electronically by registration"."[29] This is entirely feasible in an electronic conveyancing system.

If the registration gap is removed in its entirety then completion will be simultaneous with registration.[30] The power to transfer could be removed from the land owner and given to the registrar so that only the registrar can alter title. This is already feasible given that the physical act of execution may be separate from the legal act of completion.

This would necessitate changes in Irish conveyancing practice particularly as the discharge of the prior charge would need to be ready for registration at completion and not done subsequently.

Title to Greenacre would pass from A to B and the change of ownership would be registered at the same time. T's prior charge would be paid and discharged and registration of the discharge would occur also at the same time allowing C's charge to be registered on B's title.

In the transfer of Whiteacre title would pass from X to Y. Any prior encumbrance would also be discharged and registration of that discharge would occur simultaneously.

In this scenario there would be no risk of a prior encumbrance on the title not being cleared and left on the title after completion. There would be no risk from T the prior lender. B and Y would obtain an unencumbered title and C's charge would be registered simultaneous with the release of the loan funds.

Removal of the registration gap also has an impact on the other risks identified. If U, the third party or V, if a successful property claimant, have their right registered before the registration of B then they gain priority as first registered prevails. This would not be possible if there is no registration gap. As a volunteer, Y is subject to U and V's right regardless of registration. If, however, V's claim is not successful then his property claim will fail and there is no risk to B, C or Y.

In *ACC Bank plc v. Johnston*[31] Mr. Johnston was acting as solicitor for ACC Bank. He released monies to the borrower's solicitor on foot of an undertaking given to him to the effect that the monies would be applied in the purchase of specific properties and ACC Bank would have a first legal charge over the lands. It turned out that the borrower never owned the lands in question and thus the loan could not be secured by a first legal charge. The undertaking could not be honoured. Clark J. noted that if:

[27] Kelway (2004), p. 8.

[28] Harpum (2000), p. 6. See also Howell (2006), p. 553.

[29] Greed (1998), p. 1670.

[30] Harpum (2000), pp. 6–7.

[31] *ACC Bank plc v. Johnston* [2010] IEHC 236.

> conveyancing transactions could be executed and filed electronically (so as to have immediate effect), then there is no reason in principle why all relevant conveyancing and financial transactions could not be executed as part of a single integrated programme. By such a programme any existing mortgage could be released, the property could be transferred from the vendor to the purchaser, any appropriate mortgage in favour of a lending institution to the purchaser could be put in place, and all necessary financial transactions associated with each of those aspects of the overall transaction could be executed. The risks inherent in the existing system, which this case has brought into relief, could also be removed by such a process....then a fail safe method of conducting conveyancing transactions where all elements of the transaction would take place simultaneously without, indeed, the need for any of the parties to be in same place at the same time, could be put in place.[32]

A contrary view is offered by Butt who asks if it is really that important to get rid of this registration gap.

> Are house buyers really attacking the gates of the Land Registry and demanding that the registration gap be abolished? Do any of them actually know or care anything about it? Surely, the most important thing must be to speed up the part of the conveyancing process leading up to the client being able to move into his new home....What happens after that has never been of any concern to the client.[33]

This is because they assume the process is secure in their lack of knowledge of it. However, if there is a problem with registration or some other intervening interest is registered then it does become a major concern for the client. Perhaps they may wish to sell on the following day or to raise additional finance using the property as collateral and this is not feasible because of some event occurring during the gap. Just because land owners are not aware of these risks does not mean they do not exist and, if the opportunity arises to eliminate them, is it not incumbent on other more knowledgeable stakeholders to assess the merits of such a reduction in risk?

6.2.6 *Impact on Risk*

Thus removal or shortening of the registration gap does have an impact on risk. Aligning payment of the purchase monies, completion and registration has the potential to provide for:

(a) simultaneous discharge of the prior charge—risk from T to B, Y and C is removed; and
(b) no delay in registration and thus no other intervening interest can be registered—risk from U and V to B, Y and C is removed.

[32] *ACC Bank plc v. Johnston* [2010] IEHC 236.
[33] Butt (2006), p. 64.

However the question arises as to whether this is feasible even in an electronic environment particularly when the registering authority is required to sign off on the registration.[34] Even in Ontario the registration gap remains.

In Ontario if the land registrar decides that a proposed registration is in any way deficient he or she has 21 days to notify the lawyer that the application will be rejected unless the deficiency is corrected.[35] The registrar can allow a period of time between seven and 30 days for the problem to be corrected and if the request is not satisfied within that time frame then the application is rejected and priority is lost.[36] If the matter is resolved within the time frame allowed then the registration will be completed. The application will be deemed to have been registered on the day that the registrar received it and in the order that the registrar entered it into the register.[37]

Clancy expresses the view that "[e]ssentially, if the purchaser can rely absolutely on the information contained in the register and can trust the solicitor and the registration process, then there is no concern about a registration delay."[38] Unfortunately none of these absolutes apply. The reality is much different.

In both jurisdictions the register is subject to some other right getting registered in the registration gap and this right may not have been disclosed by the vendor, if indeed it was known by him. If priority has not already been secured via a priority period then there is the possibility of some other right gaining priority during the delay. Even if a priority period is secured this is dependent on the application for registration being successful. If for some reason the application is rejected then the priority is lost.

There is also the risk from a prior encumbrance on the title that has not been cleared. The example of the prior charge held by T is used above but this could be some other encumbrance on the title. The lawyer may fraudulently appropriate the funds and may not discharge the prior encumbrance in compliance with his or her undertaking.

While it may not be feasible to eliminate the registration gap entirely, particularly where the role of the registering authority is to be maintained, there is considerable scope for its reduction in Ireland and this will lead to a lowering of risk for B, C and Y. The extent of this decrease in risk will depend on how much the gap can be reduced.

The impact of this lowering of risk for B, C and Y is that there may be increased risk for U and V. U and V will have less or no time to get their interest registered or protected by a note on the title register before the transaction takes effect. Thus the

[34] In England the view has been taken that the registry must share its functions in order for the registration gap to be eliminated. This argument was being used as the rationale for implementing an automated and automatic eConveyancing system. See O'Connor (2003), p. 272.

[35] Moore and Globe (2003), pp. 142–143.

[36] Section 78(2) Land Titles Act.

[37] Section 78(5) Land Titles Act.

[38] Clancy (2007), p. 12.

possibility is that the B and C will take free from their interest. B will take free of this interest as a *bona fide* purchaser for value. C who holds a charge on B's title will also hold free of this interest.

Increasing the protection offered to those with what are perceived to be more valid and valuable rights in land (in this case B and C) at the expense of U and V may be seen as desirable and feasible in an eConveyancing environment.[39] B and C are market participants who rely on the register. Increasing the security of their rights will enhance the fluid operation of the land market and increase the potential for investment and income generation. By contrast U and V rely not on the register but on some other factor such as occupation or the status of their interest as an overriding interest.

Even if the registration gap is removed or shortened an applicant for registration will still need to comply with certain formalities for registration. This is the second risk category pertaining to pre-registration. B will seek to have his title to Greenacre registered subject to C's charge and Y will seek to have his title to Whiteacre registered. All must comply with the formalities for registration.

6.3 Formalities for Registration

B, Y and C are at risk if some other event or formality is required before registration can take place. In a paper environment these risks might arise from a failure to properly execute the deed or charge or the wrong form being used. The defect may prevent registration taking place.

Harpum notes that in England a high degree of formality is required to create proprietary rights.[40] The formalities required for contracts and deeds relating to land are strict and this is the position in all jurisdictions.[41] Traditionally the purchase of a family home was seen as the most expensive purchase a consumer would make in their lifetime and thus, in order to protect this person, who was seen to have little business acumen, a high degree of formality was required. This formality also prevented a person from inadvertently parting with their interest in property or creating new rights when they might not have intended to do so.

The formalities relate not just to the type of document that must be used but also the format of that document and the execution thereof. In Ireland traditionally deeds were handwritten on indented parchment or deed paper, signed and sealed with two witnesses to each signature. With the advent of the typewriter, and then computers, they could be typed on ordinary paper and the requirement for a seal was removed. With the move to registered land the form was set by the registering authority,

---

[39] See Sect. 9.4 for a more detailed analysis.

[40] Harpum (2000), p. 14.

[41] See Critchley (1998).

rather than by tradition, but signing and witnessing with wet signatures is still required.

Thus the type of document and its format has changed significantly over the years. Registration of title required standard documents in a standard format and this was backed by the statutory powers of the registering authority. The execution had also changed in that sealing would no longer be required. Thus there has been a continual change in the formalities for registration and eConveyancing has become part of this continuum.

Any failure to comply with the formalities may create risk in that registration may be denied. This will adversely affect B, Y and C. This failure to register may lead to a loss of priority.

6.3.1 Risk in a Paper Environment

In a paper conveyancing environment there may be

(a) a valid deed, transfer or charge and registration is successful
(b) a valid deed, transfer or charge but registration is rejected
(c) an invalid deed, transfer or charge but registration is successful
(d) an invalid deed, transfer or charge and registration is rejected

If the registrar mistakenly rejects an application for registration of a valid deed, transfer or charge, as per (b) above, then this is a registry error. The parties could re-apply for registration or could seek rectification and compensation under the provisions outlined in Chap. 7. This mistake by the registry would extend the registration gap and thus B, C and Y would be at risk for a longer period of an intervening interest being registered first and gaining priority. As there was a valid deed, transfer or charge there has been no failure to comply with the formalities for registration and, provided there is no error by the registry, registration should be successful as per (a) above.

Where there is an invalid deed, transfer or charge there is a failure to comply with the required formalities.[42] If registration is successful, as per (c), this failure might never come to light. If registration is rejected on the basis of the failure, as per (d), the parties will need to resolve the difficulty before re-lodging the application for registration. Meanwhile the registration gap is extended.

B may need to take an action against A to resolve the failure and similarly Y may need to take an action against X. C would need to take action against B who granted the charge. Such an action may be an *in personam* claim or on the basis of a breach of the covenants of title. Alternatively as the sale of Greenacre is for value B would be able to enforce the terms of the contract.

---

[42] See Battersby (1998).

If registration had been successful and a subsequent sale to D had taken place B and Y would no longer be at risk as they would have received the purchase monies for their interest in the land and C's charge would have been redeemed.

6.3.2 Changes in Formalities

In Ontario the requirement for a witness on a document was eliminated and most affidavits were replaced with law statements.[43] In 1994 Part III of the LRRA was introduced which provided for the electronic registration of electronic documents,[44] known as e-reg. Section 22 provided that the electronic document will prevail over any written document. Section 21 removed the requirement that a document be in writing and signed and thus paved the way for electronic documents. Section 23 gave authority for the direct electronic transmission of electronic documents to the title register database by authorised persons.[45] These parties are applicants in the neutral terminology as they do not alter the title register. In Ontario, as in Ireland, only the registering authority can make a change to the title register though such a change may be ordered by the Court.

The LRRA also introduced the concept of standardised forms known as POLARIS forms. Implied covenants for transfers and charges and standard charge terms were introduced. Lenders must file Charge Terms documents with the registering authority and these terms are then incorporated by reference into the standard forms. Copies of the Charge Terms are made available and a book of each year's Standard Charge Terms is published.[46] This has meant a reduction in the amount of paper stored in the registering authority and paper in the conveyancing process. These initiatives "helped streamline the document registration process by imposing consistency and simplifying the form and content of the documents that were registered in the land registration system...[and] laid the groundwork for automation and electronic registration."[47]

Similar moves towards standardisation are occurring in Ireland. The 2009 Act amended section 51(2) of the 1964 Act by deleting 'or in such other form as may appear to the Authority to be sufficient to convey the land'.[48] The discretion that could be exercised by the registering authority was removed and now it can only accept transfers of registered land in the prescribed form. More recently the Land

[43] Murray (2004), p. 3.

[44] The format could be an electronic copy, image or reproduction of a written document. See definitions in section 17 of the LRRA.

[45] Section 17 of the LRRA calls these people electronic document submitters.

[46] Murray (2004), p. 3.

[47] Murray (2004), p. 2.

[48] Schedule 1 and section 8. A similar change was made in respect of charges on registered land.

Registration Rules 2011[49] set out prescribed forms of charge that must be used from the 1 March 2012.

Section 64 of the 2009 Act removed the sealing requirement and provided that execution by an individual by signing and having their signature witnessed would be sufficient. However by virtue of section 10(1) of the Electronic Commerce Act 2000[50] deeds or transfers relating to real property cannot be in electronic form or signed electronically and this would need to be amended before the implementation of eConveyancing.[51]

Generally in an eConveyancing system the required formalities are translated into business rules that need to be complied with. These business rules are reflected in the data that needs to be put into the system. There is a common view that the electronic system will reduce the possibility for errors as the electronic system will prevent certain types of mistakes. Treacy and O'Sullivan note that "because of in-built system prompts and automatic calculation of registration fees, use of the on-line form completion is leading to a significantly lower incidence of errors in the documentation presented for registration."[52] These prompts ensure compliance with pro-forma requirements however other errors would not be picked up by the system, for example if the wrong form was used.

The system may ensure that the data input meets certain criteria and there is the possibility for data fields to be checked against the title register before the application is submitted. The data may be incorrect or the user may not have authority so there is the possibility of the formalities for registration also not being complied with in an electronic system. Rigid adherence to pro-forma requirements may also generate other types of errors as the system may be too rigid to accommodate all types of variation in transactions and may not reflect the actual agreement between the land owners.

The use of an electronic platform does drive a need for conformity not just of the required documentation but also of processes. It requires that transactions occur in a prescribed way. Thus while there may be errors these may be of a limited variety.

Simplified forms may speed up registration by reducing the amount of material that registering authority staff need to review in an application for registration. In Ontario the forms were designed in conjunction with the automated system and in a manner to compliment the screen design and automated workflow.[53] This required a reduction in the amount of information abstracted on to the register and resulted in "increased productivity because of the standardized form and workflows and improved data integrity with the simplified abstract entries."[54]

---

[49] SI 559/2011. These rules have now been replaced by a consolidated set of rules i.e. the Land Registration Rules 2012 (SI 483/2012).

[50] No 27 of 2000.

[51] Oddly the section excludes contracts which can be electronic and signed electronically.

[52] Treacy and O'Sullivan (2004), p. 8.

[53] Murray (2004), p. 3.

[54] Murray (2004), p. 3.

The question arises though as to what, if anything, might be lost as a result of this standardisation and reduction in information on the title register. Is the lack of flexibility creating invisible information leading to a consequential risk that will only come to light at a later date? Harpum points out that in "an ideal world, each and every formal requirement would be subjected to a detailed analysis to determine its precise functions."[55] This would likely reveal which formalities need to be retained and which can be removed from the process.

The function of such formalities is to provide certainty and create a symbolic representation of the important legal act taking place so the parties to that act will think carefully before undertaking the act. In this way the parties will subsequently find it difficult to claim that they did not understand the importance of the act and the consequence flowing from it. Youdan classifies the functions of formality provisions as ensuring intention, standardisation and evidence.[56] Coughlan tracks some of the changes in formalities that have occurred in Ireland while noting that there is still a tendency towards a degree of formality which seems somewhat outmoded.[57]

eConveyancing necessitates changes to the formalities required for the creation and execution of deeds. It also requires change to be made to the common law concept of 'delivery' of a deed, electronic signatures and authentication of the electronic signature through certification.[58] Statutory authority is given to the pressing of a computer key "setting off a digital reaction.... The pen succumbs to the statutory sword."[59]

Much of the change has centered around giving electronic documents validation over paper documents and changes to execution requirements so that a wet signature is no longer required. In eConveyancing an electronic document must be given the same as or preferential status to a paper document. Esigning without sealing must be facilitated. The format will be more tightly prescribed so there is less scope for inclusion of special clauses. Paper will be removed and this will mean the elimination of interests that depended on deposit of the title deeds.[60]

The lawyer may need authority to sign on behalf of the client if the type of electronic signature required is beyond the reach of clients. Supporting transactional documentation and the client authority may still exist off the register. These will be required to overcome any later difficulty with providing evidential proof of what the client authorised the lawyer to do on his or her behalf. This necessity to retain paper on the lawyers file appears to defeat one of the overall tenets of

---

[55] Harpum (2000), p. 9.

[56] Youdan (1984), pp. 314–315. See Ipp and Siopis (1989), pp. 301–317 for an examination of conflicting formal requirements. See also Dixon (2000), pp. 453–455 for the interaction between formalities and estoppel.

[57] Coughlan (1998), p. 80.

[58] Harpum (2004), p. 9.

[59] Flaws (2003), p. 397.

[60] See Sect. 8.5.3.

eConveyancing which is dematerialisation. However this can be overcome by developing digital signature solutions for land owners.

The potential conflict between paper evidence and electronic evidence of title and the fear that land owners might prefer the paper document to the electronic record probably encourages the move towards abolition of paper. As Kelway states "[i]f we are to move to a fully electronic service there cannot be a paper-based end product."[61] Lenders have generally welcomed this as the storage of paper records has become an expensive waste of space.[62] The retention of some paper may however be a necessity until all clients have an electronic signature that is robust enough to be used in the system.

While dematerialisation is an important tenet of eConveyancing it is really the knock on effect that is of interest. There may be savings in the registering authority due to efficiency of staff time, a reduction in data input, lowering of cost of paper storage and archiving and less investigation of title required as there is no need to review bundles of paper deeds. The same savings will occur in the lawyer's office. There may thus be a reduction in costs that can be passed on to the land owner.

In Ontario each electronic document statement confirms that the person signing has the authority to sign on behalf of the owner. The electronic signature is attached by the lawyer and not the land owner. These new requirements have shifted authority and compliance to the lawyer. This would suggest that it is easier for a transaction to be done without a land owner's presence, knowledge or consent. Do electronic signatures attached by the lawyer give the land owner a degree of abstraction or disassociation from the transaction and if so, what impact does this have? Is a land owner, be they transferor or transferee, more likely to repudiate the transaction as a result?

These enquiries could be seen in the context of risks that arise in all computer systems as they are not particular to eConveyancing. However, as the degree of formality associated with a paper conveyancing system is so high any perceived lowering or diluting of these formalities is generally greeted with horror. The question arises as to whether this is attitude is justified.

Clearly it would be preferable for a land owner to have the electronic signature as it is their transaction. It would also be preferable for them to make all statements about the title however these requirements may need to be traded for the other benefits that can accrue from eConveyancing.

Given that standardisation is a key requirement it is likely that the formalities will be streamlined and regardless of whether the system is paper or electronic there may be a breach of formalities. If such formalities are more clear and streamlined a breach may be less rather than more likely to occur.

[61] Kelway (2004), p. 3.

[62] Kelway (2004), p. 3.

6.3.3 *Risk in an eConveyancing Environment*

In an eConveyancing environment if the transfer or charge and registration is a simultaneous act a failure, of any type, is a complete failure. In Howell's view either a disposition is registered and takes full effect, or it is not and has no effect at all.[63] This means that under eConveyancing there can be no failure in formality as a transfer will either be registered or not.[64]

The schematic would need to be adjusted to indicate that the transfer or charge could not occur independently of its registration. It is the act of registration that is the key rather than the instrument. There may in fact be no instrument but instead registration will be based on the completion of data fields that comply with the information already on the title register, the application of an electronic signature and the click of a computer key to indicate completion of the transaction.

Making completion and registration a simultaneous act is, however, the characteristic of an automatic system where the registrant triggers the change in the title register without intervention by the registering authority. This is not the system adopted in Ontario and Ireland also proposes that the registering authority would retain the final approval of any application for registration.

In Ontario the documents may be returned by the registrar for corrections and the lawyer has 30 days to correct the problem and relodge the document.[65] Thus while the instrument may have been tendered for registration and the transaction completed based on its electronic transmission to the registrar via Teraview, until the instrument is checked, certified and entered on the register, it is not registered and has no effect.[66]

Donahue and his colleagues note that despite the risks

> current practice is to complete purchases and mortgage advances just as one would do under the [unregistered] Registry system and not await the certification of the instrument. This approach is taken in spite of the provisions in s. 78(2), which allows the land registrar to decline the registration of a document within 21 days after it was received where the land registrar decides that the document contains an error, omission or deficiency.[67]

However, even if completion and registration are not to be done simultaneously and the power of the registering authority is to be retained, it should be possible in an eConveyancing environment to reduce the registration gap to such an extent that registration follows completion almost automatically. This should certainly be feasible for straightforward transfers and charges where there is no subdivision.

Retaining a time gap, though however small, means there is always the danger that the formalities may not be complied with and an application for registration

---

[63] Howell (2006), pp. 553–576 in referring to the likely effect of the English Land Registration Act 2002 at p. 574.

[64] Howell (2006), p. 574.

[65] Section 78(2) Land Titles Act.

[66] Section 78(3) and 78(4) Land Titles Act.

[67] Donahue et al. (2003), p. 35.

might be rejected. Thus on the face of it there is no change in risk to B, Y or C through the move to eConveyancing.

If, however, the system requires a right to be registered in order for title to be conferred then a failure to register due to non-compliance with the formalities may have serious adverse consequences. If the move towards eConveyancing involves a transition from title registration to title by registration then the formalities for registration become more important. Standardised forms and workflow may make it easier to comply with the formalities and to meet the business rules but the consequence of non compliance will be more severe. Failure to register will result in the right not being enforceable. The register will not only mirror the title but will be the entire source of title to the property.[68]

Given that Ireland already operates a title by registration system it is possible that the changes in formality brought about by standardisation and dematerialisation will result in a more streamlined, efficient and cost effective conveyancing process. In built system prompts are likely to reduce the risk of a breach of formalities occurring though this may need to be balanced against any rigidity introduced if there is a lack of flexibility in the system.

If the system design is robust it presents the opportunity to build in less risk for B, Y and C. It may make it easier for them to comply with the registering authority requirements. As the formalities are translated into business rules the system may indicate if there is a problem with the data. If data is pre-populated from the title register then there is less possibility of getting the name of the transferor or property identifier wrong. Errors may be identified and resolved in advance of completion so that there is less likelihood of the application for registration being rejected. The system may also show in advance what effect a successful application will have on the title register so the applicant can be sure the application will effectively implement the transaction.

Conclusion

The implementation of eConveyancing is likely to impact on the risk profile of certain participants as a result of changes occurring in the pre-registration period.

eConveyancing in Ireland will not eliminate the registration gap but has the potential to reduce it. The remaining gap may be covered by a priority period. Reducing the registration gap lowers risk for B, Y and C and increases risk for U and V. This is likely to be seen as a desirable outcome and U and V are unlikely to be protected against this change.

(continued)

[68] Murphy (2013), p. 10.

In relation to changes to the formalities for registration there may be the opportunity to further reduce the risk for B, Y and C. This will not lead directly to a corresponding increase in risk for other parties.[69]

Thus eConveyancing will benefit those applying for registered title at the expense of third party rights. B, Y and C's title will be registered more promptly and more easily however these changes will not entirely eliminate risk for B, Y and C. Given the increased emphasis on registration the effect of an error in the register may be more severe and this risk is examined in the next chapter.

References

Battersby, G. (1998). Informally created interests in land. In S. Bright & J. Dewar (Eds.), *Land law themes and perspectives*. Great Britain: Oxford University Press.

Butt, P. (2006). *Electronic conveyancing: A practical guide*. London: Thomson Sweet & Maxwell.

Clancy, D. (2007). *Benchmarking land registration*. In Registering the World Conference, Dublin, 26–28 September 2007. http://www.prai.ie/uploadedfiles/conference20071/papers/s5p4.pdf. Accessed 14 May 2014.

Connolly, F. (2007, October). *E-Conveyancing: Who will benefit?* (B.Sc. Hons Dissertation).

Cooke, E. (2003). E-conveyancing in England: Enthusiasms and reluctance. In D. Grinlinton (Ed.), *Torrens in the twenty-first century*. Wellington: LexisNexis.

Coughlan, P. (1998). *Property law* (2nd ed.). Dublin: Gill & Macmillan.

Critchley, P. (1998). Taking formalities seriously. In S. Bright & J. Dewar (Eds.), *Land law themes and perspectives*. Great Britain: Oxford University Press.

Dixon, M. (2000). Estoppel, unconscionability and formalities in land law. *Cambridge Law Journal, 59*.

Donahue, D. J., Quinn, P. D., & Grandilli, D. C. (2003). *Real estate practice in Ontario* (6th ed.). Canada: LexisNexis Butterworths.

Flaws, J. (2003). Compensation for loss under the Torrens system – Extending state compensation with private insurance. In D. Grinlinton (Ed.), *Torrens in the twenty-first century*. Wellington: LexisNexis.

Greed, J. A. (1998). No, I shan't register. *New Law Journal, 148*.

Harpum, C. (2000). *Property in an electronic age* (Modern studies in property law, Vol. 1). Oxford: Hart.

Harpum, C. (2004). *English experience: Title by registration – Preparation for e-conveyancing*. In Law Reform Commission Annual Conference. http://www.lawreform.ie/Annual%20Conference%202004.PDF. Accessed 18 Feb 2009.

Howell, J. (2006). Land law in an E-conveyancing world. *The Conveyancer and Property Lawyer*.

Ipp, D. A., & Siopis, A. N. (1989). Formalities relating to contracts for the sale of land revisited. *University of Western Australia Law Review, 19*.

Kelway, S. (2004). *Electronic conveyancing – Experiences in England and Wales*. In Law Reform Commission Annual Conference.

[69] There may be indirect consequences for U and V. See Chap. 8 which deals with the destructive effects of a registered transaction.

Law Society of Ireland. (2013). *A guide to good professional conduct for solicitors* (3rd ed.). Law Society of Ireland. http://www.lawsociety.ie/Documents/committees/conduct-guide.pdf. Accessed 29 June 2014.

Law Society of Ireland. (2008). *eConveyancing: Back to basic principles. Vision of an electronic system of conveyancing ('eVision').*

Moore, M. E., & Globe, J. M. (2003). *Title searching and conveyancing in Ontario* (5th ed.). Canada: LexisNexis.

Murphy, S. (2013). *An examination of eConveyancing: A comparison of the treatment of overriding interests in the context of eConveyancing: Ireland with England and Wales* (Master of Law thesis). National University of Ireland, Galway.

Murray, K. (2004). *Electronic registration and other modernization initiatives in Ontario's land registration system.* In Law Reform Commission Annual Conference. http://www.lawreform.ie/Annual%20Conference%202004.PDF. Accessed 18 Feb 2009.

O'Connor, P. (2003). Information, automation and the conclusive land register. In D. Grinlinton (Ed.), *Torrens in the twenty-first century*. Wellington: LexisNexis.

Treacy, C., & O'Sullivan, J. (2004). *Land registration in Ireland – Current position and future developments.* In Law Reform Commission Annual Conference. http://www.lawreform.ie/Annual%20Conference%202004.PDF. Accessed 10 Mar 2009.

Wylie, J. C. W. (1996). *Irish conveyancing law* (2nd ed.). Dublin: Butterworths.

Youdan, T. G. (1984). Formalities for trusts of land, and the doctrine in *Rochefoucauld v. Boustead. Cambridge Law Journal, 43.*

Chapter 7
The Register

7.1 Introduction

This chapter examines the impact of the register itself. On the face of it the land owner has made a successful application for registration but due to some error in the transaction or by the registering authority their interest is at risk.

All parties are at risk from an error in the register. Due to the error A's ownership of Greenacre and X's ownership of Whiteacre may be at risk from a claim of prior ownership. If this occurs B is at risk in the purchase of Greenacre and Y is at risk in the transfer of Whiteacre. They are at risk from the fact that A and X did not have title to sell or gift. C is also at risk in the purchase of Greenacre as B did not have title to grant the charge. D may also be at risk if a subsequent transaction has occurred.

This chapter will examine where the error occurs in the modeled transactions so that B and Y are subject to a claim of prior ownership by A and X.

The unauthorised or illegitimate alteration of the title register could occur due to an action by a person who is not entitled to act at all, an action by a person who is entitled to act but not in the actual circumstances or alternatively due to an error made by the registering authority. An entry on the title register might have been allowed when it should not have been or alternatively the title register is not amended when it should have been. Alternatively the error might involve amending the wrong entry on the title register. The registering authority may fail to register the interest correctly or at all.

Cooke makes the distinction between transactional errors and register errors.[1] Transactional errors being where the transfer is void and thus should not have been registered; its registration is an error. Alternatively there may be an administrative mistake where the transaction is fine but the process of registration produces an error. Register errors occur where the register is wrong before the transaction takes

[1] Cooke (2004), pp. 401–405.

G. Brennan, *The Impact of eConveyancing on Title Registration*,
DOI 10.1007/978-3-319-10341-9_7

place i.e. there was an error on first registration of the title or because a prior transfer was void and should not have been registered.[2]

A transactional error may be capable of being corrected by the parties to the transaction, though there may be no incentive to do so if the transfer has successfully been registered. A transactional error that is not corrected may become a register error in subsequent transactions. This distinction by Cooke is primarily about which transaction has created the error i.e. the current transaction or a prior transaction.

How errors are dealt with by registration systems has, however, less to do with the transaction that created the error and more to do with the specific type of error. The exception is in the case of fraud where the person buying from the fraudster may be treated differently to a subsequent purchaser and this is examined later in the chapter.

The terms transaction errors and registry errors are used below but with a different meaning. Transaction errors are those errors that arise outside the registering authority. Registry errors refer to errors that originate in the registering authority. These errors arise purely due to some mistake by the registering authority and are not based on some fault in the transaction. For example staff in the registering authority amend the wrong entry or the title register is not amended when it should have been.

Where there is a fault in the transaction and as a result the application for registration should have been rejected but was not, this will be referred to as a combined transaction and registry error. The entry was allowed by the registering authority when it should not have been. Such errors present a danger to the participants in that the transaction may have been void or voidable for any one of a number of reasons. The transfer may have been forged or there may have been some fraudulent misrepresentation, illegality or breach of statutory duty.[3]

Thus the types of errors can be divided under the following headings:

1. Transaction errors
2. Registry errors[4]
3. Combined transaction and registry errors

Transaction errors that do not result in a registry error fall outside the remit of this examination.[5] If the error occurred prior to lodgement of the application or in the preparation of an application then the rectification is a matter for the parties affected.[6] This may mean that a deed of rectification is required or the parties may need to dispute the matter in Court.

[2] Cooke (2004), p. 402.

[3] For some examples of breach of statutory duty see O'Connor (2005), p. 45.

[4] The examination is limited to errors in the title register.

[5] Examples include where the wrong purchase monies are stated or the transferee transfers in the wrong capacity e.g. as personal representative and not as beneficial owner.

[6] Fitzgerald (1995), p. 445.

Also registry and combined errors of a minor nature are peripheral to this research. This may include where there is a mapping error or a name is spelt wrong on the register. The major risk arising from a registry error or combined error is where a party to the system loses title by being dispossessed and it is this risk that is examined in detail.

The most severe consequences for the idealised participants will be where the system allows rectification of the register, based on the error, and this adversely affects the party in question by dispossessing them. This party may be B, C, Y or D. Equally if the system does not allow rectification and upholds the register then some other idealised participant may be dispossessed instead. This would be A or X. The consequences of rectification will always be severe either for one party or another. It may be the party who would be, or have become, the 'owner' if not for the error i.e. B, C, Y or D. Alternatively it may be the 'registered owner' who should not have become so i.e. B, C or Y or the subsequent transferee D who relied on the error.

As our abstracted 'pure' participants act correctly at all times the focus is on when such an alteration or correction of the error is due to the fault of someone else or the registering authority. The error could be corrected by rectification or the system may provide for compensation to be paid to the injured party. Ruoff and his colleagues refer to these as complementary remedies[7] but in many instances both rectification and the lack thereof may lead to a claim for compensation though the claimants will differ.

Rectification may be the remedy for an error in the title register or alternatively indefeasibility may mean that the title register is immune from rectification. Where rectification is refused on the grounds of indefeasibility the registration system may provide for compensation to be paid. Compensation may also be payable if a person suffers loss due to a title being rectified when they have relied upon the erroneous registry entry. Such rectification arises on the grounds of defeasibility of the title register.

Thus the extent to which the system of registration is defeasible will determine whose interest is to be upheld as being guaranteed by the state and whose ownership is to be displaced by the error. Such displacement may have already taken place by virtue of the error and the system may let the error stand. Alternatively the title register may be rectified and this may trigger a claim for compensation.

Using the schematic the impact of combined errors and registry errors are examined in the context of both Ireland and Ontario. A number of possible scenarios arise which demonstrate the risk.

[7] Ruoff et al. (1986), p. 75.

7.2 Risk from Combined Transaction and Registry Errors

The impact of a fraudulent transaction provides the clearest demonstration of how a transaction error becomes a registry error. Where the transfers to B and Y are based on fraud the schematic presents a number of different scenarios. Each scenario pits one or more participants against other participants.

Scenario 1 examines where a fraudulent transaction takes place in the transaction for value.

Scenario 1(a)

A fraudster steals A's identity in order to sell Greenacre to B and B becomes the registered owner on foot of the fraudulent transaction. In this situation A is an innocent prior registered owner. When A becomes aware of the transfer he seeks to have the register rectified to restore his title. This would only be possible where the charge held by T had already been paid and removed from the register however the transaction would have been financed by C whose interest is now at risk.

If the register is rectified in favour of A, then B and C lose title. If the register is not rectified and the interests of B and C are upheld then A loses title.

Scenario 1(b)

Before A became aware of the fraud, B sold Greenacre to D and D is now the registered owner. In this situation A is an innocent prior registered owner but D purchased in reliance on the register. A seeks to have the register rectified in his favour while D resists the rectification and requires his ownership to be upheld. D may have purchased on foot of financing provided by a lender and this acquisition lender will be called 'C2'.

The register could be rectified in favour of A so that D and C2 lose title. Alternatively the ownership of D and C2 could be upheld so that A loses title.

Scenario 2 examines where a fraudulent transaction takes place in the transaction not for value.

Scenario 2(a)

A fraudster steals X's identity in order to gift Whiteacre to Y and Y becomes the registered owner on foot of the fraudulent transaction. In this situation X is an innocent prior registered owner. When X becomes aware of the transfer he seeks to have the register rectified to restore his title.

(continued)

The register could be rectified in favour of X so that Y loses title. Alternatively if the register is not rectified and the ownership of Y is upheld, X loses title.

Scenario 2(b)
Before X became aware of the fraud, Y sold Whiteacre to D and D is now the registered owner. In this situation X is an innocent prior registered owner but D purchased in reliance on the register. X seeks to have the register rectified in his favour while D resists the rectification and requires his ownership to be upheld. Again D may have purchased on foot of financing provided by a lender and this acquisition lender will be referred to as 'C2'.

The register could be rectified in favour of X so that D and C2 lose title. Alternatively the ownership of D and C2 could be upheld so that X loses title.

7.3 Risk from Registry Errors

A registry error originates in the registry and as a result a party is in danger of being dispossessed. Where such errors occur the schematic presents a number of other different scenarios.

In order to examine these, additional parties need to be introduced to the schematic. These will be the stranger 'S' and the stranger's lender 'SL'. D will remain the subsequent *bona fide* purchaser for value and C2 will be D's acquisition lender.

Scenario 3 examines where the error takes place in the transaction for value.

Scenario 3(a)
Instead of registering the title to Greenacre in B's name subject to the charge held by C, the registrar registers S as the owner and SL as the lender. When B and C become aware of the error they seek to have the register rectified.

Scenario 3(b)
Before B and C become aware of the error, S sold the property to D who has purchased in reliance on the error in the register. If D purchased using loan funds then C2 will also be at risk.

Scenario 4 examines where the error takes place in the transaction not for value.

Scenario 4(a)
Instead of registering the title to Whiteacre in Y's name, the registrar registers S as the owner. When Y becomes aware of the error he seeks to have the register rectified.

Scenario 4(b)
Before Y became aware of the error, S sold the property to D who has purchased in reliance on the error in the register. If D purchased using loan funds then C2 will also be at risk.

Thus in total there are four possible scenarios and each has two elements. Part (a) deals with the position where the erroneous transaction or registration has been entered on the title register and part (b) examines the position of the parties after a subsequent transaction has been registered. The idealised participants have been used above to demonstrate the error in question and each scenario will be examined to determine how the error is addressed by the registration systems in Ireland and Ontario.

As already stated the extent to which each system is defeasible will determine whether the error will lead to rectification or an upholding of the register. Either may then trigger a claim for compensation from a participant who has suffered loss.

Before applying these scenarios it is necessary to explain the position in general in each jurisdiction and also the law on rectification and compensation.

7.4 The Position in Ireland

Much of the Irish case law on rectification of the register arises in relation to the provisions of the Local Registration of Title (Ireland) Act 1891 (the 1891 Act) rather than under the current provisions of the 1964 Act.[8] This is explained by two factors. Firstly it could be argued that the 1891 Act allowed rectification in a broader set of circumstances. Section 34(2) referred to errors occurring in the registration of the ownership of land whereas section 32(1) of the 1964 Act is limited to errors originating in the Land Registry.[9] Secondly under the 1891 Act

[8] See Dowling (1993), pp. 113–129 for an examination of these cases. See also chapter IX, McAllister (1973).

[9] Confirmed by Carroll J. in *Geraghty v. Buckley* High Court Unreported (6 October 1986). Though the Supreme Court in *Persian Properties Ltd v. The Registrar of Titles and the Minister for Finance* [2003] IESC 12 held that the fact that the initial application to the Land Registry contained an inaccuracy did not relieve the defendants of their obligation to pay compensation to the plaintiff pursuant to section 120(2) since the error in registration had not been caused, or substantially contributed to, by the plaintiff.

only the court had power to rectify and thus any act of rectification is in the public domain and is accompanied by a court decision setting out the reasons for the rectification.

This is contrasted with the position post the 1964 Act where decisions of the registrar to rectify under the provisions of section 32 remain hidden as they are not made public.[10] There is an argument that, as this rectification is based on consent, it should remain a private agreement between the parties. The counter argument is that because the error was on the part of the registry and may form grounds for compensation public policy dictates that such decisions be made publicly available.

Given however that the decisions of the registrar are not available there is in fact very little modern case law that provides guidance in this area. *In re Erris Investments Ltd.*[11] a lease was disclaimed by a liquidator of a tenant company and the landlord sought its cancellation as a burden on his title. The registrar refused rectification and the court agreed. In *Boyle v. Connaughton*[12] the court ordered rectification of the register on the basis that the plaintiff was aware of the defendant's actual occupation of part of his land before the transfer and thus the plaintiff's title was subject to that overriding interest. Notwithstanding the conclusiveness of the register the rights held by the Connaughtons were preserved and protected by section 72 of the 1964 Act by their actual occupation. In addition a mistake in mapping was made when the original lands were subdivided so that the intention of the transfer was not given effect to. The maps were amended to more accurately reflect the position of both properties on the ground.

The case of *Crumlish v. Registrar of Deeds and Titles*[13] is of more interest as the same piece of land was sold twice and then the two transfers were by mistake registered in two different folios. Giving priority to the transfer that was lodged for registration first, the registrar sought to rectify the error by cancelling the second transfer to the applicant. Lynch J. in the High Court held that the registrar only had power to rectify with the consent of the parties and the applicant in this case had specifically refused consent. The court would not make an order on the basis of proceedings by way of judicial review heard only on affidavit. Unfortunately there is no further public record of how this dispute was ultimately resolved.

The lack of judicial guidance means that it is a matter for speculation as to exactly how the Irish courts might approach certain aspects of indefeasibility. However, the power of the registrar to rectify with consent means that often insignificant practical changes to the register can be accomplished without an application to court. Of course, significant changes could also be made provided there is consent.

[10] Deeney (2014), pp. 347–348 does make reference to some related case law but these decisions are not publicly available and shed little light on the core issue.

[11] *In re Erris Investments Ltd.* [1991] ILRM 377.

[12] *Boyle v. Connaughton* [2000] IEHC 28.

[13] *Crumlish v. Registrar of Deeds and Titles* [1990] 2 IR 471.

If the registrar discovers an error he may enter an inhibition on the folio in order to freeze the folio and thus protect the fund in the event of a claim.[14] This power must be exercised in a judicial manner and, unless the urgency of the situation requires otherwise, prior notice should be given to any person whose rights may be affected.[15] The registrar would not be permitted to freeze the folio indefinitely as this would make the land inalienable. The inhibition may be a prelude to a consensual change by rectification or the matter being decided in court in favour of one party or the other.

7.4.1 Rectification

Sections 31 and 32 of the 1964 Act set out the grounds for rectification of the register in Ireland.

Section 32(1)[16] provides that any errors originating in the Land Registry may be rectified by

(a) the Authority with the consent of the registered owner and all interested parties upon such terms as may be agreed in writing by the parties; or
(b) the Authority where it is of the opinion that the error can be rectified without loss to any person after giving such notices as may be prescribed; or
(c) the court upon such terms as to costs or otherwise as it thinks just, if of the opinion that the error can be rectified without injustice to any person.

The error can be one of misstatement, misdescription, omission or otherwise whether in a register or registry map.[17]

Thus the registrar can only rectify errors originating in the registering authority with the consent and written agreement of the relevant parties or, having notified the parties, if the rectification is without loss to any person. This severely limits the power of the registrar to rectify the register. Equally the court can only rectify the error under section 32 if there would be no injustice caused to any person. "Presumably this would imply that the court would not upset the registration of a registered owner who was registered on foot of a transfer for value and who purchased the lands in good faith."[18]

---

[14] Section 121 of the 1964 Act.

[15] *The State (Christopher Philpott) v. The Registrar of Titles* [1986] ILRM 499. Gannon J. also stated that this measure should only be used to protect the fund from a real probability of a claim for compensation and should relate to an identifiable error made in the registry of a nature for which compensation could be payable in accordance with section 120.

[16] As amended by section 55 of the 2006 Act.

[17] See Deeney (2014), p. 344 for examples.

[18] Fitzgerald (1995), p. 446.

The role of the registrar is in effect to mediate an agreement between the parties so as to facilitate rectification with consent. Such rectification may then give rise to a claim for compensation which will be adjudicated by the registrar. Fitzgerald points out that the hearing of compensation claims by the registrar "places him in an invidious situation and this provision in the Act has been the subject of criticism."[19]

The court also has power to rectify under section 31 in the case of actual fraud or mistake and this can be on such terms as it thinks just. This does not mean that no party will suffer loss or be prejudiced by the court's decision. Instead the availability of compensation may mean that the court's decision is equitable.[20] Section 32 contains a statutory power to rectify whereas section 31 sets out the breadth of the court's equitable jurisdiction to rectify for reasons falling outside section 32.[21]

In the recent case of *Stepstone Mortgage Funding Ltd v. Tyrrell*[22] the High Court ordered the registrar to reinstate rights of way on a folio which had been cancelled without notice to all parties with an interest in the land. The plaintiff had a copy folio showing the rights which appeared on the register at the time the charge was granted and thus was entitled to rely on the conclusivity of the register. The court referred to the fact that the plaintiff, as a chargee for value, did not have to penetrate the "Iron Curtain" of the register.[23]

Thus the court has broad powers of rectification while the registrar can only rectify errors originating in the registering authority.[24] Fitzgerald notes that "no such correction or alteration [by the registrar] would of course disturb registered and legal interests"[25] presumably on the basis that anyone holding such interests would not give their consent to a rectification that would deprive them of their interest. This is confirmed by the registering authority in a practice direction which states that no correction could, of course, be made which would disturb registered legal interests.[26] In *Geraghty v. Buckley*[27] Carroll J. noted that since the registrar did not have power to transfer land unilaterally, the only way title could be transferred, in the absence of the registration of a transfer by the registered owner, was by order of the court.

---

[19] Fitzgerald (1995), p. 447.

[20] Breen (2000), p. 52.

[21] Breen (2000), p. 52.

[22] *Stepstone Mortgage Funding Ltd v. Tyrrell* [2012] IEHC 139.

[23] This is a phrase used by McAllister. See McAllister (1973).

[24] Thus the registrar's rectification is limited to errors in the registration process and excludes the possibility of correcting errors in the document presented for registration. See Deeney (2014), p. 341.

[25] Fitzgerald (1995), p. 445.

[26] Property Registration Authority (2013b).

[27] *Geraghty v. Buckley* High Court Unreported (6 October 1986).

Fitzgerald notes factors that will be considered by the Court such as:

(a) whether or not the registered owner contributed to the error[28]
(b) that he could have had the error rectified previously
(c) that he was a volunteer and his title could have been defective
(d) that there was fraud; however where the purchaser for value then sells on the property his purchaser would get a good title and rectification would not be possible.[29]

This implies that the fraudulent transaction would not be upheld but that a subsequent transaction to a *bona fide* purchaser for value would be guaranteed.

McAllister expresses the view that if there is a fraud the register will be rectified against the fraudster and any person claiming through or under the fraudster as volunteers but that if there is a transfer by the fraudster to a purchaser for value then the transfer cannot be set aside.[30] He relies on English case law for this stance[31] and notes the lack of reported Irish cases dealing with rectification of the register on the grounds of actual fraud.[32]

Thus McAllister is of the view that the fraudulent transaction will not be set aside unless it is to a volunteer whereas Fitzgerald implies that the fraudulent transaction will be set aside unless there is a subsequent transaction. Given that both Fitzgerald[33] and McAllister[34] were registrars their comments are of considerable interest. If the fraudster has transferred registered title to himself then the register would obviously be rectified in favour of the innocent prior registered owner. The difficulty arises when the fraudster has transferred title to anther party (B or Y in the schematic) and this difficulty is compounded when B or Y have sold to D. Whose title is to be upheld?

In effect the issue has yet to be settled but on principle McAllister leans in favour of immediate indefeasibility noting that in order to overcome this "it would be necessary to show a *mala fides* on the part of the purchaser (short of actual fraud) which would tip the scales of justice against him and in favour of another claimant."[35] This contrasts with Fitzgerald's comments which imply a policy of deferred indefeasibility.

---

[28] Section 120(2) refers to the loss not being caused or substantially contributed to by the act, neglect or default of the person or his agent. This was argued in *Persian Properties Ltd v. The Registrar of Titles and the Minister for Finance* [2003] IESC 12 but Keane C.J. found this submission was not well founded.

[29] Fitzgerald (1995), p. 446.

[30] McAllister (1973), pp. 283–284.

[31] *Assets Co Ltd v. Mere Roihi and Others* [1905] A.C. 176 and *Re Leighton's Conveyance* [1937] Ch. 149.

[32] McAllister (1973), pp. 284 and 282.

[33] Fitzgerald was Registrar of Deeds and Titles from 1983 until 1988.

[34] McAllister was Registrar of Deeds and Titles from 1957 until 1974.

[35] McAllister (1973), p. 289.

Section 32(1) uses the word 'may' and thus the registrar has a general discretion to refuse rectification. Deeney, former Deputy Registrar, in a more recent work, is of the view that where a transferee for value is registered prior to discovery of the error, such error is not capable of rectification, and the remedy is a claim for compensation.[36] He also expresses the view that a fraudulent transfer to a party to the fraud or a volunteer would be set aside but any transfer for value cannot be set aside.[37] He does not distinguish between an immediate transaction or a deferred transaction but implies that no transaction or charge for value would be set aside. In support of this he quotes Glover as follows:

> If a registration has been made under a fraudulent disposition, the disposition can only be set aside as against parties and privies to the fraud, and volunteers claiming under them; it cannot be set aside as against a registered transferee for value, or a registered chargee for value, claiming under a party to the fraud.[38]

Thus like McAllister, Deeney leans in favour of immediate indefeasibility.

The High Court case of *Moore v. Moore*[39] is of interest. The first two defendants sold the property to the third defendant on the basis that they believed the plaintiff to have predeceased their father and that he was the sole owner of the property as surviving joint tenant. The third defendant became the registered owner and took out a charge on the property. The plaintiff alleged fraud on the basis that the first two defendants relied on a death certificate of someone with the same name as the plaintiff however the court found that there was no evidence of fraud or concealment as the first two defendants did attempt to ascertain the whereabouts of the plaintiff. Murphy J. held that the register is conclusive evidence of title and if the plaintiff sustained loss as a result of fraud then she would be entitled to compensation under the provisions of section 120. She was not entitled to rectification in circumstances where the third named defendant was a *bona fide* purchaser for value without notice of the alleged fraud. Also the charge holder was a *bona fide* purchaser for value without notice.

In this case there was no originating error by the registry. It relied upon an affidavit sworn by the first and second named defendants to put the property into the sole name of their father and they then sold to the third named defendant as personal representatives. The court could have rectified under section 31 on the basis of mistake but chose not to do so. There had been a transfer and charge to *bona fide* parties without notice. The court refused the plaintiff's claim as against the third named defendant.

This case is more consistent with a policy of deferred indefeasibility however the Irish Supreme Court has yet to issue a seminal judgment on the exact nature of Irish indefeasibility so the issue remains to be settled.[40]

---

[36] Deeney (2014), p. 341.

[37] Deeney (2014), pp. 374 and 343.

[38] Glover (1933), pp. 282–283.

[39] *Moore v. Moore* [2010] IEHC 462.

[40] Deeney (2014), p. 346.

7.4.2 Compensation

One of the defining features of the title register is the state guarantee of title underpinned by a compensation fund. If any of the parties suffer a loss as a result of an error in the register they may be entitled to compensation from the government. This compensation is intended to put them as far as possible in the position they would have been in had they not been deprived of the interest.

Compensation is payable under section 120[41] of the 1964 Act to a person adversely affected by a rectification who suffers loss provided the loss was not caused or substantially contributed to by the act, neglect or default of that person or his or her agent.[42] Section 120 provides the grounds to claim compensation for error, forgery or fraud in relation to registration. The five grounds of loss which can lead to a claim for compensation are:

(a) loss must arise from the rectification of an error in registration under section 32 (1);
(b) any error originating in the registry which is not rectified;
(c) any entry in or omission caused or obtained by forgery or fraud;
(d) an error in an official search; or
(e) the inaccuracy of any extract from the register.

The error originating in the registry may be a misstatement, misdescription, omission or otherwise.

Previously the claimant was required to show that he had exhausted all other avenues before he would be entitled to compensation. The case law that provided for this was according to McAllister "obviously absurd and largely negatives the notion of a State guaranteed title."[43] The Land Registry practice direction however confirms that this position was overruled by the Supreme Court in 1982.[44] This was confirmed by the Supreme Court in *Persian Properties Ltd v. The Registrar of Titles and the Minister for Finance*.[45] Keane C.J. held that a submission by the plaintiff that it was obliged to resist a claim to a strip of disputed ground and engage in expensive litigation in the High Court before applying to the defendants for compensation was wholly unsustainable. He could not see any basis on which the registrar could have required the plaintiff developers to engage in such expensive and unnecessary litigation. Reimbursement of the costs of taking or defending legal proceedings does not depend on the consent of the registering authority but will depend on the circumstances of each case.

---

[41] As amended by section 69 of the 2006 Act.

[42] Deeney refers to this as a clear restriction on the right to compensation. See Deeney (2014), p. 347. See also p. 348 for relevant case law.

[43] McAllister (1973), p. 301.

[44] Property Registration Authority (2013b).

[45] *Persian Properties Ltd v. The Registrar of Titles and the Minister for Finance* [2003] IESC 12. See Deeney (2014), pp. 347–348 for some background to this dispute.

It is not just the person adversely affected who is entitled to compensation but also any person deriving title from him or her.[46] If the loss arises from rectification of an error originating in the registry then the applicants' costs and expenses in obtaining the rectification are also covered.[47] The time limit for claiming under the section is 6 years from the time when the right to compensation accrued.[48]

Since the compensation is paid by the state,[49] section 120(6) provides that the Minister for Finance shall then be able to recover the amount from the person who caused or derived advantage from the loss. No such compensation has ever been recovered from any person.[50] This may be because there has been no significant compensation claim against the register. There has also been no rectification of the register or compensation paid arising from the use of electronic services by the registry save recovery of costs due to errors in data capture.[51]

7.4.3 How Errors Are Addressed by the Registration System in Ireland

The following sets out how the registration system in Ireland would deal with the scenarios above. Given that the exact nature of indefeasibility has yet to be definitively addressed the possible options are considered below along with the risk to each participant.

Scenarios 1 and 2 relate to a fraudulent transaction. The error did not originate in the registry but was a transaction error that became a registry error when the application for registration of the fraudulent transaction was accepted. As this error did not originate in the registry the registrar and court have no power to correct it under section 32. Instead any application for rectification must be made to the court under section 31.

Section 32 does apply to scenarios 3 and 4 as these relate to registry errors. Section 31 may also apply to those errors as this section of the legislation relates not just to fraud but also to mistakes.

Scenario 1(a)

An application to court for rectification on the grounds of actual fraud would need to be made by A under section 31. The court has the power to order rectification on

[46] Section 120(2).

[47] Section 120(3).

[48] Section 120(5)(c). The time is extended in the case of disability. See Deeney (2014), p. 347 for some relevant case law.

[49] Section 120(4) provides that all compensation is paid out of moneys provided by the Oireachtas.

[50] Interview with Greg McDermott ICT Manager Property Registration Authority 1 March 2012.

[51] Interview with Greg McDermott ICT Manager Property Registration Authority 1 March 2012.

such terms as it thinks just. In this scenario an innocent prior registered owner, A, is pitted against a *bona fide* purchaser for value, B, and his lender, C.

As idealised participants neither A, B or C will have contributed to the error and thus the scales of justice could tip either way. The court may order rectification in favour of A or may uphold the fraudulent transaction, deprive A of his interest and affirm the registered title of B and C.

Section 120 will provide for compensation to be paid to the person who suffers loss as a result of the entry in a register caused or obtained by forgery or fraud provided the participant's agent did not cause or substantially contribute to the loss. If A loses title he will be entitled to compensation, or if the court deprives B or C of their title, they will be entitled to compensation.

Such compensation may be sufficient recompense for C whose only interest in the property is of a financial nature but either A or B will suffer a loss of use.

Scenario 1(b)

Again section 32 does not apply and A must apply to the court under section 31. The court has power to order rectification on such terms as it thinks just. In this scenario an innocent prior registered owner, A, is pitted against a subsequent *bona fide* purchaser for value, D, and his lender C2. B has been paid for his interest in the property and thus is only at risk of a loss if rectification is ordered and D reclaims the purchase monies.

The court may order rectification in favour of A or may uphold the transaction to D and deprive A of his interest thus affirming the registered title of D and C2.

Section 120 will provide for compensation to be paid to the person who suffers loss as a result of the entry in a register caused or obtained by forgery or fraud provided the participant's agent did not cause or substantially contribute to the loss. If A loses title he will be entitled to compensation, or if the court deprives D or C2 of their title, they will be entitled to compensation.

Such compensation may be sufficient recompense for C2 whose only interest in the property is of a financial nature but either A or D will suffer a loss of use.

While a court may order rectification in scenario 1(a) as B took title from a fraudster it is less likely to order rectification in this scenario as there is now a *bona fide* purchaser and lender (D and C2) who relied on the register.

Scenario 2(a)

An application to court for rectification on the grounds of actual fraud would need to be made by X under section 31. The court has the power to order rectification on such terms as it thinks just. In this scenario an innocent prior registered owner, X, is pitted against a volunteer, Y.

As idealised participants neither X nor Y will have contributed to the error and thus the scales of justice could tip either way. The court may order rectification in favour of X or may uphold the fraudulent transaction, deprive X of his interest and affirm the registered title of Y. However as Y is a volunteer and did not pay for the property it is more likely that the court will order rectification in favour of X.

If Y loses title he will be entitled to compensation under section 120. Since Y did not pay for the property he will not be subject to any monetary loss but instead will suffer a loss of enrichment and loss of use value which may be difficult to quantify.

It is difficult to conceive of a fraudster gifting a property he has effectively 'stolen' to someone who is entirely innocent. It is more likely that he will sell or charge the property to make as much money from the theft as possible.

Scenario 2(b)

X must apply to the court under section 31. The court has power to order rectification on such terms as it thinks just. In this scenario an innocent prior registered owner, X, is pitted against a subsequent *bona fide* purchaser for value, D, and his lender C2. Y has been paid for his interest in the property and thus is only at risk of a loss if rectification is ordered and D reclaims the purchase monies.

The court may order rectification in favour of X or may uphold the transaction to D and deprive X of his interest thus affirming the registered title of D and C2.

Section 120 will provide for compensation to be paid to the person who suffers loss as a result of the entry in a register caused or obtained by forgery or fraud provided the participant's agent did not cause or substantially contribute to the loss. If X loses title he will be entitled to compensation, or if the court deprives D or C2 of their title, they will be entitled to compensation.

Such compensation may be sufficient recompense for C2 whose only interest in the property is of a financial nature but either X or D will suffer a loss of use. As D relied on the register the preference of the court may be not to rectify in order to uphold D's reliance on the register.

Scenario 3(a)

All parties could consent to the rectification under section 32. Alternatively the registrar could serve notice and rectify this error without loss to any person. S and SL have no grounds to object to the rectification as any enrichment they might seek would be unjust.

If S or SL do claim that they have suffered a loss, the court can rectify under section 32 or alternatively under section 31 on the basis of mistake. If a loss has been sustained compensation will be payable under section 120 and B and C would be entitled to recover the costs and expenses incurred in obtaining the rectification. This is available under section 120(3) where the error originated in the registry.

Scenario 3(b)

In this scenario B and C are the rightful registered owner and chargee but, as a result of a mistake in the registry, a stranger was registered as owner and has now sold the property to D. The charge held by SL would have been redeemed on that sale so this party is not subject to any risk. The interests of B and C are pitted against a subsequent *bona fide* purchaser for value and subsequent acquisition lender.

B and C seek to have the register rectified in their favour. If the register is rectified to restore B and C's title then D and C2 will lose title. If the register is not rectified D will remain the registered owner, C2's charge will be protected but B and C will lose title. D and C2 will not consent to rectification as this would deprive them of their interests. Neither the registrar nor court could rectify under section 32 as such rectification would cause loss and injustice.[52] The court can however rectify under section 31 on the basis of mistake.

If no rectification is ordered then S has been allowed take advantage of the error. B and C would have a personal action against S on the basis of unjust enrichment. B and C would also be entitled to compensation. If rectification is ordered then D and C2 would be entitled to compensation and also to recover their costs and expenses.

D and C2 are *bona fide* parties without notice who relied upon the register so the court is more likely to uphold their interests and refuse the request for rectification.

Scenario 4(a)

All parties could consent to the rectification under section 32. Alternatively the registrar could serve notice and rectify this error without loss to any person. S has no grounds to object to the rectification as any enrichment he might seek would be unjust.

If S does claim that he has suffered a loss, the court can rectify under section 32 or alternatively under section 31 on the basis of mistake. If a loss has been sustained compensation will be payable under section 120 and Y would be entitled to recover the costs and expenses incurred in obtaining the rectification. This is available under section 120(3) where the error originated in the registry.

Scenario 4(b)

In this scenario Y is the rightful registered owner but, as a result of a mistake in the registry, a stranger was registered as owner and has now sold the property to D. The interest of Y is pitted against a subsequent *bona fide* purchaser for value and subsequent acquisition lender.

Y seeks to have the register rectified in his favour. If the register is rectified to restore Y's title then D and C2 will lose title. If the register is not rectified D will remain the registered owner, C2's charge will be protected but Y will lose title. D and C2 will not consent to rectification as this would deprive them of their interests. Neither the registrar nor court could rectify under section 32 as such rectification would cause loss and injustice.[53] The court can however rectify under section 31 on the basis of mistake.

If no rectification is ordered then S has been allowed take advantage of the error. Y would have a personal action against S on the basis of unjust enrichment. Y would also be entitled to compensation. If rectification is ordered then D and C2 would be entitled to compensation and also to recover their costs and expenses.

Monetary compensation may be sufficient for C2 whose only interest in the property is its exchange or investment value however monetary compensation is unlikely to compensate D for its use value. Y did not pay for the property but will still be entitled to compensation for loss of the ownership and loss of use value if the gift is denied.

[52] Unless the view was taken that compensation was an adequate remedy.

[53] Unless the view was taken that compensation was an adequate remedy.

As D and C2 relied on the register, and Y did not, the court is more likely to uphold their interests and not rectify the register in favour of Y. Also the interests of D and C2 as *bona fide* parties for value will likely merit a greater degree of protection than the interest of Y, a volunteer. D and C2 paid value for their interests while Y did not and this may be a factor in the court dispensing justice between their respective positions.

7.5 The Position in Ontario

The Ontario registration system has been subject to significant legislative change and seminal court decisions on the nature of its indefeasibility and thus the position is in many respects more clear cut.

The nature of indefeasibility in Ontario has been subject to a high level of public controversy since a decision of the Ontario Court of Appeal in 2005. In *Household Realty Corporation Ltd. v. Liu*[54] a wife forged her husband's signature on a power of attorney and she then mortgaged their home three times. The court held that an instrument, once registered, was effective and the mortgagees were entitled to enforce against the husband and wife who were joint owners. This was on the basis of section 78(4) of the Land Titles Act which deemed a registered instrument to be effective according to its nature and intent and to create, transfer, charge or discharge, as the case requires, the land or estate mentioned in the register. Section 78(4) was held to override section 155 which provided that a fraudulent instrument, if unregistered, would be fraudulent and void is, despite registration, fraudulent and void in like manner. The mortgages having been given for valuable consideration and without notice of the fraud were held, once registered, to be effective and could be relied upon.

The decision was "received with widespread dismay. There was a barrage of criticism from legal commentators, the media and the provincial government."[55] The government moved quickly to introduce a Real Estate Fraud Action Plan[56] and amending legislation. "[E]ven though the Ontario online registration system maintained registrars' review it moved in 2006 from immediate to deferred indefeasibility."[57]

The Ministry of Government Services Consumer Protection and Service Modernization Act 2006[58] (hereafter the Modernization Act) introduced amendments to the Land Titles Act to deal with registration of forged and void instruments and, in

[54] *Household Realty Corporation Ltd. v. Liu* 2005 CanLII 43402 (ON CA). Also referenced as *CIBC Mortgages Inc. v. Chan.*

[55] O'Connor (2009a), p. 211.

[56] See Murray (2007) for details of the stakeholders involved in agreeing this initiative.

[57] Arruñada (2010), p. 117.

[58] S.O. 2006 Chapter 34.

effect, introduced deferred indefeasibility.[59] While *Household Realty Corporation Ltd. v. Liu* was subsequently overturned in *Lawrence v. Maple Trust Co.*[60] the Modernization Act introduced two new provisions in the Land Titles Act. Section 78(4.1) provided that section 78(4) would not apply to a fraudulent instrument registered on or after 19 October 2006 and section 78(4.2) provided that section 78(4.1) does not invalidate the effect of a registered instrument that is not a fraudulent instrument including instruments registered subsequent to such a fraudulent instrument. The registrar already had power to delete a fraudulent document and rectify the register[61] but definitions of fraudulent instrument and fraudulent person were added to the Land Titles Act to address concerns about levels of fraud.[62] In addition the LRRA was amended to strengthen the ability of the registrar to suspend and revoke access to the electronic title registration system.[63]

As a result of the changes introduced by the Modernization Act property owners are protected from fraudulent documents. "The registration does not validate the fraudulent mortgage or transfer, and it will not be enforceable against the property owner."[64] The registrar may order the fraudulent instrument be deleted from the register, thus returning title to the true owner.[65] However non fraudulent instruments registered subsequently will be effective. This is in line with sections 66, 68, 86 and 93 of the Land Titles Act whereby only the registered owner can transfer or charge land. Title cannot be given through a forged transfer since such a transfer was not made by the registered owner but a subsequently registered owner can transfer or charge land.

Thus a fraudulent instrument is void despite registration and nothing in the legislation invalidates the effect of a registered instrument that is not a fraudulent instrument including instruments registered subsequently. This enshrined the principle of deferred indefeasibility in legislation.

Lawrence v. Maple Trust Co. involved a fraudster who forged Mrs. Lawrence's signature on a contract for sale to Thomas Wright. A person purporting to be Thomas Wright then applied to Maple Trust Co. for a mortgage to finance the purchase. "Mr. Wright" used false identification to obtain the mortgage and then absconded with the funds. The transfer was registered along with a new mortgage in favour of Maple Trust Co. Mrs. Lawrence was no longer the owner noted on the title register and her house was now subject to a mortgage that she was not party to. At

[59] The Act provided protection against the registration of fraudulent instruments, improved the ability to rectify titles, streamlined the Land Titles Assurance Fund (LTAF) process, gave the registrar additional powers to suspend or revoke an individual's access to the electronic registration system and also increased the fines for real estate related offences.

[60] *Lawrence v. Maple Trust Co.* 2007 CanLII 74 (ON CA).

[61] Section 157(1) and section 57(13).

[62] Section 1.

[63] Murray (2007), p. 7. See sections 23.1–23.4.

[64] Murray (2007), p. 6.

[65] Section 57(13) of the Land Titles Act.

the initial hearing the judge was bound by *Household Realty Corporation Ltd. v. Liu* and held that the transfer was void but the mortgage was valid and enforceable. The Court of Appeal found that the transfer to Wright was void and registration did not cure the defect. Thus Wright did not become the registered owner and could not transfer or charge the title.[66] Thus Maple Trust Co. could not rely on section 78 (4) to gain an indefeasible title and the mortgage was invalid. Gillese J.A. found that the wording of the Land Titles Act could be consistent with both deferred and immediate indefeasibility but that deferred indefeasibility was preferable for policy reasons and that it would take clear and unequivocal language in the Act to abrogate or displace common law principles. He felt this was in line with the earlier decision of the Supreme Court of Canada in *United Trust v. Dominion Stores et al.*[67]

Deferred indefeasibility placed the risk of loss on the mortgagee as this was the party with the best opportunity to avoid the fraud, encourages lenders to be vigilant and protects a subsequent purchaser. This was based on the courts decision to treat the acquisition mortgagee as an "intermediate" rather than a "deferred" owner.[68] The indefeasibility would rest with the next *bona fide* purchaser or encumbrancer without notice. Because the fraudulent transfer and charge were registered contemporaneously Maple Trust Co. did not rely on the register and there was no opportunity for Ms. Lawrence to recover the land before the second transaction i.e. the charge. Thus the Court of Appeal in effect bundled the two transactions i.e. the fraudulent transfer and acquisition charge together ensuring that Mrs. Lawrence's right to set aside both transactions was not lost by registration of the charge. This case was decided following the introduction of the Modernization Act but before it was enacted.

A similar bundling occurred in *Home Trust Company v. Zivic*[69] and *Rabi v. Rosu*[70] where the transfer and the mortgages were to all intents and purposes registered simultaneously and thus were treated as one transaction.[71] A signification factor in these decisions was the fact that the mortgagees did not rely on the register.

Generally deferred indefeasibility allows the original owner a window of opportunity to set aside a registered transaction before a second transaction is registered but these decisions provide an enhanced form of deferred indefeasibility and extend that widow. O'Connor refers to "deferred indefeasibility-plus which denies

[66] Under section 68(1) of the Land Titles Act only a registered owner is entitled to transfer or charge registered land.

[67] *United Trust v. Dominion Stores et al* 1976 CanLII 33 (SCC).

[68] O'Connor (2009a), p. 214.

[69] *Home Trust Company v. Zivic* 2006 CanLII 38359 (ON SC).

[70] *Rabi v. Rosu* 2006 CanLII 36623 (ON SC). Echlin J. said Ontario was experiencing a serious mortgage fraud plague.

[71] Contrast this with the earlier decision of *Durrani v. Augier* 2000 CanLII 22410 (ON SC) where an innocent bank's mortgage was deemed valid even though the borrower was held not to be the owner of the property. Title was restored to the original registered owner subject to a mortgage they had nothing to do with. See Troister (2004), p. 5. See also *Toronto-Dominion Bank v. Jiang* 2003 CanLII 38078 (ON SC).

indefeasible title to the second purchaser in a double-transaction fraud case."[72] The second purchaser in these cases being the acquisition lender. Holding the transfer and charge to be in effect 'one' transaction provides that indefeasibility does not pass until there is a further transaction on the title.

A similar type bundling of the transfer and charge has occurred in England and Wales but to different effect. In *Abbey National Building Society v. Cann*[73] Mr. Cann purchased a leasehold flat for his mother to live in, with the benefit of a mortgage from Abbey National and with monies provided by his mother, from the sale of a previous property. It transpired that the mother had been let into occupation some 35 min before completion of the mortgage. Mr. Cann subsequently defaulted in payment of the mortgage and Abbey National sought possession. The mother claimed that by reason of her contribution to the purchase price coupled with her actual occupation of the property prior to completion, she had an overriding interest which took priority to Abbey National's mortgage.

The House of Lords held that the correct date for determining the existence of an overriding interest was the date of registration, rather than the date of completion but the relevant date for determining whether an interest in registered land was protected by actual occupation and had priority over the holder of a legal estate was the date of transfer or creation of the legal estate and not the date of registration. Where a purchaser relied on a bank or building society loan to complete his purchase, the transfer and charge were one indivisible transaction and there was no *scintilla temporis*[74] during which the property vested in the purchaser free of the mortgage.[75]

By this decision acquisition lenders gained a new status and a super priority that automatically protected them from many new adverse claims. In England and Wales acquisition lender are thus treated better than subsequent lenders whereas in Ontario subsequent lenders are given enhanced priority.

In Ontario in the more recent case of *Isaacs v. Royal Bank of Canada*[76] the mortgage was however upheld as the plaintiff actively assisted the fraudsters in perpetrating the fraud. She was not herself privy to the fraud but was not a completely innocent victim. She had been paid to act as guarantor on a mortgage for a borrower with a bad credit rating. Molloy J. distinguished between the original owner who has no knowledge of the fraud, the intermediate owner who dealt with the fraudster and the deferred owner who took the property from the intermediate owner without knowing of the fraud. He noted that it is only the intermediate owner who has any opportunity to avoid the fraud and thus as a question of policy it makes

---

[72] O'Connor (2009a), p. 213.

[73] *Abbey National Building Society v. Cann* [1990] 1 All ER 1085

[74] Moment in time.

[75] See *Thompson v. Foy* [2009] EWHC 1076 (Ch) in respect of determining the date when an interest is protected by actual occupation.

[76] *Isaacs v. Royal Bank of Canada* 2010 CanLII 3527 (ON SC).

more sense to place the burden on this party. The intermediate owner will be subject to having his or her title defeated by a claim from the original owner.

Thus Ontario operates a system of deferred indefeasibility.[77] In moving from immediate to deferred indefeasibility Ontario moved from dynamic towards static security. It favours static security by deferring indefeasibility to subsequent transferees though the system also attempts to balance dynamic security by favouring subsequent, non-infected by fraud, transferees.

7.5.1 Rectification

Section 57(13) of the Land Titles Act allows the registrar or court to rectify the register if (a) a registered instrument would be absolutely void if unregistered; (b) either is satisfied, on the basis of evidence, that a fraudulent instrument has been registered; or (c) the effect of the error, if not rectified, would be to deprive a person of land of which the person is legally in possession or legally in receipt of the rents and profits. If rectification is based on these grounds members of a prescribed class are entitled to compensation under section 57(4.1) or 57(4.2) and these are dealt with below.

Under section 163(1.1) the registrar may make orders specifying what evidence is required for the purposes of clause 57(13)(b) to enable rectification of the register because a registered instrument was fraudulent.[78] Fraudulent instrument and fraudulent person are defined in section 1. Fraudulent instrument means an instrument under which a fraudulent person purports to receive or transfer an estate or interest in land, that is given under a forged power of attorney, transfer of a charge where the charge is given by a fraudulent person or that perpetrates a fraud as prescribed.[79] Fraudulent person is a person who executes or purports to execute an instrument if the person forged the instrument, is a fictitious person or, who holds oneself out to be, but knows that the person is not, the registered owner.

The registrar can also rectify errors and supply omissions in the register, or in an entry in it, under section 158(2) upon evidence that appears sufficient. This is not limited to the correction of minor errors.

The Court may also order rectification under section 159 where it decides that a person is entitled to an estate, right or interest in or to registered land or a charge and as a consequence rectification is required. In such circumstances the court can order the register to be rectified in such manner as is considered just.

[77] See Bucknall (2008–2009), pp. 1–53 for a detailed analysis of the case law from 1999 to 2007, the legislative amendments introduced by the Modernization Act and the impact of these developments. See also Troister (2004), p. 5.

[78] Order of the Director of Titles ODOT-2007-01 available at http://files.ontariogovernment.ca/ont06_018793.pdf.

[79] Section 63 of O. Reg. 690/90 as amended by O. Reg. 439/11 prescribes this as the cessation of a charge or encumbrance and the person who purports to register it is a fraudulent person.

Section 160 allows a person aggrieved by an entry, omission, default or delay to apply to the court for an order of rectification and the court can refuse, with or without costs to be paid by the applicant, or may if satisfied of the justice of the case, make an order for the rectification of the register.

Thus in Ontario the registrar and courts have wide ranging powers to rectify the register.

7.5.2 Compensation

In Ontario compensation is paid out of the Land Titles Assurance Fund (LTAF). The LTAF applies to errors in the electronic record in the same manner as it does to paper records.[80] "The existence of the [LTAF] fund acknowledges that the principle of certainty of registration can lead to circumstances in which innocent parties lose legal title to the property."[81]

Under section 57(1) of the Land Titles Act a person wrongfully deprived of land by reason of some other person being registered as owner through fraud or misdescription, omission or some other error in an entry on the register can recover compensation or damages from the person on whose application the erroneous registration was made or who acquired the title through the fraud or error. In addition a person wrongfully deprived of land or of some estate or interest therein by reason of the land being brought under the Act can also recover compensation or damages.

Thus a person wrongfully deprived of land or some estate or interest therein can recover from the person on whose application the erroneous registration was made or who acquired the title through the fraud or error. However, under section 57(3), a purchaser or mortgagee in good faith for value is not liable by reason of the vendor or mortgagor having been registered as owner through fraud or error or having derived title from or through a person registered as owner through fraud or error, whether the fraud or error consisted of a wrong description of the property or otherwise. In these instances a *bona fide* purchaser or lender for value will not be liable directly to the person wrongfully deprived of their interest.

Section 57(4) provides for compensation from the fund for a person wrongfully deprived of land or some estate or interest in land by reason of the land being brought under this Act, some other person being registered as owner through fraud, or any misdescription, omission or other error in an entry on the register. The person must be unable to recover compensation from the person who made the application or who acquired title through the fraud or error or otherwise recover just compensation for the loss. In addition under section 57(4)(b) in order to be entitled the person must have demonstrated 'requisite due diligence' if some other person was

[80] Moore and Globe (2003), p. 229.

[81] Bucknall (2008–2009), p. 42.

registered as owner through fraud. Under section 163(1.1) the registrar can make orders specifying what constitutes due diligence[82] for the purposes of clause 57(4)(b) or 57(4.1)(b).

A mortgagee will be required to demonstrate that it took reasonable steps to verify the identity of the person mortgaging the property and to verify that the registered owner was, in fact, selling or mortgaging the property.[83] Similarly a purchaser must demonstrate that they took reasonable steps to verify that the registered owner was selling the property.[84] Thus both must verify the transaction and a lender must also verify identity.[85]

Section 57(4.1) relates only to members of a prescribed class of persons who are entitled to compensation from the fund if certain conditions are met. The person must have been wrongfully deprived of land or some estate or interest in land or have not received land or some estate or interest in land because under section 57(13)(b) the registrar or court has directed that the registration of a fraudulent instrument be deleted from the register, or, under section 57(13)(a) or (c) rectification of the register is ordered on the basis that a registered instrument would be absolutely void if unregistered or the effect of an error, if not rectified, would be to deprive a person of land of which the person is legally in possession or legally in receipt of the rents and profits.

Section 57(4.2) also provides for compensation to be paid to members of this prescribed class if the person suffers loss due to the deletion of a fraudulent instrument whereas section 57(4.1) is broader. It provides for compensation if there is rectification of the register under any of the grounds in section 57(13). However under section 57(4.1) the person must have demonstrated the requisite due diligence with respect to the instrument that is the subject of the rectification. There is no corresponding requirement in section 57(4.2).

Previously all claimants were required to seek compensation under the law before claiming against the fund. Now a person who is a member of this prescribed class can, where a fraudulent instrument is registered against their interest in land, claim against the LRAF without having to pursue the fraudster.[86] Members of the prescribed class are individuals who were registered owners of land used for residential purposes and individuals who are purchasers in good faith for valuable consideration of land used for residential purposes.[87] Lenders are not included.

---

[82] Order of the Director of Titles ODOT-2007-02 available at http://files.ontariogovernment.ca/ont06_018794.pdf.

[83] Murray (2007), p. 9. Similar type provisions exist in parts of Australia. See O'Connor (2009b), pp. 158–159.

[84] Murray (2007), p. 9.

[85] Sections 57(4)(b) and 57(4.1)(b).

[86] Thus there are two separate procedures; one for members of this prescribed class and one for others. See Service Ontario.

[87] Section 64 of O. Reg. 690/90 as amended by O. Reg. 439/11.

For these parties the LTAF is now a fund of first resort provided they are a victim of fraud and the loss is not covered by title insurance.[88] Those within the prescribed class who are protected by title insurance will have no claim against the fund.[89]

A person who suffers damage because of an error in recording an instrument can also recover compensation from the fund under section 57(5). Under section 57(8) it is the registrar who determines the amount of compensation to be paid and the registrar can then recover from any person in respect of a loss to the fund.[90]

A person is not entitled to compensation from the fund in respect of an interest existing at the time the land is brought under the Act unless that interest was registered in the unregistered system or notice of it was given to the registrar before the first registration under the Act.[91] The application for compensation must be made within 6 years from the time of having suffered the loss.[92]

Section 59 sets out a number of restrictions on the payment of compensation. For claims in relation to rights existing at the time of first registration, no compensation is payable out of the fund if the person first registered could have conveyed good title, as against the claimant, to a purchaser in good faith for value without notice of any defect and no caution was registered and the registrar did not have actual notice of the defect prior to first registration. No compensation is also payable if the claimant had notice of registration proceeding and failed to act. No compensation is payable for any claim where the claimant's negligence caused or contributed to the loss, the claimant knowingly participated or colluded in a fraud, if it is a subrogated claim or made on behalf of an insurer.

Thus a claimant will not be compensated from the fund if he or she has caused or substantially contributed to the loss through their own act, neglect, default and/or omission. This would include the failure to register a sufficient caution, notice or appropriate registration under the Act.[93]

7.5.3 How Errors Are Addressed by the Registration System in Ontario

Where there is a fraudulent transaction rectification can be made by the registrar or the court under section 57(13). This will automatically trigger an entitlement to compensation. Members of the prescribed class will be entitled to compensation under section 57(4.1) or 57(4.2). Under section 57(4.1) the person must demonstrate the requisite due diligence but there is no such requirement under section 57

[88] Murray (2007), p. 8. See also LawPRO (2009) p. 24.

[89] See Bucknall (2008–2009), pp. 1–53 for an examination of real estate fraud in Ontario.

[90] Section 57(12).

[91] Section 57(2).

[92] The period is extended in the case of minority or incapacity.

[93] Moore and Globe (2003), p. 380. See section 59.

(4.2). Section 57(4.2) refers to a person suffering loss whereas 57(4.1) refers to a person being wrongfully deprived of land or of some estate or interest in land or has not received land or some estate or interest in land by reason of the registration of the fraudulent instrument that is now to be deleted from the register.

Those who are not members of this prescribed class must claim under section 57 (4). They must show the requisite due diligence and must not have been able to recover compensation from the applicant or the new owner under section 57(1). Also the person must have been wrongfully deprived of land or some estate or interest in land.

The registrar has also a general power to rectify errors under section 158(2) and the court, under section 159, can rectify the register in such manner as is considered just where it decides that a person is entitled to an estate, right or interest in or to registered land or a charge and as a consequence rectification is required. Rectification under these two sections does not automatically trigger an entitlement to compensation.

Where there is a registry error the registrar can correct the error on foot of section 158(2) and the court can rectify under section 159. Either can rectify under section 57(13) and again this will automatically trigger an entitlement to compensation under section 57(4.1). Compensation for the error may be claimed in the following circumstances:

1. under section 57(4.1) for members of the prescribed class who have demonstrated the requisite due diligence and the effect of the error, if not rectified, would be to deprive a person of land of which the person is legally in possession or legally in receipt of the rents and profits;
2. under section 57(5) to a person who suffers damage because of an error in recording an instrument; or
3. under section 57(4) where a person is wrongfully deprived of land or of some estate or interest in land by reason of any misdescription, omission or other error in the register. The person must not have been able to recover compensation from the applicant or the new owner under section 57(1).

The idealised participants will not have caused or contributed to the loss or knowingly participated or colluded in the fraud. It is presumed that the loss is not covered by title insurance though this does form a feature of conveyancing in Ontario and as such will be examined in Chap. 9. Only some of the idealised participants in the modeled transactions fall within the prescribed class of persons for the purposes of the Land Titles Act.

Both A and X are members of the prescribed class. B is also a member but Y is not a member. C and C2 are not members. Only those who are members can claim compensation under section 57(4.1) and section 57(4.2). Those who are not members must claim compensation under sections 57(4) or 57(5). The law distinguishes between registered owners and *bona fide* purchasers for value of residential property and all other parties.

As noted previously, under section 57(3), a purchaser or mortgagee in good faith for value is not liable by reason of the vendor or mortgagor having been registered as owner through fraud or error or having derived title from or through a person registered as owner through fraud or error, whether the fraud or error consisted of a wrong description of the property or otherwise. This will apply in the case of all of the (b) scenarios as D will have derived title from or through a person registered as owner through fraud or error i.e. B, Y or S. In the case of scenario 1(a) C is also protected if it is a mortgagee in good faith for value as it derived title from a person registered as owner through fraud or error i.e. B. However B, Y, S and SL will not be protected by section 57(3) as they did not derive title from or through another person registered as owner through fraud or error.

Scenario 1(a)

The registrar or court will rectify the register by deleting the fraudulent instrument under section 57(13)(b). This will restore A as the registered owner. B and C will lose title. As a *bona fide* purchaser for value B will automatically be entitled to compensation as he will have suffered loss as a result of the deletion.

C is not a member of this class and thus will need to claim compensation under section 57(4). C will need to show that it was wrongfully deprived of an estate or interest in land by reason of some other person being registered as owner through fraud. In this scenario that person was B. C will also need to demonstrate the requisite due diligence i.e. that it took reasonable steps to verify the identity of B and to verify that A was, in fact, selling the property. C will also need to show that it cannot recover compensation from B or the fraudster. If the fraudster has disappeared or was prosecuted but the proceeds of the fraud are gone then only B will be available.

It is interesting to note that if the cancellation of T's charge had been done fraudulently the legislation includes this in the definition of fraudulent instrument and the register could also be rectified under section 57(13)(b).

Scenario 1(b)

As there has been a subsequent transaction on the title the registrar and court will not order rectification of the register. A will lose title while the ownership of D and C2 will be upheld. They relied on the register. A is a member of the prescribed class but section 57(4.2) only applies when the fraudulent instrument is being deleted so it does not apply in this instance. Also section 57(4.1) only arises similarly if there is a rectification. So A is only entitled to claim under section 57(4) which requires that A must not be able to recover from B under section 57(1). A will not be able to claim against D or C2 as they are protected by section 57(3) as a purchaser and mortgagee in good faith for valuable consideration.

Scenario 2(a)

The registrar or court will rectify the register by deleting the fraudulent instrument under section 57(13)(b). This will restore X as the registered owner. Y will lose title. As a volunteer Y is not a member of the prescribed class and thus cannot claim compensation under section 57(4.1) or 57(4.2). Also Y cannot claim under section 57(4) since it was not some other person registered as owner through fraud; it was in fact Y who was registered through fraud. Thus Y is not entitled to compensation.

Scenario 2(b)

As there has been a subsequent transaction on the title the registrar and court will not order rectification of the register. X will lose title while the ownership of D and C2 will be upheld. They relied on the register. As soon as D purchases the register is secure regardless of the fact that the transfer to Y was a gift.

X is a member of the prescribed class but section 57(4.2) only applies when the fraudulent instrument is being deleted so it does not apply in this instance. Also section 57(4.1) only arises similarly if there is a rectification. So X is only entitled to claim under section 57(4) which requires that X must not be able to recover from Y under section 57(1). X will not be able to claim against D or C2 as they are protected by section 57(3) as a purchaser and mortgagee in good faith for valuable consideration.

Scenario 3(a)

The registrar or court will rectify the register under section 57(13)(c) if the effect of the error, if not rectified, would be to deprive B of land which he is legally in possession or legally in receipt of the rents and profits.[94] This would appear to also cover C if C was a mortgagee in possession. If this provision does not apply the registrar can rectify the error under section 158(2) or the court can rectify under section 159.

In this case B and C will not have been deprived of land or some estate or interest and there has been no fraud so compensation can only be claimed under section 57 (5) on the basis that they suffered damage because of an error in recording an instrument. S and SL would also be able to claim under this section but only if they suffered damage.

Scenario 3(b)

The registrar or court will rectify the register under section 57(13)(c) if the effect of the error, if not rectified, would be to deprive B of land which he is legally in possession or legally in receipt of the rents and profits. This is unlikely to be the case as D would have sought vacant possession. The registrar can however rectify the error under section 158(2) or the court can rectify under section 159.

D and C2 will have been deprived of their interests and thus will be able to claim compensation under section 57(5) or section 57(4). In order to claim under section 57(4) D and C2 would need to demonstrate that they cannot recover from B or S under section 57(1). It is unlikely that they would be able to recover from B since he is entirely innocent in this scenario but they should be able to recover from S. S is not a *bona fide* purchaser for value and thus would not be protected by section 57 (3).

If the court does not order rectification and the interests of D and C2 are upheld on the basis that they relied on the register then B and C will have been deprived of their interests and will be entitled to compensation under section 57(5) or section 57 (4). In order to claim under section 57(4) B and C will need to demonstrate that they

[94] This is presumably to cover a situation where B had let the property.

cannot recover from S or D. D will be protected from such a claim under section 57 (3) but S will not.

Scenario 4(a)
The registrar or court will rectify the register under section 57(13)(c) if the effect of the error, if not rectified, would be to deprive Y of land which he is legally in possession or legally in receipt of the rents and profits. If this provision does not apply the registrar can rectify the error under section 158(2) or the court can rectify under section 159.

In this case Y will not have been deprived of land or some estate or interest and there has been no fraud so compensation can only be claimed under section 57(5) on the basis that he suffered damage because of an error in recording an instrument. The fact that Y is a volunteer has no impact on the situation. S would also be able to claim under this section if he suffered damage.

Scenario 4(b)
The registrar or court will rectify the register under section 57(13)(c) if the effect of the error, if not rectified, would be to deprive Y of land which he is legally in possession or legally in receipt of the rents and profits. This is unlikely to be the case as D would have sought vacant possession. The registrar can however rectify the error under section 158(2) or the court can rectify under section 159.

If D and C2 are deprived of their interests they will be able to claim compensation under section 57(5) or section 57(4). In order to claim under section 57(4) D and C2 would need to demonstrate that they cannot recover from Y or S under section 57(1). It is unlikely that they would be able to recover from Y since he is entirely innocent in this scenario but they should be able to recover from S. S is not a *bona fide* purchaser for value and thus would not be protected by section 57(3). Similarly Y is not protected as a volunteer.

If the court does not order rectification and the interests of D and C2 are upheld then Y will have been deprived of its interest and will be entitled to compensation under section 57(5) or section 57(4). In order to claim under section 57(4) Y will need to demonstrate that it cannot recover from S or D. D will be protected from such a claim under section 57(3) but S will not.

7.6 Impact on Risk

The above scenarios demonstrate the choice to be made between dynamic security and static security. In cases of conflict between two innocent parties will the Irish courts hold that the register is defeasible or indefeasible and, if indefeasibility is supported, will it be immediate or deferred? Will the interests of B and C or D and C2 be bundled together to the detriment of the lender? Or will lenders be given more preferential status?

A policy of defeasibility may be likely where there is no subsequent transaction. Under section 31 the register could be rectified in favour of A and X. B, C and Y would be entitled to compensation under section 120.

A policy of indefeasibility would mean no rectification. If immediate indefeasibility is adopted then A will be at risk from the destructive effects of a registered transaction. A would be treated the same as U and V in Chap. 8 as title would pass to B and C2 even if there was some fault in the transaction and it was based on error or fraud. Under section 120 A would be entitled to compensation.

X is unlikely to be at the same risk in respect of Whiteacre. A court is unlikely to treat Y the same as the other parties and rectification is likely to be ordered against him if his registered title conflicts with that of X, an innocent prior owner, as Y is a volunteer. Y would however be entitled to compensation under section 120.

If there is a subsequent transaction a policy of deferred indefeasibility would mean that the innocent prior owner of Greenacre, A, would lose title.[95] Title would pass to the subsequent purchaser D and his lender C2. The first holders of the defective title, B and C, would not be at risk as they got repaid on the sale to the new owner who relied on the register i.e. D and C2. With deferred indefeasibility it is the original owner A who looses out. Similarly in the transfer of Whiteacre X would be at risk. Y would be paid on the sale to D so he would not lose out and the title of D and C2 would be upheld.

All the parties suffering loss would be entitled to compensation under section 120. In this instance A and X would be entitled to compensation and no distinction is made between a lender, volunteer or *bona fide* purchaser for value. Each is equally entitled to claim compensation though the amount of such compensation may differ. It is interesting to compare this to the preferential treatment given to B in Ontario as a *bona fide* purchaser for value versus the restrictions on Y and C in claiming compensation as they are not members of the prescribed class.

Some data is available on the number of claims made and amount of compensation paid out by the registries in Ireland and Ontario. These claims can be placed in the context of the total amount of changes made to the title register in Ireland and total number of electronic registrations in Ontario.

---

[95] In effect A would be treated the same as U and V in Chap. 8 i.e. destructive effects of a registered transaction.

7.7 Claims

7.7.1 Claims in Ireland

In Ireland over the 10 year period from 2004 to end 2013 a total of 276 payments were made to the value of €1.95 million.[96] Table 7.1 sets out details of the changes to the title register, the number of claims and compensation paid for this period.[97]

No data is available as to the nature of these claims. It may be that many relate to the recovery of costs for rectifications agreed between the parties under section 32 of the 1964 Act.

7.7.2 Claims in Ontario

More detailed data is publicly available from Ontario on claims, payment of compensation and rectifications.

In 2006 the Land Titles Act was amended to provide for the registration of a caution by the registrar[98] if it appears that a registered instrument may be fraudulent in order to prevent any further transactions on the title. If such a caution has been entered the registrar may hold a hearing before ordering rectification of the register. If the hearing determines that the registered instrument is a fraudulent instrument as defined under section 1 of the Land Titles Act then an order is issued to rectify the title by deleting the instrument from the parcel register.[99]

Since this power was granted to the registrar 60 such cautions have been registered and these have led to 43 rectifications of the register as set out in Table 7.2.[100] This also lists the volume of electronic registrations for each year.[101] This caution/hearing process only relates to allegations of fraud. Table 7.2 thus lists where an order for rectification is made when there is a determination that a fraudulent instrument has been registered.

[96] James O'Boyle Financial Controller Property Registration Authority by email 13 June 2014. More detailed data from other jurisdictions may be found. For example see Griggs (2001) for an examination of claims made on the Tasmania assurance fund from 1993 to 2000. 22 claims were made during this period and only one claim for fraud. Similarly see Ruoff et al. (1986), p. 904 re claims data for England. HM Land Registry publish details of claims in its annual report. See HM Land Registry (2013), pp. 40–41.

[97] Property Registration Authority (2013a), p. 14, Property Registration Authority (2011), pp. 37 and 42, Property Registration Authority (2008), p. 32. Also information from James O'Boyle Financial Controller Property Registration Authority by email 13 June 2014.

[98] Note that this is the Director of Titles as per the neutral vocabulary in Chap. 2.

[99] Alex Radley Legal and Technical Officer Service Ontario by email 7 June 2012.

[100] Ken Crawford Sr. Legal and Technical Analyst Service Ontario by email 27 June 2014.

[101] Vicki McArthur Teranet by email 18 June 2014.

Table 7.1 Total compensation claims and amounts in Ireland

Year	2004	2005	2006	2007	2008	2009	2010	2011	2012	2013
Changes to the title register[a]	[b]	221,815	220,072	217,954	572,604	612,910	575,019	529,506	445,112	387,123
Number of claims paid	29	22	33	33	23	32	27	32	26	19
Amount of euros of compensation paid	87,169	227,596	101,266	397,200	344,698	281,542	167,557	208,627	58,363	74,942

[a]Pre 2008 the figures relate to dealings completed which can lead to one or more registrations so the figures from 2008 are more accurate

[b]An accurate 2004 figure is no longer available

Table 7.2 Electronic registrations and fraud rectifications in Ontario

Year	2005	2006	2007	2008	2009	2010	2011	2012	2013
Electronic registrations	1.73 million	1.80 million	1.94 million	1.89 million	1.74 million	1.86 million	1.83 million	1.79 million	1.66 million
Fraud rectifications	N/A	N/A	4	6	11	7	7	7	1

Table 7.3 Total compensation claims and amounts in Ontario

Year	2005	2006	2007	2008	2009	2010	2011	2012	2013
Number of compensation claims	9	3	29	10	8	15	7	3	4
Amount of Canadian dollars of compensation paid	1,086,591	394,423	1,835,588	1,821,726	524,876	821,523	1,024,914	335,538	184,405

Table 7.4 Breakdown of compensation claims and amounts: fraud and non-fraud Ontario

2005-Fraud	2005-Non fraud	2006-Fraud	2006-Non fraud	2007-Fraud	2007-Non fraud
5—$889,672	4—$196,919	2—$387,097	1—$7,326	17—$1,398,121	11—$421,837
2008-Fraud	2008-Non fraud	2009-Fraud	2009-Non fraud	2010-Fraud	2010-Non fraud
9—$1,821,726	1—$157,871	6—$522,172	2—$2,704	8—$593,127	7—$228,396
2011-Fraud	2011-Non fraud	2012-Fraud	2012-Non fraud	2013-Fraud	2013 Non fraud
6—$1,021,698	1—$3,215	2—$334,803	1—$734	3—$183,978	1—$427

Only nine of the 43 caution/hearing rectifications have resulted in claims to the LTAF paying out a total of $105,275.[102] It may be that the parties affected by the other rectifications did not seek compensation or they may not have qualified on the basis of being covered by title insurance.[103]

There is a separate process whereby each of the individual land registrars can register a caution and serve notice of intention to rectify title on all parties having an interest where an error in a record has occurred.[104] If no objections are received the correction will be made or if there are objections then a hearing will take place. These are not tracked separately[105] and there are no statistics available on the number of such rectifications.

Information is however available on compensation claims for fraud and non fraud cases. Table 7.3 gives the total number of LTAF claims for compensation and the total amounts paid out while Table 7.4 provides a breakdown between the claims and amounts for fraud and non fraud cases.[106]

If a claim cannot be paid out completely the registrar, acting in the capacity of an administrative Tribunal,[107] may choose to hold a hearing. The decisions of this Tribunal are made available online to the public and the decisions from 1986 are currently available.[108] These decisions issue when a determination has been made that the loss does not meet the requirements under the Land Titles Act and is not

[102] Ken Crawford Sr. Legal and Technical Analyst Service Ontario by email 27 June 2014.

[103] Where a prior registered owner has title insurance they must claim against the insurer rather than seeking compensation from the LTAF.

[104] For example Ministry error or an error in the conversion of records.

[105] Alex Radley Legal and Technical Officer Service Ontario by email 7 June 2012.

[106] Ken Crawford Sr. Legal and Technical Analyst Service Ontario by email 27 June 2014.

[107] Service Ontario, pp. 1, 5 and 8.

[108] See LTAF Decisions at http://www.ontario.ca/home-and-community/land-titles-assurance-fund-decisions. Accessed 23 June 2014.

Table 7.5 Decisions of tribunal in Ontario

Application	Outcome	Reason for decision	Other relevant information
Tannenbaum 2007	Applicant paid compensation to cover his costs and transfer void; deleted from title to the property and the applicant reinstated as the registered owner	Fraud: Imposter posed as registered owner, incorporated a company, transferred the property to that company and then charged the property	Chargee gave consent to rectify title to put title back into the name of the applicant free of the charge. *Lawrence v. Maple Trust Co.* cited
Sam Morreale Investments Inc. 2007	No compensation paid	Contributory negligence under section 59. Also applicant did not take reasonable steps to mitigate the loss	An error in an entry on the register had been made. Failure to notify is not an error which can be compensable out of the fund
Jarvis 2007	Application dismissed	Fraud alleged but transfer already held to be valid in court hearing	No evidence that the court proceedings were improper in any way. Any reconsideration of the matter would be an abuse of process
Flanagan 2007	No compensation paid	No error made in an entry on the register	
Binnie 2007	Compensation paid to cover costs	Recording errors when title administratively converted from the unregistered to the registered system	Misdescription also alleged but these found to have existed prior to the administrative conversion of title
Tim 2008	No compensation paid	No error on the part of the registrar	
RA & J Investment 2008	Paid compensation and costs	Substantive issues determined by court	Fraudulent discharge of charge
G.R. 2009	No compensation paid	Applicant did not have an interest in the property because he had obtained title through the use of a fraudulent power of attorney. He met the definition of "fraudulent person"	The applicant himself was the person registered as owner through fraud. He did not meet the definition that would place him in the prescribed class; section 57 (4.1)
J.W. 2010	No compensation paid	Discharge of charge was fraudulent but claiming an amount for compensation without proof that he suffered a loss in that amount	Applicant obtained court judgment by default, without a hearing and without proving to the court the amount of his loss

(continued)

Table 7.5 (continued)

Application	Outcome	Reason for decision	Other relevant information
C.G. 2010	Application dismissed	Held to be fraud but could not find that the payment of compensation would be just due to contradictory and unexplained evidence	Law pre the Modernization Act applied. Also held that there was contributory negligence under section 59
J.L. 2012	Paid compensation and costs	Direct loss suffered as a result of fraudulent statement in affidavit and transfer	Lost entitlement to enforce writ against the property

compensable or less than the full amount claimed will be compensated.[109] They are not included in the above statistics. Table 7.5 is a review of the decisions since 2006.[110]

Service Ontario[111] also provide details of compensation paid by notice of determination of liability when no written decision issues.[112]

The registry report that the incidence of title fraud involving unauthorised changes to the title register is extremely low relative to the number of registrations each year. Over the 10 year period from 2002 to 2011, there were on average 10.2 claims of title fraud each year to the LTAF out of an average of 1.8 million registrations.[113]

By 2010 fraud had moved from being the fifth most common cause of claims in conveyancing to third place and fraud costs are going up.[114] Though this may be attributed in part to increases in property prices. Murray distinguishes between mortgage fraud, where the value of the property may be artificially inflated or when a mortgage is fraudulently obtained, based on false information or identification, and title fraud which involves fraudsters using stolen identity or forged documents to transfer title or obtain loan funds without the true owner's knowledge.[115]

---

[109] Alex Radley Legal and Technical Officer Service Ontario by email 7 June 2012.

[110] Only decisions issued after the Modernization Act. This excludes one decision made in 2007 which was a French language hearing and decision.

[111] Service Ontario is the means by which the government of Ontario delivers services to its citizens.

[112] http://www.ontario.ca/home-and-community/land-titles-assurance-fund-decisions. Accessed 23 June 2014.

[113] Alex Radley Legal and Technical Officer Service Ontario by email 7 June 2012.

[114] See MacInnes and Pinnington (2010), p. 19.

[115] Murray (2007), pp. 2–3.

Murray is of the view that, as "there have been few claims to the Land Titles Assurance Fund resulting from...[the automation] process, it has been a successful initiative."[116] Moore and Globe provide a different perspective on the low level of claims. They are of the view that that

> [i]n practice, claims against the Land Titles Assurance Fund and professional practice claims against LawPRO are difficult and expensive to pursue. Case law, combined with restrictions in the statute, bar potential claimants in most cases from recovering against the fund, particularly with respect to criminal fraud.[117]

This, in their view, explains the extent of title insurance in Ontario as it "provides a practical, non-litigious alternative for clients who wish to arrange additional protection against fraud or defects in the title or legal services related aspects of a real estate transaction."[118] They refer to the fact that over half of residential transactions include the purchase of title insurance[119] however this was in 2003. The percentage is now much higher.[120] This relationship between state compensation and title insurance is examined further in Chap. 9.

There is a question mark over the value of such information and its comparability between jurisdictions. Is a low level of claims, where little money is paid out, evidence of a careful and robust registration system or are the rules just too tight? Does a deficit of applications for compensation indicate an inherently fairness in the rules of registration and that few people are disadvantaged? Or does it indicate the opposite i.e. that the system is inherently unfair, there can be few valid claims and this unfairness is hidden because the detail of applications for compensation are hidden?

Certainly in Ireland there is a lack of hard data about errors in registration and many disputes only come to light when there is a court judgment. This is a challenge for research in this area and makes it difficult to explore samples of types of transactions where errors arise and also to weigh incidences of errors as against fraud. A high incidence of errors and claims against the register would make indefeasibility unsustainable however if indefeasibility was abandoned and insurance removed then the register would become a mere deeds register.[121]

---

[116] Murray (2004), p. 5.

[117] Moore and Globe (2003), p. 380.

[118] Moore and Globe (2003), p. 380.

[119] Moore and Globe (2003), p. 380.

[120] Waters (2010), p. 14.

[121] There would be no compensation available to ameliorate the risk of an error and the title conferred would not be guaranteed by the state.

Conclusion

Subject to there being no change in the underlying legislation the question arises as to whether eConveyancing will lead to a higher or lower incidence of errors. A high incidence of errors would lead to a backlash against the move towards eConveyancing or a demise of the protection afforded by registration by judicial decisions that erode that protection. If the register cannot be relied upon and errors are frequent then there will be a reluctance to move towards eConveyancing with its increased reliance on registration.

In some instances this reliance is based on increasing the obligations of lawyers who use the system. Muir is of the view that the registration system has always relied on the integrity and honesty of conveyancing professionals and thus there is nothing new in New Zealand's automatic system.[122] eRegistration reinforces the role of lawyers as trusted professionals in the conveyancing process and questioning this "would portray a very dim view of the competence and integrity of the legal profession."[123] However this disregards the transfer of increased liability to such professionals and the danger that, in time, the compensation fund would be disbanded in favour of direct liability being imposed on such users of the system or on land owners who may of necessity turn to title insurance.[124]

As Ireland is not proposing to implement an automatic system there will be no passing of the registrars function to lawyers. Changes to the title register will not be opened up to a wider pool of people which would potentially increase the likelihood for error or fraud.[125] The registrar only will continue to be responsible for making changes to the register. There will be no passing of liability for registration and no argument that the compensation fund provisions or cover should be amended or diluted.[126] This aspect is explored further in Chap. 9.

Ireland has a robust registration system which has been subject to few challenges and the likelihood is that further advances in eRegistration and eConveyancing may only serve to strengthen this. Initial evidence suggests that errors in registration applications are reduced due to the automatic compliance checks built into the electronic system. Thus the threat to all

(continued)

[122] Muir (2003), p. 317.

[123] Muir (2003), pp. 317 and 321.

[124] See Flaws (2003) for the impact of agency registration in New Zealand on compensation.

[125] See the United Nations Economic Commission for Europe Working Party on Land Administration (2011) for details of how land registries are combatting fraud particularly in the context of increased online access to land registration information.

[126] See O'Connor (2003), pp. 1–27 for details of jurisdictions where legislation has been introduced to exclude or restrict the right to indemnity, thus shifting risk to land owners or their representatives.

parties from an unauthorised or illegitimate alteration of the register may reduce in an eConveyancing environment.[127]

In both Ontario and Ireland rectification is allowed by the court or the registrar. Compensation may be payable from the indemnity fund as a first resort and there is no need for the disposed homeowner to sue the wrongdoer.[128]

Rectification in Ireland by the registrar is limited to errors originating in the registering authority. In those circumstances the title register can be rectified and compensation will be payable to any person who suffers loss as a result of the error. In the case of errors not originating in the registering authority rectification can be ordered by the court if there is actual fraud or mistake. Compensation will be payable to anyone who suffered a loss.

The legislation is broad enough to allow Ireland a choice between following the Torrens systems which gives an absolute guarantee of title to D (deferred indefeasibility) or the Australian and New Zealand systems which give an absolute guarantee of title to B (immediate indefeasibility).[129]

The question of fairness arises and whether immediate indefeasibility awards ownership to the 'wrong' person. When there are a number of innocent parties how does the law determine which person's interest is to be valued the most? To award title to the new owner offends against the principle *nemo dat quod non habet* and deprives A of his title without his consent. There is a conflict between the registered ownership of B, C, D or C2 and A's claim for reinstatement. The law must balance between the title register giving no guarantee at all, thus becoming a deeds register, and the potential unfairness of absolute and immediate indefeasibility.

In Ontario the register will be rectified in favour of A and against B and C except when the title has been sold to D. Once the subsequent transaction to D has taken place no rectification will be ordered and A may be entitled to compensation. The sale to B and charge in favour of C will be seen as one transaction and indefeasibility will be deferred to D with a knock on benefit for C2. Ontario favours deferred indefeasibility and certainty of the register thus D, who has relied on the register, will prevail over an innocent prior registered owner, A.

This deferred indefeasibility protects those market participants that rely on the register, thus upholding dynamic security however when there is no subsequent transaction static security prevails. As Bucknall notes deferred

(continued)

[127] For example British Columbia appears to have a robust eRegistration system. In the past 10 years the LTSA processed over nine million transactions but only two claims related to fraud causing loss of title occurred and were paid from the compensation fund. See BC OnLine.

[128] In Ontario this is limited to members of a prescribed class.

[129] Cooke (2004), p. 402.

indefeasibility means that the circumstances in which a landowner loses his or her legal title through a fraud will be extremely rare.[130]

Ireland has not had a landmark fraud case with an innocent prior owner pitted against an innocent registered transferee. Cooke notes that Irish writers are untroubled by the issue of indefeasibility as it is not clear from the legislation or comment upon it what would be the position of an innocent purchaser tracing title through a forged disposition.[131] She notes that either it has never arisen or has been dealt with by the registrar and remains unreported but the likelihood is that an English approach would be taken based on section 31.[132]

According to Cooke the English approach expresses indefeasibility in money, not in land.[133] The transferee, who took from a fraudster, will be paid compensation while an innocent prior owner will get his land back. In England however, if the transferee is in possession, he will keep the land and the innocent prior owner will get compensation. Surely this comment by Cooke clouds two different aspects of title registration. Firstly, indefeasible title as being conclusive and unimpeachable[134] and secondly the compensation provisions which ameliorate the adverse impact of that indefeasibility. These are distinct elements which are not interchangeable.

Title indefeasibility will protect ownership of the specific piece of land but compensation indefeasibility treats ownership in general as equivalent to wealth. The nature of title indefeasibility is not merely to preserve value or wealth but instead, for land owners, it will mean that their title to that specific piece of property is preserved. Compensation indefeasibility puts a financial value on ownership and this can only be equivalent to title indefeasibility when the owner is interested in the exchange value and not the use value of the land. This is generally the case with lenders.

In Ireland the registrar does not have the power to rectify where there is a forged disposition and the Irish courts have not had opportunity to examine these issues. Thus it is not surprising that Irish researchers and writers have failed to examine the matter in any depth. There may be an examination of rectification or compensation but it is not couched in the cloak of indefeasibility.

If deferred indefeasibility is adopted then A would be entitled to compensation and the subsequent owner D would retain title. If immediate

(continued)

[130] Bucknall (2008–2009), p. 45.

[131] Cooke (2003), p. 169.

[132] Cooke (2003), p. 169.

[133] Cooke (2003), p. 105.

[134] See Ruoff (1952), p. 118.

indefeasibility is adopted then A would again be entitled to compensation and title would pass to B however if the title was held to be defeasible A would retain title and B would be entitled to compensation.

The key decisions are policy ones. How should Ireland decide the balance between indefeasibility (immediate or deferred) and defeasibility of the register, dynamic and static security, the right to title and the right to compensation?

The Ontario experience shows a high level of electronic integration is compatible with a policy that respects and protects static security while placing due diligence requirements on those parties most able to systematically police and keep the system honest. In order to show justice the system attempts to balance static and dynamic security and this determines which risks are indemnified by compensation and which are not.

Chapter 8 now examines the remaining risk categories arising after registration.

References

Arruñada, B. (2010). Leaky title syndrome? *New Zealand Law Journal*.

BC OnLine. Title security in BC. http://www.ltsa.ca/cms/title-security-in-bc. Accessed 18 June 2014.

Breen, O. (2000). Registration of title and overriding interests – Another crack in the mirror? *Conveyancing & Property Law Journal*, *5*(3).

Bucknall, B. (2008–2009). Real estate fraud and systems of title registration: The paradox of certainty. *Canadian Business Law Journal*, *47*.

Cooke, E. (2003). *The new law of land registration*. Oxford: Hart.

Cooke, E. (2004). Land registration: Void and voidable titles. *Edinburgh Law Review*, *8*.

Deeney, J. (2014). *Registration of Deeds and Title in Ireland*. Great Britain: Bloomsbury.

Dowling, A. (1993). Rectification of the title register. *Northern Ireland Legal Quarterly*, *44*.

Fitzgerald, B. (1995). *Land registry practice* (2nd ed.). Dublin: Round Hall Press.

Flaws, J. (2003). Compensation for loss under the Torrens system – Extending state compensation with private insurance. In D. Grinlinton (Ed.), *Torrens in the twenty-first century*. Wellington: LexisNexis.

Glover, W. E. (1933). *A treatise on the registration of ownership of land in Ireland*. Dublin: John Falconer.

Griggs, L. (2001). Torrens title in a digital world. *Murdoch University Electronic Journal of Law*, *8*(3). http://www.murdoch.edu.au/elaw/issues/v8n3/griggs83_text.html. Accessed 13 June 2014.

HM Land Registry. (2013). Annual Report and Accounts 2012/2013. HM Land Registry. http://www.landregistry.gov.uk/__data/assets/pdf_file/0016/46222/Land-Registry-Annual-Report-and-Accounts-2012-13.pdf. Accessed 19 June 2014.

LawPRO. (2009, July). Minister discusses changes to Land Titles Assurance Fund. *LawPRO Magazine*. http://www.practicepro.ca/lawpromag/default.asp. Accessed 13 June 2014.

MacInnes, N., & Pinnington, D. (2010, December). Real estate claims trends. *LawPRO Magazine*. http://www.practicepro.ca/lawpromag/default.asp. Accessed 23 June 2014.

McAllister, D. L. (1973). *Registration of title in Ireland*. Dublin: Council of Law Reporting for Ireland.

Moore, M. E., & Globe, J. M. (2003). *Title searching and conveyancing in Ontario* (5th ed.). Canada: LexisNexis.

Muir, R. (2003). Electronic registration: The legislative scheme and implications for the Torrens system in New Zealand. In D. Grinlinton (Ed.), *Torrens in the twenty-first century*. Wellington: LexisNexis.

Murray, K. (2004). *Electronic registration and other modernization initiatives in Ontario's land registration system*. In Law Reform Commission Annual Conference. http://www.lawreform.ie/Annual%20Conference%202004.PDF. Accessed 18 Feb 2009.

Murray, K. (2007). *Legislative amendments relating to real estate fraud and the Ministry of Government Services Real Estate Fraud Action Plan*. In Registering the World Conference, Dublin, 26–28 September 2007. http://www.landregistry.ie/eng/Dublin_Conference_2007/Conference_Papers/. Accessed 9 Sept 2010.

O'Connor, P. (2003). Double indemnity – Title insurance and the Torrens systems. *Queensland University of Technology Law & Justice Journal, 3*(1). https://lr.law.qut.edu.au/article/view/123. Accessed 23 June 2014.

O'Connor, P. (2005). Registration of invalid dispositions: Who gets the property? In E. Cooke (Ed.), *Modern studies in property law* (Vol. III). Oxford: Hart.

O'Connor, P. (2009a). Deferred and immediate indefeasibility: Bijural ambiguity in registered land title systems. *Edinburgh Law Review, 13*.

O'Connor, P. (2009b). Immediate indefeasibility for mortgagees: A moral hazard? *Bond Law Review, 21*(2).

Property Registration Authority. (2008). Annual Report 2007. The Property Registration Authority. http://www.prai.ie/eng/Publications/Annual_Reports/PRA_Annual_Reports_html. Accessed 5 June 2014

Property Registration Authority. (2011). Annual Report 2010. Property Registration Authority. http://www.prai.ie/eng/Publications/Annual_Reports/PRA_Annual_Reports_html. Accessed 5 June 2014

Property Registration Authority. (2013a). Annual Report 2012. Property Registration Authority. http://www.prai.ie/eng/Publications/Annual_Reports/PRA_Annual_Reports_.html. Accessed 5 June 2014

Property Registration Authority. (2013b). Practice direction rectification of error and claims for compensation (updated 1 February 2013). http://www.prai.ie/eng/Legal_Professional_Customers/Legal_Practices_Procedures/Practice_Directions/17_Rectification_Of_Error_And_Claims_For_Compensation/. Accessed 5 June 2014.

Ruoff, T. (1952). An Englishman looks at the Torrens system: Part 1: The mirror principle. *Australian Law Journal, 26*.

Ruoff, T. B. F., & Roper, R. B. (1986). *Ruoff & Roper on the law and practice of registered conveyancing* (5th ed.). London: Stevens and Sons.

Service Ontario. Information regarding the land titles assurance fund and the tribunal's rules of procedure. http://files.ontariogovernment.ca/ont06_023546_1.pdf. Accessed 23 June 2014.

Troister, S. (2004, June). Can we really rely on the land titles register? *LawPRO Magazine*. http://www.practicepro.ca/lawpromag/default.asp. Accessed 13 June 2014.

United Nations Economic Commission for Europe Working Party on Land Administration. (2011). Study on the challenges of fraud to land administration institutions. United Nations. http://www.unece.org/fileadmin/DAM/hlm/documents/Publications/fraud.study.e.r.pdf. Accessed 23 June 2014.

Waters, K. A. (2010, December). There's more to title insurance than meets the eye. *LawPRO Magazine*. http://www.practicepro.ca/lawpromag/default.asp. Accessed 13 June 2014.

Chapter 8
After Registration

8.1 Introduction

The interest of a registered owner may be subject to claims, whereby U or V seek such relief as a court may grant. The claim may be legal or equitable and may arise from rights which the registered owner created whether by contract or by conduct in favour of U or V. In such circumstances the court may order the registered owner to give up the whole or part of their registered interest[1] or to note a burden, such as a judgment mortgage, on it.

Where the registered owner is ordered to give up their interest to U or V this may be due to a number of factors. A volunteer will have taken the land subject to all prior unregistered rights held by U or V. Alternatively there may have been some defect in the transfer that makes the title void or voidable at the instigation of U or V. The court may order rectification of the register.

Section 57(13) of the Ontario Land Titles Act allows the registrar or court to rectify the register if a registered instrument would be absolutely void if unregistered. There is no similar provision in Ireland. Section 30(1) of the 1964 Act does provide that any disposition or charge which if unregistered would be fraudulent and void, shall, notwithstanding registration, be fraudulent and void in like manner. This however is subject to the provisions of the Act with respect to registered dispositions for valuable consideration. In the absence of fraud, rectification could be ordered by the court under section 31 on the basis of mistake. In this way U and V could enforce a claim or right against the registered owner.

Chapter 7 has already examined the position where a claim leads to rectification of the register. This chapter examines other lesser type claims. The registered owner is not dispossessed but his interest may be impacted by the claim if it is successful.

[1] See Deeney (2014), p. 173 for examples of cases where ownership passes to another person otherwise than by transfer from the registered owner. This is subject to notice being given to the registered owner except where their estate or interest is overreached. See p. 175.

G. Brennan, *The Impact of eConveyancing on Title Registration*,
DOI 10.1007/978-3-319-10341-9_8

Alternatively the claim may not be recognised or the registered owner may be able to transfer free of it. When this happens the interest of the claim or right holder is at risk.

This chapter deals with these remaining risk categories as identified in Chap. 5. These are interests off the register which affect title, the destructive effects of a registered transaction and interests not recognised and not capable of registration. Each category demonstrates how third party rights are impacted by the registration system and the effect of those rights on the other participants.

8.1.1 Interests Off the Register Which Affect Title

All parties to a conveyancing transaction are at risk with respect to interests off the register which affect title.

These risks can be divided into two categories. Firstly the risk from overriding interests. Overriding interests bind the registered owner whether shown on the register or not.[2] Those who hold such an interest possess an invaluable benefit[3] as their interest binds the world even a *bona fide* purchaser for value. These present a risk to all parties. The risk is from U and V.

Secondly there is the risk from other interests and claims. They may be interests already held by U or arise when V makes a successful property claim and becomes U. This presents a risk to all parties and the risk is from the prior owner or from U and V. The risk from those other interests and claims arising during the registration gap has already been examined in Chap. 6. Chapter 7 has dealt with the position where a claim of prior ownership might arise after registration thus leading to rectification of the register. Thus this chapter will examine the risk from overriding interests and this is the first risk category to be examined in this chapter.

8.1.2 Destructive Effects of a Registered Transaction

A registered transaction poses a risk to U the third party and V the property claimant.

It may be that some other right has priority and destroys the third party right or property claim. Any system of registration that requires an interest to be registered if it is to survive a disposition entails the risk of non-compliance and subsequent destruction. These failed property interests are lost. They are void against a

[2] Gray and Gray (2009), p. 191 refer to a 'crack in the mirror' which detracts from the mirror image the title register is meant to reflect.

[3] Fitzgerald (1995), p. 219. See section 37(3) of the 1964 Act.

purchaser for want of protection by registration. When this occurs it could be said that the interest is overridden by registration.

This is due to the destructive effects of a registered transaction. Due to the transaction B, C or Y's right may take priority over the right held by U or asserted by V. U may hold an equitable interest by virtue of a direct or indirect financial contribution or as a result of some agreement or arrangement with A or X. If that interest is not an overriding interest and U does not register a note on the folio, or the interest itself, if it is capable of registration, then a purchaser who registers subsequently will take free of the unprotected equitable interest.

The registered transaction may transfer the claim of V or the right of U to some other property, devalue the claim or destroy it entirely. In circumstances where the claim is transferred it would be more accurate to say that the right is defeated as a claim against the land but it may continue to be a claim against other property i.e. the fund.

This transfer is known as overreaching.[4] This may arise in relation to property rights that are capable of affecting title but which cannot be registered directly. An example is the beneficial interest under a trust. It survives a purchase but the interest of the beneficiary may be overreached by the purchaser and the right of the beneficiary becomes a right to the trust funds. While the right is not destroyed by a disposition it does become different in nature. The beneficiary may also have a personal claim against the trustee if the trustee acted in breach of the trust. In some instances these rights are not overreached and this is the situation where the transfer is to a volunteer such as Y.

This is the second risk category to be examined in this chapter.

8.1.3 Rights Not Recognised

In the schematic U and V are at risk if their claim or right is not protected by the registering authority as it is not recognised as a right capable of registration by the legislation. The state acting through the registrar will refuse registration. This will apply if the right is purely personal and cannot be converted into a property right, the right is not a registrable right or the claim by V is not mature. Where rights are not recognised by the registration system they cannot gain the protection offered by registration. This is the third and last category of risk examined in this chapter.

---

[4] See Megarry and Wade (2000), pp. 124 and 127–128 for the distinction between interests being overreached and overridden. See also *City of London Building Society v. Flegg* [1987] 3 All ER 435.

8.1.4 *Scenarios*

In order to examine these risks in detail a number of scenarios are presented to demonstrate the impact of different types of rights and claims on the participants in the schematic.[5]

Scenario 1(a)
A grants a short term tenancy of Greenacre to U for a period of 2 years. Under the terms of the tenancy U is in occupation of Greenacre.

Scenario 1(b)
X grants a short term tenancy of Whiteacre to U for a period of 2 years. Under the terms of the tenancy U is in occupation of Whiteacre.

Scenario 2(a)
U gave A the purchase monies for Greenacre.

Scenario 2(b)
U gave X the purchase monies for Whiteacre.

Scenario 3(a)
U claims that he has a right of way by prescription over Greenacre.

Scenario 3(b)
X expressly grants U a right of way over Whiteacre.

Each of these scenarios is examined in detail in the context of the conveyancing systems in Ireland and Ontario.

8.2 Overriding Interests

Some overriding interests are detectable if the appropriate enquiries are made. Some are interests which are deemed to be in need of protection such as rights held by someone in occupation and others are deemed unsuitable for registration.

The existence of such overriding interests makes the register an incomplete reflection of the state of the title at any given moment. Where such interests exist the state guarantee of title is qualified. The register will warrant that the title of the land owner is as stated on the register. It will not warrant that the title cannot be

---

[5] See Megarry and Wade (2000), pp. 130–131 for similar type examples to illustrate the position in England and Wales.

affected by anything off the register. These interests make the guarantee of title less effective and are seen as being one exception to indefeasibility.

The overriding interests that apply in Ontario and Ireland are set out in Chap. 2 under neutral vocabulary. Examples of overriding interests are short term leases, rates, taxes, easements or the rights of someone in occupation. They may be apparent by an inspection of the property or identifiable from some public source of information. Purchasers are expected to check such registers, make appropriate enquiries and inspect the property. They may also seek a declaration from the transferor stating that no such interests arise.[6] Overriding interests "operate outside the registered system and are treated as being like unregistered land. They have to be ascertained by the traditional methods of investigation of inquiry and inspection."[7] Consequently the existence of such interests make it difficult to implement a full eConveyancing system.

There are in effect two different types of overriding interests but they are given the same degree of protection. Some overriding interests do not require occupation while scenario 1 relates to an overriding interest contingent upon occupation. The rights of an occupier should be distinguished from the fact of his occupation. In the English case of *Wallcite Ltd. v. Ferrishurst Ltd.*[8] an option to purchase was an overriding interest whereas in the Irish case of *Honiball v. McGrath*,[9] which cited the English case, rights to receive care facilities were not considered to be rights in land.

Any interest in land may be protected by actual occupation[10] however, a personal right cannot be an overriding interest even if the claimant is in occupation As per Lord Templeman in *City of London Building Society v. Flegg*[11] there had to be a combination of an interest which justified continuing occupation plus actual occupation to constitute an overriding interest; actual occupation was not an interest in itself. The right must be a property right in its nature and capable of binding land. This is demonstrated by the English case of *National Provincial Bank Ltd. v. Ainsworth*[12] where a wife who remained in the former family home was held to have a personal right against her husband and she had no right good against third parties. She did not have an overriding interest under section 70(1)(g) of the Land Registration Act 1925 and the bank was entitled to possession.[13] This subsection was replicated in section 72(1)(j) of Ireland's 1964 Act.

---

[6] A section 72 declaration is automatically sought on completion in a registered conveyancing transaction in Ireland.

[7] Harpum (2000), p. 14.

[8] *Wallcite Ltd. v. Ferrishurst Ltd.* [1999] 1 All ER 977.

[9] *Honiball v. McGrath* [2000] IEHC 33.

[10] See the list of overriding interests in Ireland at Sect. 2.3.2.

[11] *City of London Building Society v. Flegg* [1987] 3 All ER 435.

[12] *National Provincial Bank Ltd. v. Ainsworth* [1965] 2 All ER 472.

[13] See Murphy (2013), pp. 30–34 for further case law.

8.2.1 Short Term Tenancy

Short term tenancies are capable of being overriding interests in both Ireland and Ontario provided the tenant is in occupation.[14]

In Ireland the term must be for less than 21 years and in Ontario there must be an unexpired term of less than 3 years. The short term tenancies granted by A and X in scenario 1 are for 2 years and the tenant is in occupation. The tenancies fall within the category of overriding interests in both Ireland and Ontario and have the same effect.

If U was not in occupation under the tenancy then his interest would not be an overriding interest. Similarly if U held an option to purchase or a beneficial interest then it would not be overriding until he goes into occupation. If U does not hold an overriding interest his tenancy will be treated the same as the expressly granted right of way is treated in Ireland in scenario 3(b).[15]

The interest will be an overriding interest providing there is occupation under the tenancy or lease. This contrasts with the position in Ireland for other rights where there is occupation. Those rights are overriding except where, upon enquiry the rights are not disclosed by the person holding them.[16]

Scenario 1(a)

If the tenancy was not disclosed by A, B will buy subject to it but will have a claim against A. If it was disclosed by A on the sale, B will still be subject to it but will have no claim against A. Such an interest will bind B despite the fact that it is not reflected on the register and even if B had no notice of its existence. C's interest will also be subject to it but C may have a claim against B if the existence of the interest was known by B but was not disclosed and it has an impact on the value of C's security.

For example if B defaults on the repayments then C may not be able to enforce its charge and sell as a mortgagee in possession while the tenancy exists as U is in occupation of Greenacre.

Scenario 1(b)

Y will take Whiteacre subject to the tenancy and Y will have no claim against X unless X gave a warranty that there was no such interest. This is unlikely given the fact that this is a gift. Again notice or the lack of notice of the interest is irrelevant.

---

[14] Section 72(1)(i) of the 1964 Act and section 44(1) paragraph 4 of the Land Titles Act.

[15] It is a burden which may be registered under section 69(1)(g) of the 1964 Act. This refers to any lease where the term granted is for a life or lives, or is determinable on a life or lives, or exceeds 21 years, or where the term is for any less estate or interest but the occupation is not in accordance with the lease.

[16] See Sect. 2.3.2. In England and Wales where there is an interest protected by actual occupation consideration is given to the discoverability of that occupation. A transferee is not bound by such an interest where the occupation would not have been obvious on a reasonably careful inspection of the land at the time of the disposition. See the Land Registration Act 2002, Sch 3, para 2(c).

8.2.2 Effect of Overriding Interest

The effect of an overriding interest is that the interests of B, Y and C may be devalued and they will suffer a loss of investment. If the overriding interest includes the right to occupation B and Y will not have the use value of the property and C may not be able to enforce its charge so that it will have little or no value as security.

These interests bind the world and it is irrelevant that B, C or Y did not have notice of the existence of the interest. In the case of these interests there is no difference in risk between B and Y. Both are equally bound by such interests. It does not matter whether the interest could have been registered, and was not, or that the interest is unregistrable. Equally it is of no relevance whether the overriding interest existed prior to completion of the transaction or came into existence during the registration gap.

This can occur if a right capable of being overriding is granted by A or X or matures during the registration gap. This right is granted to or held by V who then becomes U. Such a right will be good against A or X and B or Y will take the property subject to it.

In practical terms both B and Y would have sought vacant possession. They are also likely to have inspected the property and discovered the occupation by U if it had not already been disclosed by A and X. In the case of Greenacre if A contracted to give vacant possession but was not able to do so, B would have a right of rescission.

Unlike Ireland, Ontario does not protect the rights of those in receipt of rents and profits.[17] This can be more problematic to determine but again B and Y would likely be warned of the interest when finding a lessee in occupation. If such interests or potential interests come to light U may be required to join in the transaction to release the property or asked to postpone their claim in order to give C's charge priority.

All parties are at risk from overriding interests. This risk to A, B, X, Y, C and D on a subsequent transaction is the same regardless whether the participant is a *bona fide* purchaser for value or a volunteer. All are equally at risk though some parties may have a claim against another. In the modeled transactions B may have a claim against A, C may have a claim against B and D may have a claim against his vendor. Y is unlikely to have a claim against X as he is a volunteer and takes subject to all unregistered rights, whether or not they are overriding interests.

[17] This is an alternative to actual occupation under section 72(1)(j).

8.3 Destructive Effects of a Registered Transaction

The transfer of a legal estate or interest may overreach any over-reachable equitable interest held by U. Overreaching will not occur if the transfer was expressly subject to the equitable interest. There may also be certain formalities that have to be adhered to.

The trust provides a clear demonstration of how a registered transaction may have this destructive effect by virtue of overreaching the beneficial interest held by U. If overreaching occurs it does not destroy the equitable interest but removes it as a claim against the land and instead the claim attaches to the trust fund. Overreaching will cleanse the title taken by the transferee of the equitable interest and protect the security of his registered interest. The title will be simplified as U will have no claim on the title. In terms of the idealised participants U will become V. In the case of a wrongful sale, V may then have a personal action against the transferor.

If the transferor uses the trust fund to buy another property then V's beneficial interest will once more be in the land. V will become U again.

8.3.1 Trust

In Ireland section 21(1) of the 2009 Act provides for the overreaching of trusts and settlements where there are two trustees or a trust corporation but in some instances only a single trustee is required.[18] The overreaching is provided for the protection of transferees where there is the transfer of a legal estate or interest.[19]

Thus a transferee can overreach existing equitable interests provided he or she acts in good faith and pays the purchase monies to the appropriate people i.e. in this instance the trustees.

A transferee does not gain this protection if the conveyance was made for fraudulent purposes and the transferee had actual knowledge of this at the time, or was a party to the fraud. In addition overreaching will not occur if the transfer was subject to the equitable interest, or the equitable interest is protected by the deposit of title documents,[20] or in the case of a trust was protected by registration, or takes effect as a burden protected by section 72(1)(j) of the 1964 Act. Section 72(1)(j) protects the rights of persons in actual occupation of the land or in receipt of the rents and profits, save where, upon enquiry made of such persons the rights are not disclosed. The exception for a trust protected by registration or occupation only applies where there is a single trustee.[21] Thus where there is a single trustee the trust

[18] See section 21(2).

[19] See Sect. 8.3.2 for the reason for its introduction and the effect of overreaching.

[20] This is contradictory given the move towards dematerialisation in the 2006 Act.

[21] Section 21(3)(b)(iii).

will not be overreached if the beneficiary is in occupation and the interest is protected as an overriding interest.

Where there are two trustees or a trust corporation the statutory overreaching provisions will be activated. This is similar to the position in England and Wales where occupation does not prevent overreaching if the correct formalities are complied with. In *City of London Building Society v. Flegg*[22] the beneficiaries of a trust were found to have no right to continue in occupation when their interests were overreached by the legal charge. Their rights were transferred to the equity of redemption and they were prejudicially affected by the breach of trust, not by the overreaching provisions.

While the term overreaching is not used there are other statutory provisions with similar effect in that they free purchasers from equitable claims. These provisions apply to sale by a personal representative[23] or a mortgagee exercising a power of sale.[24] In the former case the interests of the beneficiaries will be overreached and in the later it will be the borrower's interest that is overreached.[25] The transferee will take free from the mortgage and the borrower's equity of redemption. These provisions are more widely drafted in that a purchaser does not have to comply with any formalities about how the purchase monies are to be paid.[26]

When overreaching occurs the equitable interest continues to exist but it cannot be asserted against the title. Instead it is transferred to the money. In effect the right or claim is not destroyed by the registered transaction but it does take a different form. The beneficiary will only get a portion or the whole of the monies and this is obviously preferable to the interest or claim being destroyed in its entirety. However, there is the possibility that such monies may have been dissipated. The transferor may have disappeared or there may be no funds left where a lender has been paid on foot of a charge. Thus V may be left with no recourse. In effect their right has been devalued.

There are no overreaching provisions in the Ontario legislation and purchasers are entitled to ignore the existence of any trust. Section 62(1) of the Land Titles Act provides that trusts are not recognised. Describing an owner as trustee is deemed not to be notice of a trust, those dealing with the owner have no duty to enquire as to his power and the owner may deal with the land as if such description had not been inserted.[27] This was confirmed in *Randvest Inc. v. 741298 Ontario Ltd.*[28]

In the case of a sale by a mortgagee, the mortgagee can deal with the property as if they were the registered owner of the land provided they have a power of sale and

---

[22] *City of London Building Society v. Flegg* [1987] 3 All ER 435.

[23] Section 51(1) of the Succession Act 1965.

[24] See sections 104 and 105 of the 2009 Act.

[25] For other examples see Deeney (2014), pp. 175–176.

[26] See Deeney (2014), p. 175 for other examples of overreaching.

[27] Section 62(2).

[28] *Randvest Inc. v. 741298 Ontario Ltd.* 1996 CanLII 8207 (ON SC).

provide certain evidence to the registrar.[29] Section 99(1.1) of the Land Titles Act says that this evidence is conclusive evidence of compliance with the requirements and upon registration of a transfer is sufficient to give a good title to the purchaser. In the case of a personal representative he can be registered as owner under section 121 of the Land Titles Act if he has an express or implied power of sale. While the term 'overreach' is not used this is the effect of these sections.

Scenario 2(a)

Because U gave A the purchase monies for Greenacre the court found, on application by U, that A holds Greenacre on trust for U. A has now sold Greenacre to B.

In Ontario B does not need to concern himself with the existence of the trust and does not need to make any enquiries about A's entitlement to sell. A and B can deal with the property as if the trust did not exist as U's beneficial interest has no impact on the sale.

In Ireland B can only take Greenacre free of the trust provided a number of conditions are met. The transfer must not have been subject to the trust or made for fraudulent purposes. In addition the trust must not have been protected by registration and U must not be in occupation as his interest would then be protected as an overriding interest.

If B meets these conditions he will take Greenacre free of the trust. U's claim will transfer to the trust fund. While U loses any prospect of enjoying the land itself he has a corresponding interest in the trust fund. Also if A acted wrongfully, U will have a personal claim against A for breach of trust.

The trust cannot be protected by registration in its own right but if U had protected his interest by registering a note on the folio before the sale of Greenacre to B then overreaching would not automatically occur. Such a note on the register will put B on notice of the existence of the trust and he will then need to be careful to comply with the correct formalities. A would need to apply for a second trustee to be appointed in order to facilitate the sale and allow overreaching.

In the interim, as there is only a single trustee, U can protect his interest against a transfer to B by occupation. In this situation if B proceeded with the purchase he would take Greenacre subject to the beneficial interest as U would hold an overriding interest.

Scenario 2(b)

Because U gave X the purchase monies for Whiteacre the court found, on application by U, that X holds Whiteacre on trust for U. X has now gifted Whiteacre to Y.

The position in Ontario is the same as above. X and Y can deal with the property as if the trust did not exist.

In Ireland the position of Y as a volunteer is different to that of B as Y will take subject to the interest of U. The definition of purchaser in the 2009 Act requires the transaction to be for value and the definition includes a mortgagee.[30] Thus B and C

[29] Section 99(1) of the Land Titles Act.

[30] Section 3.

can overreach but Y cannot. The gift of Whiteacre from X to Y will not pose any risk to U and his beneficial interest will continue to affect the title to Whiteacre.

8.3.2 Effect of Overreaching

Section 21 was introduced because the 2009 Act provided that the only legal estates capable of being created or disposed of are a freehold estate and a leasehold estate. All other estates and interests take effect as equitable interests only.[31] Thus trustees are registered as owners and the interests of the beneficiaries are by way of an equitable interest only and these are not registrable interests.[32] They can, however, be protected by registration of an inhibition. The position now in Ireland is that the trust may not be evident from the title register unless an inhibition has been entered.

As demonstrated above Y will take subject to the interest but there is a risk for B and C. If they are not aware of the existence of the trust then they may not comply with the correct formalities and overreaching may not occur. There is no corresponding risk in Ontario. The existence of the trust can be ignored as B and C will take free of any claim. In Ontario U automatically becomes V when a sale or transfer of the land occurs.

In Ireland the 2009 Act simplified and standardised property rights and thus trusts were moved off the register. In implementing this change section 21 tried to effect a compromise between ensuring that land held in trust is freely alienable and protecting the interests of the beneficiaries in preserving their rights. The difficulty with section 21 is that on a practical level the compromise may leave transferees and lenders unwittingly subject to an equitable claim that was not evident from an inspection of the title register or any other register.

Where there is no inhibition on the title register a single trustee can readily hoodwink a purchaser into falling foul of section 21. Mee was critical of the original provision in the Bill and expressed the view that it downgraded beneficial interests in family homes.[33] He referred to the English system which requires two or more trustees all of whom must execute the deed[34] and notes that while a family relationship is going well it is most unlikely that a non-owning partner will take steps to register their beneficial interest.[35]

[31] Section 11 of the 2009 Act.

[32] Property Registration Authority (2012).

[33] Mee (2006), p. 71.

[34] This is a reference to section 2(1) and section 27 of the Law of Property Act 1925.

[35] Mee (2006), pp. 70–71. Mee does not deal with how this section interacts with the protection provided by the Family Home Protection Act 1976 as amended and he obviously could not address the provisions of the subsequently enacted Civil Partnership and Certain Rights and Obligations of Cohabitants Act 2010.

The main thrust of the section is to protect transferees, by transferring the interest of the beneficiary to the trust fund, but it appears to have failed somewhat in achieving this. In Ontario even if the trust is evident from the register the registered owner can deal with the property as if there were no such beneficial interest. The beneficiary is V and has no claim against the land. This policy is a more definitive stance on the issue and has much to recommend it. B, Y and C take free of the trust and the beneficiary V must seek recourse from the transferor and trustee, A or X.

8.4 Rights Not Recognised

If rights are not recognised and not capable of registration then there is a risk posed to U the third party and V the property claimant. Rights may not be recognised and capable of registration for a number of reasons. The right may be a personal right that cannot be converted into a property right. For example breach of a contract of employment will result in an *in personam* claim and these type of claims fall outside this examination.

Some rights fall outside the registration system in that they are not registrable rights. Other rights may be rights that are capable of being registered but the claim by V is not sufficiently mature to effect the land.

8.4.1 Easement

In Ontario easements, including rights of way, are overriding interests under section 44(1) paragraph 2 of the Land Titles Act but there is a caveat to this in section 44(3). This provides that such rights are not overriding if notice of the application for first registration of the land was served on adjoining owners and no objection to the first registration was filed. If no objection was filed at the time the adjoining owner's easement is not protected as an overriding interest. This means that subsequent transferees will not need to concern themselves with easements existing prior to first registration provided this notice was served.

After first registration easements by prescription are prohibited by virtue of section 51(1) of the Land Titles Act. This provides that no title, right or interest can be acquired adverse to or in derogation of the title of the registered owner by any length of possession or by prescription. In effect the Act prevents the maturing of claims for adverse possession or easements and a matured prescriptive easement may be lost if the owner does not contest the registration of the servient lands. This position was confirmed in *394 Lakeshore Oakville Holdings Inc. v. Misek*.[36] Thus

[36] *394 Lakeshore Oakville Holdings Inc. v. Misek* 2010 CanLII 6007 (ON SC).

after first registration easements can only be obtained by express or implied grant such as easements of necessity.

In Ireland the 2009 Act abolished the acquisition of an easement by prescription at common law and provided that acquisition at law shall only arise on registration of a court order under section 35(1). Section 40 does retain the right to an implied grant, easements of necessity and the doctrine of non-derogation from grant. Prospective purchasers require registration as section 39 provides that after 12 years continuous non-user the easement is extinguished unless protected by registration.

Until extinguished the easement is protected as an overriding interest under section 72(1)(h) of the 1964 Act unless created by express grant or reservation after first registration. Express grants or reservations can be registered as burdens under section 69 of the 1964 Act. If the easement is not an overriding interest the threat from a prospective purchaser to the easement requires it to be registered to secure the right and avoid the possibility of extinguishment.

There is a contradiction between the 2009 Act which pushed towards registration of easements and the 1964 Act which accords them status as overriding interests binding the world. It is a shame that the opportunity presented for reform of the general land and conveyancing law in 2009 did not also encompass the law on registration (which was only reformed in part by the 2006 Act). Alignment and consolidation of these twin pillars might make any future reforms more robust.[37]

The explanatory memorandum to the 2009 Act notes that section 35(1) was designed to facilitate conveyancing by relieving purchasers of the need to make enquiries or search for possible rights not mentioned in any documents of title as all new rights acquired by prescription will have to be registered.[38] However purchasers will still have to enquire if a court order has been made but not yet registered as such rights may be overriding interests and purchasers will also have to enquire if any proceedings have been initiated.

This move to bring easements on to the register caused consternation in legal circles as previously lawyers relied upon statutory declarations from prior owners as to length of user.[39] Now a deed or court order seemed to be required.[40]

The non-expressly granted easement is an important user right and the neighbour is a monopoly supplier. Forcing the claimant to contract or obtain a court order imposes cost and raised the possibility of a dispute. Servient owners could decline to execute a deed and force the dominate owner to go to the expense of a court application. This has been remedied somewhat by amending provisions in the Civil

---

[37] It should be noted that landlord and tenant law also remains to be reformed. The Law Reform Commission has published draft reforming legislation. See Law Reform Commission (2007). In April 2011 a version of this draft Bill was published by the Department of Justice and Equality but unfortunately this has not progressed further. See http://www.justice.ie/en/JELR/Pages/PR11000046. Accessed 23 May 2014.

[38] Explanatory memorandum Land and Conveyancing Law Reform Act 2009, p. 22.

[39] Brennan (2010).

[40] See Deeney (2014), p. 309 for more detail of the difficulties which were caused by section 35.

Law (Miscellaneous Provisions) Act 2011[41] which allows the registrar to register the easement when there is no dispute between the parties. Notice is served on all interested parties and in the absence of the application being contested, registration may proceed.[42]

Thus the dominant owner can avail of this simple procedure to register subject to their being no objection by the servient owner who may be a friendly and co-operative neighbour. This extension of the registrar's power is in line with the increased emphasis on title registration in the move towards eConveyancing.

Scenario 3(a)

U is claiming a right of way by prescription over Greenacre.

In Ontario U cannot claim a right based on prescription after first registration of the land and thus his claim will be rejected by the courts. U becomes V as his claim is defeated. The right is not a registrable right and is not recognised.

In Ireland U will need to demonstrate 12 years user.[43] If U does not have sufficient user to be successful in asserting his right his claim is not yet mature and will not be recognised by the courts. U may be able to register a note on the register temporarily, while proceedings are pending, but when the claim fails the registrar will remove the note from the register. In the interim period the title is effectively frozen as B would likely not purchase Greenacre until the matter is resolved. U becomes V as his right is not recognised and cannot be registered against the land.

If U can demonstrate 12 years user and his claim is successful the court order can be registered as a burden under section 69(1)(h) of the 1964 Act. This will protect his interest from extinguishment. This registration is required under section 35(1) of the 2009 Act for a legal easement. If U does not register the court order he would have an equitable easement. This is protected as an overriding interest under section 72(1)(h) of the 1964 Act.

The status of such a right as an overriding interest contradicts the aims of the 2009 Act in attempting to bring prescriptive easements onto the register. As noted previously this demonstrates a lack of co-ordination between general conveyancing law and the law in relation to registration of title and the detrimental effect of piecemeal reform. Mee argues that more consideration should have been given to developing a conception of how eConveyancing might work before settling on the approach to reforming the substantive law.[44]

---

[41] No 23 of 2011.

[42] Property Registration Authority (2013b).

[43] Under sections 33 and 35(2).

[44] Mee (2006), p. 68. He notes that the Law Reform Commission report on eConveyancing came almost a year after the publication of its report setting out the substance of the Bill which was enacted as the 2009 Act.

Scenario 3(b)

X expressly granted U a right of way over Whiteacre. This right is recognised in Ontario and Ireland. The question of the right maturing does not arise as it comes into being when the grant is executed.

In Ireland this right is not an overriding interest.[45] Instead it is a burden which may be registered as affecting registered land under section 69(1)(j) of the 1964 Act. The easement cannot be extinguished by 12 years non-user as section 39 of the 2009 Act only applies to those acquired by prescription or implied grant or reservation.

If this was Greenacre U would be advised to register the easement in order for it to survive a sale by A to B. In the case of Whiteacre as a volunteer Y will take subject to all unregistered rights to which X held the land so it does not matter if U failed to register the easement. It will survive the gift.

The easement was created after first registration by way of express grant from X. U can register a note of it on the register in Ontario under section 39(4) of the Land Titles Act. If U fails to register it will still be protected as an overriding interest under section 44(1) paragraph 2 and on a sale or transfer both a purchaser for value and volunteer will be bound by the interest. In Ontario the easement is treated the same as the tenancy in scenario 1. B, Y and C will take their respective interests subject to the right of way.

8.4.2 Effect of Rights Not Recognised

Lyall notes that registration of title is not merely procedural, but affects substantive law in a number of respects as it produces a new classification of interests in land.[46] This classification of registered interests overlaps with the legal and equitable estates and interests that can generally exist. Some legal and equitable estates and interests will be capable of registration and others will not.

The prescriptive easement is not registrable and not recognised by the title register in Ontario. In Ireland the prescriptive easement needs to be mature to affect the title. The expressly granted easement is an overriding interest in Ontario but in Ireland it is a burden which should be registered to survive a transfer from A to B.

The above scenarios demonstrate how third party rights are dealt with by the registrations systems in Ireland and Ontario and the effect of those rights on other participants in the land market. It is clear that registration systems do not deal with or acknowledge all third party rights.

---

[45] Section 72(1)(h) excludes easements created by express grant or reservation after first registration.

[46] Lyall (2010), p. 936.

The title register is not a complete reflection of the title at any given moment[47] and this can be viewed in a number of contexts. It may be seen as detracting from the value of the register by adding enquiries and cost to conveyancing transactions. As Stewart-Wallace puts it so articulately "[a] partial register is rather like a boat with a leak in it. You may not be drowned, but you are sure to be uncomfortable. The register must be final and conclusive in all cases and for all purposes, or its utility is diminished".[48]

Woods is of the view that "[o]verriding interests, which operate to bind a purchaser of registered land despite not appearing on the register, were not part of Torrens' original vision."[49] They are just one exception to indefeasibility which negate the effectiveness of registration. By contrast, as noted already in Chap. 4, Mason argues that indefeasibility does not mean, and has never meant, absolute indefeasibility and that some of the problems with the Torrens system were "unreal expectations of what the system of registered title would deliver, engendered by the notion of indefeasible registered title."[50] He notes that when introduced in Australia registration under the Torrens system was voluntary and that equitable unregistered interests can be created in respect of registered land.[51]

A disparate view is offered by Park who believes the ideal espoused by the originators of land title registration was that of a complete and comprehensive register.[52] To investigate and ascertain legal rights or obligations a person only needed to inspect the register as "title is not affected by anything not shown on the register. It is not only unnecessary but also impossible to establish a right in the land by other means."[53] He notes however that this and other absolute statements regarding the integrity of the various title registers are not justified as the register is less than perfect and overriding interests exist which are not disclosed on the supposedly conclusive register.[54]

[47] In England and Wales the Law Commission has endorsed making the register a complete and accurate reflection of the state of the title at any given time. See Law Commission and HM Land Registry (2001), p. 2.

[48] Stewart-Wallace (1924), p. 92.

[49] Woods (2009), p. 34.

[50] Mason (2003), pp. 3–4.

[51] Mason (2003), p. 3.

[52] Park (2009), p. 8.

[53] Park (2009), p. 8.

[54] Park (2009), p. 8.

8.5 Effect of eConveyancing

The changes being implemented to advance eConveyancing bring a different perspective to these debates. While the scenarios above demonstrate transactional risk, illuminated by the model, the imperative of eConveyancing can reveal other systemic risks.

In Ontario, Ireland and England and Wales it is widely acknowledged that eConveyancing can only be implemented in respect of registered land and this has led to an accelerated push to complete the title register. For example the Ontario e-reg system has only been introduced for registered titles. This generally means there is no further attempt to keep the registered and unregistered systems in line with each other.[55]

There is one exception to this widely held view. Arruñada says it is easer to fully automate a registry of deeds rather than a register of rights *stricto senso* in which only purged, clean titles are entered.[56] He is of the view that agency registration, i.e. an automatic system, will debase a registry of rights into a recording of deeds given the imperative to speed up registration.[57]

It is easier to fully automate a deeds system because it lacks a register of rights and thus Arruñada warns "there is a risk that the introduction of electronic registration inadvertently interferes with the broader decision about the choice of titling system".[58] This view that eRegistration will push towards deeds registration is an interesting perspective as most commentators feel that eConveyancing can only take place in respect of registered titles. In many jurisdictions and contrary to Arruñada's view it has led to a push from deeds to title registration.

Thus Arruñada's perspective has not found favour. This may be due to the fact that to date no jurisdiction has reduced the protection offered by its registry in order to speed up registration thus debasing the register of rights into a recording of deeds. In Ontario for example new improved classes of title were created instead.[59]

While Arruñada may be correct that it is easier to automate a registry of deeds, many jurisdictions embracing eConveyancing initiatives have instead chosen to advance their title register at the expense of the deeds register. This advancement has focused attention on completion of the title register and also on its efficiency. Both Ireland and Ontario have made significant movement towards extending the title register to all land parcels. This focus on completion of the title register is not just limited to its geographical spread. It also impacts on the very nature of title and

[55] Harpum (2004), p. 4.

[56] Arruñada (2010), p. 118.

[57] Arruñada (2010), p. 118.

[58] Arruñada (2010), p. 118.

[59] LTCQ AND LT Plus. See Sects. 2.3.2, 4.8 and 8.5.3.

how rights are categorised. The aim is not just to extend the register to the entire land mass but also to all rights and interests,[60] or at least those deemed worthy of protection by the registry. This can be described as both a wide extension and a deep intension of registration.

Such changes have the potential to significantly effect how the registration system deals with rights and interests and particularly the type of third party rights examined earlier in this chapter.

8.5.1 Moving Rights on to the Register

Under eConveyancing it will be registration, and registration alone, that will 'create' a property right.[61]

> The overall effect is to weld concepts of 'title', 'estate' and 'proprietor' into a form of statutory ownership of land which begins to resemble the civilian model of proprietorship. The 'registered proprietor' now holds a 'registered title' which is inseparable from – indeed has no meaning apart from – the 'registered estate' in the 'registered land' to which it relates.[62]

This increased emphasis on registration involves an examination of all rights and interests to see if those off the register should be moved on to the title register. The aim is to make the register definitive, conclusive and all encompassing.[63] This move towards certainty comes at the expense of some land owners. Any change in categorisation may have a positive or negative impact. An interest previously not given the protection of registration may be deemed sufficiently important to be reclassified as a right capable of registration. A right which previously affected without registration may now require registration and thus the land owner will need to comply with the required formalities. A right previously protected by registration or which affected without registration may no longer be deemed worthy of protection and may be cast out. This would be a significant policy shift and raises the issue of compensation for the loss.[64]

Any reclassification of property rights poses a risk to all land owners. Some rights may be downgraded and others upgraded. The interests currently not protected by registration may, on a review, be deemed worthy of being reclassified

---

[60] Deeney notes that it will be necessary to have the title to all estates and interests affecting registered land registered in the title register and this will necessarily mean a fundamental review of the conclusiveness of the register as such an extension of the register might have implications for the state guarantee i.e. the compensation provisions. See Deeney (2014), p. 366. This aspect is explored further at Sect. 9.6.

[61] Howell (2006), p. 554.

[62] Gray and Gray (2009), p. 183 in referring to a new form of register-based title which compresses the historic terminology of English land ownership into an amalgam of interchangeable concepts.

[63] Law Society of Ireland (2008), p. 1.

[64] See Sect. 8.5.3.

as rights capable of registration. U and V may benefit from a change in the legislation. Until this reclassification is completed the rights held by U and V are subject to increased risk. The danger is that they will be deemed as not being sufficiently important to be reflected on the new all encompassing register and thus will be deemed not to be recognised as rights.[65]

There is also the possibility of other interests or even estates in land being examined and challenged. The likelihood of this occurring, however, is slim. It is one thing to remove third party rights but it is quite another to remove from land owners or lenders rights which were previously capable of registration. Such a major re categorisation would throw the entire conveyancing system into disarray.

A reclassification of property rights to make the register definitive and all encompassing would mean being true to one of the original principles of title registration i.e. the register being a mirror of the title.[66] Such a reclassification could mean that any rights on the register would be protected and any rights not on the register would not. In effect equitable interests and overriding interests would no longer be enforceable and those holding such interests would have no remedies and no protection.

> Following the arrival of electronic conveyancing it will not be possible to generate or dispose of most interests *except* by means of some contemporaneous entry in the register. Unregistered transactions will, quite simply, have no effect either at law or in equity.... entitlement will be conferred by 'registration and registration alone'.[67]

In referring to overriding interests Deeney is of the view that the difficulties in mapping, establishing title, registering and updating such interests would far outweigh the benefits to be gained by their entry on the register.[68] Murphy also sees difficulties and refers to the need for the electronic register to be capable of recording all rights and interests as "the Achilles heel of eConveyancing".[69] However Deeney notes that in order to successfully implement eConveyancing it will be necessary to have the title to all estates and interests affecting registered land registered in the register and the provisions relating to burdens which affect without registration will have to be repealed.[70]

Attempting to enter all interests onto this all encompassing title register would be a challenging task, possibly involving delay and expense. Those holding such interests are generally given an interim period to register their interest but if registration does not occur within the time given then the interest is deemed to be

---

[65] Murphy notes that property rights which cannot be brought on to the register will cease to exist. Murphy (2013), p. 10.

[66] See Ruoff (1952), p. 118.

[67] Gray and Gray (2009), p. 194.

[68] Deeney (2014), p. 133.

[69] Murphy (2013), p. 8.

[70] Deeney (2014), p. 366. This is a reference to section 72 of the 1964 Act. See also Law Society of Ireland (2008), p. 1.

lost or may only be enforced as a personal right.[71] Alternatively old rights could be protected independently but all new rights of the same type refused and then eventually those types of rights would fade away.

Hansmann and Kraakman express the view that the recognition of new classes of property rights generally involves a shift in wealth towards the user of those rights at the expense of nonusers and society at large or whoever bears the system costs for the new rights.[72] Thus reforms promoting or abolishing property rights are likely to be influenced strongly by different interest groups.[73]

Thus it is important to ask a number of questions. Is it reasonable to expect all parties to register their rights even if those rights arise informally such as by virtue of occupation, under a constructive trust or by estoppel? Or are there circumstances where it is reasonable to give protection to interests off the register? Can eConveyancing truly be effective without a complete title register that encompasses all rights, interests and estates in land? Or should it be accepted that the title register is not capable of dealing equitably with all interests in land and there will be an ever expanding category of unregistered interests and rights that must be accommodated?

8.5.2 *Interest Recording*

Some jurisdictions have tried to mitigate the impact of increasing the categories of off register interests by providing for interest recording systems to be combined with title registration. This was recommended in 1990 by the Canadian Joint Land Titles Committee *Renovating the Foundation: Proposals for a Model Land Recording and Registration Act for the Provinces and Territories of Canada*.[74] The Committee was of the view that "the law cannot effectively guarantee ownership of all interests in land and would seriously mislead people if it were to try extend title registration to all interests."[75] It would not be appropriate to register an almost indefinite range of estates and interests.[76] The Committee also expressed the view that title registration should not change substantive real property law but instead

[71] See Sect. 8.5.3 for examples.

[72] Hansmann and Kraakman (2002), pp. S402–S403.

[73] Hansmann and Kraakman (2002), p. S403.

[74] Joint Land Titles Committee (1990). See McCrimmon (1994), pp. 300–316 for details of the recommendations. This Committee favoured discretionary indefeasibility in order to achieve fair results. See Mason (2003), p. 18. Mason is inclined to agree that it might generate fairer results but was not sure if the benefits would outweigh the detriments of change, particularly as there would be uncertainty for a significant period of time as to how the courts would exercise the discretion.

[75] Joint Land Titles Committee (1990), p. 14.

[76] Joint Land Titles Committee (1990), p. 20.

"should float upon the general law."[77] This Committee included representatives from Ontario but its main recommendations have not been adopted there.[78]

November and Rendell note that such interest recording confers priority, but does not in itself confer ownership, while title registration confirms priority and ownership.[79] Unregistered interests are recorded on the title register but are not actually registered. This could be seen as an amalgam of the title register and deeds register systems. Does such a proposal accept the distinction between unregistered rights and title registration and reinforce it? The reality is that many jurisdictions already operate forms of interest recording within title registration.

Australia has caveat provisions which allow for the protection of equitable interests.[80] New Zealand has a limited example of such a system with its notification of restrictive and positive covenants on the title register.[81] Though the benefit of a covenant or easement does not constitute a claim of ownership to the burdened land so the difference may be in the nature of the claim rather than the status of any registered entry. A recording may be a means of accommodating all types of equitable interests within the system or only have the short term function of protecting interests prior to their registration. The former may not require that the interest be registrable[82] in its own right.

Both Ontario and Ireland already operate limited forms of interest recording. In Ireland those holding unregistered interests in registered land or registered charges may protect them by registering a caution or inhibition.[83] A caution is for the temporary protection of an unregistered right[84] pending its conversion into a registered interest.[85] It restricts any disposition by the registered owner without notice to the cautioner. No notice is required for dealings by someone other than the registered owner. A transfer for value will be stayed pending litigation by the cautioner to establish their right as the registrar does not decide between the relative

[77] Joint Land Titles Committee (1990), p. 19.

[78] Where registration is based on a forged or unauthorised transfer the Model Act leaned in favour of restoring a displaced registered owner and compensating the innocent successor of the fraudulent party as the displaced owner is statistically likely to have a closer connection with the land and to suffer loss which will be harsher as well as greater and less easy to quantify, than the loss suffered by the recent acquirer of the interest. See Joint Land Titles Committee (1990), pp. 3 and 25.

[79] November and Rendell (2010), p. 169.

[80] McCrimmon (1994), pp. 300–316. She notes that while Torrens was critical of the interference of equity he did not advocate the abolition of equitable interests as the original statute permitted the registration of trusts and the caveat. Some commentators disagree. See Hughson et al. (1997), p. 495 who state that Torrens did not foresee the continuing validity of equitable interests.

[81] November and Rendell (2010), p. 151.

[82] Hughson et al. (1997), p. 464.

[83] Property Registration Authority (2013a).

[84] Defined in section 3(1) of the 1964 Act as any estate, interest, equity or power.

[85] Section 97 of the 1964 Act. Cautions are not given in respect of section 69 burdens or section 72 overriding interests. See Brennan and Casey (2012), chapter 14 for a detailed explanation of cautions, inhibitions and priority searches.

merits of each side.[86] A transfer to a volunteer would however be registered as a volunteer will take subject to any unregistered rights. This is a strong limit on the register and means that there is no general principle of immediate indefeasibility as some titles are clearly defeasible i.e. those of volunteers.

Unregistrable rights that cannot be converted into registered rights can be protected by an inhibition.[87] It will usually restrict transactions without certain consent or within a specified time period. For example it may protect beneficiaries under a trust. In the case of a conflict the registrar will prevent any registration pending a determination by the court. Another means of protection is provided by a priority entry[88] and this has already been examined in Chap. 6.

Section 69 of the 1964 Act also lists burdens that may be registered as 'recordings' against registered title. The title held by C is a clear example of this as its charge cannot be registered its own right, it can only be registered as an encumbrance against B's registered title. Some, but not all of these, are U interests and V claims thus allowing for entries on the title register that may protect U and V.

Similarly in Ontario under section 71(1) of the Land Titles Act any person entitled to or interested in any unregistered estates, rights, interests or equities in registered land may protect same by entering a notice, caution, inhibition or other restriction on the register. Where this is done every registered owner and every person deriving title through the registered owner, except prior owners, are bound by notice. Again this restriction only prevents the interest being impaired by an act of the registered owner.

Those claiming to have an interest in registered land or in a registered charge can apply for registration of a caution to prevent dealings without the consent of the cautioner.[89] This can be used to prevent dealings both by the registered owner or any other person named in the caution however it expires after 60 days and cannot be renewed. A registered owner can also place a restriction on the register to prevent a transfer or charge without notice, consent or the doing of some other matter or thing.[90]

Thus such a recording or caveat on the title[91] may take the form of a caution, inhibition, priority search or registration of an encumbrance. Any such recording gives a warning to potential purchasers. It may not confer any validity on the interest but it will prevent registration of a dealing that affects the interest of the person who made the recording.

November and Rendell express the view that interest-recording is a relatively blunt way to protect unregistered interests and requires a person to be aware of the

[86] Deeney (2014), p. 278.

[87] Section 98 of the 1964 Act.

[88] Section 108 of the 1964 Act, as substituted by section 66 of the 2006 Act.

[89] Sections 128–135 of the Land Titles Act.

[90] Section 118 Land Titles Act.

[91] November and Rendell (2010), p. 175 refer to this as a settlement notice.

existence of the interest in order to record it.[92] They note the potential problem of making conveyancing more complex if the distinction between recording and registration becomes blurred.[93]

To date the distinction does not appear to have caused any great difficulty for lawyers but such interest recording may need to be examined if unregistered interests themselves are under scrutiny in the move toward eConveyancing. Could C's first legal charge be upgraded from an encumbrance to an interest capable of registration in its own right perhaps facilitating wealth generation and an improved market in land?[94] This has echoes in the recent creation by the Irish registering authority of a new register of charges taken over by the National Asset Management Agency (NAMA).[95]

Could those holding overriding interests be required to register them as 'recordings'? Should someone in occupation be required to register even though such occupation is surely apparent to any transferee who inspects the property? A complete 'recording' system linked to title registration would need to be mandatory and to bind the world to truly be of benefit to transferees relying on it as a comprehensive reflection of the title. Recording only would be effective to protect unregistered interests and other forms of notice, such as from inspection, thus become irrelevant.

8.5.3 Reclassification of Interests in land

Some interests have already been reclassified. An example arises in Ireland with the removal of the status of land certificates and certificates of charge which was driven by the dematerialisation aspect of eConveyancing.

Prior to 1 January 2007 the Land Registry would on request issue a land certificate. This was an important document of title and was required to be produced if there was any change in registration. Section 73 of the 2006 Act, which came into effect on 1 January 2007, provided that these certificates would no longer be issued. All existing certificates ceased to have effect from 1 January 2010 and in the intervening 3 year period a person who held a lien through deposit or possession

[92] November and Rendell (2010), p. 175.

[93] November and Rendell (2010), p. 175.

[94] See Sects. 4.3 and 8.5.5 on the different property markets with particular reference to the complex commodities market.

[95] Property Registration Authority 'Strategic Plan 2013–2015' (2013), pp. 31 and 39. NAMA was established in 2009 as a means of addressing the problem with Ireland's banking sector created by excessive lending. The agency acquired loans with a nominal value of 74 billion from participating financial institutions. Note that the registration of NAMA is not compulsory and any transfer to NAMA takes effect as a deed registered on the date on which it took effect. See Deeney (2014), p. 351.

of such a certificate could apply to the registrar to have a lien registered as a burden on the folio. Section 73 related similarly to certificates of charge.

Thus as of 1 January 2010 it was no longer possible to create an equitable charge on registered land by lodgement of the land certificate with a lender. Any lender previously holding such a charge was given 3 years to protect their interest by registering it on the folio. Any lender who did not exercise this right was left holding a worthless document and an interest that could no longer be enforced.[96] In effect a type of security that was low in cost, easy and quick to effect was abolished despite the fact that it was commercially valuable. Lenders must now take the risk of unsecured credit or put the borrower to the expense of putting a charge in place.

This demonstrates how a party may lose their claim by not registering within the time allowed and collectively a category of land owners may lose their claim if their right or interest is no longer recognised by the registration system. There is an inherent risk in registration systems and these risks are amplified in any reclassification of what the system protects.

A clear example is the change to trusts introduced by the 2009 Act[97] whereby the distinction between registration as 'full owner' and registration as 'limited owner' was abolished. Limited owners can no longer be registered owners, their ownership being an equitable interest only.[98] This means that such limited owners, whether a minor or someone holding a life interest, remainder or reversion, no long have power to transfer legal title. Trustees are registered as owners and the interests of the beneficiaries are not registrable interests.[99]

Another example of reclassification is provided in the case of rent charges which were previously capable of registration as a section 69 burden. Section 4 of the 2009 Act provided that such rent charges are only enforceable as a simple contract debt. The Act also prohibited the future creation of rent charges in law or in equity except those created by the court or under statutory provision. Thus a "commonplace registration"[100] was no longer possible i.e. where an annuity is payable to a donor by a donee.

Other interests may not be lost but may be downgraded or rendered inferior in the process or indeed there may be a perception among consumers, legal professionals and the market place that the new interest is inferior even if the reality is very different. In Ontario the protection offered by the registry has been extended in the move towards electronic services with the automation and conversion of registry records. This is reflected in the creation of two new types of registered titles.[101]

---

[96] The Act did contain compensation provisions to protect vulnerable people whose right might be extinguished without their knowledge but no applications for such compensation have been made. See Deeney (2014), p. 362.

[97] See Sect. 8.3.

[98] Section 11 of the 2009 Act.

[99] Property Registration Authority (2012).

[100] Deeney (2014), p. 117.

[101] See Sects. 2.3.2 and 4.8.

The new land title parcels are "commonly referred to as "Qualified Land Titles" among real estate practitioners, with the connotation that the parcel is inferior to an Absolute title" or traditional land title parcel.[102] The LT Plus and LTCQ are however both qualified to a lesser degree than the previously best title available i.e. the absolute title. Murray says it is unfortunate that these parcels are referred to as "Qualified"[103] as the guarantees given mean that for most conveyancing purposes they are superior to absolute title.[104] Thus eConveyancing may lead to an improvement in the quality of registered titles being offered by the registry.

eConveyancing may also require the development of a different system of principles to determine the circumstances in which it is possible to acquire title to registered land by adverse possession. This reflects "the fact that the basis of title in a registered system is the *fact of registration* and not possession as it is in an unregistered system"[105] This enhances the status of registration which becomes an integral and essential part of the conveyancing process.[106]

Thus jurisdictions such as England and Wales have because of the conclusive nature of registration, in an eConveyancing environment, severely restricted the circumstances in which a squatter can acquire title to registered land by adverse possession.[107] Gray and Gray refer to this as illustrating "the emergence of a much more robust and deeply stabilised form of state-endorsed title."[108] The Land Registration Act 2002 reduced the scope and number of overriding interests, created some new registrable interests and introduced a new regime for adverse possession based on the premise that registration and registration alone confers title.[109] Dixon points to schedules 1 and 3 of this Act as having enhanced free alienability of land[110] by reducing the number of overriding interests[111] in the move towards an eConveyancing system with a near complete electronic register.[112]

---

[102] Murray (2004), p. 7.

[103] Their exact title is Land Titles Converted Qualified (LTCQ).

[104] Murray (2004), p. 7.

[105] Harpum (2004), p. 4.

[106] Harpum (2004), p. 10.

[107] Harpum (2004), p. 11.

[108] Gray and Gray (2009), p. 183. Interestingly in discussing realism about title they examine physical possession versus proprietary ownership and refer at p. 1165 to "the unattractive rumble of state-sanctioned *force majeure*."

[109] See Chamberlain (2002), p. 1093. See also Gray and Gray (2009), pp. 191 and 1106 and O'Sullivan (2013), pp. 43–63. O'Sullivan advocates that a similar early warning notification system of adverse possession of registered land should be introduced in Ireland.

[110] Dixon (2003), p. 145.

[111] Though Harpum expresses the view that the Law Commission and Land Registry in England and Wales adopted a rather cautious approach to the abolition or downgrading of overriding interests. See Harpum (2000), p. 16.

[112] It is interesting to note that no compensation was provided for anyone suffering loss due to these reforms.

Ontario has gone even further and has provided that no claim for adverse possession can be made in respect of registered land unless rights were acquired before the lands were brought into the registered title system. The Law Reform Commission in Ireland has also made radical proposals[113] in relation to adverse possession but these proposals have not yet been introduced into legislation.[114] In particular the draft Bill produced by the Law Reform Commission requires that the court grant a vesting order which must be registered on the title register even in the case of unregistered land. This it notes will be one way of extending registration of titles.[115]

As mentioned previously[116] this extension of registration can be described as both a wide extension and a deep intension. It is linked to the expansion of the role of the registering authority beyond its traditional remit.[117] An example of such expansion in Ireland is the creation of a register of charges taken over by NAMA.[118]

These reforms may be looked at in the context of a drive towards a stricter *numerus clausus* and the implications this may have on the operation of the land market.[119] As noted in Chap. 2, it is more difficult to build an electronic system that is flexible enough to accommodate estates and interests that may not be determined for some years to come.[120] The move towards eConveyancing may trigger further examination and reclassification of interests in land thus creating risk for all those holding, to trying to assert, such interests.

The Irish legislature does not however have an unfettered right to interfere with the land market at will. Two factors may impede any reclassification of property rights particularly where there may be a lessening of protection for particular interests. Firstly the constitutional protection given to property rights in Ireland and secondly Article 1 of the First Protocol of the European Convention for the Protection of Human Rights and Fundamental Freedoms.[121]

Two provisions of the 1937 Constitution are of relevance.[122] The first is Article 40.3 and the second is Article 43.

Under the heading 'Personal Rights' Article 40.3 provides that:

[113] Mee (2006), p. 67.

[114] The Law Reform Commission (2005) and O'Sullivan (2013), pp. 43–63. O'Sullivan notes at p. 43 that in recent years the doctrine has been fuelled with uncertainty and confusion and subject to immense criticism. He advocates the adoption of the English notification system.

[115] The Law Reform Commission (2005), p. 327.

[116] See Sect. 8.5.

[117] See Sect. 3.3. Deeney notes that implementation of eConveyancing will require a fundamental review of the present functionality of the Irish land register. Deeney (2014), p. 365.

[118] Property Registration Authority 'Strategic Plan 2013–2015' (2013), pp. 31 and 39.

[119] See Sect. 8.5.6.

[120] See title to land at Sect. 2.3.2.

[121] Available at http://conventions.coe.int/Treaty/en/Treaties/Html/009.htm.

[122] Available at http://www.irishstatutebook.ie/en/constitution/.

1. The State guarantees in its laws to respect, and, as far as practicable, by its laws to defend and vindicate the personal rights of the citizen.
2. The State shall, in particular, by its laws protect as best it may from unjust attack and, in the case of injustice done, vindicate the life, person, good name, and property rights of every citizen.

In Article 43 the State both acknowledges the right to private property and asserts that this right may be curtailed by the State in certain circumstances.

Under the heading 'Private Property' Article 43 states as follows:

1.1 The State acknowledges that man, in virtue of his rational being, has the natural right, antecedent to positive law, to the private ownership of external goods.
1.2 The State accordingly guarantees to pass no law attempting to abolish the right of private ownership or the general right to transfer, bequeath and inherit property.
2.1 The State recognises, however, that the exercise of the rights mentioned in the foregoing provisions of this Article ought, in civil society, to be regulated by the principles of social justice.
2.2. The State, accordingly, may as occasion requires delimit by law the exercise of the said rights with a view to reconciling their exercise with the exigencies of the common good.

Article 43 defines the attitude of the State to the concept of private ownership, acknowledges that a natural right to private ownership exists and that the State will not attempt of abolish this right or the associated right to transfer, bequeath and inherit property. The Article does however recognise that the State may as occasion requires delimit by law the exercise of this right with a view to reconciling their exercise with the exigencies of the common good. Thus Article 43 prohibits the abolition of private property as an institution but permits, in certain circumstances, the regulation of the exercise of the right to private property. Article 43 does not deal with a citizen's right to a particular item of property. This is dealt with in Article 40.3 as a person right.

The relationship between these two articles was explored in the seminal cases of *Madigan v Attorney General*[123] and *Blake and Ors v Attorney General*[124] which examined parts of the Rent Restrictions Act 1960. The Rent Restrictions Acts, 1960–1981 placed a statutory restriction on the rents payable by tenants of dwelling houses with rateable valuations which did not exceed specified sums. The Supreme Court held that part of the Rent Restrictions Act 1960 was an unconstitutional interference with the property rights of landlords as the Act restricted the exercise of these rights without providing for compensation and did so for the benefit of tenants without taking into account the financial means of either landlords or tenants.[125] The two actions were heard together in High Court and subsequently on appeal by the Attorney General in the Supreme Court.

The Court found that the provisions of Part 2 of the 1960 Act did restrict the property rights of one group of citizens for the benefit of another. The restriction was held to be both "unfair and arbitrary" on the basis that it applied only to some

[123] *Madigan v Attorney General* [1982] IR 117.

[124] *Blake and Ors v Attorney General* [1982] IR 117 at 127; [1981] ILRM 34.

[125] As a result of these cases the Housing (Private Rented Dwellings) Act 1982 was enacted.

houses and dwellings and not to others, that the basis for the selection was not related to any established social necessity and the restriction applied without compensation and without regard to the financial capacity or the financial needs of either group. O'Higgins C.J. stated that the legislation could only escape the description of being unfair and unjust by including some adequate compensatory factor for those whose rights were so arbitrarily and detrimentally affected.

However in the later cases of *Dreher v Irish Land Commission*[126] and *O'Callaghan v The Commissioners of Public Works in Ireland*[127] the Irish Courts have accepted the principle that every case of infringement of a citizen's property rights does not require compensation at market value. This issue has also arisen at a European level when land owners have appealed to the European Court of Human Rights under Article 1 of the First Protocol of the European Convention for the Protection of Human Rights and Fundamental Freedoms.

Wylie cites the case of *Mellacher v Austria*[128] as evidence that it is doubtful any further protection, over and above that in the Irish Constitution, for property rights is given by Article 1.[129] In that case the European Court of Human Rights ruled that rent reductions introduced by Austria's Rent Act 1981 did not violate Article 1.

Article 1 provides that:

> Every natural or legal person is entitled to the peaceful enjoyment of his possessions. No one shall be deprived of his possessions except in the public interest and subject to the conditions provided for by law and by the general principles of international law. The preceding provisions shall not, however, in any way impair the right of a state to enforce such laws as it deems necessary to control the use of property in accordance with the general interest or to secure the payment of taxes or other contributions or penalties.

In *James v United Kingdom*[130] the landlords of property in Belgravia, London alleged that the compulsory transfer of the property under the Leasehold Reform Act 1967 as amended gave rise to a breach of Article 1. This Act provides tenants residing in houses on long leases with the right to purchase compulsorily the freehold on prescribed terms subject to prescribed conditions. The Court found that the leasehold reform legislation was not *ipso facto* an infringement of Article 1 merely because the immediate beneficiaries of the compulsory transfer of property it empowers are private parties. A taking of property effected in pursuance of legitimate social, economic or other policies may be in the public interest even if the community at large has no direct use or enjoyment of the property.

The Court felt that the margin of appreciation available to the national legislature in implementing social and economic policies should be a wide one and thus would respect the legislature's judgment as to what is in the public interest unless that judgment was manifestly without reasonable foundation. In the Court's view

[126] *Dreher v Irish Land Commission* [1984] ILRM 904.

[127] *O'Callaghan v The Commissioners of Public Works in Ireland* [1985] ILRM 364.

[128] *Mellacher v Austria* ECHR 19 December 1986, Series A No. 169; 12 EHRR 391.

[129] Wylie (1998), p. 17.

[130] *James v United Kingdom* ECHR 21 February 1986, Series A No. 98; 8 EHRR 123.

Article 1 did not guarantee a right to full compensation as the legitimate objectives of public interest, such as pursued in economic reforms or righting social disequilibria, might call for less than full reimbursement of the market value.

Deputy McDowell, in a discussion about the Irish ground rents legislation,[131] pointed out in the Dáil that

> [p]roperty rights do not necessarily carry with them constitutional immunity for change or abrogation or conversion to something else. . .. If it can be shown and demonstrated that the common good is served by the extinction of certain property rights in certain circumstances then that can be done.[132]

Professor Sweeney in referring to the same legislation after its enactment stated that

> [i]t is not as revolutionary as one might think that, in the public interest, property rights should be interfered with without notice to the owner. . .. Here we are concerned not merely with interference with property rights but with their actual acquisition, an acquisition not required in the interests of the health and safety of the public but required rather as a necessary solution to a vast conveyancing problem with a socio-economic dimension.[133]

Thus both the Irish and European courts permit state regulation of property rights provided the legislation serves the common good and does not amount to an unjust attack on those rights. In addition it is clear that both the Irish and European courts have accepted the principle that land owners may not automatically be entitled to full compensation.[134]

Even if compensation is to be paid this can be problematic. Land owners value land differently depending on their perspective. They may value the property as the price paid on the open market, the revenue from renting, the construction cost or the 'emotional value' of a home.

8.5.4 An (In)complete Title Register

The commentary on overriding interests and other 'off-register' interests provides a clear demonstration of the debate between those that support a complete title register and those that see a benefit in having some interests which affect title off the register.

O'Connor notes that the term overriding interest

> does not designate a homogenous group of interests. It is best understood as a legislative device for subjecting registered titles to interests that are deemed worthy of 'passive'

[131] The Landlord and Tenant (Ground Rents) (No. 2) Act 1978 (No. 16 of 1978) which introduced a new test and procedure for tenants to purchase the freehold.

[132] 373 *Dáil Debates* 3267–3268 (24 June 1987) http://historical-debates.oireachtas.ie/D/0373/D.0373.198706240004.html. Accessed 23 June 2014.

[133] Professor Sweeney (1992), p. 67.

[134] See Hogan and Whyte (2003), pp. 1989–2023 for further case law on these points.

> protection, in circumstances where the persons entitled to the benefit of the interests cannot reasonably be expected to enter them on the register.[135]

In a more detailed examination[136] she breaks them down into transitional safeguards against errors in first registration, those arising from legislation that create taxes, rates or other charges in favour of public agencies, interests where the cost is disproportionate to the benefits of registering e.g. short term occupation tenancies and those that it would be inconvenient or unreasonable to expect people to register e.g. created informally, public rights or those that have become obscure with the passage of time. She notes that there is no general criterion for determining when a right should override registered title.[137]

Often the criteria are based on achieving a public goal via the registration process.

> National laws prescribe stringent, multi-step procedures that must be followed to achieve a legally valid transfer of ownership. These restrictions are intended first and foremost to protect the parties involved, but also to further other public goals.[138]

Examples include where land owners cannot register their title until tax is paid.[139] In some jurisdictions interested parties must produce certification from a public agency by way of permission before registration can occur in order to ensure that the transaction does not negatively affect the public goals.[140]

The most usual category of overriding interests arise in relation to rights of those in occupation or in receipt of rents and profits. In *Boyle v. Connaughton*[141] the court found that the plaintiff was aware of the defendant's actual occupation of part of his lands before the transfer and thus the plaintiff's title was subject to the rights of the defendant.[142] If the plaintiff had not visited the property or asked about such rights he would still have been bound. If, however, he enquired and the rights were not disclosed then the rights would not have been overriding. In Ireland non disclosure by the right holder where the overriding interest is contingent upon occupation will mean that the interest is not overriding.[143]

---

[135] O'Connor (2003c), p. 89.

[136] O'Connor (2003b), pp. 258–259.

[137] O'Connor (2003b), p. 258.

[138] Stubkjær et al. (2007), p. 8.

[139] In Ireland the stamp duty certificate must be lodged with the application for registration.

[140] Stubkjær et al. (2007), p. 12.

[141] *Boyle v. Connaughton* [2000] IEHC 28.

[142] This overriding interest is listed at section 72(1)(j) of the 1964 Act. Breen states that the right which accrued to the benefit of the defendants in this case was the right to rectification of the register. She explores whether a right to rectification is itself an overriding interest. See Breen (2000), pp. 52–57. However, it should be noted that the Court in this case also found that there was a mistake in mapping and the actual rectification involved correction of those maps. See Murphy (2013), p. 26 for details of an attempt to repeal this provision which was not successful.

[143] This proviso does not apply in respect of tenancies.

In *The Right Honourable The Lord Mayor Aldermen and Burgesses of Dublin v. Burke*[144] Geoghegan, J. was of the view that during the registration gap the respondent purchaser, only held an unregistered right and thus, in a sense, the question of section 72 burdens did not yet arise but if the appellant held a tenancy on the property the purchaser's unregistered right would be subject to it.

It is one thing for the legislature and courts to permit such protection in certain circumstances but it is quite another for them to actively encourage the proliferation of such overriding interests.

> [T]he complexity of modern law, with its multiplication of rights, often makes apparently simple cases more complex than they appear. For instance, the increasing number and variety of rights that have been granted over the family home to spouses who are not owners make it necessary to collect their consents; otherwise, the acquirers' titles would be burdened with overriding interests.[145]

In Ireland a spouse's consent is required for sale of a family home and in the case of other property a declaration is obtained.

Park asks how people are to ascertain such interests that are not recorded and why a registered title system permits such off-register interests.[146] He blames the legislature for enacting statutes providing for exceptions to the fundamental principle of a complete and comprehensive register and also the courts in their interpretation of those statutes.[147] The thrust of title registration is to provide transparency and certainty and thus enhance transferability thereby encouraging commerce and trade in land. But legislation has subjugated the interests of transferees by providing for categories of overriding interests.

The aim of the register as a "bridge that transports...[the transferee] safely across the morass of trusts and equities through which the purchaser of unregistered land must struggle at his peril"[148] has surely been defeated by the existence of such overriding interests.

> The fact that there is a category of property right that can bind a purchaser of a registered title without either that interest appearing on the register or necessarily being discoverable is thought by many to be an anathema to the very idea of a registration system.[149]

This category of interests is capable of surviving a disposition of the legal title and binding a transferee notwithstanding the fact that they were not registered. The "effect of such interests has been to limit the absolute protection afforded to a purchaser who examines the register."[150] If there are always rights that must be

---

[144] *The Right Honourable The Lord Mayor Aldermen and Burgesses of Dublin v. Burke* [2001] IESC 81.

[145] Arruñada (2010), p. 118.

[146] Park (2009), p. 8.

[147] Park (2009), p. 8.

[148] Glover (1933), p. 14.

[149] Dixon (2003), pp. 137–138.

[150] Fox (2000). See this thesis for an examination of the policy behind the creation of overriding interests in England and Wales.

protected without registration, then the register will never be capable of giving an absolutely accurate reflection of the title at any given point in time. It will never fulfill the mirror principle.[151]

Stubkjær and his colleagues note that it

> is tempting for the legislator to burden the transfer of ownership in real estate with various other social goals. It seems difficult to achieve an assessment of the benefits and compare them with the cost: they fluctuate according to politics and with the times. Whether or not the costs outweigh the benefits is a political matter.[152]

The enquiries necessary to close off a threat from overriding interests may add cost to conveyancing transactions but this cost on its own is unlikely to prevent the operation of the land market. It is really a question of the extent to which that market can be trusted. If costs are higher due to the risk of overriding interests then this may discourage non-acquisition mortgages. Land owners will however still move home and thus will require acquisition mortgages. If land can be bought and sold it will be traded even if it is slow and expensive. The costs would need to be prohibitive to affect the volume of transactions to any degree.

Dixon is of the view that there is nothing inherently wrong with a category of non-registrable binding right, even in a system of land registration, "provided that the category is well-bounded, well known and can be justified by reference to some stronger legal, social or economic need."[153] He refers to the rights of those in occupation as deserving of such protection. Fitzgerald is similarly of the view that overriding interests are a useful and necessary compromise between the ideal and the practical in a public register of title.[154]

Deeney however is of the view that a prerequisite of an electronic system would be the repeal of the legislative provisions relating to overriding interests.[155] Murphy also questions the role played by such overriding interests in the current taxonomy of property rights so as to give them protection within an eConveyancing system but argues that any attempt to abolish those rights should be approached with caution as they "bring about a just and equitable order to a registered title."[156]

This is a key point. Does the imperative of legal, social or economic need outweigh the values of certainty, transparency and efficiency in land transfer? The latter would be enhanced if the register was both the sole and exclusive evidence and the origin of a person's title.[157] The former would dictate that there are certain rights which should be protected without entry on the register.

[151] See Ruoff (1952), p. 118.

[152] Stubkjær et al. (2007), p. 12.

[153] Dixon (2003), p. 138.

[154] Fitzgerald (1995), p. 219.

[155] Deeney (2014), p. 366.

[156] Murphy (2013), pp. 14 and 80.

[157] Dixon (2003), p. 138.

The existence of such overriding interests adds to the cost for all parties by expanding the administrative burden, reducing efficiency, adding uncertainty, time and work.

> [T]he possibility of hidden property rights increases the information asymmetry between the conveying parties: the seller knows better than the acquirer about hidden property rights. More generally, the need to know which conflicting property rights exist, finding out who their right holders are, bargaining with such right holders to obtain their consent and contracting or somehow formalizing an agreement with them, all increase the costs of transforming and conveying rights. This may in turn hamper investment, trade and specialization.[158]

The benefits of a 'clean' complete, definitive register is to be balanced against one which protects latent rights.

The impact of eConveyancing on land registration brings a different perspective to these issues.

> The very point of e-conveyancing where the act of electronic registration is to be the act of creation or transfer of a property right would be undone if it were possible to claim protection for rights created off-register through a substantial category of overriding interests.[159]

Overriding interests run contrary to the policy aims of eConveyancing.[160]

The goal of conveyancing reform is that the process should be capable of being conducted by computer and "[i]f that goal is to be achieved, the role of over-riding interests must be reduced to a bare minimum."[161] Harpum also notes that the goal of making the register, in so far as possible, be an accurate reflection of the state of the title at any given moment "can be achieved only if over-riding interests are eliminated as far as possible."[162] Elimination means to remove the protection currently given to these interests however an alternative would be to require these interests to be put on the register and protected by registration.[163] This would involve a reclassification of such interests as mentioned previously.

If overriding interests were eliminated any interest not reflected on the register would not be enforceable against a *bona fide* purchaser for value. Overriding interests as a category of interests in land would no longer exist and the title register would become definitive, conclusive and all encompassing.[164]

Demands for certainty, transparency and efficiency mean that the continued existence of overriding interests is thrown into doubt. On a scale of eliminate,

---

[158] Arruñada (2011), p. 4.

[159] Dixon (2003), p. 138. See also Sect. 6.3.3 in relation to changes in formalities.

[160] Murphy (2013), p. 67.

[161] Harpum (2000), p. 4.

[162] Harpum (2000), p. 14.

[163] Murphy notes that it may prove impossible to bring them on to the register due to their organic and intangible nature. See Murphy (2013), pp. 69–70.

[164] See O'Connor (2003b), pp. 271–272 for moves towards this goal in England. See also Law Society of Ireland (2008), p. 1.

reduce, keep the status quo or expand, eConveyancing reform drives towards reduction and elimination. If overriding interests are eliminated as a category of right "[t]he role of the traditional methods of investigating title, including on-site inspections, will therefore become largely obsolete."[165] There would be no need for enquiries about occupation or declarations to be sought relating to rights off the register. This would make the conveyancing process more efficient and could lead to reduced costs.

However this has the potential for the register to become entirely removed from reality on the ground. The true ownership may in fact not be reflected in the register at all and if so, there is a danger of the land market operating in the dead capital, extralegal sector referred to by De Soto.[166] The elimination of such overriding interests would not be welcomed by tax authorities, those holding easements[167] or short term tenancies and, in particular, is likely to be vigorously opposed by social activists given the impact on spouses in occupation.

The question arises as to whether one single form (title registration) can fulfil multiple principles; the security of debt, a land owner's autonomy of disposition, protection for those who contribute to the purchase price, protection of occupation rights and so on. The difficult is that right holders with legislative influence and commercial power, e.g. revenue collection and lenders, tend to gain an unwarranted level of protection. Those who are not organised such as transferors, transferees and spouses may be neglected.

If the register is to fulfil all functions then it would be necessary to put temporary rights on and off very quickly. There would need to be incentives to do so otherwise the register will be cluttered and will quickly be out of date. Instead of having to search for the possible existence of rights off the register participants would need to spend time and money checking the rights on the register to see if they are still relevant.

If overriding interests as a category of rights was removed the status of the register would be enhanced but this would reduce, and perhaps even remove, the freedom of the courts and land owners to create and enforce new rights. It could lead to a lack of flexibility that in the long term could undermine the register and force land owners to find alternative means of dealing with title to land.

The risks and rewards of erasing overriding interests are extremely difficult to quantify. There is a need to balance specific interest groups with the overall interest of society in having a fluid land market. The change may benefit some participants but not others and it raises questions about the overall purpose behind control of land and how that control is reflected in land and registration policy. "The result of

[165] Harpum (2000), p. 4.

[166] De Soto (2001), pp. 23 and 30.

[167] Murphy refers to the case of *Walsh and Cassidy v. Sligo County Council* [2010] IEHC 437, [2013] IESC 48, [2014] IESC 22 in relation to public rights of way as an example of the lengths and expense that land owners are prepared to go to protect their property and how rigorously claimants of overriding rights will defend those rights. See Murphy (2013), p. 78.

this [land policy] control is to force market players into a certain kind of behaviour, so that transactions help to underpin the achievement of society's general objectives."[168]

The question arises as to what those objectives are. Do we value the use of land as a home[169] and place of shelter or does its value lie in monetary terms as a commodity that can be realised and transacted, and whose interests do we wish to protect?

> Property rights in land and buildings, as defined in private law, do not give the right holder the (total) control that is sometimes assumed. In the general interest of society (or at least of the administration) the control of the right holder over his property is limited in many ways.[170]

How the land market is structured will meet the objectives society has defined as important but such structure needs to be balanced so as not to place an undue burden solely on any one of the parties. It must be remembered that title registration is a considerable public investment and is, of itself, an interference in how the land market is structured. It provides for a category of registered interests that is overlaid on top of the estates, rights and interests that can generally exist.

So there is precedent for significant reform of interests in land and how they can be enforced but there are many considerations that must be taken into account in any restructuring.

Clancy argues that a multi-purpose register might solve the problem. "Only those rights appearing in the register would create interests that attached to the land."[171] This is one option if one accepts that not all rights are capable of registration on the title register. There would still be the difficulty of getting overriding interests onto this multi-purpose register. This is likely to be just as problematic as getting them onto the title register and a more effective long term option is reform.

O'Connor notes that this could lead to a two-tier interest registration and interest recording system whereby

> [c]ertain classes of interests, such as legal fee simple and major leasehold estates, would be registered with a full State guarantee, as at present. Lesser interests, including many that are presently unregistrable, would obtain priority upon being recorded in the register, but would not attract a State guarantee. This is because it is uneconomic for registries to examine and assume the risk of interests that are of short duration or are variable in their incidents.[172]

It may be argued that in a modern developed society citizens are sufficiently educated so they should be required to register their rights in order to gain the

[168] Ferlan et al. (2007), p. 31.

[169] Fox (2006).

[170] Zevenbergen et al. (2007), p. 261.

[171] Clancy (2008), p. 3.

[172] O'Connor (2003a), p. 11 in referring to law reform proposals in Alberta, Canada and the UK. See Sect. 8.5.2 for more information on mixing interest recording with title registration.

protection of the state. Should overriding interests be destroyed by registration of a transfer unless the claimant took action to enter a caveat or assert their right in court? Should they be treated like prior unregistered interests which are destroyed by first registration? Or does such an approach take advantage of the most vulnerable in society?

These arguments for and against a complete title register reflect the conflict between certainty and flexibility of the registration system. If the system is too rigid it is felt that participants will operate outside the land market but if the system is too flexible it will introduce uncertainty. Are the rights to be protected limited in nature or does the legislature permit new rights to be created? The 2007 Registering the World conference report suggested that in the future land registries might be called upon to recognise and record information about climate change, energy ratings, public utilities information, topography, infrastructure such as cables and pipes, carbon trading, water rights, mining tenure leases and in some jurisdictions native title rights.[173]

New rights being created is a threat to legal certainty but gives the system flexibility. The system of rights creation and transfer can thus adapt to the ever changing needs of society.

8.5.5 *Certainty Versus Flexibility*

This flexibility is provided by equity which operates to mitigate potentially harsh consequences of strict adherence to legal certainty. Gummow is of the view that "equity has oiled the mechanisms that operate the statutory system. Indeed, without recourse to equitable doctrines and remedies and their adaptation it is not easy to see how the statutory system could be self-sufficient."[174] The extent to which interests off the register can be created and either put on the register or impeach or postpone a registered interest will demonstrate the scope for equitable intervention in the registration system.

The traditional view is that the register must be sufficiently flexible to facilitate alterations to mirror court orders creating or adjusting property rights or changes in ownership brought about by events for example the bankruptcy of the land owner. There is a threat to the register if it cannot accommodate these changes as informal local transactions could spring up to counter its inflexibility.

One way of keeping the register flexible but only to a degree is to introduce a veto system which allows registration in the absence of an objection by the registered owner. An example of this is the system of adverse possession in England

173 United Nations Economic and Social Council (2007), p. 5.

174 Gummow (2003), p. 66.

and Wales.[175] Such rights would then only be registered after notice is served on the registered owner. Deeney notes that over 40 years ago in Ireland forgery notices were served on the registered owner prior to the registration of transfers or charges but they were "discontinued as they had the effect of considerably slowing down the registration process and causing unnecessary enquiries and cost."[176] Such notices are an option in the current eDischarge process and he says consideration should be given to the service of notices as a feature of eRegistration projects as they are rolled out.[177]

If no new rights can be created there is a danger that the system will prove unable to meet the demands and needs of land owners. There is then the possibility of interests being created and traded off the register thus creating a separate market-place. This devalues the register. However if too many new rights can be created then land owners and lenders will hesitate to invest in property as there may be unknown threats to their investment that cannot be determined. Land owners may wish to create novel interests or push the boundaries of existing interests e.g. the restrictive covenant, easement of storage[178] but the register may not be flexible enough to accommodate those new interests. Generally registers tend to restrict what new rights can be registered. The question arises as to the extent to which a land owner can freely create new interests in his land and then expect those new interests to be protected.

In Ontario under section 68(2) of the Land Titles Act a person having sufficient estate or interest in the land may create estates, interests and equities in the same manner as the person might do if the land were not registered.

In Ireland further legal interests can be created by statute. Other estates and interests take effect as equitable interests.[179] The 2009 Act acknowledges judicial recognition of equitable interests.[180] Thus the courts remain free to exercise their equitable jurisdiction to develop the law in order to accommodate the changing needs of Irish society. Examples include the equitable doctrines of proprietary estoppel and constructive and resulting trusts.[181]

Rajoy has explored the risks to legal certainty and the impact this has on investment in the property market.[182] He identifies two risks. The first is allowing public administrations to decide who holds property rights and the potential abusive or arbitrary use of this authority for political gain and the second is the opposite extreme in allowing the traders in the market to assign, define and decide the order

[175] For an examination of adverse possession and its role in relation to registered land in England and Australia, see McCrimmon (2003).

[176] Deeney (2014), p. 378.

[177] Deeney (2014), p. 378.

[178] Such an easement exists in England and Wales but not in Ireland.

[179] Section 11(6) of the 2009 Act.

[180] Section 11(7).

[181] Explanatory memorandum Land and Conveyancing Law Reform Act 2009, p. 5.

[182] Rajoy (2008).

of rights.[183] He implies that there are only two markets, primary and secondary.[184]

This is a simplistic view as it could be said that there are in fact four markets.[185] Firstly a primary market in buying and selling land. A secondary market in non-acquisition, but involving secured lending on land. This market meets the needs of these who want to unlock equity and who borrow to spend cash by using their house as collateral. This may involve a secondary mortgage and during the boom this type of lending became socially and economically viable with its focus on wealth creation and consumption. As a result of this free availability of credit many land owners now find themselves overextended and in financial difficulty. A tertiary market may be a derivative of the first and second and then fourthly a complex commodities market involving the re-sale of mortgage books. This market is reflected in the refinancing and securitisation or repackaging of loan books and its failure to deal adequately with risk is reflected in the subprime[186] crises being suffered by many jurisdictions.[187]

Thus there are many difficulties besetting private legal certainty in the property market. How a jurisdiction deals with the competing demands of certainty and flexibility will have an impact on the market. Greater certainty will lead to a strong, secure market but lack of flexibility may restrict investment and lead to interests being traded off the register. A great degree of flexibility will allow changes to meet the needs of owners but may also restrict investment as it would be difficult to establish the threats to ownership. Thus the extremes of both certainty and flexibility would be detrimental to the market and a balance must be achieved between them.

8.5.6 *A Stricter* Numerus Clausus

Arruñada identifies the danger that contractual constraints[188] may be imposed if a stricter *numerus clausus* is necessary to make an automated system viable.[189] In 1952 Ruoff warned that the strict undeviating insistence upon the use of authorised

---

[183] Rajoy (2008).

[184] Rajoy (2008).

[185] See also Sect. 4.3 noting Wallace and Williamson who refer to five land market stages. Wallace and Williamson (2004).

[186] See Williams (2008).

[187] See O'Connor (2009), pp. 133–159 for details of the moral hazard arising from such securitisation and other 'predatory' lending practices. See also Tuffin (2009), pp. 280–310.

[188] Arruñada (2010), p. 118.

[189] See Gray and Gray (2009), pp. 138–139 for an explanation of the *numerus clausus* principle. They also offer the alternate view that the modern drive towards comprehensive recordation of land rights in a publicly accessible register has reduced the need to constrict the menu of rights deemed capable of proprietary status.

printed forms and, no others, acts as a clog upon the dispositive powers of the owner.[190] He could in fact have been talking about the move to eConveyancing.

Constraints on contractual autonomy may be required for rationalisation of the system. In addition to the speed versus legal-quality trade off, Arruñada refers to the "hidden dilemmas" relating to the standardisation of property rights.[191] While there is no doubt that there will be winners and losers in a move towards standardisation and the reclassification of property rights this trade off is not just about speed versus legal-quality. There may be rights protected as a result of a social or political environment which no longer exists. There may be fundamentally sound reasons why such rights should no longer have the importance that they once had.

For example the Irish family home protection legislation[192] was introduced at a time when non-owning spouses could find the family home sold out from under them. This primarily disadvantaged women who were at home with the children and had no independent means of support. The social protection imperative for this legislation no longer exists and lending policy now dictates that the family home be registered in joint names. Should this legislation now be revisited in light of the changing nature of our society? Though the lending policy was implemented purely to avoid lenders being caught by the spouses' right and, if the protection is removed, lending policy may revert thus exposing these parties to risk. These are the type of policy issues that will need to be explored in any reclassification of property rights.

If the register is all then the distinction between legal and equitable interests would disappear. A contract for the sale of registered land would not confer an equitable right.[193] "Either a disposition is registered and takes full effect, or it is not and has no effect at all. There is no intermediate position....the centuries old categorisation of legal and equitable interests in land will have no meaning."[194] The categorisation of interests into legal and equitable will, in eConveyancing, "be devoid of any meaning, other than that given by the land registration legislation itself."[195]

Merrill and Smith do not see much distinction between the *numerus clausus* explicit doctrine of the civil law world and the common law principle that property rights must confirm to certain standardised forms.[196] They argue that what we want

[190] Ruoff (1952), p. 162.

[191] Arruñada (2010), p. 119.

[192] The Family Home Protection Act 1976 (No 27 of 1976). Note that this legislation has been amended on numerous occasions by piecemeal reform of the law in part to accommodate civil partners and cohabitants.

[193] At the moment section 52 of the 2009 Act provides that the entire beneficial interest passes to the transferee on the making of an enforceable contract for the sale of land.

[194] Howell (2006), pp. 553–576 in referring to the likely effect of the English Land Registration Act 2002 at p. 574. He notes at p. 554 that legal and equitable interests have a life of their own outside any registration system but under eConveyancing they may not. He notes also at p. 554 that the traditional distinction and dividing line between 'personal' and 'property' interests will change.

[195] Howell (2006), p. 553.

[196] Merrill and Smith (2000–2001), pp. 1–70.

from a social point of view is optimal standardisation with the objective of minimising the cost of measuring the attributes of the right, frustration costs and administrative costs.[197]

> By permitting a significant number of different forms of property but forbidding courts to recognize new ones, the *numerus clausus* strikes a balance between the proliferation of property forms, on the one hand, and excessive rigidity on the other.... Permitting free customization of new forms of property would impose significant external costs on third parties in the form of higher measurement costs. On the other hand, insisting on a "one size fits all" system of property rights would frustrate those legitimate objectives that can be achieved only by using different property rights that fall short of full ownership. Optimal standardization is the solution, and the *numerus clausus* moves the legal system closer to the optimum, although we do not claim it generates a perfect mix of forms.[198]

Hansmann and Kraakman refer to Merrill and Smith's optimal standardisation as a "trade-off between the utility of having more forms and the confusion that more forms would engender" and they disagree with this analysis.[199] In their view the restriction on the creation of property rights that deviate from the recognised forms in each jurisdiction serve not to standardise rights but rather serve to aid verification of the ownership of rights offered for conveyance.[200] Transferees need security as to the interest they are purchasing otherwise they will spend time and resources on investigations of title in an attempt to remove the insecurity and this will drive up transaction costs.

The achievement of this optimal standardisation according to Merrill and Smith is best done through legislative decision making[201] rather than by the courts. The rule change will be quicker and more informed than when it "must be teased out of court opinions",[202] such changes will be universal in their application which decreases the costs of ascertaining the rule and comprehending its meaning, the change will be more stable and less likely to be transitory, legislation will be prospective whereas judicial changes apply retroactively to the parties and legislated change can devise the means for compensation whereas courts are endowed with a limited set of options for devising remedies.[203]

For Van Erp the numerus clausus doctrine "if strictly applied, creates the risk that innovation takes too much time, which might hamper the further development of new categories of property rights that are being developed in legal practice."[204] He argues that flexibility is required which enables property law to be more responsive to economic developments in the law. However he also notes that

[197] Merrill and Smith (2000–2001), p. 38.
[198] Merrill and Smith (2000–2001), p. 69.
[199] Hansmann and Kraakman (2002), p. S374.
[200] Hansmann and Kraakman (2002), p. S373.
[201] Merrill and Smith (2000–2001), p. 61.
[202] Merrill and Smith (2000–2001), p. 61.
[203] Merrill and Smith (2000–2001), pp. 62–65.
[204] Van Erp (2003), 7.2.

closing legal categories creates more legal security and reduces information costs.[205]

There is no doubt that eConveyancing would work more easily with a *numerus clausus* system. Standardisation, simplification and certainty come more readily when there is a fixed list of property rights recognised as being capable of registration and when the law dictates that only those rights on the register bind the world. This would cut down the enquiries that have to be carried out as no right would exist off the register. Land owners would be required to actively protect their rights by registration and could not rely on the law to protect them otherwise. According to Lyall "[i]n a more secular age it may no longer be regarded as a moral requirement to avoid taking advantage of the failure of others to protect their own interests where they are able to do so."[206]

For example in England and Wales under section 93 of the Land Registration Act 2002 certain dispositions will only have effect if they are electronically registered. Thus "failure to observe mandatory electronic formalities will not even result in the creation of an equitable right, let alone one existing at law."[207]

Non owning spouses or those in possession would not be protected without the positive act of registration. The law would not intervene by default as a back up to any failure to register. The matter would be clear cut; the register would be all.

Conclusion

eConveyancing with its increased emphasis on registration poses a threat to the ongoing existence of the overriding interests that can be asserted. Legislative reform will likely trigger an examination of all overriding interests and their possible rationale. This could lead to such rights being devalued, undermined or completely lost. Third parties such as U may be required to bring their rights on to the register. At the moment there is no incentive for those holding overriding interests to register them. This may change in an eConveyancing environment.

Even in 1995 Fitzgerald advised that a revision of the formidable list of overriding interests in Ireland might be timely.[208] There is no doubt but that some of the overriding interests in section 72 of the 1964 Act are relics of the

(continued)

[205] Van Erp (2003), 7.2.

[206] Lyall (2010), p. 963.

[207] Dixon (2003), p. 154.

[208] Fitzgerald (1995), p. 219.

past.[209] Examples include those relating to the Land Purchase Acts, Land Commission and Labourers Act 1936.[210] Similarly there may be no necessity for those in occupation under a short term tenancy to be given the status of an overriding interest as such tenancies are now required to be registered with the Private Residential Tenancies Board (PRTB) under the Residential Tenancies Act 2004.[211] Given the reforms implemented by the 2009 Act it is also questionable as to whether any customary rights arising from tenure still exist[212] and those overriding interests relating to fee farm grants will now become obsolete as such interests can no longer be created.[213]

These particular overriding interests could likely be removed without giving rise to injustice or practical difficulties. The position may be less clear cut in respect of others, such as the rights of those in occupation or covenants which continue in force after enlargement.[214]

While there may not be compelling social or economic reasons to remove overriding interests entirely there is certainly merit in a reexamination of their value as part of the ongoing reform process. The move toward eConveyancing provides a landscape against which this reform can be measured.

U will be at increased risk if the greater emphasis on registration means that he has to register in order to protect his interest against a *bona* fide purchaser for value. Otherwise the interest will fall into the category of interests that are destroyed by a transaction for value.

However there is a cost to enforced registration and because the cost is not rolled into a transaction, it is highly visible and will be resented by U. If the enforced registration costs ten million a year but B and C only save five million in reduced legal and search fees then there is no overall cost saving. Given that U is likely to be a non-commercial land user any imposition of increased cost is likely to be resisted.

If eConveyancing leads to an increased emphasis on registration and further standardisation of property rights then a registered transaction may be given more impact, with an increase in its destructive effects. Additional

(continued)

[209] Murphy notes that some no longer have relevance in a modern conveyancing context. Murphy (2013), p. 21.

[210] These relate to the resettlement of large estates by the Land Commission to tenant farmers. The Land Commission was dissolved in 1992 after over 100 years in existence. See Sect. 2.3.2.

[211] No. 27 of 2004.

[212] Lyall (2010), p. 944.

[213] There are two such overriding interests; a perpetual yearly superior rent and covenants and conditions created in an instrument creating the superior rent.

[214] Where a tenant has acquired the fee simple. See section 28 of the Landlord and Tenant (Ground Rents) (No. 2) Act 1978 (No. 16 of 1978) as amended by section 77 of the 2006 Act.

overreaching provisions may be introduced. Alternatively if the operation of provisions, such as section 21 of the 2009 Act, are found to be overly complex and detrimental in practice, then the legislature may move towards more clear cut and definitive legislation along the lines of Ontario's section 62(1). While this does not destroy the trust there is the danger of the money being more readily lost from the beneficiary's reach.

Standardisation of rights puts the focus on policies which decide how many interests and how those interests are to be protected from transactions or dealings with the title. The legislature may require the courts to limit the availability of equitable relief and this will lead to a reduction in successful claims impacting on the ownership of land. The strengthening of the register with its all encompassing remit will require parties to register to have any entitlement. This will herald the reduction or even elimination of third party interests held by U and successful property claims by V.

The power of the courts to recognise novel claims would be fettered. In the choice between certainty and flexibility, eConveyancing pushes towards a stricter *numerus clausus* which facilitates ease of transaction, security of registration and the commoditisation of ownership of land. Thus certain rights may be reclassified into the category of rights that are not recognised and not capable of registration.

Such major changes can have unintended consequences on risk. Chapter 9, the concluding chapter, looks at the shift in risk and identifies suggestions for reform and research in the move towards eConveyancing. As Ireland is in the early stages of its eConveyancing programme there remains the potential to minimise any adverse consequences for participants in the land market while maximising the benefits of an electronic system.

References

Arruñada, B. (2010). Leaky title syndrome? *New Zealand Law Journal*.

Arruñada, B. (2011). Property titling and conveyancing. In K. Ayotte & H. E. Smith (Eds.), *Research handbook on the economics of property law*. UK: Edward Elgar. http://www.econ.upf.edu/docs/papers/downloads/1177.pdf. Accessed 14 May 2014.

Breen, O. (2000). Registration of title and overriding interests – Another crack in the mirror? *Conveyancing & Property Law Journal, 5*(3).

Brennan, G. (2010). *Aspects of the Land and Conveyancing Law Reform Act 2009 likely to arise before a Circuit Court Judge*. In Circuit Court Judges Conference, Adare, 9 July 2010.

Brennan, G., & Casey, N. (Eds.). (2014). *Conveyancing* (7th ed.). Oxford: Oxford University Press.

Chamberlain, L. (2002). The Land Registration Act 2002: A "Conveyancing Revolution" – Pt I. *New Law Journal, 152*.

Clancy, D. (2008). *From caveat emptor towards full disclosure – Developments in Ireland*. In United Nations Economic Commission for Europe's Working Party on Land Administration Workshop on the Influence of Land Administration on People and Business. http://wpla.

uredjenazemlja.hr/prezentacije/Presentation%20Caveat%20Emptor%20to%20Vendor%20Disclosure%208-9-08.pdf. Accessed 14 May 2014.
De Soto, H. (2001). *The mystery of capital*. London: Black Swan.
Deeney, J. (2014). *Registration of Deeds and Title in Ireland*. Great Britain: Bloomsbury.
Dixon, M. (2003). The reform of property law and the Land Registration Act 2002: A risk assessment. *Conveyancer and Property Lawyer*.
Ferlan, M., Šumrada, R., & Mattsson, H. (2007). Modelling property transactions. In J. Zevenbergen, A. Frank, & E. Stubkjær (Eds.), *Real property transactions: Procedures, transaction costs and models*. Amsterdam: IOS.
Fitzgerald, B. (1995). *Land registry practice* (2nd ed.). Dublin: Round Hall Press.
Fox, L. (2000). *Co-owners, co-occupiers, co-habitees: The role of policy in disputes between creditors and non-debtor occupiers* (Ph.D. thesis). Queen's University of Belfast.
Fox, L. (2006). *Conceptualising home: Theories, law and policies*. Oxford: Hart.
Glover, W. E. (1933). *A treatise on the registration of ownership of land in Ireland*. Dublin: John Falconer.
Gray, K., & Gray, S. F. (2009). *Elements of land law* (5th ed.). Great Britain: Oxford University Press.
Gummow, W. M. C. (2003). Equity and the Torrens system register. In D. Grinlinton (Ed.), *Torrens in the twenty-first century*. Wellington: LexisNexis.
Hansmann, H., & Kraakman, R. (2002). Property, contract, and verification: The *Numerus Clausus* problem and the divisibility of rights. *Journal of Legal Studies, 31*.
Harpum, C. (2000). *Property in an electronic age* (Modern studies in property law, Vol. 1). Oxford: Hart.
Harpum, C. (2004). *English experience: Title by registration – Preparation for e-conveyancing*. In Law Reform Commission Annual Conference. http://www.lawreform.ie/Annual%20Conference%202004.PDF. Accessed 18 Feb 2009.
Hogan, G. W., & Whyte, G. F. (2003). *JM Kelly: The Irish constitution* (4th ed.). Great Britain: Tottel.
Howell, J. (2006). Land law in an E-conveyancing world. *Conveyancer and Property Lawyer*.
Hughson, M., Neave, M., & O'Connor, P. (1997). Reflections on the mirror of title: Resolving the conflict between purchasers and prior interest holders. *Melbourne University Law Review, 21*.
Joint Land Titles Committee. (1990). Renovating the foundation: Proposals for a Model Land Recording and Registration Act for the Provinces and Territories of Canada. http://www.law.ualberta.ca/alri/docs/Model%20Land%20Recording%20Act.pdf. Accessed 13 June 2014.
Law Commission and HM Land Registry. (2001). Land registration for the twenty-first century: A conveyancing revolution (Report) [2001] EWLC 271. http://www.bailii.org/ew/other/EWLC/2001/271.html. Accessed 18 June 2014.
Law Reform Commission. (2005). Report on reform and modernisation of land law and conveyancing law. The Law Reform Commission (LRC 74 – 2005). http://www.lawreform.ie/Reports_Published/Default.135.html.
Law Reform Commission. (2007). The law of landlord and tenant. The Law Reform Commission (LRC 85 – 2007). http://www.lawreform.ie/Reports_Published/Default.135.html.
Law Society of Ireland. (2008). *eConveyancing: Back to basic principles. Vision of an electronic system of conveyancing ('eVision')*.
Lyall, A. (2010). *Land law in Ireland* (3rd ed.). England: Round Hall.
Mason, A. (2003). Indefeasibility – Logic or legend? In D. Grinlinton (Ed.), *Torrens in the twenty-first century*. Wellington: LexisNexis.
McCrimmon, L. A. (1994). Protection of equitable interests under the Torrens system: Polishing the mirror of title. *Monash University Law Review*, 20.
McCrimmon, L. A. (2003). Whose land is it anyway? Adverse possession and Torrens title. In D. Grinlinton (Ed.), *Torrens in the twenty-first century*. Wellington: LexisNexis.

Mee, J. (2006). The Land and Conveyancing Law Reform Bill 2006: Observations on the law reform process and a critique of selected provisions – Part 1. *Conveyancing & Property Law Journal, 11*(3).

Megarry, R., & Wade, W. (2000). *The law of real property* (6th ed.). London: Sweet and Maxwell.

Merrill, T. W., & Smith, H. E. (2000–2001). Optimal standardization in the law of property: The *Numerus Clausus* principle. *Yale Law Journal, 110.*

Murphy, S. (2013). *An examination of eConveyancing: A comparison of the treatment of overriding interests in the context of eConveyancing: Ireland with England and Wales* (Master of Law thesis). National University of Ireland, Galway.

Murray, K. (2004). *Electronic registration and other modernization initiatives in Ontario's land registration system.* In Law Reform Commission Annual Conference. http://www.lawreform.ie/Annual%20Conference%202004.PDF. Accessed 18 Feb 2009.

November, J., & Rendell, J. (2010). The "Mirror" principle and the position of unregistered interests in the Torrens system. *New Zealand Law Review.*

O'Connor, P. (2003a). Double indemnity – Title insurance and the Torrens systems. *Queensland University of Technology Law & Justice Journal, 3*(1). https://lr.law.qut.edu.au/article/view/123. Accessed 23 June 2014.

O'Connor, P. (2003b). Information, automation and the conclusive land register. In D. Grinlinton (Ed.), *Torrens in the twenty-first century.* Wellington: LexisNexis.

O'Connor, P. (2003c). Registration of title in England and Australia: A theoretical and comparative analysis. In E. Cooke (Ed.), *Modern studies in property law* (Vol. II). Oxford: Hart.

O'Connor, P. (2009). Immediate indefeasibility for mortgagees: A moral hazard? *Bond Law Review, 21*(2).

O'Sullivan, E. (2013). The law of adverse possession in Ireland: Is the doctrine in need of radical reform? *Hibernian Law Journal, 12.*

Park, M. M. (2009). *Removing the disharmony from Victoria's land title registration system.* In Land Surveying Commission Seminar, 21 May 2009. http://papers.ssrn.com/sol3/papers.cfm?abstract_id=1537710&http://www.google.ie/search?hl=en&q=park%2B%22removing+the+disharmony%22&meta=&aq=f&aqi=&aql=&oq=&gs_rfai. Accessed 28 Oct 2010.

Property Registration Authority 'Strategic Plan 2013–2015'. (2013). Property Registration Authority. http://www.prai.ie/eng/Publications/Strategic_Plan/. Accessed 5 June 2014.

Property Registration Authority. (2012). Practice direction trusts of land (updated 1 February 2012). http://www.prai.ie/eng/Legal_Professional_Customers/Legal_Practices_Procedures/Practice_Directions/18_Settlements_and_Trusts_2006_/Trusts_of_Land.html. Accessed 5 June 2014.

Property Registration Authority. (2013a). Practice direction cautions and inhibitions (updated 1 February 2013). http://www.prai.ie/eng/Legal_Professional_Customers/Legal_Practices_Procedures/Practice_Directions/Cautions_and_Inhibitions_published_30_November_2009_/. Accessed 5 June 2014.

Property Registration Authority. (2013b). Practice direction registration of easements and profits á prendre acquired by prescription under Section 49A (updated 1 February 2013). http://www.prai.ie/eng/Legal_Professional_Customers/Legal_Practices_Procedures/Practice_Directions/Easements_and_Profit_%C3%A1_Prendre/. Accessed 5 June 2014.

Rajoy, E. (2008). 'Presentation' CINDER XVI International Congress on Registration Law Valencia Spain, 20–22 May 2008. http://www.cinder2008.com/ingles/contenidos.cfm?id_web=565. Accessed 27 Aug 2010.

Ruoff, T. (1952). An Englishman looks at the Torrens system: Part 1: The mirror principle. *Australian Law Journal, 26.*

Stewart-Wallace, J. S. (1924). Land registration under the Law of Property Act, 1922. *Conveyancer, 9.*

Stubkjær, E., Frank, A., & Zevenbergen, J. (2007). Modelling real property transactions. In J. Zevenbergen, A. Frank, & E. Stubkjær (Eds.), *Real property transactions: Procedures, transaction costs and models.* Amsterdam: IOS.

Sweeney, (1992). The vesting certificate: Magic wand or Pandora's box? *Dlí, 7.*

Tuffin, J. (2009). Responsible lending laws: Essential development or overreaction? *Queensland University of Technology Law & Justice Journal, 9*(2). https://lr.law.qut.edu.au/article/view/32. Accessed 23 June 2014.

United Nations Economic and Social Council. (2007). Report on the Dublin Conference "Registered the World", United Nations. http://www.unece.org/fileadmin/DAM/hlm/documents/2007/ece/hbp/wp7/ece.hbp.wp.7.2007.9.e.pdf. Accessed 13 June 2014.

Van Erp, S. (2003). A numerus quasi-clausus of property rights as a constitutive element of a future European property law? *Electronic Journal of Comparative Law.* http://www.ejcl.org/72/art72-2.doc. Accessed 13 June 2014.

Wallace, J., & Williamson, I. (2004). Developing cadastres to service complex property markets. In FIG Conference on Standardization in the Cadastral Domain. http://www.fig.net/commission7/bamberg_2004/papers/ts_03_04_wallace_williamson.pdf. Accessed 13 June 2014 (PowerPoint Presentations).

Williams, S. (2008). *Real estate investment on level playing fields.* In United Nations Economic Commission for Europe's Working Party on Land Administration Workshop on the Influence of Land Administration on People and Business. http://wpla.uredjenazemlja.hr/prezentacije/1_S.%20Williams_Real%20Estate%20Investment%20on%20Level%20Playing%20Fields.pdf. Accessed 13 June 2014.

Woods, U. (2009). The English law on adverse possession: A tale of two systems. *Common Law World Review, 38.*

Wylie, J. C. W. (1998). *Landlord and tenant law* (2nd ed.). Dublin: Butterworths.

Zevenbergen, J., Frank, A., & Stubkjær, E. (2007). Pre-emption rights compared. In J. Zevenbergen, A. Frank, & E. Stubkjær (Eds.), *Real property transactions: Procedures, transaction costs and models.* Amsterdam: IOS.

Chapter 9
Conclusion

9.1 Introduction

This analysis has examined the management of risk in conveyancing transactions in the context of the move from paper based to electronic conveyancing. Legal, descriptive, analytical and comparative techniques have been deployed in order to determine the likely impact of technological change on the distribution of legal risk with particular reference to Ontario and Ireland. The impact is the extent to which a change in transactional process may unintentionally affect risk. Risk being the consequence of change and the likelihood of that consequence having a negative effect.

The particular focus has been on risks that impact on title registration and the security, protection or lack thereof that this registration offers to land owners, third parties and property claimants. The methodological approach to this investigation of risk has been by use of a model of two conveyancing transactions.

This chapter is the concluding chapter. It provides an overarching view on the impact of eConveyancing on risk and examines potential mechanisms for removing, minimising or distributing the risk or takes the view that the risk is worth bearing given the other benefits accrued. Finally it seeks to draw conclusions to inform the reform process in Ireland.

9.2 Risk Versus Reward

In implementing technological change there is a change in the distribution of risk in conveyancing transactions as the protection offered to different property rights is strengthened or weakened. "Any major business process re-engineering of a long

G. Brennan, *The Impact of eConveyancing on Title Registration*,
DOI 10.1007/978-3-319-10341-9_9

established system such as conveyancing will raise the question for all participants of costs and benefits and changes to risk profile."[1]

If the risk cannot be removed, minimised or distributed is it worth bearing given the other benefits of eConveyancing? Even if the risk can be mitigated, is there some factor, such as time, money or complexity that would make it undesirable? Generally when risk is allocated it should not fall on those least able to bear the consequences. This is a policy driven area where standards may be set, though this often results in the risk being borne by banks and bureaucracies with the benefit falling on consumers. Compensation may not be a feasible option, as not all risks are directly comparable when realised in monetary terms.

eConveyancing has the potential to deliver numerous benefits. There may be a reduction in the cost of title registration and greater accuracy of the register with the priority of interests more readily apparent and more transparent. There will be increased access to live register data and the possibility for quicker completion and registration. The protection of registration will be granted at an earlier stage, closer to completion, and if the register is all encompassing then there will be less searching required which will lead to lower costs.

Legal rules should minimise and balance the risks between present and would-be owners but Baird and Jackson point out that rules which increase the information about property ownership, presumably reducing the risks, bring their own costs and these must be weighted against the benefits.[2] Improvements in transparency however benefit all participants.

Transaction time may be reduced. Electronic messaging will be virtually instantaneous versus postal delivery which takes at least a day. If lawyers are able to deliver information and documentation more readily to each other, then they will be able to respond in a more timely manner and while the details of the transaction are fresh. Less administration will be required as documentation can be pre-populated; it will be sufficient to type data in once. This data will then be validated by the registering authority so that any difficulties can be addressed before completion. The improved efficiencies and improved collaboration between stakeholders will benefit all participants in the process.

There is no merit in governments, registries or citizens attempting to halt the march of technology. That argument has already been lost and technology is now an integral part of daily life. Instead it is preferable to make technological advances work to the advantage of processes that require improvement.

> There is no doubt that the move towards electronic conveyancing will continue unabated. The information technology experts have an unshakeable grip on the psyche of society and the need to reduce the human element in transactions. In conveyancing terms, this offers a promise of greater accuracy, more certainty of title, and provided the security concerns of access to central databases can be overcome, the opportunity for reduced claims on the assurance fund.[3]

[1] Sneddon (2007), p. 22.

[2] Baird and Jackson (1984), p. 301.

[3] Griggs (2001).

The achievement of the savings and efficiencies from eConveyancing will, if realised, accrue to all land owners however this comes with increased risk for some participants.

While this analysis focused on the management of risk in relation to land owners, third parties and property claimants it must not be forgotten that eConveyancing offers considerable benefits to the state through its title register. There may also be benefits to professionals involved in the conveyancing process. Those benefits may however come at the cost of increased risk for those professionals and this would merit further study.

9.3 Impact of eConveyancing on Risk

eConveyancing will move risk from one participant to another by the substantive and procedural rules it imposes. Conveyancing itself is a risk distribution system and this does not change in an eConveyancing environment. As Keating notes "[c]onveyancing is a process which requires an ability to recognise and minimise risks; the risk that the vendor is acting fraudulently or the risk that another party such as a lender may have a greater form of interest or estate in the property."[4]

Chapter 5 set out a model in order to provide a transaction unit analysis. This involved the creation of two abstracted conveyancing transactions; an arms length transaction for value and a gift. This schematic allowed risk to be allocated to the abstract participants in order to determine how each risk is impacted by the move to eConveyancing. Some conclusions can now be drawn from the analysis of each risk category.

9.3.1 Registration Gap

The elimination or compression of the registration gap does have an impact on risk in conveyancing transactions. It lowers risk for B, Y and C. There is less delay in achieving the protection of registration and reduced possibility for an intervening interest to be registered.

While the risk to B, Y and C is reduced there is increased risk for U and V. They have less time to register their right or claim before it may be destroyed by a registered transaction.

Y will still be subject to all unregistered rights to which X held the land unless his status is improved. There are law reform proposals in other jurisdictions suggesting this but it has not been proposed in Ireland and would be unlikely to be adopted. From the perspective of a complete register it would make sense to treat

[4] Keating (2012), p. 7.

Y the same as B. However, X would then be able to use the gift of Whiteacre to Y to destroy valuable unregistered interests and there would be no direct market interest to counter balance. Also there is no market claim for Y and there are many instances where X has attempted to use a gift to Y to circumvent his creditors so treating Y and B the same is not recommended.

Given that the registering authority is to remain the gatekeeper of the title register it is unlikely that the registration gap in Ireland can be eliminated entirely but there is merit in reducing it as much as possible. There is discussion in Ireland about bringing priority entries[5] into the next phase of eRegistration which may reduce some of the current risk between completion and registration but this has a cost associated with it. Also if a priority entry becomes standard practice, does it remove the incentive to reduce the registration gap? It would be preferable to reduce or eliminate the registration gap in so far as this is feasible while not implementing an automatic system. As a small gap will remain a priority entry could be used to seal this gap.[6]

The reduced risk to B, Y and C affirms the value of title registration as a feature of the Irish land administration system and enhances the security of the market. This provides increased protection to land owners at the expense of U and V.

9.3.2 Formalities for Registration

Initial indications are that electronic systems with more streamlined formalities result in less errors in applications for registration. In built system prompts provide the opportunity for problems to be corrected in advance of completion. If there are less registry errors all parties who participate in the registration system will benefit from the increased accuracy. The registering authority will also benefit from a reduction in claims.

This will decrease the risk for all participants as applications for registration are less likely to be rejected. It will also facilitate closing of the registration gap. The benefits of standardisation and simplification must, however, be balanced against any contractual constraints that might result. If eConveyancing prevents new interests in land, that currently cannot even be conceived, then this will fetter land owners, make the market less responsive to changes in society and limit new U interests and V claims.

---

[5] This would provide a mechanism for a priority period to bridge the registration gap. See Sect. 6.2.

[6] According to Deeney it is arguable that such an entry ought to be the norm as such a registration "effectively safeguards" the position of an intending purchaser or chargee against transactions for value that might defeat them. See Deeney (2014), p. 377.

9.3.3 Error in Register

It is difficult to establish if eConveyancing of itself will lead to increased fraud. There is no evidence that more fraud occurs in an electronic environment[7] though this is one of the reasons most often cited for caution in implementing eConveyancing. An increase in property fraud may be attributable to the increasing globalisation of our society, new methods of squeezing cash from land ownership and property booms and busts rather than being in any way directly attributable to electronic systems. The disassociation of dealing with a virtual environment may be in part to blame but there is a strong argument that it is linked to predatory lending practices as much of the case law on fraud relates to mortgage fraud and particularly identity theft perpetrated on lenders.[8] This is one reason why many jurisdictions including Ontario have moved to introduce more stringent controls on lending practices with specific provisions around the necessity for due diligence.

The analysis of the system in Ontario provides grounds for determining how the Irish courts might deal with similar challenges and provides a framework for writers and academics to explore how the nature of indefeasibility might develop in Ireland. This research opens this debate in advance of any consideration by the courts. The low levels of fraud claims against the LTAF in Ontario may be due to the nature of the claim system and the profileration of title insurance rather than proof that electronic systems can be robust enough to withstand fraud. This aspect requires further research.

Who bears the risk under this heading will be determined by whether the Irish courts find the register defeasible or indefeasible and if it is the latter whether this is immediate or deferred. In the absence of a subsequent transaction the law allows the court to rectify in favour of A but it by no means certain that this would occur if B is in occupation.

A policy of immediate indefeasibility would benefit B and C at the expense of A who would only be entitled to compensation. Y is however likely to lose out to a claim of prior ownership by X. If there is a subsequent transaction a policy of deferred indefeasibility would benefit D and C2 at the expense of A, who again would only be entitled to compensation. This is presuming that the courts will not distinguish between the title of B and C or that of D and C2. As one is a purchaser and the other a lender the courts may choose to give them differing levels of protection rather than bundling their interests together.

In relation to errors there is the potential to reduce these through the system design. eConveyancing may not, of itself, create more errors and increased loss but may reveal errors and losses already in the conveyancing system. Those errors and

[7] HM Land Registry does not accept any link between eConveyancing and fraud noting that the rise in fraud in England has occurred during a period when apart from a small number of electronic charges it was not possible to use or submit electronic documents for registration.

[8] See Tuffin (2009), pp. 280–310 and O'Connor (2009), pp. 133–159. Both explore risk arising from bad lending practices and particularly the lack of due diligence by lenders.

losses may previously have been hidden from the general public and policy makers and illumination provides the opportunity for them to be acknowledged and addressed. Thus the system can be designed to close off some current risks in the process. This would benefit all parties who rely on registration and also benefit the registering authority through reduced claims.

9.3.4 Interests Off the Register Which Affect Title

eConveyancing with its increased emphasis on the title register leads to an examination of which interests should be protected by the register and which should not. Overriding interests as a category of property rights require a review and, if this category is to be retained, the individual interests should be examined to determine whether reform is required. Some of these interests are out of date and may no longer have the same relevance. The efficiency resulting from the removal of this category of rights needs to be balanced against any injustice that might be caused to those holding such rights.

The general rationale for this category of rights is that they keep the register flexible and applicable but many of the individual rights, when examined closely, do not fulfill these criteria. If these rights are reduced or removed as a category this will increase risk for U and V. This may not immediately correspond to any decreased risk or lower costs for other participants but will impact future transactions when B and C don't have to enquire about such rights.

9.3.5 Destructive Effects of a Registered Transaction

With the increased emphasis on the register the power of a registered transaction is likely to increase. This will have a negative impact on the interests of U and V. Their interests may become rights that have no impact on the ownership of land. An assessment would need to be carried out to determine if there is some other means of providing sufficient protection for those holding such rights or are there some interests which should survive a registered transaction.

A claim that was previously a property claim may become a personal claim. This would change the nature of some claims fundamentally but will have less impact on others. For example, could the claim to an easement or reliance on a restrictive covenant exist without some link to the title? In relation to trusts and equitable charges the claim will continue to exist provided there are funds to meet the claim. Other rights are temporary such as an option to purchase but if they are not recognised then there is no market as they cannot be bought and sold. This may close off areas of the land market that currently exist.

9.3.6 *Rights Not Recognised*

The re-classification of interests in land has already commenced and is likely to be driven further by the demands of standardisation and simplification to make an electronic system viable. The impact of any re-classification of rights needs to be carefully assessed and should form part of an overall reform strategy.

Such a re-classification may put the right of certain participants at risk. In particular the interests of U and V may be open to scrutiny. Third party rights are most at risk of being downgraded to personal rights or rights which can be defeated by a registered transaction. If it is the latter and the registration gap is eliminated or compressed then there is little possibility of such rights intervening between the registered interests of A and B. If overriding interests are also downgraded to rights which can be overridden by a registered transaction then U and V will have few, if any, opportunity for enforcing their right or claim against the land.

9.4 Risk to U and V

Thus the parties who are most at risk in any move towards eConveyancing will be U and V. There is the potential for all other parties to benefit from efficiencies in the system of title registration. This is indicative of the fact that all other parties are already participants whose interests are embedded in the title register. As a general rule all the other participants (A, B, C, X and Y) will seek to have their interest protected by the registration system. Whereas U and V may seek to rely not on the register but on some other factor such as:

(a) the status of their interest as an overriding interest;
(b) a personal claim against the grantor of the interest;
(c) some personal relationship with the registered owner; or
(d) occupation of the property.

The registered owner may accept that the right or claim held by U and V has merit as often the facts speak for themselves. U is in occupation. V is married to A. U did contribute to the purchase monies or X did give V an option to purchase the land. A conflict between U and V and the other participants in the land market may not be about the existence of the claim or right but instead be a conflict about the breadth and depth of the claim.

The existence of such a claim or right may not, in reality, have any impact on the title register but in seeking to ensure priority of registration B and C are required to carry out enquiries about potential claims or rights held by U and V. This adds to the cost of conveyancing and undermines the effectiveness of the title register.

When examining the key objective of each participant as set out in Chap. 5 it appears that eConveyancing may defeat the resilience sought by U the third party and V the property claimant. The extent to which this occurs will depend on how U and V are to be dealt with and there are a number of options.

U rights and V claims may be reduced or downgraded to personal rights or rights which can be defeated by a registered transaction. This would make the system cleaner and easier, reduce risk and cost for B and C but adversely affect U and V.

Alternatively U and V could be brought onto the register. This imposes cost on U and V. If these rights or claims would previously have been personal rights or defeated by a registered transaction, then bringing them onto the register will have a detrimental effect on the interest of land owners. If however they were overriding interests that affected without registration then it would benefit future land owners to have these reflected on the register.

Another option is to provide compensation for U and V if their interest or claim is downgraded or defeated or compensation for purchasers if U and V cannot be disposed of or brought onto the register.

Requiring U or V to register or downgrading their interest or claim would be an interference in the land market and this should be considered carefully. There is a general acceptance of De Soto's argument that a secure and efficient land market creates more credit and investment and thus generates economic growth.[9] If we accept this argument we interfere with the market at our peril.

9.5 Interference in the Land Market

Property rights are maintained and enforced through governmental support via legislation and the operation of state agencies such as the registering authority and all land ownership will incur some form of regulation.[10] However the practical and economic implications must also be considered when major changes are being introduced, particularly if this is done within a short period of time.

Rapaczynski notes that every jurisdiction engages in regulation that impairs or encroaches on the value of people's investments and most are not considered "compensable takings" however the political system and economic pressure groups will ensure the state does not go "too far" in interfering with an owners control over his assets.[11] This may be true of lenders or investors but is less true of consumers. They are a dispersed group with diverse interests and have less organised representation. Often it is the state that finances and controls the consumer lobby.

Thus a conflict may arise. On the one hand consumers are seen as being more vulnerable than other participants in the land market and often merit increased protection which manifests itself in consumer protection legislation. On the other

---

[9] De Soto (2001).

[10] Gray and Gray note that title "as self-authenticating social reality has given way to title as state-regulated bureaucratic fact." See Gray and Gray (2009), p. 180.

[11] Rapaczynski (1996), pp. 92–93.

hand consumers do not have the same level of representation at policy level and this may make it easier for a government to subvert the interests of the consumer to economic or public policy considerations. The legislation may go too far in one direction or the other and as a result may not achieve either objective.

Any enhanced reliance on registration of title will need to factor in the maintenance of security of title so that the market can operate efficiently and effectively. Sneddon notes the importance of ensuring continued confidence in the marketplace for conveyancing.[12] "If the right land administration system is defined, it will show 'emergent properties', in this case 'trustworthiness'; the fact that people can and will rely on and contribute to the system."[13] The Irish registering authority currently has this trustworthiness and maintaining it is vital.[14] As Deeney notes "[i]t is essential that the system of registration of title maintains the confidence of the Court, the legal profession and the general public."[15]

According to Ruoff the Torrens system has five objects, namely, reliability, simplicity, cheapness, expedition and suitability.[16] This is equally true of all title registration systems and eConveyancing will only succeed if it moves land registration closer to these fundamental objectives. The challenge is that these objectives may not be totally congruous and the move towards eConveyancing may reveal tensions between them. One object may need to take precedence over another. For example if the register is to be completely reliable all interests should be registered, including those held by U, but this will impose cost on those holding overriding interests, for example, who are now required to register.

Such interference in the land market may be more acceptable where the increased risk can be mitigated. The question arises as to whether this is possible. Third parties and property claimants like U and V could be given a period of time to register their right and thereafter it would be lost. If U or V were successful in registering, then their interest is protected as a property right and if their claim is unsuccessful and fails then the interest is destroyed. After a period of time no new interests or claims of that nature would be allowed.

As Holmes points out in referring to statutes of limitation and the law of prescription "what is the justification for depriving a man of his rights, a pure evil as far as it goes, in consequence of the lapse of time?" but he also notes that "[s] ometimes it is said that, if a man neglects to enforce his rights, he cannot complain if, after a while, the law follows his example."[17] This may be a useful argument when depriving an individual of rights that he has failed to protect but has less merit when used to justify the removal or downgrading of an entire category of rights.

---

[12] Sneddon (2007), p. 10.

[13] Zevenbergen (2006).

[14] See Property Registration Authority 'Annual Report 2011' (2012), p. 22 for results of a customer survey undertaken in November/December 2011.

[15] Deeney (2014), p. 21.

[16] Ruoff (1952), p. 198.

[17] Holmes (1896–1897), p. 476.

To extend a prohibition to all new interests or claims would be a drastic move by the legislature which throws up public policy and justice issues. This may, in effect, mean a definitive move towards the civil law *numerous clausus*, the removal of the Courts and land owners discretion to create new interests in land thus introducing a lack of flexibility into the common law system that would overturn centuries of tradition.

The gains would be certainty, the register becoming all encompassing and the state having a more direct role in the nature and existence of title. Estates, rights and interests whether legal or beneficial would be of no relevance as the registered legal title would be all. This may have been the original aim of the Torrens registered title system but the reality of such a system would send shock waves through the common law world.

Despite this clear moves are already afoot in various jurisdictions with the limiting or removal of adverse possession claims, reduction in overriding interests, trusts being moved off the register and the attempt to move easements onto the register. Dematerialism also throws any interest dependent on the holding of paper evidence of the interest into doubt.[18]

None of the risks to the parties holding those interests have been mitigated by a general compensation scheme[19] or through insurance but interference in the land market can be softened by indemnifying parties adversely affected by change. Thus it is important to consider the merits of this as a risk avoidance mechanism.

Title registration systems use a combination of risk management strategies to reduce the incidence of conflicts between different interests. O'Connor refers to the generation of publicity for interests to reduce the likelihood of conflict, establishment of new priority rules that provide an incentive to register, the transfer of some risks to the State and the spreading of risk through an indemnity scheme.[20]

Thus mitigation of risk can be done by existing insurance or compensation or new provisions may be required. However new insurance must be paid for and additional claims on existing insurance will be paid for by increased premiums. Additional claims on the registering authority compensation fund will come from central exchequer and will likely be passed on to land owners through higher registration fees. The question arises as to whether the state should bear the loss or is there a role for private insurance?

---

[18] See impact of the removal of the status of land certificates and certificates of charge dealt with in Chap. 8.

[19] The removal of land certificates and certificates of charge in Ireland was accompanied by a compensation provision to protect vulnerable people whose right might be extinguished without their knowledge but no application for compensation was made. See Deeney (2014), p. 362. See Sect. 8.5.3.

[20] O'Connor (2005), p. 48.

9.6 Indemnity for Loss

9.6.1 Title Insurance Versus State Compensation

Title insurance is a form of insurance that generally protects a land owner's title against loss incurred as a result of unknown or undetected title defects for as long as the land owner owns the title. Depending on the nature of the policy it can protect against fraud, errors in title registration and overriding interests. It is "an after-the-fact indemnity."[21] Thus an actual loss must occur.

Title insurance is insurance purchased privately by the land owner and may add an additional cost to the transaction though this may be offset by other costs which are removed from the process. For example, if B is relying on title insurance his lawyer may see no need to carry out the same level of detailed enquiries about encumbrances.

The question arises as to whether the use of title insurance encourages title defects to be hidden. In a system where title insurance is standard it provides no encouragement for title defects to be remedied before a conveyancing transaction is concluded. Comprehensive searches may not be done to identify potential difficulties with the title that would properly inform the transferee B or acquisition lender C. This may reduce the cost of the transaction but is it worth it? As Moore and Globe point out

> [s]imple reliance on title insurance as protection against financial loss and a narrowed focus on the bottom line can interfere with a purchaser's awareness of the personal and financial values of being fully informed on all matters relating to land ownership and enjoyment.[22]

Is financial compensation likely to be adequate compensation for loss of title, possession or enjoyment of the property? In the case of a family home this is unlikely to be the case.

Manthorpe is of the view that the title insurance system

> seems to be an inferior system offering less protection and at greater expense than the land registration systems in other countries. . . .Although it provides financial recompense if title is later to be found to be invalid this is usually only to the value of the purchase price at the time the property was bought. It does not protect the owner's possession of a property bought in good faith.[23]

Not every commentator is as critical. Bucknall is of the view that in Ontario title insurance provides a useful and economic supplement to conventional conveyancing practices.[24] He asks if "title insurance [should] be put in place as a private protection against losses created by the statutory registration scheme? Should

---

[21] O'Hara and Husa (2008), p. 2.

[22] Moore and Globe (2003), p. 391.

[23] Manthorpe (2007), p. 6. He is referring specifically to the US title insurance system.

[24] Bucknall (2008–2009), p. 44.

landowners expect to protect themselves when statutory protection is obviously inadequate?"[25]

Donahue *et al.* listed the benefits as including less searching, avoiding surveys, insuring existing defects, providing broad coverage and the covering of post-closing events.[26] However one could be forgiven for being skeptical about these claims. Surely if all of these benefits could be realised the entire world would have adopted title insurance?

There are some searches or enquiries that cannot, or it is argued, should not, be covered by title insurance. For example O'Hara and Husa note that "title insurance is not a substitute for a survey prepared by a professional land surveyor."[27] This was made abundantly clear by the Ontario Superior Court of Justice in *Ontario v. Syvan Developments Ltd.*[28] When the title to the property was converted from the unregistered to the registered system a right of way was inadvertently included and the error was not discovered until after the transaction closed. It was argued that a prudent developer in the plaintiff's position would have obtained an up to date survey prior to completion and this would have disclosed that the right of way no longer existed and the court agreed.

Thus

> an act or omission that would otherwise be a neglect or default within the meaning of the provision [i.e. s 59(1)(c)] will not cease to be so if is [sic] has been insured against. In other words, a defect is a defect is a defect. While title insurance may indemnify a party from defects in title, it does nothing to guarantee title or cure defects...Title insurance is not a substitute for due diligence.[29]

The lawyer is still required to properly advise their client and to disclose material information that would affect the client's decision to enter into the transaction.[30] Also title insurance only protects a transferee and may be provided only for a certain period of time. It is not "a one-size-fits-all policy that eliminates the need for searches or surveys".[31]

In *Bertrand v. Trites*[32] the court denied a claim for compensation partly on the grounds that the purchasers choose to obtain title insurance but not a land survey prior to closing. "[T]he Plaintiffs elected to take title insurance rather than obtaining a survey to inform themselves.... By doing so, they undertook the risk, and sequentially the cost, if necessary, of relocating the barn and garage or obtaining a minor variance" as their location infringed local set back provisions.

---

[25] Bucknall (2008–2009), p. 44.

[26] Donahue et al. (2003), pp. 262–263.

[27] O'Hara and Husa (2008).

[28] *Ontario v. Syvan Developments Ltd* 2006 CanLII 32430 (ONSC).

[29] O'Hara and Husa (2008), p. 3.

[30] See Lemieux (2010), pp. 29–32 for details of 'legal service coverage' which relates to errors or omissions on the part of the lawyer. It also includes examples of title insurance claims.

[31] Haynes (2010).

[32] *Bertrand v. Trites* 2006 CanLII 37959 (ON SC).

Title insurance can cover a wide range of risks including errors or defects in the title, imperfect legal services, reimbursement for legal fees and expenses and losses caused by fraud or forgery.[33] However MacInnes and Pinnington warn that title insurance will not protect if there has been a "valid fraud" i.e. the lender will be protected if the charge is fraudulent and invalid but not if the financing is greater than justified by the true value of the property.[34]

Title insurance is the business of accepting risk in return for payment of a premium. A title insurance company that does not collect more premiums than claims paid will quickly go into liquidation. Thus there may be strict requirements to be met before compensation is paid. It is not a failsafe last resort as contributory negligence will be taken into account and the policy will provide for subrogation. Thus title insurance will not protect in every instance. Each policy will have differences in relation to covered risks, due diligence requirements, exclusions and time periods. Title insurance

> provides owners and lenders with comprehensive no-fault protection against both title and legal services risks inherent in real estate transactions...[however like all forms of insurance] coverage is subject to numerous detailed exclusions, exemptions and endorsements.[35]

The view could also be taken that the risks protected by title insurance rarely occur and thus it is of no value however its merits must be compared as against other methods of closing off the same risk.[36]

State compensation similarly does not cover everything. There are exceptions in the legislation, overriding interests, *in personam* claims, interests incapable of registration and also dangers faced by volunteers who have less protection. State compensation will generally only arise if the state is responsible for the loss or the operation of the system overrides someone's interest; it is not a blanket insurance against risk but neither is title insurance.[37] *In personam* claims are not likely to be covered by title insurance and certainly not claims arising from post completion acts.

It could be argued that title insurance is used by lawyers purely as a means of diminishing their own exposure to negligence[38] however Irish lawyers have chosen not to use title insurance in this manner and in Ontario title insurance has not resulted in less claims by clients against their lawyers.[39]

[33] See Donahue et al. (2003), p. 261 for further examples.

[34] See MacInnes and Pinnington (2010), p. 21.

[35] Moore and Globe (2003), p. 381.

[36] Ziff (2003), p. 395.

[37] Flaws examines the differences between state and private title insurance in respect of New Zealand. See Flaws (2003), pp. 407–413. It should be remembered however that this system provides for automatic registration. See p. 414.

[38] Reevy notes that by getting the client to use title insurance the risk to the practitioner of a subsequent negligence action is diminished. See Reevy (2003), p. 902. However Rolph is of the view that title insurance is not the panacea solicitors in Ontario had hoped for. See Rolph (2010).

[39] Rolph (2010), pp. 26–28.

Moore and Globe noted in 2003 that

> real estate transactions, and more particularly title, execution and adjoining lands searches, give rise to a disproportionate number of negligence claims against lawyers. Traditionally, real estate claims have accounted for almost one half of all claims made annually against LawPRO, the Lawyers Professional Indemnity Company.[40]

This statement is not supported by the figures produced by LawPRO but conveyancing malpractice claims are the second highest after civil litigation and these claims account for a higher percentage of claims costs.[41] Over the 10 years prior to 2010 the claims averaged 29 % of claims and 30 % of claims costs.[42]

The penetration of title insurance in the Ontario conveyancing market has an impact on risk however it is worth noting that title insurance is not a standard feature of conveyancing in Ireland. In Ireland it may be used where there is a particular defect on title that cannot be remedied until some time has passed. It was previously used by sub-prime lenders for re-mortgages during the property boom however most of these lenders are no longer lending and only retain a presence in Ireland for enforcement purposes.

The experience in other jurisdictions shows that there are dangers in the widespread adoption of title insurance as a means of mitigating risk in conveyancing. If title insurance is introduced:

> [t]he insurers' strategy of risk assumption could result in increased claims upon the… indemnity fund, by reducing standards of due diligence in conveyancing. If changed conveyancing practices induced by title insurance adversely impact upon the fund, it is likely that governments will propose measures to shift the risks back to the insurers. Legislatures will bar title insurers from exercising the subrogated rights of the insured to claim…and exclude claims on the fund by privately insured persons for losses covered by their policies.[43]

O'Connor provides examples of jurisdictions where the state indemnity provisions have been limited effectively shifting risk to claimants and their representatives particularly where there has been fraud or negligence.[44]

If private title insurance is used to mitigate risk there is a danger that this will result in the statutory scheme operated by the registry being downgraded. This will result in further increased emphasis on private title insurance with a corresponding decrease in claims against the indemnity fund. A continual shift has the potential to eliminate the indemnity fund entirely with only title insurance remaining. This private title insurance will be optional and thus some participants may choose not to pay and assume the risk instead. This shift in risk assumption from the state to individuals can be seen in Ontario.

---

[40] Moore and Globe (2003), p. 379. See also http://www.lawpro.ca/AboutLawpro/default.asp.

[41] MacInnes and Pinnington (2010), p. 16.

[42] MacInnes and Pinnington (2010), p. 16. In Ireland there has also been an increase in conveyancing claims. See Fingleton (2010), p. 8.

[43] O'Connor (2003), p. 8.

[44] O'Connor (2003), p. 8.

Title insurance prevails and dominates the conveyancing system in both the United States[45] and Ontario.[46] In Ontario the consideration of title insurance is now a required step in both purchase and lending transactions.[47] Waters estimated in 2010 that 95 % of residential purchase transactions in Ontario were title insured.[48] This may account in part for the low level of claims against the LTAF as set out in Chap. 7 but it is also an indication of lack of public confidence in the system of title investigation and transfer. In a system where title insurance is standard it provides no encouragement for the defects to be remedied before a conveyancing transaction is concluded.

The profileration of title insurance in the market has led to this area being regulated by legislation and also by rules of professional conduct laid down by the Law Society of Upper Canada.[49] Indeed the rules themselves may have contributed to the penetration as rule 2.02 of the Rules of Professional Conduct relates specifically to title insurance in real estate transactions.[50]

The LTAF and title insurance co-exist but the LTAF will not pay out if the claim is covered by title insurance. Thus the state indemnity has been diluted with the penetration of title insurance in the market. Though as a matter of public policy and equity, surely the state indemnity fund should pay out if the loss is due to inbuilt risk in the system regardless of fault and regardless of whether the claimant has another recourse. The state should not be encouraged to avoid liability for its errors and place the onus on individual land owners.

Title insurance as a method of socialising risk puts the onus on individuals rather than on the state. If a land owner chooses not to take out title insurance he may have recourse to the LTAF for some losses and he avoids the cost of title insurance. He must pay for registration but this is a cost that has to be incurred independent of any potential claim. Alternatively if he chooses to take out title insurance, he may have recourse to the title insurer for losses not covered by the LTAF, but he paid for this via a premium. Of course some losses may not be covered at all.

Flaws suggests that private insurance and state compensation are complementary and that such insurance is not a threat to the quality of conveyancing.[51]

> Rather, it can be used as a commercial tool to cover the gaps created by many of the limitations and exceptions of state compensation and to provide economic protection against a broad range of property law risks that the state has no business or interest in covering.[52]

---

[45] For a brief explanation of the United States land title system and the role of title insurance see Thomas (1997).

[46] See Ziff (2003) for the development and growth of the title insurance market in both jurisdictions. Title insurers are also attempting to break into other markets. See O'Connor (2003), pp. 1–27. See also Donahue et al. (2003), pp. 262–263 for an argument in favour of title insurance.

[47] Moore and Globe (2003), p. 381.

[48] Waters (2010), p. 14.

[49] See Moore and Globe (2003), pp. 382–384.

[50] The Law Society of Upper Canada 'Rules of Professional Conduct' (2013).

[51] Flaws (2003), p. 399.

[52] Flaws (2003), p. 399.

However in a choice between state compensation and title insurance, state compensation is to be preferred for many reasons. The social insurance model operated via the state compensation fund facilitates distribution of risk by maximising the pool of insured persons and allows for cross-subsidisation. O'Connor describes this as "[t]he right to indemnity is not confined to contributors. Persons who have had no dealings with the registry may suffer loss through a registry error or omission".[53] By contrast only those who take out title insurance will be able to claim against the policy.

While acknowledging that private title insurance may be able to transfer to an insurer certain risks

> [t]he worst scenario would see governments abandoning universal social insurance in favour of optional private insurance, many people opting to go without cover and the occasional person suffering disastrous loss without recourse to compensation.[54]

The experience in Ontario and other jurisdictions shows that the penetration of title insurance allows the government to narrow its liability and this is to be avoided. While there might be some argument for a reduction in the state liability where an automatic eConveyancing system is being implemented, and the registering authority is no longer responsible for changes to the title register, there is no such argument in the implementation of an automated (but not automatic) eConveyancing system.

Regardless of whether compensation is provided via title insurance or state compensation it is not a perfect remedy. A land owner will likely not consider money to be adequate compensation for loss of title, possession or enjoyment of the property particularly in the case of a family home. As Ziff points out title insurance is not a guarantee of title but rather a source of indemnity[55] and coverage can be limited in several ways.[56]

Similarly monetary compensation may not be adequate for U and V if their right or claim cannot exist independently of the land. The real merit of the state compensation lies in its complimentary interaction with the rectification provisions. Any attempt to decouple these and insert title insurance between them is surely likely to allow certain claims to fall through the cracks.

If the increased risk to U and V is to be mitigated by private insurance or the general compensation scheme then loss allocation rules may provide assistance in examining which, if any, mechanism should be used to compensate U and V.

---

[53] O'Connor (2003), p. 8.

[54] O'Connor (2003), p. 8.

[55] Ziff (2003), p. 372.

[56] Ziff (2003), pp. 386–388.

9.6.2 *Imposition of Loss*

These have already been considered by Sneddon in the context of eConveyancing.[57] In looking at maintaining confidence in the move to eConveyancing in Australia, he set out three principles, from the economic efficiency approach to liability and loss allocation rules, as follows:

1. liability should be allocated to the party or parties that can reduce the incidence of losses at the lowest cost ('least cost avoider')[58];
2. liability should be allocated to the party or parties best able to spread the losses (liability for substantial losses may be spread over a wide class by insurance or a claim fund to which all members of the class contribute)[59]; and
3. liability allocation rules should be simple, clear and decisive so as to minimise the costs of administering them and disputes about their application.[60]

He refers to Cooter and Rubin who explain rules of loss imposition, loss spreading, and loss reduction.[61] Cooter and Rubin note that most people are risk averse and when facing a possible loss will pay out more than the loss's average value to eliminate the risk and the widespread use of insurance is evidence of this.[62]

Griggs and Low note that the principle of loss imposition asks who should enforce or have the loss imposed on them and the clearest solution is to let the loss lie where it occurs but this fails to take into consideration that the consumer is less likely to be able to enforce their rights.[63]

Loss reduction would mean identifying the least cost avoider and this would be B and C.[64] The party who can guard against the loss most easily should incur the cost. This would in effect maintain the current position but provide compensation to

---

[57] Sneddon (2007).

[58] This 'cheapest cost avoider' principle introduced by Guido Calabresi is widely used in the interdisciplinary field of law and economics. See Calabresi (1970). See also Coleman (2005), pp. 337–354; and Posner (2005), pp. 12–23.

[59] Griggs and Low (2011), pp. 285–308 are of the view that the guiding economics behind loss allocation and loss spreading is that the risk should be borne by the person who can achieve risk neutrality at the lowest level i.e. a financial institution or insurer. See p. 289.

[60] Sneddon (2007), p. 10.

[61] Cooter and Rubin (1987–1988), p. 70. Griggs and Low refer to this as the seminal article on loss spreading, loss reduction and loss imposition. See Griggs and Low (2011), pp. 285–308.

[62] Cooter and Rubin (1987–1988), pp. 70–71.

[63] Griggs and Low (2011), p. 290.

[64] O'Connor notes that the Ontario Court of Appeal invoked the cheaper cost avoider analysis in support of deferred indefeasibility thus placing the burden of the fraud on the lender rather than the innocent homeowner. See O'Connor (2009), p. 141. She notes at p. 134 that very few jurisdictions extend immediate indefeasibility to mortgagees and argues that there are sound policy reasons for denying immediate indefeasibility to mortgagees even if the rule is adopted for transferees. As between the mortgagee and land owner the mortgagee can at the least cost avoid identity fraud by adjusting their behaviour in the transaction. The courts in British Columbia adopt a similar approach; see Keating (2012), pp. 94–96. In British Columbia unless a mortgage is granted by

B and perhaps C if U and V cannot be disposed of or brought onto the register. Such compensation would likely be subject to due diligence putting the onus on B and C to enquire about U and V. This due diligence or notice requirement would maintain the status quo as it applies to overriding interests except that compensation would be payable in the event that U and V were undiscoverable as this would be a systematic risk. This makes sense as B and C should not be at risk due to undiscoverable U interests and V claims. This option however retains the cost of off register enquiries and searches and mitigates against a complete all encompassing register. In the current recessionary climate any suggestion that the state compensation scheme be extended is likely to be rejected. In addition the option of compensation for B and C provides less incentive for U or V to make and register their interest or claim.

In referring to the lowest cost avoider Griggs and Low note that in Australia there are obligations imposed on mortgagees to verify identity yet little is imposed on the owners of real estate.[65] They question what it is reasonable to expect of owners of land noting that if responsibility and liability is solely imposed on financial institutions then there is little incentive for homeowners to take precautions and requiring them to

> take precautions will only be of use if the behaviour of those people alters. If it does not, imposing liability makes little sense. For this reason, whereas loss spreading clearly favoured the imposition of liability on the bank in a land transaction, the result is not as clear for loss reduction.[66]

Loss spreading could also mean to either impose such loss on the state, paid for by all citizens, or on all those who avail of the protection of title registration through increased fees.

A scheme to compensate U or V for any loss, however it occurred, would be difficult to justify. Compensation for losses caused to U and V by the registration system is more justifiable when there is a gain for other users of the system, in disregarding the interests of U and V, particularly when there is an overall public benefit. Such a scheme would avoid human rights issues by giving compensation for the de facto expropriation of the property interest.

The downgrading or destruction of U's interest may bring a net public gain and thus it seems fair to compensate U, however V is more problematic as the nature of the interest may be subject to dispute. Any compensation scheme would have to resolve the validity of the claim before its value could be assessed.

The existing, or a new compensation fund, could be utilised with payment of compensation dependent on the taking of reasonable action by U and V. For example U or V may be required to bring their interest or claim to the notice of land owners, or those engaged in a transaction, or, U and V may be required to make

the true owner of a property the mortgage is invalid and the owner's title will be returned to its original state. See BC OnLine.

[65] Griggs and Low (2011), pp. 289–290.

[66] Griggs and Low (2011), pp. 289–290.

their claim within a set time scale to avoid the difficulty of unquantifiable liabilities to the system. A claimant with sufficient claim against the land owner may not be eligible so as to avoid the potential for land owners to be relieved of obligations they had undertaken. Instead the land owner could be required to compensate U and V directly.

U and V could be given an opportunity to assert their right so as to reduce the incidence of losses and if a new simple, efficient and cost effective scheme was put in place this would fulfil the loss reduction rule. Currently if there is a dispute between a land owner and third party or property claimant this can only be resolved by a court case which is expensive and lengthy. A new scheme would benefit U and V if the rules were simple, clear and precise.

Alternatively private insurance could be offered but this would be an imperfect solution as it would likely not cover all claims or claimants. In addition, as noted already, there are dangers associated with the penetration of title insurance as it has the potential to unravel the state compensation scheme adversely affecting all participants in the land market.

From the standpoint of those relying on the register it would be better to bring U rights onto the register. They are likely to be interests that already exist and bind but are just not shown on the register. The advantage of having them on the register for future transactions is that they are less likely to be overlooked. This would also benefit U and V where their interest or claim is vulnerable to the effects of a transfer.

As a general principle it is reasonable to ask people to protect interests that are of value to them. Thus U and V should be asked to produce formal and verifiable documentation and to lodge those with the registry in order to bring such interests onto the register. It would be preferable not to have interests arising without such documentation.

U and V, however, are a disparate group and include some parties who would not be able to avoid the loss. For example those holding family interests or contributory rights in a family setting may, in the absence of legal advice, not know that they have a claim. If they do not know they have a claim, they cannot act to protect it. Also some claims do not produce documents. For example those based on adverse possession or prescription and informal interests generally. A problem with proofs will make registration difficult to achieve. Questions arise as to who pays for the cost of proving the claim, what mechanisms for poof are needed and what if the proof accepted by the registering authority is then challenged in court?

Thus a significant claimant group may suffer if U and V are disposed of or required to come onto the register. Any solution designed for a particular type of U interest or V claim is likely to throw up issues for another type of U interest or V claim. An overarching mechanism for dealing with all U interests and V claims is likely to have unintended consequences for other participants in the land market. Without examining each potential interest or claim it is not possible to be prescriptive in making recommendations for how to deal with U and V. Instead some key principles are set out in the context of asking if the advantages of eConveyancing are sufficient to merit the injustice that might be caused to individual third parties or property claimants.

9.6.3 *Grounds for Increased Risk to U and V*

The benefits of eConveyancing to land owners are significant and may provide grounds for the increased risk to U and V. In particular it appears that many of the benefits of eConveyancing can only be realised by increased reliance and certainty in land registration. This lends itself to the elimination of exceptions to indefeasibility. Moving U and V onto the register may be a desirable and feasible solution that provides the benefits of eConveyancing and allocates the reduction in risk in the longer term among the greatest number of participants in the land market. B, C and to a lesser extent, Y would benefit.

In Mason's view the essence of the system, the Australasia Torrens system in his commentary, must be to provide a regime of registration that provides security of title, is inexpensive and enables prompt registration of interests.[67] eConveyancing may provide the means to achieve all of these to a greater degree than heretofore. In eConveyancing the participants who already register their interest will continue to do so and they will be able to achieve the protection of registration in a more timely manner. Such protection will then be of increased quality. This will likely lead to a more secure and effective land market.

As eConveyancing drives towards simplification and standardisation of property rights, certainty of the register will be valued above flexibility. Security of registered title is likely to be enhanced and this will lead to a reduction in the exceptions to indefeasibility. *In personam* claims, equitable interests, adverse possession and overriding interests may be limited or eliminated. eConveyancing may achieve what has eluded the title register to date; the register and the register alone becomes the arbiter of title.

9.7 Recommendations

The following recommendations are made in order to maximise the benefits of eConveyancing while also mitigating the potentially harsh effect of these changes on participants in conveyancing transactions:

(a) An automated eConveyancing system retains the role of the registering authority and keeps the state compensation scheme intact.[68]

---

[67] Mason (2003), p. 18.

[68] See conclusion to Chap. 7.

(b) Reduce or eliminate the registration gap without implementing an automatic eConveyancing system.[69]
(c) Priority entry is a useful tool to seal any remaining registration gap.[70]
(d) The lesser protection given to a volunteer should be maintained.[71]
(e) Robust system design provides the opportunity to reduce the risk of non compliance with the formalities for registration however this must be balanced against any contractual constraints that might be imposed.[72]
(f) Further research is required to establish if eConveyancing of itself will lead to increased fraud.[73]
(g) The nature of indefeasibility as it applies to the title register in Ireland requires debate and discussion. Examining the results of various measures across the common law world may provide some guidance to the courts in assessing the impact of risk to participants in the conveyancing process.[74]
(h) Robust system design has the potential to reduce registry errors.[75]
(i) Review overriding interests as a category of property rights to establish how this category will operate in an eConveyancing environment or to determine if these rights should be reclassified. If this category is to be retained review all overriding interests individually to update but where possible overriding interests should be abolished, subject to the policy imperatives of the law, the practicalities of the conveyancing and land administration processes and the due protection of property rights under the Irish Constitution and the European Convention for the Protection of Human Rights and Fundamental Freedoms.[76]
(j) Further research is required to determine the impact of the increased emphasis on registered transactions so that valuable rights are not inadvertently destroyed. Consideration should be given to moving vulnerable rights onto the register.[77]
(k) The negative impact of any re-classification of property rights should be carefully assessed. Piecemeal reform is to be avoided as an overall strategy would provide a more cohesive approach.[78]
(l) Title insurance is not recommended as an alternative to state compensation.[79]

[69] See Sects. 6.2.6 and conclusion to Chap. 6.

[70] See Sect. 6.2.

[71] See Sects. 5.4 and 5.5.

[72] See Sects. 6.3.2, 6.3.3 and 8.5.5.

[73] See Sect. conclusion to Chap. 7.

[74] See Chap. 7.

[75] See Sects. 6.3.3 and conclusion to Chap. 7.

[76] See Sect. conclusion to Chap. 8.

[77] See Sect. 8.5.1.

[78] See Sects. 8.5.1, 8.5.3 and 8.5.4.

[79] See Sect. 9.6.1.

(m) It must be acknowledged that eConveyancing will copper fasten registration of title and registration of title will enhance eConveyancing.[80]

(n) Given the success of the initial eRegistration initiatives and the move towards a complete title register the timing is right for Ireland to implement eConveyancing.[81]

(o) While the experience in other jurisdictions provides valuable insights Ireland must develop its own system.[82]

Conclusions

Treacy and O'Sullivan are of the view that while any model of how an electronic service should work "can draw heavily from experiences in other countries, especially other common law jurisdictions, it must also be designed to take account of practices and procedures unique to Ireland."[83] Thus an eConveyancing system must accommodate local conditions and practice variations. A unique case in point is the federal system in Australia which has to meet the needs of all states and territories[84]

Countries have a wide range of different cultures, sizes, politics, populations, traditions, philosophies, resources, development needs, stakeholders, systems, regional and geopolitical requirements and thus what is best for one may be unworkable for another.

> The development and maintenance of land markets involves the interaction of complex political, economic, social and cultural issues, legal frameworks, fiscal policies and environmental controls. Their impact on society and the local economy varies from nation to nation and depends much upon what is happening in other parts of the national and global economies.[85]

Best practice must be society specific and no one size fits all. While lessons can be learned from other countries only each individual jurisdiction can decide what is best for its citizens.

The Irish conveyancing process has specific practices and procedures that will need to be taken into account in designing any model of eConveyancing. Such contextual factors will make some elements of the model more vital and others less important when compared with models developed elsewhere. For example, closing the registration gap may be less of an imperative in jurisdictions where completion and registration are closely aligned.

(continued)

[80] See Sects. 8.5, 8.5.1 and conclusion to Chap. 8.

[81] See Sect. 3.4.1.

[82] See Sect. conclusion to Chap. 9.

[83] Treacy and O'Sullivan (2004), p. 12.

[84] Douse (2005).

[85] Dale et al. (2006), p. 3.

There is merit in further legislative reform to review the category of overriding interests but also to align and consolidate the registration of title statute, the 1964 Act, with the primary piece of conveyancing legislation; the 2009 Act. Also the current recessionary climate in Ireland has introduced additional delay in the conveyancing process[86] and tight constraints on lending.[87] The high percentage of home ownership and affinity for land means that the security of the conveyancing process and registration system is an essential part of the social fabric in Ireland and cannot lightly be tinkered with.

In many jurisdictions progress towards eConveyancing has been slower than previously anticipated. Developing the technology has been more difficult and costly than expected and the costs have proved harder to justify whilst the benefits have seemed less assured in the context of government retrenchment, a slow land market and a general economic recession. Thus empirical data must be gathered to clearly show the merits of the business case for all stakeholders. In order to do this more progress has to be made in developing methodologies and ontologies. This will allow the definition of concepts and terminology for further research and establish appropriate indicators to compare conveyancing and eConveyancing systems and processes.

Any conceptualisation must take into account conceptualisations already established in other domains such as economics, political sciences and geosciences, given the relationship of land to other socio-economic fields. In referring to research on the cadastre Sliva and Stubkjær point out that the methodologies used are largely those of the social sciences as the cadastre relates as much to people as it relates to land and that cadastral systems, which in their view includes the land register,[88] are shaped by social, political and economic conditions, as by legal and technological factors.[89] Thus the conveyancing system must not be viewed in isolation.

Taking into account the overall tenets of eConveyancing it is possible to design a system that introduces new controls on existing risks and provides for a net reduction in risk for land owners compared with paper based conveyancing. Any increase in a specific risk will be compensated by an overall increase in benefits however there must be a recognition that no

(continued)

[86] Among other changes, additional property taxes and charges have been introduced which add to the enquiries that need to be carried out by a transferee.

[87] Loan offers are valid for shorter periods and can be withdrawn at any time. Loan to value ratios have reduced. Only those in very secure employment are in a position to obtain loan funds so generally the market is restricted to cash purchasers.

[88] Silva and Stubkjær (2002), p. 410.

[89] Silva and Stubkjær (2002), p. 420.

commercial activity is completely without risk. Each jurisdiction will need to assess the risk and reward and this will be judged in light of the aversion to or appetite for risk.

The arguments for and against eConveyancing has resonance in many spheres be they cultural, political, social, judicial, economic or constitutional. Principles about the ownership of property and the protection of interests in land impact on every citizen and every activity and thus major changes should not be lightly implemented. Sufficient thought must be given to the overall strategy and impact of the goals of reform. Thought must be given to the fact that conveyancing is not just a process of transferring land but it has a wider remit as a tax and social control mechanism.

However,

> [o]nce we have. . .[eConveyancing], it is a safe bet that few would want to be without it. It will become a part of life, just like electronic rail tickets or theatre bookings. Reluctance will become the province of the few because any streamlining exercise has its victims, and it will be a tremendous challenge. . .to find an acceptable way to safeguard those whose interests appear to be squashed by the new requirements....As electronic conveyancing is implemented, we may well be able to say that we have moved from a state of general reluctance with a few enthusiasms, to one where a few are reluctant and enthusiasm is general.[90]

To date such enthusiasm has manifested itself primarily in the development of eRegistration systems. These provide an easier route to reform through the control and force of central government. While this demonstrates the art of the possible, it is eConveyancing that provides the potential for re-engineering of the conveyancing process for the twenty-first century.

The experience in Ontario provides valuable insights into how Ireland might move into such unchartered territory but ultimately Ireland must decide for itself how it will balance the risks and rewards of implementing eConveyancing.

References

Baird, D., & Jackson, T. (1984). Information, uncertainty, and the transfer of property. *Journal of Legal Studies, 13*.

BC OnLine. Title security in BC. http://www.ltsa.ca/cms/title-security-in-bc. Accessed 18 June 2014.

Bucknall, B. (2008–2009). Real estate fraud and systems of title registration: The paradox of certainty. *Canadian Business Law Journal, 47*.

Calabresi, G. (1970). *The costs of accidents; A legal and economic analysis*. United States: Yale University Press.

Coleman, J. (2005). The costs of The Costs of Accidents. *Maryland Law Review, 64*.

[90] Cooke (2003), p. 293.

Cooke, E. (2003). E-conveyancing in England: Enthusiasms and reluctance. In D. Grinlinton (Ed.), *Torrens in the twenty-first century*. Wellington: LexisNexis.

Cooter, R. D., & Rubin, E. L. (1987–1988). A theory of loss allocation for consumer payments. *Texas Law Review, 66*.

Dale, P., Mahoney, R., & McLaren, R. (2006). Land markets and the modern economy. *Royal Institution of Chartered Surveyors*. http://www.knowedge.co.uk/Papers/Land_markets.pdf. Accessed 23 June 2014.

De Soto, H. (2001). *The mystery of capital*. London: Black Swan.

Deeney, J. (2014). *Registration of Deeds and Title in Ireland*. Great Britain: Bloomsbury.

Donahue, D. J., Quinn, P. D., & Grandilli, D. C. (2003). *Real estate practice in Ontario* (6th ed.). Canada: LexisNexis Butterworths.

Douse, B. (2005). Progressing a national approach to electronic conveyancing. Department of Lands, New South Wales Government. http://www.lands.nsw.gov.au/_media/lands/pdf/electronic_conveyancing/publications/ProgressingANationalApproach.pdf. Accessed 28 Jan 2008.

Fingleton, K. (2010). PI claims – Trends and developments. *Parchment, 45*.

Flaws, J. (2003). Compensation for loss under the Torrens system – Extending state compensation with private insurance. In D. Grinlinton (Ed.), *Torrens in the twenty-first century*. Wellington: LexisNexis.

Gray, K., & Gray, S. F. (2009). *Elements of land law* (5th ed.). Great Britain: Oxford University Press.

Griggs, L. (2001). Torrens title in a digital world. *Murdoch University Electronic Journal of Law, 8*(3). http://www.murdoch.edu.au/elaw/issues/v8n3/griggs83_text.html. Accessed 13 June 2014.

Griggs, L., & Low, R. (2011). Identity fraud and land registration systems: An Australian perspective. *The Conveyancer and Property Lawyer, 4*. http://eprints.qut.edu.au/46059/1/45749.pdf. Accessed 24 June 2014.

Haynes, M. (2010, December). Title insurance: Separating face from fiction. *LawPRO Magazine*. http://www.practicepro.ca/lawpromag/default.asp. Accessed 13 June 2014.

HM Land Registry. *Report on responses to e-conveyancing secondary legislation part 3*. http://www.landregistry.gov.uk/__data/assets/pdf_file/0006/3102/econveyancing_cons.pdf. Accessed 19 June 2014.

Holmes, O. W. (1896–1897). The path of the law. *Harvard Law Review, 10*.

Keating, S. (2012). *Digital signatures and electronic conveyancing* (LL.M. thesis). National University of Ireland, Galway.

Lemieux, T. (2010, December). TitlePLUS claims: What the numbers tell us. *LawPRO Magazine*. http://www.practicepro.ca/lawpromag/default.asp. Accessed 13 June 2014.

MacInnes, N., & Pinnington, D. (2010, December). Real estate claims trends. *LawPRO Magazine*. http://www.practicepro.ca/lawpromag/default.asp. Accessed 23 June 2014.

Manthorpe, J. (2007). *Land registration – A health check*. In Registering the World Conference, Dublin, 26–28 September 2007. http://www.prai.ie/uploadedfiles/conference20071/papers/keynote%281%29.pdf. Accessed 14 May 2014.

Mason, A. (2003). Indefeasibility – Logic or legend? In D. Grinlinton (Ed.), *Torrens in the twenty-first century*. Wellington: LexisNexis.

Moore, M. E., & Globe, J. M. (2003). *Title searching and conveyancing in Ontario* (5th ed.). Canada: LexisNexis.

O'Connor, P. (2003). Double indemnity – Title insurance and the Torrens systems. *Queensland University of Technology Law & Justice Journal, 3*(1). https://lr.law.qut.edu.au/article/view/123. Accessed 23 June 2014.

O'Connor, P. (2005). Registration of invalid dispositions: Who gets the property? In E. Cooke (Ed.), *Modern studies in property law* (Vol. III). Oxford: Hart.

O'Connor, P. (2009). Immediate indefeasibility for mortgagees: A moral hazard? *Bond Law Review, 21*(2).

O'Hara, W., & Husa, A. (2008). A place for everything and everything in its place: Why title insurance cannot take the place of a survey. http://www.gardiner-roberts.com/documents/articles/A_place_for_Everything_-_Article_-_O_Hara_Husa.PDF. Accessed 23 June 2014.

Posner, R. A. (2005). Guido Calabresi's *The Costs of Accidents*: A reassessment. *Maryland Law Review, 64*.

Rapaczynski, A. (1996). The roles of the state and the market in establishing property rights. *Journal of Economic Perspectives, 10*(2).

Reevy, J. (2003). Property transactions – The new risk controllers. *New Law Journal, 153*.

Property Registration Authority 'Annual Report 2011'. (2012). Property Registration Authority. http://www.prai.ie/eng/Publications/Annual_Reports/PRA_Annual_Reports_.html. Accessed 18 June 2014.

Rolph, D. (2010, December). Title insurance – Not the panacea solicitors had hoped for. *LawPRO Magazine*. http://www.practicepro.ca/lawpromag/default.asp. Accessed 13 June 2014.

Ruoff, T. (1952). An Englishman looks at the Torrens system: Part III: The insurance principle. *Australian Law Journal, 26*.

Silva, M. A., & Stubkjær, E. (2002). A review of methodologies used in research on cadastral development. *Computers, Environment and Urban Systems, 26*.

Sneddon, M. (2007). *Risk assessment and management in electronic conveyancing*. In Registering the World Conference, Dublin, 26–28 September 2007. http://www.prai.ie/uploadedfiles/conference20071/papers/s4p1.pdf. Accessed 14 May 2014.

The Law Society of Upper Canada 'Rules of Professional Conduct'. (current to 24 January 2013). http://www.lsuc.on.ca/WorkArea/DownloadAsset.aspx?id=2147489377. Accessed 23 June 2014.

Thomas, D. (1997). Accessing US land title records through the internet. *Journal of Law, Information and Science, 8*(2). http://www.austlii.edu.au/au/journals/JlLawInfoSci/1997/11.html. Accessed 13 June 2014.

Treacy, C., & O'Sullivan, J. (2004). *Land registration in Ireland – Current position and future developments*. In Law Reform Commission Annual Conference. http://www.lawreform.ie/Annual%20Conference%202004.PDF. Accessed 10 Mar 2009.

Tuffin, J. (2009). Responsible lending laws: Essential development or overreaction? *Queensland University of Technology Law & Justice Journal, 9*(2). https://lr.law.qut.edu.au/article/view/32. Accessed 23 June 2014

Waters, K. A. (2010, December). There's more to title insurance than meets the eye. *LawPRO Magazine*. http://www.practicepro.ca/lawpromag/default.asp. Accessed 13 June 2014.

Zevenbergen, J. (2006). Trustworthiness of land records – The basis of land administration systems. *GIS Asia Pacific, 10*(6). http://www.geospatialworld.net/uploads/magazine/925d04_apJune2006.pdf. Accessed 13 June 2014.

Ziff, B. (2003). Title insurance: The big print giveth but does the small print taketh away? In D. Grinlinton (Ed.), *Torrens in the twenty-first century*. Wellington: LexisNexis.

Glossary

Term	Meaning	Related jurisdiction (if any)
ARTL	Automated Registration of Title to Land	Scotland
AVMs	Automated Valuation Mechanisms	
CFR	Compulsory First Registration	
CROBECO	Cross Border Electronic Conveyancing	European Union
DRA	Document Registration Agreement	Ontario
EAS (now landdirect.ie)	Electronic Access Service	Ireland
EFS	Electronic Filing System	British Columbia
EFT	Electronic Funds Transfer	
eDRS	Electronic Document Registration Service	England and Wales
ELRA	European Land Registry Association	European Union
EU	European Union	European Union
EULIS	European Land Information Service	European Union
GDP	Gross Domestic Product	
HIP	Home Information Pack	England and Wales
ICT (or ICTS)	Information and Communication Technology (Information and Communication Technologies)	
IMC	Irish Mortgage Council	Ireland
IMF	International Monetary Fund	
IT	Information Technology	
ITRIS	Integrated Title Registration Information System	Ireland

(continued)

G. Brennan, *The Impact of eConveyancing on Title Registration*,
DOI 10.1007/978-3-319-10341-9

Term	Meaning	Related jurisdiction (if any)
LTSA	Land Title and Survey Authority	British Columbia
LAS	Land Administration System	
LINZ	Land Information New Zealand	New Zealand
LRC	Law Reform Commission	Ireland
LSUC	Law Society of Upper Canada	Ontario
LT Plus	Land Titles Plus	Ontario
LTAF	Land Titles Assurance Fund	Ontario
LTCQ	Land Titles Conversion Qualified	Ontario
Ministry (or Ontario Ministry)	Ministry of Government Services	Ontario
NAMA	National Asset Management Agency	Ireland
NLIS	National Land Information System	England and Wales
OECD	Organisation for Economic Co-operation and Development	
OSi	Ordnance Survey Ireland	Ireland
PEXA (previously NECS or NECDL)	Property Exchange Australia (previously National eConveyancing System or National eConveyancing Development Limited)	Commonwealth of Australia
POLARIS	Province of Ontario Land Registration Information System	Ontario
PRA (also PRAI)	Property Registration Authority of Ireland or Property Registration Authority	Ireland
PFI (PPP)	Private Finance Initiative (or Public Private Partnership)	
PRTB	Private Residential Tenancies Board	Ireland
QeD	Quick electronic Discharge	Ireland
UML	Unified Modelling Language	
UN	United Nations	United Nations
UNECE	United Nations Economic Commission for Europe	United Nations
UNECE WPLA	United Nations Economic Commission for Europe's Working Party on Land Administration	United Nations
WTO	World Trade Organisation	

MIX
Papier aus verantwortungsvollen Quellen
Paper from responsible sources
FSC® C105338

If you have any concerns about our products,
you can contact us on
ProductSafety@springernature.com

In case Publisher is established outside the EU,
the EU authorized representative is:
Springer Nature Customer Service Center GmbH
Europaplatz 3, 69115 Heidelberg, Germany

Printed by Libri Plureos GmbH
in Hamburg, Germany